VOYAGE TO DESTRUCTION

The Moroccan Letters of Alfred Chester

Edited and Introduced by
Edward Field

SPUYTEN DUYVIL
New York City

The Norman Glass letters are from Kent State U.
Paul Bowles' letters are from U. of Delaware

Some of these letters have been previously published in:
Les Episodes
The New York Native
Exquisite Corpse
Confrontation
Christopher Street
Open City

Cover photo: Paul Bowles and Alfred Chester in Morocco, 1963

Library of Congress Cataloging-in-Publication Data

Names: Chester, Alfred, 1928-1971, author. | Field, Edward, 1924- editor.
Title: Voyage to destruction : the Moroccan letters of Alfred Chester /
    edited and introduced by Edward Field.
Description: New York City : Spuyten Duyvil, 2022. |
Identifiers: LCCN 2021043912 | ISBN 9781956005097 (paperback)
Subjects: LCSH: Chester, Alfred, 1928-1971--Correspondence. | Chester,
    Alfred, 1928-1971--Travel--Morocco. | Authors, American--20th
    century--Correspondence.
Classification: LCC PS3505.H679 Z48 2022 | DDC 816/.54 [B]--dc23
LC record available at https://lccn.loc.gov/2021043912

VOYAGE TO DESTRUCTION

GLOSSARY OF NAMES

Diana Athill	Chester's Editor Andre Deutsch Publishers London
Jane Bowles	Writer, Paul Bowles's Wife
Paul Bowles	Writer, Longtime Tangier Resident
Elia Braca	Actress Wife Of Painter Herman Rose
George Broadfield	Former NYU Classmate. Visited Bowles In Tangier, Later Murdered In New York
William Burroughs	Novelist, Tangier Resident
Remy Charlip	Dancer And Writer Of Childrens' Books
Ira Cohen	Beat Poet, Editor *Gnaoua*, *Jilala* Magazines, Resident Bat Palace Tangier Medina
Jess Collins	Painter, Robert Duncan's Partner
Columbine And Skoura	Alfred Chester's Dogs
Candida Donadio	Alfred Chester's Agent
Avel De Knight	Greenwich Village Artist
Neil Derrick	Novelist, Author with Edward Field *The Villagers*
Robert Duncan	San Francisco Poet
Dris	Moroccan Fisherman, Alfred Chester's Intimate Friend
Jason Epstein	Alfred Chester's Editor Random House
Extro	Canadian Youth, Accompanied Chester To Mexico
Irene Fornes	Playright, Part Of The Sontag/Sohmers Circle
Elliot Fremont-Smith	New York Times Columnist
Maurice Girodias	Olympia Press Paris. Publisher Of Chester's *Chariot Of Flesh*
Norman Glass	Expatriate English Writer, Occasional Tangier Resident
Brion Gysin	Novelist, Burroughs Collaborator
Hajmi	Moroccan Hustler, Friend Of Dris
John Hawkes	Novelist
Sir David Herbert	English Aristocrat. Lived On The Mountain In Tangier

Ted Joans	Poet
Lincoln Kirstein	Patron Of New York City Ballet
Philip Lamantia	Beat Poet
Larbi	Paul's Houseman. Dictated To Paul Bowles *A Life Full Of Holes* And Other Books Bowles Translated And Published Under Pseudonym Of Driss Ben Charhadi
Taylor Mead	East Village Poet, Actor
Scott Meredith	Chester's Literary Agent Who Succeeded Candida Donadio
Sonya Orwell	Widow Of George Orwell
John Rechy	Author *City Of Night*
Rosetta Reitz	Owner Four Seasons Bookstore Greenwich Village 1947-1956
Rosalind Schwartz	Ira Cohen's Girlfriend
Irving Rosenthal	Beat Writer, Tangier Resident. *Sheeper,* Grove Press, 1967
Sharifa	Jane Bowles' Moroccan Lover
Richard Seaver	Editor Grove Press
Dennis Selby	Author *Sanctity: Or There's No Such Thing as a Naked Sailor*
Hubert Selby	Author *Last Exit To Brooklyn*
Robert Silvers	Editor New York Review Of Books
Harriet Sohmers (Zwerling)	Artist's Model/Writer, Pregnant At Start Of Correspondence
Ian Sommerville	Burroughs Muse Featured In *The Lost Boys*
Gilbert Sorrentino	Editor, Novelist, Author *Mulligan Stew*
Milo	Harriet's Newborn Son
Theodore Solotaroff	Editor *Commentary*
Susan Sontag	Essayist/Novelist
Ted Wilentz	Owner 8th Street Bookshop
Charles Wright	Greenwich Village Novelist

THE MOROCCAN LETTERS OF ALFRED CHESTER

INTRODUCTION

Alfred Chester's meeting with Paul Bowles at a New York dinner party was the most fateful of his life, for it set in motion a chain of events that led to his death eight years later. In the winter of 1962-1963, Bowles, that old wizard of *The Sheltering Sky* and long the resident guru of Tangier, was in New York writing music for a Tennessee Williams play on Broadway, "The Milk Train Doesn't Stop Here Anymore," when he was introduced to Chester, then at the top of his form as a critic and one of the darlings of the New York literary establishment. At the same time, Bowles was in his lowest period of creativity from the exhaustion of years of coping with his wife Jane Bowles' psychological and physical problems. Her decline, through breakdowns, shock treatments, strokes, and alcoholism, is chronicled in painful detail in Millicent Dillon's biography, *A Little Original Sin*. That winter, Paul Bowles was in desperate need himself.

Alfred Chester, thirty-four years old at the time of their meeting, was in awe of Bowles. Chester, like the rest of our generation, had been electrified in the late forties when Bowles' short story, "Pages From Cold Point," came out in a New Directions Annual, which set off endless debates over whether the boy actually seduced his own father at the story's murky end (Bowles later confirmed to Alfred Chester that he did). But even before that publication, we were aware of Bowles as a figure on the international arts scene, hobnobbing with the legendary Gertrude Stein and Alice B. Toklas in Paris, before settling in Morocco.

Now, at a low ebb, Bowles must have recognized in Alfred Chester a brilliance similar to his wife's, the "food" his own creativity needed. For like Jane Bowles, Alfred was Jewish, homosexual, self-destructive to the point of masochism, and even had a physical "defect"—her crippled leg, his total hairlessness from a childhood disease—that would allow Bowles to be the golden boy to their "monsters." Later, Chester would write that Bowles was the only mind on his level in Tangier, but it must have been true the other way round also.

Since childhood, Chester had worn a wig, that made the meagerest attempt to suggest real hair, making him, with his pudgy form, look very odd indeed, though this had never hindered his success with a series of handsome partners. But the attraction on both his and Bowles' sides was never sexual. Bowles seemed to need the stimulus of Chester's energies, as he had once needed, and used, perhaps used up, his wife's. In the forties, he had shifted from music composition to fiction, psyching himself into writing stories by tuning in on Jane's quirky craft, making it his own, and, as her infantile psyche probably interpreted it, taking writing away from her. Her difficult behavior, in the years of her decline, after her writing became overshadowed by his, when she continually interrupted his writing schedule, might be seen as her only means of revenge, as well as a kind of "leftover life to kill."

Alfred and Jane's lives followed a similar path. Enthralled with Morocco and its exoticism, they both threw themselves into the life there with abandon, living for the moment and to the hilt, as a more cautious Bowles had never done. They had fairytale relationships with Moroccan lovers (in Jane's case she married the Witch, as in Alfred's it was Beauty and the Beast), used alcohol and drugs immoderately, went crazy, and died in exile within a few years of each other. Jane, though devoted to Paul, described him as a spider, referring to a spider's talent for capturing his victims in a web and draining them of their fluids— and indeed "dryness" was a quality, a physical characteristic even, of Paul Bowles. (Later, he would learn a less destructive, more creative, use of the same devouring impulse, by taping the stories of Moroccan illiterates, then transcribing and translating them into English.)

To play the kind of psychic games he craved, Bowles had to have a "receiver" who could read his subtext, those messages that can be conveyed underneath the apparent level of the conversation, requiring a sensitivity enhanced by the use of kif, the Moroccan form of marijuana. This took a special kind of person, a borderline psychotic perhaps—like Jane, or Alfred. At the New York dinner party, that winter of 1962-1963, where he met Alfred Chester, Bowles must have unconsciously recognized a perfect foil for his mind games, which explains why he invited him so insistently, so inscrutably, to Tangiers. Bowles may have thought it was true when he claimed that he never invited anyone to Morocco, but according to the letters I received from Alfred Chester in the spring of 1963, it was clear that Bowles made one exception to his rule:

"[Bowles] wrote me a fascinating gossipy letter and insists I come there. He and I are linked together in the new Transatlantic [Review]—we both have fables. It made me feel good." But Chester is still resisting Bowles, for he adds, "If I get the Guggenheim I'll come to Europe." (March 13, 1963)

"If things work out with Random House I'll come to Europe, although Paul keeps writing and saying come to Tangier. It sounds so full of beats that it makes me nauseated." (April 3, 1963)

"I had a letter from Paul Bowles today and he makes me want to come to Tangiers like mad. What if I went at the end of May?" (April 17, 1963)

"Whoever thought the day would come that Paul Bowels [sic] would be anxiously awaiting my appearance in Tangier and I would be thinking what an asshole fucking place it seems to be." (April 22, 1963)

Perhaps another explanation for Bowles' eagerness in this case was that he saw Alfred Chester as a companion, similarly flawed as both were, for his wife Jane, to look after her, amuse her, lighten the load on him that her mental illness had caused. And it is true that Alfred and Jane immediately became intimate friends, and she often looked after him maternally. She got him to a doctor when a fungus sprouted on his eyelids, and loaned him money when he was broke. There is a touching scene, in the Millicent Dillon bio, of Alfred at a café with Jane, helping her write a letter of apology to Paul for having given away all the money in his checking account while she was drunk, and promising never to do it again. For she was aware that her uncontrollable, irrational behavior would necessitate his putting her into the asylum in Malaga, as he had done before.

Jane's use of money in rebelling against Paul's control was crucial, for Bowles was famous for being close, if not tightfisted, with his resources, as well as with his privacy, and his emotions. Therefore, it is particularly revealing that Bowles actually offered to allow Alfred to stay in his house in Morocco with his dogs until he found a place of his own. Alfred's dogs were two large and barely manageable mongrels he had rescued from an island in Greece, who tore up apartments and bit people everywhere Alfred went. It was with untypical considerateness that Alfred wrote to Paul that, since he was coming with the dogs, Paul had better rent him a place nearby. And with equally untypical generosity, Bowles offered to loan Chester passage money.

I was in Europe on a Guggenheim fellowship with my friend, Neil Derrick, when, early in July 1963, we drove down from Paris to Gibraltar where Alfred Chester disembarked from his ship on his way to Morocco. On board, he told us, he had had an affair with a young woman going on to Israel, though he professed a certain disgust for her, mysteriously likening her to a bowl of oatmeal.

The next day, together with his two half-wild dogs, Columbine and Skoura, on leashes, and a footlocker weighed down with manuscripts and an old standard typewriter, the three of us took the ferry across the Straits to Tangier, a two-hour trip from the modern world to a place that might be described as medieval, but is essentially timeless. As picturesque a country as anywhere on earth, the populace swarms through the streets in biblical robes and skullcaps, the women still mysteriously veiled and hooded, the medina a movie set of whitewashed cubist dwellings clustered on the slope above the harbor, with mysteriously twisting alleys leading up to the casbah, the walled fortress, at the peak.

Like Jane, Chester was nervous about being alone with Paul, and begged my friend and me to accompany him to the house that Bowles had rented for the summer in Asilah, a fishing village about 30 miles from Tangier on the Atlantic coast, which was not then the artsy resort it is today. Tennessee Williams had visited Bowles there earlier, and had used it as the model for the town with rapacious boys in his play

"Suddenly Last Summer." Though I loved the play, after experiencing the real Asilah I can attest that one ludicrous aspect of it is the script's contention that the boys needed to be aroused by a beautiful woman like Elizabeth Taylor before they would have sex with the poet Sebastian, for Asilah boys were born hustlers and, as Jimmy Baldwin used to say to me about himself, "could fuck a snake."

Similar to the movie version of the play, as our taxi arrived and the boys on the beach spotted us above the ancient sea wall of the picturesque town, they raced up the crumbling stone stairways to surround us, and were only prevented from "devouring" us, as Sebastian was in the movie, by Paul Bowles coming out of his house to shoo them away in Arabic.

Overlooking the sea, Bowles' rented house was built into the ramparts of the town's old fortifications that also incorporated a derelict palace. He was obviously not happy that Neil and I had come along with Alfred, any more than we were comfortable about showing up uninvited. But delighted with Alfred's arrival, he agreed to put the three of us up for the night. Alfred would stay on as planned, and Neil and I would move into a hotel in Tangier the next day. Paul had Larbi, his manservant, serve us lunch, though after several severe bouts with typhus, he himself would only eat a can of salmon, and when I questioned him about the delicious-looking goat cheese I had seen in a market stall on the way, round white cakes nesting on fresh grape leaves, he dismissed them as "typhoid pie." I had always thought of Bowles as an adventurer, but this was the first indication to me of his complex, of his self-protective yet paradoxical nature, choosing to live in a place that he saw as dangerous. But quite the opposite of him and never cautious when it would have been wiser to be, it could be argued that both Jane and Alfred fully embraced, and were destroyed by, Morocco.

Lending weight to my supposition that one of the reasons Alfred had been invited as a "playmate/nurse/companion" for Bowles' disturbed wife, Jane seemed to have been primed to meet Alfred, and almost immediately showed up from Tangier with her Moroccan lover, Sharifa, a silent, saturnine butch in Levis. Jane, looking proud, announced right off that Sharifa carried a doctor's certificate attesting to her virginity. We all sat on Paul's terrace overlooking the Atlantic Ocean, as Jane chattered on in a tone of sophisticated mockery that I found quite unnerving.

After Jane and Sharifa left, we all lay on mats on the terrace and our first kif pipe was passed around, leading to a strange reaction on Alfred's part, in which he saw my face distorted hideously—he looked at me, his best friend, with horror—indicative of his ultrasensitivity to drugs. It was a premonition of his rejection of me several years later when in his madness he claimed I was not the "real" Edward. He was always both alarmed and fascinated by the effects of the kif, and during his stay in Morocco wouldn't stop taking drugs, even if they brought on terrors and panic.

In the late afternoon, Bowles led us down to the beach where the town's fishing fleet had come in and, before the boats drawn up on the beach, the fisherman had spread the day's catch on the sand to sell to the townspeople. We had barely descended from the sea wall and started across the beach, when a young Moroccan left the crowd haggling over fish and approached us, a large fish dangling from one hand. Tall, muscular, and graceful, with a face almost Greek, but too rugged to be classical, the fisherman, whose name was Dris, was introduced by Paul to Alfred, beginning a passionate, stormy, and exalting relationship that Alfred described to me in his letters over the next two and a half years, and the loss of which he mourned for the rest of his life.

Many years later, Paul Bowles described to me how he had set up this relationship in advance: "The first time I met that young man," he wrote, "I decided never to have anything to do with him. He struck me as bad news, and I admit I was afraid of him. His conversation consisted solely of accounts of assaults he had made on European men, and this seemed to me a very bad sign. So, (this may sound like a non-sequitur) as soon as Alfred wrote me he was definitely coming to Morocco, I began to coach Dris on how to behave with him. We would meet for tea every afternoon in the public garden, when I'd tell him all

I knew, and what I surmised, about Alfred. Reason for this behavior: I was curious to see what would happen...."

This gives a good idea of Paul Bowles' strange morality, or amorality, his preference for setting up situations (in fiction and in life) that he can stand outside of and watch impassively while the characters destroy themselves. In his eighties when I last saw him, he was very much like that yet. While not discouraging visitors, he does nothing to make one feel at home, and merely sits back and watches while you stammer and make a fool of yourself.

In this case, the New York Jew was more than a match for the young Moroccan, who quickly fell under his spell. Bowles said that he never knew anyone who dared throw himself into Moroccan life as fast as Alfred Chester, and Jane Bowles added that Chester had had more from Morocco than anyone she'd ever known. And, indeed, from the first day, Alfred started picking up the language, a dialect of Arabic called Moghrebi, recognizing its similarity to Hebrew, which he had studied as a boy in Brooklyn. And his relationship with his Moroccan friend, Dris, and his family gave him an unparalleled entrée into Moroccan life. His letters to his friends at home reveal a Morocco as seen from the inside, as well as portraits of the expatriate, literary, and beatnik colony, both in the Medina and on The Mountain, the fashionable suburb where snobbish, titled Englishmen like the Honorable David Herbert lived.

He became an expert on Bowles, revealing the power he felt Bowles had over him. "Sometimes I think Gerald is God," Alfred Chester wrote in a short story, "Safari," disguising Bowles as Gerald, "at least a local god, or more exactly, a local demon. Africa is not the same as other continents, despite its revolutions, and Gerald has lived here so long that magic and sorcery are more part of his nature than science or the Ten Commandments. I do actually hear drums at his approach; I can see the bone and the ring through his nose; I can see the hideous paint on his face. He is a witch doctor using the body of a mild English missionary. I believe his mind can create things, can make them up as he goes along, real things (so to speak), like this road we were on, or the valley we'd just crossed over, or the mountain above us. If the world is illusion, why shouldn't Gerald be the cause of some of those illusions? I know this sounds insane. I probably am insane. Still and all, can't a madman be logical and right?

"If I see too much of Gerald, he spreads insidiously through my life like ink on blotting paper. I go out at night and hear a strange bird cry in the trees, and I think: that's Gerald. Or a dog baying. If I'm with someone else—but it is rare that I am—I might easily say, "Listen! Do you hear that bird? It's Gerald. He can turn himself into a bird...a demon bird....

"One summer afternoon I went bathing at the vast empty beach on the cape. After a while I started feeling strange, maybe a little sunstruck—giddy and nauseated, but yet exultant. Trying to calm myself, I paced around in the sand; Gerald was much in my mind, like a huge dirty joke. Then suddenly I was looking at the towering sand cliffs to the east, and I felt sure—without fright, mind you, with laughter, rather—that Gerald's smiling head would appear above those hills like a gigantic puppeteer over his stage, like a dripping leviathan surfacing out of a swimming pool."

As Gerald, Paul Bowles is portrayed as a wizardlike demonic figure, sometimes benign but more often satanic, his behavior arbitrary, speaking in an unsettling subtext, a game Paul seemed to love at that time, perhaps part of his druggy mentality, for he was a lifelong smoker of kif. Bowles later denied he ever spoke in subtext, as Alfred claimed, and treated it as one of Alfred's inventions, but it is this view of Bowles that also comes through the many letters I received from Alfred, the Bowles that presided over Alfred Chester's Moroccan years.

The Paul Bowles myth with its image of the unruffled, imperturbable, neutral facade is altered by these letters, which reveal a more human Bowles. Yet Bowles particularly denied Chester's reports of his throwing tantrums and smashing things. I conjecture that it is likely that for a brief time Bowles, uncharacteristically, was trying out being like Alfred, imitating his unleashed self-expression, which he later felt uncomfortable about and wished to deny. But if Bowles was suffering from a writer's block and couldn't write anymore, as Alfred reported to me soon after settling in Morocco, experimenting with erratic, loosening up behavior, Alfred-like excesses, would have made sense as a kind of therapy.

Whatever the ups and downs of their relationship during Chester's Moroccan years, after his expulsion from Morocco in 1965 he referred to Bowles as his "Magic Father" who had given him Morocco and kif. Daily smoking of kif by itself may not have been the culprit that disordered Chester's mind, but in combination with habitual use of dexedrine and liquor, plus occasional LSD and opium, it was dangerous. Still, drugs allowed Chester to write and complete his novel, *The Exquisite Corpse*, a web of shifting and multiple "selves," reflecting, often playfully, his obsession with not knowing who he was, not having a fixed "I," and his suffering over this "situational" self, which was determined by whom he was with. In his first letter to me from Morocco, he complained that "there isn't any me now.... There is no one or thing around to establish my past."

It is a theme that he had been obsessed with throughout the preceding decade in France and America, struggling to finish his novel, *I, Etcetera*, parts of which were cannibalized as stories for his collection of short fiction, *Behold Goliath*, which appeared in 1964, and precipitated his first major mental breakdown, with the realization that it was not going to be a success. Not that he ever admitted he wanted to be famous. He even fled from Time magazine's reporters and photographers whenever, over the years, they had tried to get an interview. It was a quirk of our generation of bohemians, so different from today's, that believed a true artist should flee the blandishments of the world in order to create his great works, and if you become famous it must only happen in spite of rejecting it, preferably after death, when you can no longer "sell out." It was partly to escape fame that Chester had come to Morocco, but he was clearly in conflict about it.

More than fame, he needed enough money to live on. Though he came from comfortable, middle-class people, Chester had struggled with poverty ever since he dropped out of graduate school at Columbia University in 1950 and defied his business-oriented Brooklyn family, that never understood his literary ambitions, by going to live in Paris for nearly a decade. During those apprentice years, living on a shoestring, he did manage to earn some money legitimately, selling stories to the literary quarterly Botteghe Oscure, which paid what seemed fabulous sums, getting an occasional writing fellowship, even writing a dirty novel, *Chariot of Flesh*, under a pseudonym for Olympia Press. But to survive, he also, less nobly, invented a number of scams, one of which involved announcing a fake marriage to squeeze money out of his family, or bilking insurance companies by "losing" insured luggage, the latter a trick he succeeded in pulling off successfully in Tangier and even recommended to his friends.

Returning from Europe to New York in 1959, he soon found himself sought after, not for his fiction, to his dismay, but for his essays and reviews, by such high intellectual journals as Commentary, Partisan Review, NY Review of Books, which have been collected in *Looking For Genet* (Black Sparrow Press, 1992). His reviews were never hackwork, though, and if occasionally unfair, even bitchy, were the product of his shrewd literary intelligence. I think he, himself, saw them primarily as performances, or entertainments. He would never have admitted it, but writing for money brought his splintered character into focus and coherence. Not only Esquire magazine, which published one of his stories, but Mademoiselle, placed him among the "hottest" writers of 1963, including Anthony Powell, Dawn Powell, Robert Lowell, W.D. Snodgrass, James Baldwin, and William Gaddis, which could not but be flattering. But he remained uncomfortable with that part of his career. It was to escape this success as a literary critic that was sidetracking his unfinished novel that, after throwing a wild party and burning his furniture, he left New York with not much more money in his pocket than the landlord was paying him for vacating his apartment.

In Tangier his first mental breakdown came about in the winter of 1963-1964, with his funds depleted and struggling to survive on an occasional check from a periodical or a publisher. Later called "The

Mistake" by Jane Bowles, he conceived a plan to blackmail Paul and Jane who, he reported to me, were supported by what he called "Jane's millionaires," not only old friends like Truman Capote, Tennessee Williams, Libby Holman, but patrons from the Mountain, the Tangier suburb where the wealthy and titled expatriates lived. While the Bowleses were freely homosexual in their personal lives, their marriage and the remoteness of Tangier had protected them from scandal for several decades of an era that was quite intolerant about such things. They were terrified of anything coming out publicly, fearing that they would lose their glamorous image and be no longer welcome at parties and receptions in the fashionable milieus they enjoyed, nor, with their high-class artistic reputations tarnished as known homosexuals, would they continue to get grants from prestigious foundations, as Paul had been doing for years. (When Paul became a successful writer, Virgil Thompson, known for his wicked wit, said that after Paul had garnered all possible grants as a composer, he had switched to writing to be eligible for all the writing fellowships.) But perhaps Bowles' fear of being openly exposed as homosexual, in that benighted age, was primarily grounded in his WASP tradition of presenting a conventional appearance to the world, including a wife, no matter what you did in private.

Alfred's blackmail plot, "The Mistake," was based on a reference to Paul in an article written by Irving Rosenthal in a forthcoming issue of poet and Medina denizen Ira Cohen's magazine Gnaoua, which was about to come out in Tangier. The offending sentence, an oblique reference to Paul's supposed failings as a cocksucker because of a dry mouth, now seems almost innocuous, but at that time was seen by Paul as threatening and he demanded that it be deleted. Even William Burroughs got into the act to appeal for its removal. Ira Cohen refused to censor the piece, and Alfred and Ira got the idea of demanding $10,000 from Paul to remove the line. But after Cohen backed out of the plot, Alfred went ahead with it on his own.

Faced with Bowles' cold eyes as he made his extortion pitch, Alfred suddenly became terrified at what he was doing, and recalled a letter

Paul had previously sent Cohen in which he said he was going to have Alfred Chester "rubbed out." This note had been written by Bowles the previous September, fed up after one of the stormy fights Alfred provoked, probably for the pleasure of getting a rise out of Bowles. During the blackmail attempt, Alfred became fully conscious of the fact that Paul Bowles was part of a world where murder was no big deal: After all, Jane's good friend, the singer Libby Holman, had killed her husband, and the novelist William Burroughs, his wife, accidentally in both cases, perhaps, but neither was convicted. And as Alfred told me, Paul himself, perhaps indulging in kif fantasies, liked to brag how easily you could arrange to have anyone done away with in Tangier for a pittance.

Terror for his life sent Alfred into a tailspin, as these letters so vividly describe, and he wired me in New York to come get him out of Morocco and take him home. I went a little crazy myself with worry over him, trying to reach him by telephone. Eccentrically, Paul never had a telephone, but Jane who lived in an apartment on a lower floor of the same building did, and I eventually got through and asked her about Alfred, shouting over the crackling transcontinental telephone lines that were routed through Paris. With me, Jane Bowles put on her usual act to the outside world, reassuring me that nothing was wrong, and that there was nothing to worry about. In fact, Alfred, in his panic, even went to the US Consulate about the death threat from Paul, who then had to smooth things over by convincing the authorities that the note was a joke and Alfred was unbalanced to have taken it seriously.

There is also the possibility that his Moroccan friend, Dris, who cooked for Alfred, put into his food mind-altering substances, prescribed by a local witch to keep the "Nazarene," which referred to all Europeans, Christian or otherwise, faithful. Alfred and Dris frequently resorted to a local "witch," who once gave them a vial of mercury to blow under the door of a troublesome upstairs neighbor, did spells to influence Alfred's mother to send him money, or get manuscripts accepted by editors in New York. There is a scene in "The Foot" where Alfred awakens in the night to find Dris performing magic before the fireplace, chanting and inscribing egg shells. Much as Sharifa, Jane's lover, was said to use magic to keep Jane with her, Dris might have used poisonous ingredients bought from the witch to keep Alfred—for it is said that the Moroccan never leaves the Nazarene, but vice versa.

When Alfred recovered from this first crackup, brought on by The Mistake, he soon gave up writing critical articles and reviews to concentrate on writing his novel, *The Exquisite Corpse*. All of us at home were relieved that he seemed so happy in Morocco, now living with his Dris in a charming apartment in Tangier, when a crucial event occurred: The wig he had worn from childhood burned up by accident on the kitchen stove. Surprisingly, he did not fall apart, and it looked as if his growing maturity allowed him to go about revealing his baldness for the first time in his life. He even invited the Bowleses to lunch, to display his newly-bald head, though Paul claimed to me that he never noticed any change, because, as he put it, he never noticed people.

I was reassured when Alfred continued sending long, fascinating letters full of information about Morocco, his sometimes-stormy, sometimes-blissful, relationship with Dris, his eternal lawsuits, battles with his family, agents and publishers, with reports of his hilarious relationship with Paul and Jane Bowles woven throughout. His letters also give vivid pictures of the writer at work, especially his strategies in writing his novel *The Exquisite Corpse*. His epistolary style was neither that of his fiction nor his essays, but a livelier, more informal amalgam that went beyond both. This is made obvious when he quotes what he is writing, from his Jean Genet essay, for example, where the prose excerpts, even at their sassiest, stand out for their formality and hardly need quotation marks. The charm of these letters, and what makes them his most important writing, I believe, is that the voice of his entire being is expressing itself, the demanding, querulous, impossible, brilliant, and entertaining Alfred Chester, the voice he was always seeking in his prose and never quite achieved, all the while lamenting the fragmentation of his "I." It was not really true, but some critics even said that each of his stories sounded like someone else had written it.

When his letters arrived I always found myself overwhelmed by his orders of things to do for him, though I suspect he made these inordinate demands on all his friends. I tried to fulfill as many as I could, though being somewhat shy myself, I was not too successful confronting and fighting his battles with formidable publishers like Jason Epstein, and dealing with lawyers and agents. He was furious with his publisher and agent for not promoting his book *Behold Goliath* as vigorously as he wished, and eventually broke with his agent, Candida Donadio, switching, on Norman Mailer's recommendation and with the hope of being handled as a potentially best-selling author, to Scott Meredith, who turned out to be equally unsatisfactory. He was also convinced that his family had swindled him out of his father's inheritance, and laid out his case repeatedly in obsessive detail. Much of this material I have cut as tedious reading.

Neil and I made another visit to Tangier, though Alfred was somewhat disappointed in me this time, complaining afterwards that I had become "old maidish." Of course, it would have been difficult to live up to the idealized image he had of me, and I was not going to throw myself into Moroccan life as totally as he had. To celebrate our arrival, Alfred threw a cocktail party with martinis, a novelty in his somewhat-beatnik Tangier crowd, and invited his friends, whom he had complained about to me frequently in his letters: Ira Cohen and his girl friend Roz, who lived in a Medina house called "Bat Palace," so named after an unfortunate bat had flown in and ended being cooked and consumed in a pseudo-satanic rite; "the King of the Beatniks" and Tatiana, who after several tokes on the joint passing around the room, broke the zonked silence with sudden shrieks of mad laughter; Dale and Liz, who were hopefully opening a bar that was soon closed by the Moroccan authorities in one of their periodic sweep-ups, and expulsions, of the Medina denizens.

Alfred drove Neil and me in his battered car on a hair-raising ride to the mountaintop village of Chauen, turning around from the wheel to speak to us in the rear of the car even while negotiating hairpin curves on a road that allowed no passing room. Chauen was a holy place only recently opened to non-Moslems, where water gushed from the mountainside. In the village gardens, set within the crumbling walls of an ancient palace, we sat drinking mint tea among robed elders, as the magical night fell. Another time, he drove us out to a dusty hilltop in the country for an allnight religious festival at a Moslem saint's tomb, where we crowded into a smoky tent to watch gold-toothed boys dancing to a *jilala* orchestra. The boys had filed their teeth down and replaced them with gold "to be beautiful," Dris explained to us,

But the consequences of Alfred's giving up his wig were only delayed in coming, for he had a second breakdown a year later, when, without the protection of the wig he began to feel alien and hostile forces tuning in on his bare head. This later crackup, from which he never recovered, was precipitated, inadvertently, by a visit by Susan Sontag to Tangier in late summer of 1965. Their previous relationship in New York had been intense and complex, as all his relationships usually were, involving both rivalry and attraction on his part. In 1959, at the time Chester had returned to New York from a decade in Paris, Sontag had left her husband and was teaching philosophy, first at Columbia University, and then at Sarah Lawrence College. Adopting Chester as a model, she embarked on her own first attempts to write fiction, immediately landing a contract for a novel, *The Benefactor*, on the basis of what Alfred dismissed as little more than a collection of dreams—he claimed that Roger Straus of Farrar, Straus and Giroux, her publishers, was hot for her. But put Sontag down as he often did, and bitchily, when he left New York for Morocco he turned over to her his position as theater critic on Partisan Review, which was soon followed by her publication in that journal of her "Notes on Camp," for which she immediately became famous. The ideas for this essay, he claimed after he read it, came from discussions she had had with him about W.H. Auden's article on Oscar Wilde that had been published in The New Yorker the winter before he left for Morocco. But Alfred was impressed by another essay of hers, when he "glanced through it at

Paul's," surprised that she understood "about the true depth of a work being in the surface," a quality he was aiming for in his current novel, *The Exquisite Corpse*.

Alfred had always had powerful women around him, and suffered from a competitive spirit with them, even when he was their creative model, as he was for Sontag. She was particularly threatening because of her formidable beauty, and he liked to cut her down to size by badmouthing her legs as heavy, and her mind as conventional/academic. He had already been thrown into a tailspin once before by jealousy of her in New York, when his boyfriend pre-Morocco, the one on the trip to Mexico described in the earlier letters here, seemed to fall for Susan and started to make afternoon calls on her. Now, with her arrival in Tangier announced for the late summer of 1965, Alfred was convinced Dris would fall in love with her and leave him. Besides, he would also have felt threatened by Susan Sontag's new success and world fame as "Queen of Camp," but which because of his absence he was not fully cognizant of, which hit him like a ton of bricks after her arrival, when she moved into the most elegant hotel in Tangier, the Minzah. As can be pieced together from Alfred's somewhat incoherent account in his story, "The Foot," that he wrote later in New York, it was on an overnight trip to the heavily-romantic mountain spa of Chauen that he flipped out, sure that this would be the inevitable setting of Susan's seduction of his friend.

Nothing of the sort happened, except that his jealousy reached a critical pitch and, with his mind unbalanced by all the drugs he took, triggered his madness. Unfortunately, because of the severity of this breakdown, he didn't write me anything about these events. But according to Bowles, Sontag tried to be helpful, and even went with him to the American Consulate to get a new passport, for he was nervous that the old passport photo showed him with his wig and sans wig he wouldn't be let out of Morocco. And without the "protection" of his wig, he had developed a terror of forces beaming into his bare skull, which was intensified in official surroundings like the American Consulate. Now began the voices and drums in his head, that, unaccountably, he believed in. When Sontag reported to Bowles that Alfred Chester was crazy, Paul, airily dismissing this as mere psychology, replied that everyone in Tangier was crazy. "No, Paul," Susan said, "Alfred is really crazy."

With the onset of madness, Chester, with an onslaught of guilt over his homosexuality, rejected Dris and, following the instructions of the "voices" in his head, went out and slept with a whore. According to Bowles, his odd behavior in this period provoked his landlord to complain to the authorities, and a few months later Chester was expelled from Morocco. He returned to New York in the winter of 1965 acting very strangely, indeed, with instructions from the "voices" to marry Susan Sontag.

From the evidence of the final letters, he continued appealing to Paul Bowles to help him return to Morocco. For if Bowles was his "magic father," Morocco remained the lost paradise he longed for for the rest of his short life. There were several attempts to reenter the country by air and sea, and in 1967, he succeeded in returning for a year, but I have little documentary evidence of this stay, since he no longer believed I was "the real Edward" and didn't communicate with me. Nor was there a reunion with Dris, who was in Holland, where he had gotten married.

Tormented by his "voices," his personality disintegrating and his creative powers disrupted, the rest of Alfred Chester's life was spent in anguished wandering, with brief residences in Italy, France, England, the U.S, and finally Israel, where he died in 1971.

Alfred Chester's two and a half years in Morocco were undoubtedly the high point of his life, and these letters record the dramatic events that are almost fictional in their intensity, for it could be argued that in Morocco, under the influence of kif, the exotic culture, and Paul Bowles' powerful presence, Chester started living fictionally, as if his life had become the stuff of fiction, until he could no longer distinguish between fiction and reality.

I've deleted masses of material from the letters, much repetitive raging against family, publishers, and agents, as well as, in almost every letter to me, more orders than I could possible carry out. But I've left in most of the old literary gossip of the time about writers like Hubert Selby, Irving Rosenthal, William Burroughs and others, as well as the chilling reports of his tireless and suicidal drug taking that finally destroyed him.

EDWARD FIELD

EDEN

Postcard from Asilah, Morocco   July 11 (?), 1963
To Harriet Sohmers (Zwerling)

Love it here. Am already married. Big funny thing. Paul dreary and un-miserable. My boy is called Dris, 20, captain of fishing boat, does everything for me. It worked with the girl, and she fell in love, but I guess it isn't for me. I am happy. I am happy. The town is beautiful. The weather is gorgeous. It is cheap. I've nothing more to say on a postcard, *sauf que je t'aime et que tu me manque et je veux que tu vienne.*

Write xxx A.

To Edward Field   July 11, 1963 B.P. 14, Asilah, Morocco
Edward *dyeli* My Edward,

I'm here in my ratty little house surrounded by flies and dogs and noises from the street. And I'm tired because I bought a straw mattress to sleep on and it is hard. Dris is all aches and pains from it. I think I'm married to him, but I'm not sure. And I'm too tired and too lazy to think about it. There is one other boy who is courting me, El Hajmi (or something like that) who is gorgeous but unbelievably boring. He banged on the door for hours last night while D. and I were fucking and I think that D. has gone off to beat the shit out of him. I feel like Carmen.

It is a relief to be out of Paul's clutches. I felt more and more like a prisoner, especially because he made all sorts of shenanigans so that I couldn't be alone with D. He is an old queen vintage Edwin Denby, and I think that his brain has melted from kif. I haven't been smoking much. Dris brought me some majoun (hash fudge) the other night and I got higher than ever before. Dreams and hallucinations. Paranoia for a moment when I thought it was poison and that he'd fed it to me to make me paralyzed and impotent. Paul really wants to own me; he is so used to owning people and things here. He keeps saying "they" about the Moroccans, even when he means "he." Like Larbi

3

says something and Paul delivers a comment on "they" to me. He is incapable of a conversation. To tell the truth I loathe him. When he says "they" I always feel like vomiting and also when he says anything or when I get a whiff of his sweat or see his flesh. It repels me. He seems so unclean compared to the Moslems. Dris, like Larbi, washes himself five times a day. He is lovely in bed; all the hair on his body is shaved. "They" all do that according to Paul. And you are wrong, "they" have big cocks like the Algerians. We seem to make love more or less continually and he is sensual like a cat and affectionate and won't let me out of his arms all night. It is lovely except he wants to do all the fucking, but I think he will come around because I know he likes it and probably just wants to tell people he fucks me. I took him to Tangier last night, just to get away from Paul really. It was our first time out. And he walked me past every cafe or crowd of boys in Asilah before going to the bus, pushing me around and strutting with his thumbs in his belt, swaggering I mean. (It was ridiculous because he is a pussycat when we're alone and he just dreams.) I felt he was informing the competition that they'd better keep out or off. He brags about being a great drinker etc., but he felt sick on one sip of my martini last night and ordered a coke for himself. He is really just a baby, twenty years old. But he's captain of his fishing boat, and was a carpenter's apprentice for ten years. It is so nice. He holds my hand in the street and keeps his thigh against mine when we sit together. I'm not paying him, in case you're interested. He wants to move in on a permanent basis in two weeks when the fishing season ends and keep house for me. Paul says "they" feel like Moslem women when they go to live with a foreigner. They expect to be taken care of completely and in exchange they take care of you completely. It seems to be true, so far. Shopping in Asilah is a lot cheaper when I go with Dris than when I go with Larbi [Paul Bowles' houseman].

I love Larbi. I love him. Now that I've told him I'm a Jew (and also circumcized) he isn't so worried about me and thinks I can probably take care of myself. Before that he thought I was a helpless imbecile like Paul. *Oh, mon dieu, que j'ai des histoires à te raconter!* About Phèdre and everything.

We sat with Ted Joans last night and met the Newsweek reporter. He is doing a story on Tangier. I was out when the Esquire photographer came to Paul's the other day.

Night. If I wasn't sure I was married this morning, there is no doubt in my mind anymore nor for that matter in the minds of anyone in town. My house is suddenly furnished and Dris is bringing over a double bed tomorrow as a present. El Hajmi it now appears is working for Dris. In any case, he is back and forth on errands. Dris is cooking supper. We've just spent a couple of hours at the beach cafe where he showed me off again and made it clear to everyone that we were sleeping together. I'm really in a state of shock. He is working out a budget for us at $100 a month. Even Arthur never got me this married this fast or this thoroughly. I feel by tomorrow he'll have me wearing a laundry bag and a veil across my face. He says he knows that one day I will be able to afford radios and tape recorders like Paul and a big house, and he is content to wait.

I know I'm going to wake up any minute and find it was all a dream. In the middle of the room is a tea tray with a pot of mint and three glasses (El Hajmi is invited to dinner) and a little disgusting plastic sugar bowl which delights Dris.

Paul is stunned more than I am, I think. He admitted the Moroccans hate going to bed with him and he has to pay more and more to keep them. Can this be true? He said he hadn't spent a whole night with one in thirty years.

El Hajmi is back. He looks a movie star version of Julie Perlmutter, only sexy. But boring. D. has just announced dinner.

Love to you both, from your captured (and delighted) Alfred

Next morning. Friday. I'm so fascinated with my new life that I can't imagine you wouldn't be. So I've opened the envelope to continue the letter.

I am home alone. Dris will be on his boat until four. He didn't sleep here because of the fucking and the mattress; I mean he got up too late yesterday and missed his boat. Anyway he gave me a lecture in French (so El Hajmi wouldn't understand) and you would be surprised at how much he could say with his twenty or thirty word vocabulary. The point of the lecture was that I mustn't appear in public with other boys because then people would talk about me the way they do about the Englishman (who by the way is running a bordel right here in that big house of his). Only with him.

El Hajmi is supposed (D.s orders) to come and take me and Columbine to the vet's this morning, but I'm going to leave before he comes because I'm beginning to have the feeling that I can't do anything for myself. I'll soon become a dried out old Dr. Schweitzer like Paul. (You were right about him. He never gets fucked.) Columbine bit a little girl the other day. Quite badly, but I don't blame her a bit, the kids bothered the dogs every minute. Now they keep well away. The police came very apologetically. The neighborhood (the whole medina according to Paul) was in an uproar and they wanted to ask the government to throw all the Nisranis (Nazarenes) [foreigners] out of Asilah: me, Paul, the Englishman, and two French queens who teach school. But the police assured me it was all right and just to bring my papers to the medico. That was four days ago, but I haven't been able to find the medico, though Larbi took me there the first time.

I don't feel at all like I'm having a love affair. I'm just married, which is what I wanted and I'm glad. I can't remember Extro. I can't remember anyone really. Even you are a little vague. Maybe Dris fed me a donkey's ear. Larbi has warned me against black magic. Maybe I'm just being born over again.

Later still. There's something odd about the tone of this letter. It doesn't sound like there's any me in it. There isn't any me now, but I don't mind. A little I do. There is no one or thing around to establish my past. Even the dogs seem vague to me. I dreamt Skoura was hit by a car and was bleeding to death in my arms; she was growing grayer but no blood was evident. I woke up thinking I am no one. I am Dris (he spells it with one s) and Hajmi (he spells it this way) and Asilah. Then I thought of all the people in New York looking at each other and being inane and telling each other who they were.

I am not happy or exalted. My cup runneth over and all I can do is sit and look at it. I obviously have to get to work if I intend to support my wife. He promised me a good table this evening.

He just came by for an hour in his fishing clothes to see how I was doing and wanting to cook lunch for me. He says he will find a big house with a kitchen and a toilet for the same amount of money or less, though not on the sea. I said all right because with the two of us here and the dogs we can hardly move around.

Poor Paul. He is pathetic.

Larbi says love affairs between Christians and Moslems are wars, but he doesn't doubt I can win this one since I'm a Jew. It is like my idea of a love affair, I guess. The power struggle and all. Perhaps Larbi means I will end up Dris's slave rather than he mine. Though I am, of course, since I do just what he says and in three days I've become almost helpless without him. I couldn't buy Nescafe and light the stove this morning but had to go to a cafe, and a few days ago I bought cloth for sheets, and had it cut and sewn all by myself because Larbi was so useless. He's useless because Paul is full of money and Larbi never takes the trouble to haggle. I don't think he cheats. But it is a fact that on large sums the merchant pays ten percent to the person who brings the client. On the way back from Tangier in the cab the other night Dris gave me his ten percent of the fare.

I think he is a good boy. I hadn't thought this before. I didn't trust him at all, mainly because of Paul. But then I hadn't entrusted him with anything much yet.

Do you want to come back? I will get Dris to find you a good house or if you would live with us, one great huge house. I wouldn't even mind if you each took a turn with him. Now I think of it, I wonder why I don't mind. He'd mind if I did. I think he is probably used to being thrown over. It's so nice not to have to worry for a change. When he isn't around I feel almost as good as when he is around. I mean about him. I mean there doesn't seem to be anything to suffer about.

Will you come back?

Love, Alfred

I know about a dozen words in Moghrebi and can conjugate "to have"—*andi, andek, andu,* etc.

Next morning. Saturday. Paul brought your letter back from Tangier. He says he never knew anyone who dared throw himself into Moroccan life as fast as I have. Have I done this?

I asked Dris if it was possible he could be as good as he seemed and he said he was. He asked me to be faithful and said he would be.

I'm going to cook supper tonight and attempt to recover my wits today. Already I have made tea for myself this morning.

Paul and Larbi don't sleep together. They used to for a little while years ago. Will you ask Gait if she will display some of Larbi's jewelry? His book is being published in France.

What are you going to do in ridiculous Paris? Dris brought me two pieces of majoun as a present yesterday. I wish I could send you one (enough for two) so you could have lovely dreams about me.

I could easily be very happy now, and could love Dris except I am afraid to, out of pride I think.

xxx

Yes, you are right. P. doesn't write anymore.

(*Note on envelope*: Will you save this letter? It occurs to me I might want to remember what I first felt like. And I can't keep a journal.)

To Harriet Sohmers (Zwerling)   Asilah, 20 July 1963
Ma cherie —

I keep writing letters to you and throwing them away because I can't stand their tone. I'm glad you and your belly are big and well. It's just past dawn now and I thought I'd try a letter to you before trying to write some. I got terribly kifed last night at Paul's, worse than ever before and it was worse than being drunk. I don't know why it affected me so powerfully. I'm all right now though. Dris is at work until afternoon. The fishing season ends in another ten days and after that he's going to move in entirely. As it is now, he goes home late at night presumably because he can't wake up here at 5 a.m, but actually because he is ashamed that his family will wonder why he stays here all night. When he moves in entirely no one will wonder because he'll say he's my servant. As it is, no one wonders since everyone knows anyhow, but *la figura* is very important to him. He's a very good boy usually and does all the housekeeping here. He is tall and bronze-colored and rather handsome, though not at all pretty, with a fairly stupid look in his face, and a very lovely body. Sexy. We've taken vows of always and fidelity and so on. He says he loves me and I'm inclined to believe him, though I didn't at first. He says he will give up his rich English lover for me, which is flattering even if it isn't much of a sacrifice. (He never took money from him and didn't like him much, he says.) He likes hugging and kissing almost more than I do, if possible.

Esquire asked my agent if I would write something about Tangier for them and I think if I do it will have to be anonymous since Paul says they'll kick me out if I tell the truth. There is apparently some sort of upheaval in the country, but not as bad as the Voice of America makes out. I'm fairly happy here, I guess, sometimes very happy. Life seems more possible than it did in New York. I get on better with Paul now that I'm out of his house and now that he is reconciled to my being *casado*. He's kifed out of his mind most of the time, and is terribly unhappy. He says no Moroccan will sleep with him more than once anymore unless he pays a lot. I can understand why. There's no love in him and the boys I know respond quickly to affection, even the whores. I like Jane a lot, though seldom see her, since she is mainly in Tangier. Also Burroughs I liked—I spent one afternoon with him. My favorite person here is Larbi, the boy who works for Paul. He is the same boy who spoke the story of his life into the tape recorder and in Paul's translation is being published by Grove. I'm teaching him how to write every morning at ten. He's a saint, and has a wicked young wife, sixteen years old, who torments him. As there is a child, he won't leave her.

Asilah is beautiful. My house is sort of awful, tiny, but Dris has fixed it up into a home. It's built into the wall of the fortress that surrounds the medina and looks over the Atlantic. Paul has a great beautiful house down the wall. On the other side of me is the house of an Englishman who made a fortune selling blue jeans to Moroccans. Now he owns real estate. (No other foreigners in the medina, though some Spaniards in the European town.) The Englishman is hated by the townspeople because he is terribly promiscuous, especially with little boys. This makes him a *maricon*, disreputable, and it makes his regular lover a *puta*. It is sad. They can never sit together in town or even walk together. (There is no hope for a secret sex life here.) It is now beginning to emerge that he is using his house as a *bordel*. He has two or three Englishmen over every other night or so and supplies them with local boys.

Edward and Neil were here for a couple of days. Edward was unhappy as usual. I wanted him to take a house and stay, but Neil wanted to go back to Paris, so that was that....I saw Ted Joans a couple of times. He's gone to Norway now with wife and child. I've met various foreigners, none of whom I like especially. Dris is enough for now anyhow. I can barely write his name without getting an erection. You'd get the hots for him too if you saw him.

I want to make piles of money and buy Dris beautiful Moslem clothes to wear. I told him this and he told his father and this made his father approve of me. (As it is now, he wears awful English things.) I also want him to go to the mosque five times a day like Larbi, but it isn't likely he will.

I'm trying to concentrate on my writing, but it is difficult, though more and more possible these last days. Dris doesn't play games or try to make me jealous. If anything it's the other way around, though I don't mean to. I walked out to the country yesterday and he came back from work early. When I got back there were burrs on the back of my shirt, had I lain in the fields? Yes. Alone? Yes. No, you wouldn't lay alone. How much did you pay? Etc. We talk a crazy Spanish to each other, all infinitives. My Moghrebi stinks; I mean my ear for it. But he'll teach me it when he quits working.

In case you are wondering I wouldn't give him up for anyone else, like Extro I mean. The dogs aren't too well, and I'm not either actually. Generally debilitated. Not enough sleep, I suppose.

Volkswagens are very cheap here and maybe later I'll get one. Dris would go out of his mind if I did, because Paul wanted to buy one in my name (and for me to chauffeur him around) and I refused to D's disgruntlement.

I miss you most. xxxox and love *de ton* Alfred

To Dennis Selby   Arcila—22 July 1963
Dear Dennis:

I'm thinking of you lovingly this morning, which makes me glad. Please come to Morocco. I don't like any of the people I meet here, I mean of those I can speak some language to, except Jane, Paul's wife, and she is mostly in Tangier. Did Harriet tell you I was married? To Dris Bn Osein Kasari. But after the first ten days of passion and devotion, he now takes me for granted. This isn't true, of course, but it's how I feel today. We talk Spanish together and I am too complex for the few words I know, and whenever we disagree the only thing I can say is: *No tengo palabras para decir*, and of course he thinks I'm lying. I will have to get simpler to fit my vocabulary. When his job ends he'll teach me Arabic and I him English, then maybe we can speak to each other. My deaf mute fantasy becomes more viable with every love affair.

We have taken vows of fidelity and eternity but neither of us believes the other. Paul has made me so mistrustful of Dris that when he isn't here I imagine he is betraying me in every conceivable way. And he, I guess, pretty much the same, because whenever I go out alone he questions me closely on every move I've made, to whom I've spoken, and so on. He is not really wrong because I am propositioned roughly a dozen times a day and it is hard to say no which I invariably do because Dris would inevitably find out if I did, the town is so small here. (I mean, didn't say no.) I'm hoping things will improve when his job ends and we are together all the time.

Edward and Neil were only here for a couple of days. Paul was evidently anxious to be rid of them. He is quite monstrously possessive, an old fashioned colonial type and I was virtually a prisoner the ten days I stayed with him. And the moment he realized that Dris and I were flirting with each other, he never left us alone a minute. I don't believe he wanted to sleep with either of us (though once I had a feeling he wanted an orgy), but he worked hard at keeping us apart. Jane says he can't stand people making love. The day before I moved into my own house, he walked out of the dining room and left us alone to my great surprise. We had a whispered conversation, making arrangements for the next day, and when Paul came back he switched on the tape recorder which had been recording for fifteen or twenty minutes. I sat there feeling sick when the long silence played back at us. He is kifed out of his mind all the time. I smoke occasionally, though not too much. Dris brings me majoun, hashish fudge, but we seldom eat it and are keeping it till after his job ends. (He's captain of a small fishing boat owned by a Spanish company.) Upon two or three occasions I've been high to the point of dreams and hallucinations and my memory was completely obliterated, that is, I'd have to repeat the same action a dozen times because I couldn't remember that I'd done it. Like wiping my ass once. Also, while I was shitting I couldn't work my anus sphincter and I was terrified that my guts were going dawn the drain.

Asilah is beautiful. My house is lousy but Dris has fixed it up rather prettily. It is built into the fortress wall that surrounds the medina and is right on the Atlantic. Paul's house is just down the wall. It is very grand, rented from a Spanish consul whose secretary was Dris's first lover (when he was thirteen), first European anyway; he is only now getting around to admitting sex with Moslems. Larbi, the boy who works for Paul, is the illiterate who told a novel into the tape recorder. Paul's translation of it is being published by Grove in the winter. I'm teaching him how to write, but it's very difficult.

I met Burroughs whom I like well enough. My agent writes that Esquire asked if I'd do an article on Tangier for them. Their photographer has been rushing around ever since I've been here taking pictures of everyone, but it's been a great mystery who was going to write the text.

You should come here and have a love affair and never mind those absurd Americans. You can teach at the American school. Jane says I can do that if things get rough. I miss you.

Love from Alfred

To Harriet Sohmers (Zwerling)   (Summer) 1963—Asilah, Morocco

Mon ange emmerdante: First of all I'm not even sure I haven't mailed you one of the several letters I've written and lost or thrown away. So some of what I say may not be new.

I've just come back after three days in Tangier chez Jane. Skoura has been deathly sick for three weeks now with some horrible virus from France that affects the brain, a kind of meningitis. She was just getting better when she suddenly started having convulsions for nearly 24 hours straight, then lay paralyzed for a day, except her head which kept twitching, and she snapped if you went near her, even me. So I decided I'd better stay in town with her. Before that I'd been going in every day by taxi, back and forth, 30 miles and it had cost me a fortune. At Jane's it seemed likely she would die any minute but she didn't, and then last night and this morning she seemed much better. She started eating and getting up. But there is something even wronger with her now. She can't stop eating, everything, cigarettes, shit, piss, whatever's around, and she keeps pacing back and forth nervously and has twice so far fallen down the steps, I don't know what to expect next, but it's just gone on so long, I'm bored, and she doesn't seem like Skoura anymore, just some strange unloving animal. Columbine goes on biting every kid in town. Today when Dris took her out, she jumped on a little boy, and the father is raising hell and Dris has gone to see them, but will probably forget about it between now and the next street as is his wont. His little 14-year-old brother got carried away by soldiers the other day and he, Dris, was hysterical but chanced on a cult meeting and forgot all about looking for his brother.

Other problems, Dris got very resentful about all the money I was spending on Skoura, so I've had to buy him a ring, half a ring for 20 bucks. He's supposed to pay the other half to get it out of the jeweler's, but he isn't working so of course I will. I'm feeling not too bad about money because the Tribune wants me to do 1200 words every month on anything I feel like for 100 a time. Don't send me any more bills. I'm not interested. Susan sent Paul a copy of her book. It still looks terribly boring to me. Jane read five pages and couldn't go on. Paul, I haven't asked. He is a pain in the ass and every time he gets a chance he starts coming on to Dris, and sometimes right in front of me in Arabic. I know enough to follow. There is a new English boy in town [ed. note: Norman Glass] who is more or less Paul's constant companion now, thank God, so the old shit has someone to pal around with. I have no one except Dris and the only place I can really go with him is some small old cafe on the beach where his intimate friends go, all fishermen, and chop their kif. He is getting more and more reluctant to go through the medina with me and especially outside the walls to the Spanish town. Jane says it's because people are talking. I don't know what the fuck they can be talking about. But life at home is very nice. Except of course he is 20 and never wants to stop fucking. We either eat or fuck. Ever since he stopped working he is full of excess energy. Oddly enough, I was hotter for Extro. I don't really like being made love to.

Skoura keeps pacing back and forth.

I'm thinking of moving to Tangier so I can have somewhere to go out to and people to see. Dris will come along.

Show Magazine wrote asking me to do something for them, but not guaranteeing money. Dennis was behind it. I don't know what's happened. My agent [Candida Donadio] has been in the hospital getting tested for cancer. Her secretary wrote she is okay.

I had a huge letter from my girlfriend weeks ago and still haven't answered it. I don't know what to say. She is so sweet, but my heart stayed dead.

The Moroccans are such different people from us. I've tried everything to cure Dris of lying. Jane says they lie to cover up their tracks, even when they haven't done anything wrong, like animals. I know when he lies and I know when he tells the truth, and I always agree when he tells the truth and never agree when he lies; even though he knows this, he lies. I don't really think I'm going to fall in love with him, though I always do a little when I meet him on the street with food in his hands and he is just on his way home to cook or clean a fish. I'm beginning to accept him as he is—which actually isn't too much unlike me—but this somehow precludes falling in love. When he gets romantic I usually burst into laughter. When I get romantic he gets bored.

I'm going to mail this before the post office closes. I haven't said a word really about Morocco or Arcila. Asilah. I love it here. Or how beautiful it is. Or what the market is like. Or how the food tastes. Or how somehow absolutely pure sex is here. It has nothing to do with the mind. Mostly, in spite of any number of horrors, I feel home.

I kiss Milo, and you too, you big shit.

xxxx ton Alfred

I hope you will come here. You would be happy here.

To Edward Field   14 Aug. 1963 — Asilah, Morocco
Paidhaiki,

I keep thinking that you must be mad at me. I mean about the bed—and even if you are, please write. Everyone must be mad at me except Dick Kluger of the Tribune. He's the only one who writes. Paul got Susan's book but she didn't send me a copy. Now that I'm not in New York I feel like a literary nonentity. Though I'm working. But of course only a fuss makes you feel literary. The Tribune has asked me to do a monthly article on anything I want, 1200 words. Also Show and Esquire have inquired about articles on Tangier.

Dris and I are still married, more so than ever, though every time he's out of sight I plot ways to get rid of him. Every time I see him with food in his hand I fall madly in love. He can make me very happy and often does. He keeps house pretty well and his cooking is improving. We're still in that same awful hole. There isn't another available house, and now I'm thinking that maybe we should move to Tangier during the next few weeks. Dris has lots of friends and family here of course and is always running around, and I have no one except Paul who is really so dreary or the Englishman next door who is even drearier and whose boy anyhow is Dris' best friend and hated rival and so I can't see much of him. Jane is here for a few days now, so that's a little entertaining. And there's an English boy living here now whom I wouldn't be caught dead with anywhere but here or on a ship. Very dreary. And Paul so bitter always. If I had any fantasies left, sexual ones, my life with Dris would be a delicious reenactment. As it is, it is exhausting and frightening. But also it is giggly. He makes me laugh and laugh, I can hardly believe it. We had the clap about a week after we began. He said from me, I said from him.

Skoura has been horribly sick from some virus. The doctor gave her some pills and now for 24 hours she's been sitting in a sort of crazy trance, and I can't go near her. She doesn't recognize me and it's terrifying. I hope she hasn't become insane or something.

My feeling centers are all fucked up. I don't know what is happening to my emotions if I have any.

The money I spend on Skoura caused a crisis in the household because I'd never spent any money on Dris. He became impossible and I finally went and talked to his father, which seemed to me (and to his father) a perfectly natural thing to do. Paul was shocked and Dris was crushed. Larbi approved. It seemed natural since everyone knows what's going on anyhow, though of course you don't acknowledge it. I told his father if he didn't behave I'd send him home, and that helped

16

a little, but things didn't actually get better until I bought him a ring. (Only half of it really. He bought half himself on the bonus he got from the fishing.)

Yesterday was circumcision day in town. Two hundred fifty little boys got cut in the mosque around the corner. Of course, I couldn't watch. It was done by three barbers. Parades all day. The little boys arriving on horseback, preceded by drums and cymbals and flags and followed by keening women. It was so real. Imagine circumcising a boy for a reason like hygiene. Here they do it because God says to. The Jews don't know why they do it anymore. Paul ran around all day with his tape recorder. "What's the point in going if I can't record the music?" and explained the origins of circumcision. "How do you know?" I asked. The new English boy (who is Jewish and a queen and a sort of beatnik, who is shocked by the way I live) said "I'll bet they don't even sterilize the scissors or put penicillin on the cut." In the evening the Hamacha cult danced in the big square in the medina. They go into trances and cut their heads open with axes and rocks. Dris' father is a leading member. He is a cherif. So is Dris. This obviously makes me a cheriffa.

Jane has been with her Cheriffa for sixteen years.

He is waking up now with his gigantic erection and his voluptuous tossings. In the mornings he looks like drawings in faggot magazines. And imagine, he waits on me yet.

I got those Danish male magazines but don't have anything to send them. Dris says I should send a picture of him.

I can talk a little Arabic. Mostly swear words, but also some other practical phrases.

Will you write to me?

Jane just came by. She is so nice and is staying here for a few days.

I'm off fishing now with bamboo poles. Dris just spent two hours cooking a picnic lunch. He makes my heart glad.

We're going to have a special session of the Djilala cult tomorrow night. Aicha, the cleaning woman, is high priestess, a witch noted for black magic and murder. Her husband is high priest. Paul is agreeable to having it at his house since nonMoslems can never get into the thing when it goes on in a Moslem house. They hate foreigners here. Except the boys.

Love to you both. Alfred

To Dennis Selby   Arcila—15 August 1963

(Marginal note: Please don't send me any more bills. I'm not interested.)

Dear Dennis:

Thank you for writing me at last. I am hungry for mail and no one writes except editors.

I'm glad you're living with that boy, though Morocco has made me shift gears, and your qualms about whether or not you keep him seem silly.

That was written early morning and now it's late afternoon. I'm sitting in the so-called Cafe of the Garden, and it's cool and full of flowers and the boys are playing cards and I'm drinking mint tea and smelling like a whore. I put lots of eau de cologne on for some reason before going out. I've had a pipe of kif and am high and dry now. I just saw Paul and Larbi off on the bus to Tangier and have run away here before the awful English boy gets me. I had him to supper last Thursday and couldn't take him today.

Thursday is market day, the souk—which makes it the most exciting day of the week, unless some cult is performing on the street, and then that day is the most exciting. Though Thursday is always more so for me, since Dris goes to the market and buys lots of food and I love him with food. He bought today two pigeons (they are tied up now in the kitchen), and two hens (in his father's house) and two bulls' balls (so that each of us can have a ball) and millions of those dreary Mediterranean vegetables.

Dris just walked through the garden unexpectedly and sat down and we had a fight. Then we made up and he left me saying: Go fuck yourself and him saying, You fuck you crazin, which means: I'll fuck you until you go crazy. And he probably will too.

I don't know if I should tell you about the ants now. I'd planned to tell you about them but Dris brought me down. Anyway they're just ants hurrying by the millions underfoot. Actually, I've just remembered we had two fights now, one about postage stamps and one about kif. He hates to buy me kif. Sometimes he buys me majoun but never kif. I think it's because he thinks I should buy liquor so he can brag to his friends how we have whiskey and vermouth. He hates it that I want to do Moroccan things and don't act like an elegant European. He runs around in blue jeans and my red banlon shirt. That was a parenthesis. Anyway, I gave Larbi a dollar to buy me kif in Tangier (one-half pound) and Dris is furious, because he can't stand my asking any other Moslem boy to do anything for him. I got him to start teaching me Moghrebi by asking someone else in front of him to teach me.

I did get a letter from Show but they asked me to write the article on "spec" (as he put it). So I sent the letter to my agent. I haven't heard anymore about Esquire. I am doing a regular monthly piece for the Tribune. Not reviews. Little sort of literary essays. My first one is about Larbi and the watermelons. $100 each. Which is a nice sum each month. That is more than enough to live on splendidly here, but Dris eats like a horse and food is costing over $15 a week. Food alone, I mean. Skoura has been terribly sick for three weeks. She still is. And this too has cost a fortune. If I get my money from Girodias, I'm going to buy an old car when I finish a draft of this novel, if I finish it, insha'allah, (note local color), and go traveling around Morocco. I'm thinking of going to Marrakech in the fall to live. I mean that literally: I'm thinking. I was thinking it as I wrote it. I'd never thought it before, ever. Before I wrote it I was thinking of going to Tangier.

The soldiers are lining up in the square for an evening march.

There is always some big holiday going on, every weekend. Two weeks ago Mohammed's birthday. Last week circumcisions. All the little boys in town got cut. Very exciting. Lots of hoopla and screaming women. This weekend the Hamacha cult is having a public meeting. They slaughter a bull and then they play wild African sounding music and go mad into trances and cut their heads open. Dris says his father is head of the cult but I don't believe a word he says anymore.

Listen, you shit, I had a letter from Taylor Mead and was furious at you for about a minute, but then I got over it. It was madness the way he filled it out. I didn't get my own Ford grant and am halfsuspecting it's because of his letter. I am glad I didn't get it though, because I don't want to go back to the States.

I lead a very quiet life and am usually happy. Can you imagine? I suppose you are too. Isn't it funny the minute I left we both got lovers?

I am dry, too, though the kif has made me rather chatty. If you have a minute will you phone Walter and say I wrote him weeks ago, did he get my letter? And if perchance he didn't, give him my address. I feel a pang of longing for Extro as I write this, a conditioned reflex I suppose.

When I have time one day, I'm going to write an essay on the sexual monetary system in Morocco. Do you know *everyone* pays for sex. They even pay each other, unless they are lovers, males together or males and females. The fucker always pays the fuckee. The fee is very cheap for Moroccans. Europeans must pay—they don't have to really as it isn't payment but a gift, 500 francs=$1. They can pay less but it is very rude to do so. 500 is the price here for everyone except Paul who is an idiot and is making all the prices go up. (As I haven't been with anyone but Dris, this information is secondhand.) In Tangier of course the prices are much higher. Did I say the fucker always pays the fuckee? Yes. Unless the fuckee is a European. The European *always* pays (unless he is living *with* the boy and then he pays through the ears, especially emotionally. I mean huge scenes.) The other day Dris told me that a friend of his said he wanted to do me and I said, how much will he pay me, and Dris was in a perfect fury that I had the audacity to expect payment from a Moslem.

Well that is enough newsletter for now. The ants are dwindling but the flies are becoming impossible. My soul is swept with joy. I love the place. And the people. And the air. And Dris, when he wants to, can make me terribly happy. He had the nerve to tell me he told Paul (who'd said D. should see to it I work regularly): When I let him have peace, he works well, when I don't let him have peace, he works badly. It is true. But mostly he lets me have peace.

Twilight now. I am invaded by pleasure.

Write. Love from Alfred

Do you wait to work at the American school here? You can.

To Edward Field   Sept. 3, 1963 Asilah, Morocco

Edward

I've written you a dozen letters and hate them and loathe me.

I'm looking for a place in Tangier.

I threw Dris out two weeks ago.

I've been sick as a dog for days. Taking codeine and antibiotics.

Skoura is still sick. She hasn't wagged her tail in a month.

I want not to want love anymore. It makes me nauseous.

I get kifed every night starting at sunset.

Philip Lamantia is spending the week in Asilah. Last night I looked at him and loved him like a puppy.

I never feel like having sex. I'm surrounded by gorgeous boys but don't want any of them.

I hate this Morocco and I love this Morocco.

I'm writing this way because I am filled with contempt for myself and despise everything I feel.

I love you anyhow.

Alfred

To Dennis Selby   (early September 1963)—Arcila

Dear Dennis:

I don't know why I'm trying to write you when I'm in such a foul mood. It's been going on for days and getting worse. Chiefly, what it is, is that my love affair with Morocco, with Arcila, has ended. There's a saying here that if someone puts up a wall between you, you must build a second wall. Well, I am always building the first wall, and then when the second wall is put up, I start crying and say, no, I didn't really mean it. My wall wasn't real. Anyway I'm trying like mad to find a place in Tangier, though I don't know why. I can't think of anywhere else. I don't feel anymore that this is the place for me.

I want to be a writer again, oddly enough. I mean I want to believe in it again. I don't want love. I mean, I do of course, but it's ridiculous. I want to live alone. I don't of course, but anything else is ridiculous. I have the vaguest suspicion that Tangier will let me write, and I even have the feeling that may be why I came to Morocco. I'll be thirty-five on Saturday.

Paul has been in Tangier for the last two days, and an American poet named Philip Lamantia has been staying in a room on the beach. So Arcila has been better during the last couple of weeks. I feel as though God brought Philip here to prevent me from shriveling up. We see each other from about sunset (I'm usually in Tangier until then house-hunting), get high, and stay high until late at night. Oddly enough, he does most of the talking, and I know I am waiting for him to give me the word. I'm beginning to believe in the word again. I mean, I'm expecting to find something of value other than the hideous love-hunting. There is a new and unexpected me rising on the horizon. Please God, I shall be delivered safely of him. I feel I've got to sit it out here waiting for him, like Harriet.

Show apparently is commissioning a 2000 word letter from Tangier from me. $600. The Dris mess has become hopelessly unentangleable.

A day or two later. I've been terribly sick, still am, with some sort of flu. Paul is back. I just went out to sit on his terrace for a little. All sorts of famous queens were there. One thought I was 24. I'm very thin. I have only had one real meal since I threw Dris out. I'm thinner than I was in Mexico.

I loved your letter even though it was all gossip. How nice your garden of love couldn't be rosier, though even as I write I question. Philip has come with some marvelous hashish. It makes one gorgeously unnoticeably high.

I'm on bad terms with almost everyone in Arcila. After Dris, it all collapsed. All I do is wrangle with Paul, offend Larbi and enrage everyone. I was like this in Europe too. I wonder if I was like this in New York. This Morocco is so much living in the present. I can't believe in any other world.

I've succeeded in covering a whole page of letter without having a thing to say. I just covered it so you'd write me back a long charming letter. I'd write you a long charming letter except the qualities in me that make for length and charm I find abhorrent now and loathsome.

Though not in you.

Love and kisses to you. Alfred

To Harriet Sohmers (Zwerling)   23 Sept. 1963

Silvers said he saw you at Susan's cocktail party, so I assume you were okay then. When? Have you had the baby? What? Please write me.

I am okay. Not really. Clap again. We keep giving it back to each other. And lots of bizarre infected sores. But I am happy. I woke up this morning thinking that I'm full of shit. Dris and I are back together again. I threw him out and then he wouldn't come back for three weeks. I went through all kinds of hell because I saw what my life was all about. And just as I got reconciled he came back.

I'm doing a monthly column for the Tribune. First one appears next Sunday, 29th.

I had a huge fight with Paul and he started having a tantrum and throwing books and dishes all over the place. That was a week ago. I went into Tangier yesterday for the first time since and found he had told everyone on earth about it, or anyway it had all gotten around. He is really a shit. The pretext for my anger was Larbi (who is the Driss Ben Hamed Charhadi I write about in the Tribune) but it was really because he's done everything to mess my life up here. Tried everything to come between me and Dris, and was a good part of what made me tell Dris to get out.

I've been looking for a place in Tangier but things difficult because the sultan's here now. Do you know Irving Rosenthal? He's sweet. Ira Cohen? Ugh.

The galleys of my book came with the dedication to Edward and Irene, and I didn't know what to do about it, Irene I mean, but finally left it. I hate all my stories. They make me vomit. I'll probably be rich and famous before I've done a damn thing to merit it.

Jane says I've had more from Morocco than anyone she's ever known. She means Dris has given me more than Moroccans give. I used to think I deserved it, and I still think I do, but I don't think I've done anything to deserve it. Though I'm trying to now.

How Is Bill? Louis? Please please write me. I love you and kiss yon.
Ton Alfred

I saw the review of Susan's book in Time. It was really too bad and too stupid. It sounded personal. She didn't send me a copy of the book.

To Edward Field   2 Oct. 1963 Asilah, Morocco (Express mail)
Dear Edward

Today you're leaving so I'm writing. Probably my fifteenth letter to you. When I read them over I feel like a reel of movie film and that each letter is just a single frame, and so it is ridiculous to send it. So I save them, meaning to send all; then I hate them all and tear them up.

I am destroying the personal in me. I didn't realize this until just

24

now. I mean I am trying to become a man again, like I was before I went to America.

Everything I do is urgent. Life is becoming different for me. I am living again a little. I am grateful to this Morocco even for its deceptions and heartlessnesses.

I finally had a great fight with Paul, drove him to a tantrum, he smashed things all over the house, and I threatened to expose him to the world: He has been a monster in my life here. He wrote a letter to Ira Cohen saying he was making arrangements to have me "rubbed out" in Tangier. *Il est fou.*

I got my galleys and hate all my stories except "Behold Goliath." It (the book) is dedicated to you and Irene.

Norman Glass and Irving Rosenthal are coming to lunch here today. Dris and I are together again—God knows why. Just because I have no life of my own, probably. And he is someone to come home to like the dogs. Skoura has never recovered from her sickness. She is sort of spastic and hasn't wagged her tail in two months.

I'm working like a horse to support my idiotic menage: he eats like a Great Dane. No wonder they don't want him at home….The truth is you cannot be other than the creature of the situation. You suffer because the promise of love is implicit in Neil. But it's a lie. He cannot give it, anymore than you ever could.

xxx

Alfred

6 Oct. 1963   I've just torn open this letter which I hadn't yet mailed to ask you to send me please *d'urgence* a hundred dollars. I am suddenly down to nothing after shelling out for an apartment in Tangier, and now for terymiacin. We still have the clap. It won't go. Three months. I was getting quite scared but now they say this should do it. I've probably taken fifteen shots and Dris more.

The address of the apartment is 28 Sidi Bujari, Tangier, but probably won't move until your money comes, so wait to hear for sure. Can you send a bank check or what? I'm expecting 600 for my Show article and also 600 still from Girodias.

Irving Rosenthal loves your poetry, and says he was at Grove and was responsible for Seaver's interest two years ago and also chose the poems for Evergreen.

Love, Alfred

To Harriet Sohmers (Zwerling)   10 Oct. 1963—Tangier

Ma Lapinette Perdue: I had a wire this morning which read: *Hereuse annoncer mariage aujor'dhui obocer baisers bridaugroom zwerling.*

Please, what does *obocer* stand for?

I am happy you announce happily. I am glad you married that sweet purrson, rather than the other one. I really am, though doubtless neither you, he nor the other one will believe this. Please write me your news. I had your postcard but not the letter. Yes, much mail doesn't arrive. Please tell Louie [Zwerling] to wire me immediately the baby comes. I'd wire you now except I'm down to $20 and am moving to Tangier the above address tomorrow or after. I have a superb apartment, the nicest I've seen, $30 a month, with a terrace overlooking the cosmos, bigger than the roof on Sullivan St. Only three rooms, but two baths and fireplace. Out toward the country. Dris is coming along. If we don't fight again between now and going. I've thrown him out a dozen times this summer. I've settled for him, because Morocco is obviously not the place for anything but old genteel queens, and when I give up on him I never want anyone. I realize this last sentence is confusing, but I'm too lazy to explain.

Skoura is in a bad way. She never recovered from that meningitis and is spastic in her back legs, can barely walk, can't wag her tail. The tail wagging part is the worst. She's recovered most of her brains, all of them in fact, but she's always sad and chirps a lot as if in pain. She can't bark at all and has to piss and shit in the house. It's been two and a half months now and I don't really know if she'll ever recover. Dris says to kill her, and often enough the thought occurs to me. It's so terrible to

26

see her flopping down after every step she takes and then falling down the stairs if she gets too near them.

I had a huge fight with Paul. He went mad and smashed things. I called him a big queen and said I would expose him to the world for the monster he is. Jane poor thing was scared shitless. He rushed off to Tangier to tell her about it. He wrote a letter to a mutual friend to say he was making plans to have me bumped off, or some phrase like that. We never speak.

What else? Nothing really. I'm busy working on my article for Show magazine. On Tangier. They're paying me 600 if they take it, 150 if they don't. I get 100 a month from the Tribune. My galleys arrived for the book and I hate them too much to correct them. I saw the review of Susan's book in the Tribune. Is she famous now? Is she a name to be dropped, like off a cliff, *par exemple*. I had a love letter from a lady called Mrs. Jean Jacques Duval, Central Park West, who read my Salinger article. Doesn't the name sound familiar? She says: Relax, dear Mr. Chester, you are not about to be tracked down by a pursuing female (although I can't resist telling you that Dylan Thomas used to call me Theda Bara. Alas, poor Dylan, I knew him well.), and so on.

Darling, darling, I am so glad I have come here. Even when I'm not with Dris and walk around feeling abandoned and lonely, I thank God I'm here. If you come, we can take a huge house on the mountain for sixty or seventy a month. If you promise to keep away from Dris, and if Louie does too. And also your indubitably oversexed baby.

Going to PO now. Please write me. Please. I wish you joy all three.

Mille baisers and love from Alfred

To Dennis Selby   18 Oct. 1963—Tangier

Dear Dennis:

I ran into Paul yesterday with your letter in his hand. I had written you at length but hadn't mailed the letter. When I got home and read

27

it, I tore it up. Which is really why nobody hears from me. Not because I don't write, but because I tear it up. I interpret my life in your terms or Edward's or Harriet's and then afterwards I read it and feel ashamed, as though I'm living a life of great sin here and have to make it sound clean in letters. And besides also I'm in terrific motion, somehow, inside. Nothing seems true the minute after I say it.

We moved last Monday to Tangier finally. We is with Dris. I took a year's lease on this apartment, very lovely it is. I don't know what is happening to me really. Last night when I got home I began a letter to you saying: Dennis, I'm afraid. Sometimes I feel like I'm going mad, often, and then I think, yes it's true what they say about people coming here to go to pieces. And then often I feel more whole than ever before.

What I don't want to talk about is Dris, I suppose because I don't understand it. Sometimes I get the terrors that he is feeding me that stuff. It shocks me when people say we are lovers. He says he is my wife, though this is only very recently even remotely true as far as bed is concerned. He means he keeps house and I take care of him. He looks like a piece of classical statuary, very tall. To me, he is my ten year old friend I play marbles with, my accomplice in the murder of all Christians and Jews, my bonded servant, my omnipotent master, my third dog, the smiler with the enormous knife, that makes me feel I'm swallowing Prometheus fire and all. (Footnote: Prometheus has since awakened and decided to start a postage stamp collection. Could you please buy a few packets of stamps (foreign) at Woolworth's and send? Tell me how much and I'll send equivalent in kif or Moroccan cum.)

If I don't stop now I won't mail this. The sexual thing is at the heart of it.

I'm in the middle of the Show article, blessings on you sweetheart. I get $150 if they don't take it, $600 if they do.

The scene is sick here, sick. Sometimes I think if it ended with Dris I'd be out of here in twenty-four hours. Then I think never. I think all I want now is to write and give myself up at last to my madness.

I'm late on two deadlines and I've promised my wife socks and underwear. She is sleeping in the other room as she was up washing

28

floors until two and then fucking me until four. I've been up since seven working with dexamils I'm almost out of and then what. Yesterday for the first time he let me watch him shave his pubic hair. It was like being allowed into a mosque.

I suppose I should say, in case you keep this letter for posterity, that I was at a party for a young English nobleman at Bill Burroughs' house the other night. I took Dris in his djellaba and he made me promise I'd bring home a beatnik girl we could fuck together. Burroughs' scene is sicker even than most, he lives with two English faggots and his seventeen year old son. I despised the nobleman who alternated between trying to make me hot for him and trying to flirt with Dris.

Forgive, precious, the brevity of this note, but I must get to work. I will try to be better from now on and write more regularly. I work very hard indeed. I am glad you have your Stevie. I suppose I should tell you this isn't the best place in the world for a pair of lovers to come. But then what is?

Lots of love to you. Alfred

To Harriet Zwerling   (Telegram, dated Oct. 24, 1963,
                                          returned undelivered) Letter undated

Isn't Zwerling on the mailbox anymore?

I know it is the *djinns* and the *ifrits* that didn't want this telegram to arrive. They are trying to win me and probably will.

All the wire said was: joy blessings love kisses.

That's all I can say even now.

Does this make Milo scorpion?

God give him much courage, much strength, much laughter, an open heart, an endless appetite for life, the power to be silent or alone without pain, eyes good enough to catch sight of another's soul and suffering, a body which he need never make much of one way or the other, sicknesses which leave him healthier, wiser and more grateful, a knowledge of the French language so that he can converse with his mother, the ability to love those who love him, honor without pride, self-respect without vanity, and above everything the wit to distinguish between the work of man and the work of God.

xxxx Alfred

To Dennis Selby   1 Nov. 1963

Abandoned one, from Miss Lonelyhearts:

I am in the middle of doing my galleys for the book, weeks late and now your letter. Well, of course, it isn't over. Probably by this time you are hootching and cootching all over the place. Ah, self-deception, ain't it grand, says one self-deceiver to another. I was just lying here today with deception up my ass as usual and thinking, you know the nice thing about Morocco is that, at least for a Jew, you can forget Christendom. You can live out the whole immoral business of your character. Get angry, plot plots, revenge, etc. None of that cool detachment. It is so nice to be crazy like my ancestors.

Yes, I'm answering this as though he didn't come back, or as though you said no, though naturally he did and you didn't. It would cost you a little over a hundred to come. Which will leave you three hundred to begin with. An excellent beginning if you manage not to get married as fast as I did. No, you cannot teach. It is too late in the season. However—I am on kif now—you will find yourself able to manage. It is a difficult thing to discuss on the telephone, especially with wars on and things, but I know you trust old uncle Alfred. He recommends you insure your valuables, especially those gold cigarette boxes and the diamonds heavily. Theft is a daily occurrence here and it is too ghastly the numbers of people, myself included, who never think about insuring their baggage.

If I haven't said how I would love you to be here, let me hasten to say so now. Would you be happy here? I don't know. I have never loved anywhere so much as here. If it is love. Felt so much at home. Felt so right. I would suggest you get hold of my article, which should be arriving at Show magazine today or Monday and read it before you decide. I don't know whether they'll print it or not. It is sexy and highbrow.

Am I being thoughtless about your marital crisis? What is there to say, sweetie? All I can do is listen really. You know that yourself, I can't comfort you. The nice thing about Moslems is that they get less bored with time, more trusting, more loving. But Dris always says *il n'y a pas de confiance entre les Arabe*s. His best friend stole 10,000 francs from me the other day.

I've parted company with the Tribune as of this last article. They hauled it over without permission and I said I would write no more unless I got a written statement saying no more changes without my consent. They sent it not. My agent is obviously scared shitless because lawsuits are in my mind and she is responsible for allowing them to change. So that ends my monthly hundred. (As of now I'm expecting one hundred from them and at least one hundred fifty from Show. After that I'm on my own again. I wonder how Dris is going to take to finding out his Nazarene hasn't been kidding about poverty.

I bought Dris a box of watercolors and he is doing pretty zen trees. (marginal note: you will notice that being in Tangier is making me more like myself. Actually, it is intoxicating to watch this huge terrifying bit of rough trade making pretty watercolors and cooing over me.)

I went to Gibraltar the other day, overnight. Ghastly. I don't really know why I went. To buy socks, I think, as they're expensive here.

I have heard reports from three people today on the war, one said it was over, one (who is a correspondent for ABC) said it seems worse, and Dris who made up some story, as I am a Nazarene and must under no circumstances know the truth.

He has just came home from a round of cocksucking with the boys and we are going to study Arabic and eat.

Come soon.

I love you, dear heart. Alfred

To Harriet Zwerling   22 Nov. 1963

Maman: Tu n'as meme pas une minute pour ton pauvre vieux Alfred?
Do you want to give me complexes and sibling rivalries and things?
Can you be overprotecting Milo every minute of the day? I wish you
would write me a long long long letter, telling me how you came to
get married, all about having the baby, what about Louie, what about
everything. You must have oodles of time between tit. Put it to some
use. Remember, Milo will grow up and leave you, so don't forsake your
old darlings entirely. When you are old you will need us.

I am all right. I wish there were something to tell you about, but
there really isn't. The weather is mostly splendid still, though chilly at
night and in early morning, and occasionally gigantic rain. It would
be so nice if you were here. Would you consider it? It would be a
perfect place if there were people here one liked. But everyone is so
fucked up and mostly boring. Sometimes I think if it weren't for Dris
I'd leave, but then when I think that, I next think leave for where? And
then I think of New York and all the dead souls, and I don't want to
go there. So where is there? Anyway, this place makes me work hard,
which is nice. I have one friend, an English boy, named Norman Glass,
and I like Irving Rosenthal though he is difficult. Paul and Jane are
in Marrakech. I was supposed to go or be going, but I don't have the
money now. I was going to get presents there for Milo, so either I will
get them here or wait and get them there. What is he like, your Milo?
Dennis said he's beautiful.

I have a small but exquisite apartment and *peu á peu* I'm furnishing
it with lots of Arab junk. It's sort of a strange life that mustn't be
questioned too closely or it all falls apart. I wrote a fable for my
Tribune column, and the man says: "Every night I wake up sweating
and shaking and trembling, and with a start I ask myself: Who am I?
It's only this question that gives continuity to my life and identity to
my being. Only when I ask myself who am I, do I have any idea who I
am. I am he who doesn't know who he is. If I suddenly did know who
I was, I would no longer know who I was."

I suppose nowadays when you wake up you know just what it's all
about. Isn't that nice?

32

How are the ladies? I take it Susan's book was a big flop after all.

Skoura is a little better than she was. She's finally begun wagging her tail a teentsy-weentsy bit and she isn't so dazed-looking as she was, and even her poor little spastic backside seems somewhat better.

Will you write me a nice long happy letter? *Je t'embrasse.*

Love from *ton* Alfred

To Edward Field   27 Nov. 1963 Sidi Bujari 28, Tangier

Moushkie

I'm in the middle of war with my angel and feeling afraid about the Kennedy *complot*. It makes me nervous like some gigantic web covering the world. Lover boy and I are in the midst of another power struggle. The odd thing about power struggles is that they don't have a direct relationship to getting your way. I mean I am getting my way right now, but I have the definite feeling that I'm losing. Sometimes he gets his way and yet I know he is losing. It doesn't have to do with the surface, does it? He's just come back with the dog and is sitting here bothering me. The fight is of course about dogs and garbage. I'm damned if I'm going to be mama or Edwina again. I'm not picking up after him or, worse, complaining about it. I'm tired of complaining. He's sitting here, just sitting here, in that hideous Arab way, just sitting and looking. And I'm getting drunk because I can't keep calm in an Arab way. He's waiting for me to tell him to go to the market, so that he can say he doesn't want to. It all ends up with either my saying get out and then having to back down or else his saying I'm leaving and then he has to back down. But there always has to be the crisis. Also, we didn't fuck last night which makes the situation tenser. I'm about to burst into laughter. He can see the smile on my face and is trying to see the typewriter. The one word he can of course recognize is his own name which I'm tempted to put down but won't.

An hour later. The fight ended up where it was supposed to, and now everything is hunky dory again. My asshole is big enough to rent out as a three-room apartment. Know anyone who wants to move in? I finally got him to blow me. This is a national horror. The odd thing is that being blown is even more of a disaster. There is a story an old man tells about being blown by Paul twenty or thirty years ago. He the man, had a rock in his hand over Paul's head the whole time, saying, *ten' cuidado, ten' cuidado, si tu comes yo rompe tu cabeza.* Where was I? Yes, the trouble is Dris forgets the point of the fight. The point of the fight was that last night we quarreled about the fish and he threw it in the garbage and said he wouldn't cook. I said I was tired of having to argue about things. We fought. He went and cooked the fish that was left and made me a meal, but he didn't sit down with me. He went to bed. As I'd started smoking kif to calm down, my appetite was enormous and I ate every last scrap of everything. It now turns out that his idea about our quarrel is that I didn't leave him anything to eat. Real things matter so much to him, he is such an odd boy. When he gets gloomy I think it means some horrible Nazarene-style rejection like he is in love with someone else. But it never means anything abstract. It means I haven't given him twenty francs for the pinball machine.

Evening. I just got back from the market with Jane. It's the first time she's been to the market in years and she was very happy and ate pinchitos and was thrilled. She says everyone on earth knows the Kennedy thing is a fascist plot. I knew it all the time and it is scaring me. I just read the above paragraphs and I was drunk and also somewhat kifed or I wouldn't have bored you with all the fish and things....Show magazine was evidently struck dumb by my article. I knew they wouldn't take it, but they promised me a hundred fifty even if they didn't. But now they won't cough up and my agent is being very highhanded. She is getting to be a pain in the ass. She screwed me up at the Tribune, but now that is straightened out. I quit because she gave permission to change my second article. Also, I'm seriously thinking about writing a novel but I won't talk about it. I saw Paul for a minute while he was putting up his goodies from Marrakech. I hate him. Hajmi was there to my great shock and horror. Poor Norman is in love with Hajmi. Not really in love, but I've told him it would be good for him to get married and settle down. Hajmi is one of my Arcila rejects. Anyway Hajmi won't sleep with Norman, won't fuck that is, though he does sleep at his room. It is all a mystery why. But Dris says Hajmi is afraid of *ts'heur* [black magic] which is reasonable as I asked him once to get me some for Dris. So he thinks us white people are as wicked as they are.

This sounds like I have a social life. I haven't. I work all the time and see no one but Norman. Occasionally I see the people from bat palace who are so far gone on drugs that it's mostly impossible. Irving is nice though. I had them all over on Saturday for snake tajine, stewed that is, a specialty of Dris'. Rosalind was all squeamish about it, which was ridiculous as she once southern fried a dead bat and they all ate a piece of every part of it. Irving said the snake tasted like gefilte fish. It did too because I forgot to turn the fire down when Dris went out to buy oil.

I just realized that I'm still drunk. If I were sober all this would be terribly boring for me. I had a lot of wine at Christopher Wanklyn's.

I must stop this and do my homework. My Arab teacher comes tomorrow. I completely forgot and haven't looked at the stuff in a week.

Next morning. My novel, if I write it, I think can only be about one thing, that I was fifteen, then twenty, then twenty-five, then thirty, now thirty-five, and I have never succeeded in becoming myself, I still don't know who I want to be. Who I am is any given circumstance.

Norman and Hajmi came over last night and looked cute. They still haven't made it, but I presume would have last night. Dris and I clucked like an old married couple. Then they left and we put steaks on the fire and he fucked me twice. Sometimes I get panicky, really deeply frightened by all this sex. His ease, though, is reassuring. In the middle of it all last night he began singing me an Arabic love song.... Skoura is a little better. At least she finally wags her tail. Irving laid healing hands on her. But she is still terribly spastic and walks like a junkie....All of Burroughs' boys have moved out except his son. I feel sort of sorry for him, though I think he's a monster....When there is peace between me and Dris, like now, I can't tell you how lovely life is, as it has never been before.

Somehow this letter is all wrong, but I'm going to mail it anyway. Will you write to me? I give you both kisses.

Love from Alfred

Now Thursday evening. I've got apple sauce and stringbeans on the fire. It's thanksgiving, you see. Dris bought a great big chicken which I wanted to do in the fire, but instead he is doing it Arab. Well, compromise is the only alternative life offers us to total defeat. Abdl Krim has been—and gone. It was a great lesson. Dris sat and grunted, feeling put down by prissy miss Abdl Krim's education and moving around the place like the piece of rough trade he used to be. We had just had another terrific crisis. He packed again and I just sat and pretended not to notice. To tell the truth, I hardly did notice. It's all so tiring as you know. The other day I kept a diary for one hour. The first entry reads: Today, the old person caught up with the new life. He came through a moment with all his years, all his exhaustion. (Oops, I must go look at the apple sauce.) (another parenthesis: That's what makes everything so hard, being abstract about life at one moment and then having to look at the apple sauce; it makes us so disintegrated; we should try to be one thing for a long time.) Where was I? My diary, to continue: "There must be something else, I wept, meaning other than the mountain and the trees and the world and the piece of paper in the typewriter. In Arcila once I cried without tears. Now again, I cried without tears, he said, please God let me cry. Suddenly, but a little later, it came like a blessing. The new life is just a fresh paint job on a crumbling house. The continuity of the structure and desiccation the unity of the man (myself) is in that. Even my energy is an attitude."

But before that, where was I? Oh yes, the fight. Anyway he packed up and left three times, then rang the bell for this or that pretext. And came back in. And the third time he realized I wasn't going to come after him (of course it was only the first time it was difficult) and he came in and I knew I had to save his pride so I said stay, and he lay down on the bed. I felt terrible because I hate to win. I mean,

36

ultimately it doesn't matter to me whether I win or lose, I mean win or lose power. I just don't want to have to argue about the same things every day, it is boring and exhausting. But he is only twenty-one and an Arab and it matters to him, and I hate it when I have to defeat him. And oddly enough when I win, I just win out of fatigue because I'm too tired to go through all the dramatics and emotions of losing. Defeat brings out all my heroic postures. Anyway, that was hours ago and he just came back for a minute to tell me he'd been playing soccer with a bunch of fourteen-year-olds, and so he was happy as a lark.

Edward, if I should break up with Dris I would probably want to rush back to New York. Please promise to tell me not to, if I should give you the chance. I don't think it's good for me there.

I had the proofs of my book and hated it so kept it delayed for ages, then finally rewrote page after page; and they say it will cost me a fortune (imagine them assuming anything could cost me a fortune) and delay publication until April or May (originally Jan. Feb.). It is dedicated to you and Irene. I wanted to take Irene out, but didn't finally, though like you I have drawn the line between the sexes. I think you were about thirty-five then too. I will stop now. Happy thanksgiving to you both.

To Harriet Zwerling   29 Nov. 1963
Mumsie

I was so glad to get your letter. I thought you'd never write again. Yes, Milo de Venus would have to be beautiful wouldn't he? Actually he does have your eyes. As for the chin, well most babies have that gumpy chin, don't they? Normal ones grow out of it....*Comme le parrain* (pariah I almost wrote), I tell you that it is your first duty to try to make life as bearable as possible for Milo and not develop another ulcer case. Why don't you escape from your in-laws to Tangier; or come say in March and I'll take a big house in Arcila for all of us. Oh, no, cats and babies and dogs. Well, I'll take two houses. I'm seriously thinking of going back in the spring because the fishing season starts and it is better Dris keeps to his trade as well as to his people. Assuming we're still together in the spring. Oh, darling, if you were only here I would be so happy.

We're going to Marrakech on Monday for a week, leaving the dyke concierge to care for the dogs. Skoura, by the way, makes slow recovery. She finally started wagging her tail. I never thought I'd see that happen, and her brain is obviously improved. I mean she has started remembering me again and being afraid of Columbine [her mother] again. But she still doesn't remember anything more than three seconds. And she is still very spastic in the back legs and can't walk down or up steps. She hasn't barked once since July. Anyway I'll send you a sheepskin for the baby and slippers for both of you. Now you will think I'm telling you this because I'm going to ask a favor. But don't think that. Because I never offered anything in return when I've asked you favors, you rat. You think I want to borrow money, which is good, so when I tell you what I do want you'll be relieved. Besides I will pay you for them. I want to give Dris a pair of black cowdens for Christmas. I don't approve, and told him I would rather spend more money to get him dressed the way he is supposed to rather than like an American faggot. But you can't stand in the way of a national destiny. So. He has been dying for them and also he is dying to have a Christmas (he won't accept that I'm a Jew) now that he has a Nazarene, with tree and all. Well, if Susan could do it for David [Rieff, her son], I suppose I can do it for a Moslem. Anyway, his size is what? I just measured him with the tape measure and he is about 72 inches, 6 feet, but yet he seems taller than you. Anyway he fits into mine, which I think are a 32 waist or maybe 31. No, make it 32. I don't like his great big cock and round ass being so much in evidence with all the ferocious carnivorous and rich Englishmen around. In fact, make it 33 if there is, and as long in the leg as possible, at least 32, no, what am I saying. Very long in the leg, the longest. He doesn't like ankles and things showing. If you could get me (marginal note: I mean, also a pair for me) a pair 32 waist, 28 leg, I would be glad. (I've just had a pipe of kif which is what makes this endless conversation about nothing possible.) I'll send you the money. It should take close to a month to get here, so get them first opportunity. Tear off the labels and declare no value if you have to, because there is a stinky ridiculous customs here.

When Dris loves me, I love him very much. I hear in my head now, him going around the house as he sometimes does singing: Ay ay ay ay ay I like you berry much, ay ay ay ay ay I tink your gwand. He's out getting kifed with the boys down the street. When he doesn't like me and is bad, my heart really stops and becomes stone.

This paper is now covered with Flit. The flies never end here. It is still warm. I have to light a fire in the morning for an hour and at night, but otherwise comfy. Barely any rain so far, this is supposed to be extraordinary.

I now have four different minds, the kif mind and the old mind, the Moslem mind and the Christian/Judaic mind. Actually the Moslem mind is as much Berber and pagan as Mohammedan. It is the most exalting of them all. The Christian/Judaic mind is all full of guilts and worries. Thus, last night, while cooking applesauce, it occurred to me that the first time in my life I believed that homosexuality was not unnatural, it was just another thing in nature. I mean it didn't seem wrong in the eyes of the universe. Then I lay down and started reading Buber's Hasidic Tales and immediately my old CJ mind returned. Right away, theories. I just remembered that I'm talking to you and you'll get bored if I go on with this. There is one thing that will interest you, and this came out of a great high last night. I thought that sex is the only one of our natural acts which is impersonal in the sense of not being concerned with our individual preservation but rather of the species. Now, our egos cannot endure or accept anything except as a means of personal survival, and hence we try to absorb the object of our sexual longings into ourselves. We don't really want to admit a greater importance in any single thing to the race or the cosmos than to ourselves. This sounds improperly thought out. But I'm not kifed now. Kif makes the connections and leaves you to figure them out.

Is Susan famous? Jane and Paul couldn't read her book, it seems. This has been a year of great changes for everybody, hasn't it? The Kennedy business is atrocious. The Texans, police anyway, are shameless. It is hard to believe they could be so stupid and naïve. It's made me adore America and Kennedy, etc., doubtless a passing emotion. The old man, Joe Kennedy, is of course the tragic hero. His mechanical empire wiped out in a minute by a nobody. It is a lesson in humility.

Please write me a long long long long long long letter. Or why don't we both buy tape recorders and send voice letters?

I love you darling and give you a million kisses and also Milo and hello to Louis.

Ton Alfred

To Dennis Selby   1 December 1963

Dennis dear Dennis

I spent most of Saturday trying to write you a letter, but I kept getting stuck on the subject of jealousy. So now it is Monday morning and I will try again, and try not mentioning jealousy. It is cold—well, not really cold, I suppose about fifty and rainy and there is little wood left for the fire and no point buying any as it's rained for two days and all the wood supplies will be sopping wet. Dris is in Arcila; he goes home every Sunday, comes back Monday afternoon. I have 24 hours of solitude, which I love, though I wouldn't love it more often.

I was thinking last week, actually the day before Kennedy died, of becoming British. It seems so much safer somehow. The Kennedy thing has affected or effected (I never know which is which) me very powerfully. I knew right away, as everyone here did, but no one seems to in America, that it was some hideous rightist plot. And it has scared the daylights out of me. Everyone keeps talking about the Reichstag fire. And the French paper L'Express makes a huge appeal to Bobby Kennedy not to accept any compromises but to uncover the truth. It is all ghastly. Please get away from that awful place as soon as possible, and hurry over here where I can protect you.

Jealousy (here I go again) is, I think, greatly dependent on self-esteem. It is the old question of cuckoldry. Now I'm not going on. It's too complicated for a letter.

We're going to Marrakech tomorrow for a week. Christopher [Wanklyn], a Canadian friend with a house there, is driving us down and we'll stay with him. Dris is trying to get 15,000 francs out of his father to buy a *silham*, a sort of sleeveless djellaba, so he can ride on a horse at the *mouloud* festival, Mohammed's birthday or something and deliver little boys for circumcision, a great honor. He couldn't do it this year, not having a *silham*. When I had the money I wouldn't buy it for him, because I was all full of Paul's bullshit about not getting taken. It is so odd, I used to almost weep with frustration, saying to Dris, when will you be on my side? And it's taken me five months to realize that I wasn't on his side.

The mail just came. There was your silly letter and I am jealous, not of your happiness, but that you had the nerve to talk about it. I often feel that way lately but am embarrassed to say so or superstitious, like tempting the devil: Anyway I'm glad. What are you supposed to say, except I'm glad. Yes, one always is depressed by someone else being too happy. There is only room for one happy person at a time in this world. With your letter came nothing from my agent, the bitch, which means of course that she hasn't collected.

Dear Dennis, what shall I tell you about myself? I am slightly changed. Morocco, kif, Dris.

Dris just came back. His father didn't give him the money. His father told him: Your Nazarene is as crazy as you are, I know he just gives you money to show off with. Which is, alas, the case. Christopher says it's like putting my head into a lion's mouth, but so far it's been okay. I mean if the Moslem doesn't come home with a pile of money for his family they wonder what is the point of his living with a rich Nazarene. And Dris is naturally the biggest showoff and exhibitionist in Arcila, so when he goes home I give him practically all the money in the house to show off with. I suppose his father has finally noticed that the money doesn't stay home, it just passes through.

Since he is a retired whore, as he says, he has gone into matchmaking. He is so shrewd that he gets paid from both sides. He is wrapping up a bargain with Paul today. He says if I'll help he'll split it with me. But it seems too silly to take half of his fifty cents. He gets a sort of royalty arrangement with the boys he fixes up. They don't pay him just once. They pay him every time, unless of course it's a marriage. Then there's a lump settlement.

I picked up a couple outside the house here who just got off the boat. They came from Ibiza, a Dutch girl and a French/Japanese boy. They stopped me in their car to ask for directions. Oddly enough they were looking for the house I lived in in Arcila, as some faggots who were here in the summer had mentioned it to them. They didn't mention how ghastly it was. Anyway, I've asked them to stay here for a week and take care of the dogs, as the concierge conked out at the last minute. The dogs are even more of a problem than they used to be as Skoura still can't go up and down stairs, and so shits in the house.

Love and kisses to you, happy one.   Alfred

To Edward Field   20 Dec. 1963 Sidi Bujari 28, Tangier
Dearest heart,

Your letter came this morning and I've read it ten times I'm so happy for you. Except for the publisher, it has all worked out better than anything I imagined. So here you are America's most famous poet. Your letter also depressed me because I'm feeling like a big fake. I don't want to write articles anymore and I hate my short stories and everything. I just want to write a book, but I don't know if there is anything honest in me.

I've been starving lately. I sent Dris back to Arcila on Sunday as there was no point both of us starving, though he obviously loves me better poor than rich. He cooks beans in a variety of gorgeous ways, and he wants to go on eating them so we can have money for other things, like the pair of shoes I've been promising him since July. The check from Girodias obviously got lost in the mail; I haven't had a word from my agent in three weeks. She has done nothing about Show, and I will have to take the bull by the horns to get my guaranteed $150 and write to [the publisher] Huntington Hartford. Also the franc deal with Girodias fell through. The book [*Chariot of Flesh* by Malcolm Nesbitt, pseud. Alfred Chester, Olympia Press, Paris] was reprinted two years ago in a special white-cover edition. I hoped my mother would come through, and finally today Jane came and sent a telegram for me. I wanted to phone but the lines are impossible on account of the storms. I said to wire money today. On top of everything I've had no wood for the fire and my back is bad. I've been keeping myself high with kif and codeine tablets. I simply can't work under these circumstances and have two deadlines within the next two weeks, one for the Tribune and one on Genet for Commentary. I've been rereading *Notre Dame des Fleurs* and it is as wonderful as ever. My trouble is that I can't take these lapses into poverty anymore, I mean physically I can't take them: They aren't anymore things to be gotten through, they now just are. If I weren't a coward I'd just give up and become a bum. I feel our roles are reversed again. There you are living your glamorous life in New York, full of success, and here I am a failure. Anyway Norman's coming back. I had a card today from Marrakech saying he had sent Hajmi home, couldn't take it anymore and he is coming back soon.

My mother would probably send me money if my brother would let her. He seems to have no conscience and bears me no love. She doesn't either of course, and what is especially difficult is that she in her tradition needs to be martyred by a bad son, just like any Jewish mother. If she gave me money, she would stop suffering.

It is nice that you don't judge me. I am worn out with my own judgments of myself. I am thirty-five and still begging. Why don't I just get a job? Why don't I just forgive myself my past? Even that I can't do. I just go on living all my sorrows and shames. I have almost no love in

43

my heart. Sometimes I feel a rush of feeling in Dris, and I remember distantly what it was like.

Ts'heur is black magic, love potions, poison, etc. The Arabs all dread it. It is only two months since Dris has trusted me enough to let me do any of the cooking.

The maid just arrived. In all my poverty I have a maid. She costs $6 a month and is an idiot. I have to tell her to do the same things every day. Imagine expiring of starvation in the midst of troubles with my domestics. I phoned Dris's brother's stall this morning and told him to come back. He is so profoundly fatalistic about life that he hinders me from manipulating my circumstances. I mean, if we're broke we're broke—*suerte*, he says (that's Spanish for, I think, fortune or luck), or that's the way the cookie crumbles, and he cooches and sings. (I can sing "Tell me that you love me as I love you" in Arabic.) And then I forget. The maid is dying to know why Dris isn't here. She's always listening at the doors and probably thinks that we've had a quarrel.

It's now three p.m. which means, I believe, it is nine a.m. in N.Y. I sent the wire at eleven-thirty, or five-thirty in New York. It should have been there by eight-thirty. The banks here close at five or what is eleven there. Which means the money can't possibly be here today. Well, there are still some beans left, *suerte*, as I've been too high to eat. Oh, that woman is too horrible. The one in Arcila robbed like a demon, and this one is honest, but I can't stand her....I've had another fight with Paul. This one is my fault. I let Dris fix him up with a boy, pretending not to know about it. He gave Dris 2000 francs and I like an idiot told a mutual friend about it who went and told Paul. This was horrible to Paul as probably the main reason he let Dris fix him up is because he thought he was getting Dris to do this behind my back.

Hours later. Went to bank. *Walu,* meaning nothing. Dris is back, saying *suerte* and planning beans for supper. He brought me two drums from Arcila as presents, one that belongs to him, a big gorgeous painted one from Fez, shaped like a *compotière*, or whatever you call it, Y-ish, and a little one prettily painted but not so exotic from his niece who is my friend in Arcila. She is about eight and has a pretty face like a French girl and hennaed hair. We've been having jam sessions, just the two of us, with the tambourine drums we bought in Marrakech and the *gnaoua* [cult] clanky things, iron cymbals like dumbbells. My favorite song is the one about the U.S. soldiers arriving here and the chorus goes: Fuckie fuckie, money money, come, come come, ahhamerikun. He had to tell everyone in Arcila we'd had a fight to explain why he stayed so long; he would sink in their esteem and probably be considered a faggot if he admitted to living with a broke Nazarene. Only one he told, Mohammed Dumdum, who made Dris go back to me after the big fight in Arcila, which someday I'll tell you about in all its gory detail.

Next afternoon. I'm not long back from the consulate where they let me phone my mother as there was no money at the bank. I waited two hours to get the call through because mama kept picking up the receiver and hanging up as soon as she heard Morocco calling. I think she was afraid I might be dead. Finally she answered and just yelled and said she wasn't going to send me anything. (The call will probably cost twenty or thirty bucks, you can't call collect from here.) I kept saying in a subdued way, do you want me to die here? and she said, do what you want. I hung up on her as I couldn't think of anything to say and it would have been embarrassing to shout with all the embassy people hanging around. I came home and cried of all things, can you imagine? Dris came and lay down and gave me a lot of kisses and said *No tenemos suerte.* So I guess it does mean luck. He said he was sleepy and is now asleep. I think he plans to hibernate until money comes. I don't know when that will be now. There isn't a franc left, and though I hate to borrow more from Jane I'll probably have to and send him back to Arcila. It is good of him not to have failed me now, but of course he knows all about poverty.

Next day. I've had some sort of infection around my eyes and on the lids for weeks, mild fungusy. Now suddenly it's gotten terrible and sorey and it's breaking out on my right ear and all over my penis. Very disgusting. I look a hundred years old and very puffy. My eyelids are red lumps. It takes hours for them to clear in the morning....I started writing my piece for the Tribune yesterday and it is all about my money problems, but really I can't put my heart into literature now. But I felt great because suddenly the whole thing seemed very funny. I saw Jane and she arranged with the dykes at the French bookstore to agree to pay me the Olympia Press money if Girodias agrees. If he doesn't pull another fast one, it should start coming through next week. Then she gave me 3000 francs and I bought some meat and went home to find Dris making a stew out of two potatoes, two tomatoes and two onions. It tasted like Chinese, very good. Jane says Moroccans love when their Nazarenes go broke; it makes them equal, she says.

I know I musn't let my mother and brother get away with this. I feel somehow that the iron is hot for striking, but I don't know how to go about it. She had $100,000 in investments only when my father died in 1949. In 1959 her interest was $8,000, you can figure back on four percent or so for bluechip stock. She keeps reinvesting her interest and lives on Social Security. Of course she was caught last year for eight years' back taxes, but even so. And now she sold the house. I am not imagining money, Edward, it is really there. Aren't they ghouls? It is really quite extraordinary they can be such pigs. Do you think my brother never feels one twinge of conscience on having never offered me even a token sum for the family business, which of course is quite outside any investments. My mother knows perfectly well that I am really sitting on pins and needles waiting for her to die, and this probably bothers her so much that if she hasn't already, as she once said she did, she will leave me nothing. I was sitting with Dris this morning heaping curses on them. I put a horrible fearful curse upon them. The awful thing is that if I said something sneaking like send me 500 to come home, they would send it. I mean they want me to cheat them out of the money. I mean she doesn't want me to act as though it is mine by rights. I suppose maybe she does have a profound guilt after all, and that's why she can't admit to any money being mine. But now I have acted as though it were mine, what do I do next? Why don't you call up my cousin the lawyer and ask him why I have to starve when my mother has two hundred grand and my brother has

46

my father's business? As you are the only family I have, you have the right to interfere I suppose. His name is Samuel Chester, LO 3-4413. He will laugh at you if you call. They like to do that. They like to laugh and say, oh, ho, ho, funny little boy, oh ho ho.

Night. A miracle has just happened. Fifty dollars from Elga Duval. Did I tell you about her? She started writing me love letters during the summer because of something she'd read, and partly, mainly to get rid of her, I wrote and said I needed $2000 and would she send it to me if she could afford to. So she sent fifty instead. Oh, cherished fifty, better than $2000. Skoura knows. She's running around the house in circles for the first time since she got sick. I will begin my criminal career with this money. I just ran to Jane's to tell her the news, but she got hysterical about my eyes and started phoning the doctor. Dris is still out with the boys. I give you a thousand kisses. And will mail this tomorrow.

xxxx Alfred

To Edward Field   Jan 9, 1964 Sidi Bujari 28, Tangier
Qelbi

It's more than six months since I saw your glowing face and beheld your gleaming eyes. Listen, I have fallen in love with Dris. (Except when I hate him.) Yesterday at this time I was ready to pick up and leave. Then I kissed his foot. He said not to as it would remove the magic pebble from my ass (*soowish* is ass in Arabic.) I did that once before on the street in Arcila at three in the morning. The miracle happened, I mean the love miracle after reading something in Kierkegaard. (I attribute the miracle to him though I can't remember what it was I read.) I was suddenly inside Dris. In him. (I just thought I'd change color for fun.) [Ed's note: ink changes from green to red.] I could hardly believe it. Suddenly I was Dris at the market. And I knew exactly who he was and exactly who I was to him. I burst into laughter. It was simple and so

47

lovely. Norman thinks he's terrifying. Everyone thinks he's terrifying. I used to think so too. My gentle lamb, I told him today when he was standing at the door to the terrace that he made the sky bluer. He stuck his ass out and said: Doesn't that make it even bluer? He is void of functionless poetry. Do you know that he cannot make a graceless gesture? All those centuries of practice, perfectly executed. This new piece of information requires green ink. [ink color changes to green] He and I have the same name. I keep wanting to write you this; maybe I have. Also Castro has the same name. Dris is Kasri, which comes from Ksar, which means castle or fort. It comes from the same word as castle—castrum which means camp (of all things:). Chester (oh, if only that were my name) is the anglicization of castrum and Castro the spanolization. Does that sound superbly fateful?

[ink changes to red] By the way, *suerte* is his Spanish word for *mktoub* which means: It is written.

I can't decide now whether this letter is red against a green background or green against a red background. I'm deliciously high.

[ink changes back to green] Edward, I wrote a wicked column for the Tribune, libeling (so he said) Show, Olympia, my mother and my agent. So I revised it and my agent has quit in a huff because she still felt libeled. So I sent him a telegram. The Girodias check lost in the mail was an open Amex money order. Can you imagine their madness? I am all right for money now. The bookstores are paying me. But my career feels ruined. Thank God. My family disowned me. I wish I could do something. [ink changes to red.] I haven't yet recovered from those awful weeks before Christmas. I may enclose a photo of me, D. and Mohammed Dumdum. I can't decide whether I look like a ten-year-old bull dyke or an eighty-year-old Truman Capote. It is really a very sinister photograph. I look like the brains behind a dope racket with his two bodyguards.

(unsigned)

To Edward Field   Jan. 20, 1964 Sidi Bujari 28, Tangier

Dear love

Two letters from you today. Oh, your life is so exciting. I'm in a rush with deadlines. My Genet essay tears everything down, the whole of western civilization. It must be there by the 1st, and my column is due today for the Trib and I haven't even begun it. I want to write about Mailer as a postscript to the Genet. The Genet says that when Christ died in the 19th Century Europe woke from a sweet dream with a bloody knife in its hand. It couldn't face its guilt, 2000 years of godless murder so it had to go on believing in dead institutions. "Freud comes briefly to Europe's rescue with his brilliant diversion. He makes guilt personal; though he too denies God, he fouls from the target by making it possible for a man to ignore history in favor of his childhood. We pay attention to our mouths and anuses (tr. assholes). What a relief to be guilty of nothing worse than coveting mama. (And what a perfect totalitarian weapon psychoanalysis potentially, if not actually, is. It reduces all opposition to expressions of personal and misdirected hostility. It makes all protest infantile.)...." On and on goes my inexorable logic, until the coup: "Hitler had the genius to turn Christianity inside out, to make that of which the Christians were most guilty into the ideals of a new order. Conquest, murder, betrayal, all the crimes of man that had been for twenty centuries blessed by God, again received the blessing, and along with it the blessing of bread."

It is genius but I hate it. I am so jealous of you. I mean envious.

It's Ramadan. So Dris sleeps all day and then sits up all night in the cafe next door getting kifed. Ramadan is the holy month in case you don't know. No eating smoking fucking or anything from dawn to dark. Everything allowed at night, but everytime we have sex he has to rush off to the hammam. He mutters prayers the whole time and I think hates me a little just for being alive at this holy time.

Norman is leaving Morocco and I can't say I'm sorry, but I'll miss him as he's my only friend. Oh, it is so sick here. And I'm going through a terrific crisis. Kif. It has taken me into a new (old) level of my personality. The nothing. The no one. The brilliant fake. I hate myself. I hate myself. My stories are all impostures. They're just me showing I can fit into any pair of clothes. And be more brilliant than the man who first made them. But I am no one. Only in "Behold Goliath" a little. And my hatred. Edward, I hate people. I hate everything and everyone. Deeply I do. Under kif I wrote about Alfred Chester: He hates people and this he has refused to admit to himself. It creeps out but he pretends not to notice it. He distributes love with the ease of the unfeeling, and everyone obeys him. Love is a gigantic weapon, especially when you don't feel it and people think you do. He has been at this game for so long that he's begun to think he actually does love people. But the truth is he doesn't and I think he is getting a little tired of the game. He is tired of laughing and kissing and entertaining.... It broke off here. I just have never faced myself, really. That probably sounds so boring to you, but it is causing me gigantic anguish. Even my criticism. All I ever do in it is try to show the writers up. I am campier than Rechy, beater than Burroughs, more brainy than Nabokov, more zen than Salinger, etc etc. All you have to do is turn the dial and I'm it. Even all this is just because of Genet probably. I'm Genet now. Is there any hope of ever being Alfred?

"When one looks back at the slaughtered of Christendom   the American Indians, the Negroes, the Moslems, the Christians themselves, the Asiatics and Africans—six million Jews are a drop in the bloody bucket. Hitler was no uncouth accident in the ladylike history of Europe. He *was* the history of Europe, he *was* Europe—merciless up to its very last gasp. And if we don't know of the crimes of the humanists, it is probably only because the humanists won the war."

"To a melody by Mozart, enter Jean Genet, whom Francois Mauriac has accused of being in league with the devil."

I'm feeling a little better now. I woke Dris up on the pretext that I wanted him to go to the market and so he diverted me for an hour. As it would never occur to him that he was anything but a whole with tradition wrapped around it, he rightly thinks my profound anguish needs no more than a tickle and a kitchy to disappear. Is it awful that he should be so right?

He was enchanted, as I was, by the cock in Liberty's hand [Postage stamp of the torch in the hand of the Statue of Liberty, turned upside down] So what else should be in the hand of freedom? Did you get the photo? You don't say anything so I'm not sure you got that letter....I finally surrendered and wrote to the girl on the ship. She just kept writing and begging and I gave up. I suppose I have to be careful now....Heaven has just come back from the market and is cooking himself harira, a soup made with rancid butter and flower, flour I mean. They all eat it when the cannon goes off—which is when the moon rises. The moon looks different now. It looks holy. Then about eight o'clock the flutist plays in the street and everyone has supper. At three in the morning the drums begin to wake people up for breakfast. To the accompaniment of flutes one eats spongy bread with rancid butter, Arabic pastry and tea or coffee, kifed to the ears. I feel like Paul Bowles to whom I do not speak, thang kod....I read a letter that Irving Rosenthal sent to Norman and on the bottom it said "a kiss to mama hen." And I thought that must be me. Ever since I read it I feel like I'm laying an egg every time I open my mouth.

Do you ever read my column? The one coming in a week or two is the poor one. It's nice. I hope some rich person reads it and sends me an allowance so I can try my hand at a novel. I think maybe I could produce something. It makes me feel a little happy when I think of Marty Tucker reviewing me in the Post. Please see he gets his review in early and that he should call me a genius at least once somewhere so my relatives will read it.

I finally ran out of dexamils and to my surprise I went right on working, just as many hours and just as clearminded. Lots of coffee though. I don't need liquor either, though I might if I started on a novel. I can't write at all with kif except analytical horrors.

Tuesday. Strange you mention the golden chalice. I use it in the Genet. I say: He holds the golden chalice in his hands but he knows the Holy Water has dried out of it leaving a crust of blood around the edges. I thought I was making up the expression as an image of the cup, the holy grail. But I guess I wasn't. Yes, I think it is the cup of the tarot, since I've always assumed, or was told, that the tarot cup is the grail. What made Rosetta Reitz think of asking me?

Norman has terrific chutzpah and so he got us invited to lunch tomorrow on the Mountain at the home of an English nobleman. No one else is coming to dinner, to lunch, probably because the Hon. David Herbert doesn't want us creeping into society. I am definitely out as far as the chic people go, and as far as the beatniks go. No one wants me. Even Dris almost left yesterday when for the 10,000th time I told him I was Jewish. He refuses to accept it. But yesterday I made the mistake of saying it again *in mitten drinnen* Ramadan. He said he could never sleep with me again and was ready to go. Then he looked at my neck and said it was an American neck and would hear no more about it.

Every night now, on account of Ramadan, I go to bed alone and usually slightly or very kifed. And this is what I do: I think of awful things, incomplete things that make me suffer, and I complete them in the most ghastly way possible. It makes them happen and then they are ended. Then I do another thing. I twist my face and body and make hideous noises and laugh and scream and go generally mad. It occurred to me the other night that I was denying myself a great variety of possibilities. I mean slumping into melancholy, etc., all the time, rather than being all these other interesting things. Have you ever done this? It's fun.

Yes, you can say Alfred Chester will tour with you next year.

"But no one can be thrown out of civilization because each man contains the whole and tells the truth about the whole. A state executes in order to disavow everyone's guilt. The execution of Eichmann, for example, makes all the rest of us seem innocent, when in fact the only honorable and honest thing would be to have the whole human race hanged in Jerusalem."

Do you think Commentary will be amused by that?

Dris is going to the market so I'll pack this up and tell him to mail it.

And I send a million kisses to you, loviedovie. Did you actually take Neil to VP [Variety Photoplays, *louche* movie house on the Bowery]? On Sundays I miss it like an old sweetheart. Also certain subway stations like DeKalb Avenue.

Love

Alfred

To Dennis Selby   Tangier—26 January 1964

Dear Dennis

I've just been left too, so there. Not an hour ago. And let me tell you it is very difficult getting left by a Moroccan. In fact, so far as I know this is the first time it's ever happened. Of course, setting records is cold comfort, but I don't really need much comfort. At least not yet. It always takes me a while to react. Probably I'll be screaming in another hour. And not a soul to tell my troubles to. Norman went to Italy on Friday. I'm not sure why Dris left. It probably has to do with Ramadan, which is the name of this month, and it is holy, and fights are traditional. They're not supposed to eat, fuck, smoke, or anything between dawn and dark. Actually they're not supposed to fuck at all. But they do. Anyway, he sits up all night in the cafe next door waiting for the last minute to have his last meal. And last night I blew a fuse about it and told him to go home, to Arcila, then changed my mind. But we went on fighting this morning, and I humiliated him in front of the maid. (It is very bad taste to insult one Arab in front of another.) So he packed up and left. I didn't bother stopping him, since he does this every couple of weeks. But then he went, to my surprise. I had gin and a tranquillizer, but no kif as I want to go back to work, and shed two or three tears to commemorate the occasion.

Now it's nearly six, the sun's gone down behind the mountain and the cannon was fired to announce eating time. A roar went up from the town as usual. It sounds like the whole of Morocco is roaring.

Yesterday was like a perfect spring day in New York, and for some reason I thought with pleasure of visiting Irene up at Katherine Gravets' apartment in the Irving House: Then I thought of Spain and how nice it would be to travel. About a week ago I remembered that I hadn't come to Morocco for Dris. I don't remember why I came though. Do you? I think it was because I'd used up New York. Yes, it was time to go. Like you, that time you got left, I've spent the last two hours thinking what to do next. Now it's occurred to me not to do anything next. There's no point living here. The Europeans and Americans are corrupt completely. The Moroccans are hungry. There has been just Dris to divert me from the really gruesome life outside my work. And my own really gruesome life.

Next day. I hopped into a cab at seven p.m., and went to Arcila and brought him home. He said I needn't have bothered, which the tone of my letter seems to indicate I knew, as he was coming back anyway. So it's all hoochiecoochie again.

Did you see my column in Sunday's Trib? It just came and I loved it.

There is no news. With Norman gone I see no white people at all. In fact, I haven't spoken a word of English since last Wednesday. A little dreary. I work from eight in the morning until eight at night. Then we eat, get kifed, and go to bed. Sometimes I walk into town to mail a letter or shop, and pray that I don't run into any Americans or Europeans. I never think of sex except when Dris is around. It's gone clear out of my head. Actually I don't even think about it when he's around as he doesn't ever give me a chance to get there first.

I had an exquisite lunch on the Mountain the day Norman left at the house of the English nobleman, the Hon. David Herbert, Earl of Pembroke (I think)'s youngest son. I've known him for months but never liked him. Now I like him enough so that, with N. not around, he seems a possible someone to talk to. He has millions of peacocks and is giving me two when the new ones hatch. His house is all sort of delicious Victorian, sort of museumy. Oh, there are such rich people here. I wish I WERE RICH. I will be soon I think, I hope.

Are you miserable? Come here and you will find both love and passion, if you can put up with three or four months of lunacy. Oh, I long to see you and Edward and Harriet. Really terribly.

I send you lots of love and wish you would write to me more often. Alfred

To Edward Field   Jan. 29, 1964 Sidi Bujari 28, Tangier
Dear heart:

It is eight p.m. and I've been at the Genet since eight in the morning and yesterday and forever, and it is supposed to be there this week and I'm exhausted. It gets more and more brilliant, but I hate it—more and more. And the letter comes from Irving Rosenthal in Marrakech saying money is absolutely the only justification for writing essays and book reviews, in which case you don't tell your friends about it. So I've written him a letter (Hitler being his favorite hate) beginning *Mein lieber Adolf* and telling him I didn't know the law. And that if he was cold there was a surplus of fuel at Auschwitz. But it's made me depressed because it's true and I'm working like a dog. Anyway. I was so excited to get your letter. I made myself wait five minutes before reading it. Like eating the meat on your plate last. I'm terribly lonely now that Norman has gone, and I knew I would be. Imagine only Jane, whom I hardly ever see, and Irving Rosenthal as companions. Oh, Irving asks if he can have a free copy of your book. 2192 Tanger Socco. Can I? I seem not to have taken it with me. I thought I did. Actually I think I gave both copies away....It's so exciting about your film. You're so famous. And I'm so depressed.

Thanks for solving the teapot. I told Dris today to go have it soldered and he's gone now to do it. I'll mail it Friday or Saturday because I won't go out before then. It'll take a month to get there. It is goldy sort of and looks like a minaret and has legs and is about eight inches high, and you put in it mint and tea and you pour in hot water and you let it sit. Oh, and piles of sugar. Then you pour into little mustard jarsize glasses with gold trimmings….I don't know if pot is better than kif. Kif is different now from what it was. My mind is controllable now.

Tell them to let you read your narration in the movie. Your words really need your voice. I mean they sound like you. Not like me….What I say in the Genet is that Genet is just telling the truth. He is making the real Christian ideals—murder, pillage, treachery and robbery—into his own ideals. As he's in jail he has nothing to lose. It takes me thirty pages to say it, but that's a good sign. I'm beginning to get my wind back. I don't come out in farts now, but in streams of shit. Note how long my letters are….Your envelopes make me die of homesick. I woke Dris up to make him look at it this morning, Chinatown. He thought it was ugly like Tangier. But of course he comes from Arcila, and you remember that creampuff. Yes, I'm faithful. I often plan not to be. When he goes home for the night, I always decide to go cruising and then I never do. Or I go out and run away if anyone talks to me. I love sex with Dris, but except when we do it I never think about it. I doubt if he's faithful. They don't have that concept, except for the women. He swears he is but I don't see how he can be. I mean when he goes to Arcila and the boys all fuck each other, they'd think he was queer if he said he was being faithful to his Nazarene. Or if he didn't go along with them. I keep telling him I hate being faithful, and it's true, I do, and I never ever have been before. I'm just older, I guess. Like you. I can see your fidelity to N. in quite another light now. It isn't you think you should be, you just don't have the jism for it (infidelity), baby.

I just blew the bellows on the fire for fifteen minutes and my arms ache. I also smoked a pot cigarette. Kif. Dris chopped it last night and it is very powerful. I'm wearing his big white djellaba. The house is pretty. Jackson Heights Arabicstyle furnishings. A nickel here a nickel there and it's cosy. Where was I? Fidelity. Hm. I love his big warm genitals. They are genitals. They're not cocks and balls somehow. "You like eats my snake?" he says. Yummy. He is picking up English as you see. He is very proud of his cock as who wouldn't be and he's still young enough to be delighted by it. He hangs things on it, like shopping bags and shoes. Talking about sex gets him hot. Being close to people

56

gets him hot. He claims he never thinks, and I more and more believe it. He never gets bored. He just falls asleep. He never worries except when whatever it is to worry about is right in front of him. Like when his mother was very sick recently. He came back practically hysterical (just like a good Jewish boy should be about *mammele*), and then in an hour had forgotten about it and never bothered even phoning for the next ten days. He is afraid of me, of my anger, because I sulk, and he says that makes his heart shut. When I smile his heart opens. His heart isn't often open these days because I'm unhappy with myself. He looks very different from the photo and from when you saw him. Unless I see different. He looks young and gentle. He is like a boy. And he's beginning to like his ass fooled around with. I think they're genitals because they're so generous and so gentle nestling there in his crotch. Cocks and balls are sort of bangy and tennisrackety and not sort of complete together and whole and breasty.

I can do my Trib columns lately in a day, which is nice. The latest one is about Norman Mailer. And I took a poke at Jimmy Baldwin and I'm feeling bad about it. It just slipped out. I wrote how Norman falls in the respectable mud between the oasis of the little magazine and the desert of the national magazine, I mean his ideas are just on the verge always of becoming respectable: "He's the bronco buster of the halfbroken bronco. He rides them into acclaim, like James Baldwin." It sort of slipped out and I left it in. I felt guilty but don't care.

Dris just walked in with your *berrid* as it's called, very trilled r, Italian r, rolled. They scratched the gold off like mad and of course it never occurred to him to test it at the store. I'll tell you later if it works. I have to stop now to talk to him while he cooks. We're having tajine with artichokes. It's a stew with artichoke hearts stewed in toward the end. Nice, try it. With lots of ginger.

Next day. Almost done with Genet thank God. Will type it through tomorrow and mail it without thinking about it anymore. Your teapot works and will also mail it tomorrow or Saturday. From last part of essay: "America is Europe's knight in shining armor. But the love-starved maiden needs something a lot warmer in her arms than a

57

coffer of jewels. Beauties have been known to fall in love with beasts before; or, as Confucius said, a hot dragon is more fun in bed than a cold dollar bill...." I really need a rest after this....I get money from bookstores who owe money to Girodias. He's paying me that way....Tell Harry Goldgar that I'm the reason I left New York too. It seems odd that I who don't even exist could bother anybody that much. It's just my dybbuk. I'm not responsible. Why am I not pitied and my demon exorcized?

Saturday: Dris woke me at five this morning and I finished up the Genet in time to get it to the post office before noon when it closed for the weekend. Didn't have time to wrap the pot, so that goes Monday. Teapot I mean. It's really very cute. The Genet is called "Goodbye to Christendom." I do hope they print it. It will bring me $300 and cause a little stir. I read it over this morning and could hardly believe how good it was, though it reads like I'm in the middle of a nervous breakdown. It must be the dexadrines I use to keep going. I alternated between dex and librium as you can't get dexamils here. At night I had gin and kif to unwind with. It is like summer today. The doors to the terrace are wide open. The Genet is really an *apologia per mia vita*. It tries to explain my dybbuk. As the deadline is today the piece will be late and it isn't likely I'll see the proofs. I wrote Ted Solotaroff with the piece that if there is any important cut or change, he should consult you and if you agreed, it would be okay. I hope this is all right with you, being my literary executor and all. I mean I can't trust them or Candida. I have another copy but can't send it to you as it just cost me 1300 francs to send the one to them. So if he does call you for permission, for anything, don't agree to anything without reading the whole thing first. I hate doing this to you, my precious, but who else is there. Anyway, the essay is really such a vicious attack on everything except Genet, you, God and myself, that I don't even know whether they'll have the nerve to print it.

There were four galleys of *Behold, Goliath*, my agent writes me, and they were sent, will you believe this, to Dwight MacDonald, Norman Mailer, Terry Southern and Gore Vidal. Epstein must think my book is Esquire magazine. Imagine that asshole Terry Southern. I've written a note to James Purdy for a quote. Is it embarrassing to have a quote by you when the book is dedicated to you? If it isn't, then give me one and I'll make them put it on the jacket. Who else is there? Hortense [Calisher]. That's too ridiculous. PLEASE PAY ATTENTION. I mean try to answer my letter; lately I get the feeling nobody's paying attention to me....I got Larbi 250 from that Carnegie Fund that two years ago sent me money when I was broke. Next time you see Seaver tell him to apply for a Whitney Fellowship for Larbi. His pen name is Driss Charhadi...Would Paul's name be any good on my jacket? Oh, God, imagine making up with him....Did I ask you for a list of names and addresses for announcing my book? By the way, my Genet ends up talking about Kennedy. I quote Mailer's passage about the subterranean river of American life: "It was out of this river that the assassin's bullet came, regardless of who pulled the trigger or why. We accept, with the authorities, the guilt of the lonely psychopath because it tells a truth if not a fact. It dramatizes the refusal of Unreason to be silenced any longer by man's, Europe's, idea that he, Reason, rules the world. Humanism, however pretty, isn't for us because nature isn't human, and man willy-nilly is of nature. Nature is Unreason and God. It is the madness that runs through our lives and connects us to the stars in a way no rocket ship can ever duplicate. It connects us to all living things and to ourselves. To name this madness Holy doesn't promise peace or prosperity; it promises only a reason for being, a reinvestment of life into the dead matter of which the universe is now composed." Nice, yes?

I must close now and rest in the sun for awhile and get my strength, because next I want to write my novel, maybe. Love and kisses to you adorables.

Alfred

To Harriet Zwerling   Feb. 1, 1964

(Marginal note: I just had a fan letter from a psychiatrist who says he feels he should order me to stop writing.)

Mon ange: It's the first of February and a glorious summer day. The weather's been getting better and better ever since Christmas. I'm sitting here the way you're supposed to do in Morocco, on my gigantic terrace overlooking Spain, with my maid slaving away and my Moor sweetie out with the dog buying firewood. I'm feeling especially heavenly since I finished my Genet piece (called "Goodbye to Christendom") this morning and have mailed it and it's my first day of rest in over a month. You could practically go swimming today.

I love the photos of Milo (is it Mee-lo or Mylo?) Can I be one of his daddies? You know, when I saw your picture, I felt a wave of jealousy. That you were looking down at the baby instead of up at me. You're the only woman left in my life, except my agent, and the girl from the ship whom I've finally given into and written to. She bombarded me with letters and also from her father. Sometimes I am filled with panic that she'll show up here. The pants came with Dennis's name on the bag. Thanks to both. I'm so grateful. So is Dris, who looks a little too sexy in them. Did you get the djellaba and skin for Milo? Next on my gift list are you and Dennis. I'm sending Edward a teapot on Monday. I don't know why I'm sending presents. I miss you all terribly. I have no friends here. Work all day and Dris all night. And pot. Which is nice.

If Susan is really famous will you ask her to give me a quote for my book jacket. Even if she hates me, she owes her job at Partisan to me, after all.

Make a list of names and addresses of everyone you know who would know my name for publisher's mailing list.

I've decided Norman Mailer is terribly smart. I mention him in my Genet, and two of my Trib columns are going to be about him. The first is very mean, and as Random House asked him for a quote for my jacket I hope he gives the quote before he sees the column. The second column is very flattering.

I wish you'd come here, for awhile anyway. Tangier is cool in the summer. It's got trade winds. Why not? Everything else is trade.

Loverboy just came back thrilled that Columbine had bitten three dogs. They belong to a couple of nice French dykes, friends of Jane.

I'm going to the Socco Chico today. Ugh. To pay a 1000 franc debt to two hideous beatniks, bohemians—I don't know what to call them. The scene is really ghastly here. But the scenery is nice which helps. My only friend Norman went to Italy last week. I hate going to the medina with all its faggots, whores, beatniks. It's sort of like living nowhere here. Poised between Morocco and Europe. I hate both. But I like my apartment. And I like Dris. But he's hard to talk to, a little. I mean I can't ever be abstract with him. Today, for example. I realized for the first time that he hadn't been told the world was round or that Morocco was in Africa. It's sort of nice being like that. Everything is here and now.

I wish you'd write to me more often and stop being such a slut.

I kiss you ferociously and also my godson. And miss you terribly.

I wish I could think of a nice message for you to give Susan and/or Irene. But I can't

Lots and lots of love and kisses. *Ton* Alfred

To Dennis Selby   3 Feb. 1964—Tangier

Dennis—

This note is mainly to tell you I just heard my book is coming out April 10th. Can you get the blurb into Publishers' Weekly?

I had a huge lump of hashish fudge last night and it nearly killed me. The worst I've had so far. I laughed hysterically for three hours. And then couldn't get rid of a fantasy for the next two hours about what would happen to my body if I died. It was too gruesome. Dris kept holding me and reassuring me and being angry that I'd eaten the stuff. This morning I'm hideously hung over.

Love and kisses. Alfred

To Norman Glass in Italy   Feb. 5, 1964 Sidi Bujari 28, Tangier

Dear Warmin

Well so there you are back in some dreary hotel like you never crossed the Mediterranean. Even so, it seems terribly exciting, and all those Italian stamps on the envelope. My heart stood still a moment, enthralled by Europe. Driving to Positano. If there is a nice day and you have an extra few hundred lire just take the train to Latina, it's only a couple of hours, and rejoice in the beauties of nature.

I'm home alone as Dris is in Arcila for two days. I went to Bat Palace on Sunday to pay them the thousand. I was there for two hours during which time Ira never stopped talking, ranting, raving. About Irving, Peter, etc. He is ashamed because he thinks he is leading a middleclass sort of life. Rosalind was her as-always winning self. I got there just as the cannon went off and said jokingly, oh, just in for harira. And lo, she gave me a bowl of it. But very working class stuff it was indeed, full of flour. She really is so cute, messing around in her little kitchen all the time. Coffee came next. And last a great mess of majoun she'd been whipping up like chocolate pudding. I had a lump before going home. Laughed hysterically for three hours and then was sick all night, with Dris comforting me and admitting after he'd been scared by the way my heart was pounding. Violently. Ira said he'd wanted to come visit me but that frankly I gave off negative vibrations and he felt unwanted. I said, oh ho ho don't be silly, feel free to come. I half meant it as I haven't talked to anyone since you left. A couple of middleaged beatniks arrived just before I left. Ira and I were talking about Houdini, and the middleaged beatniks got all excited imagining that Houdini had been to the East and studied with yogis etc, you know the story. It was really too much to stomach for them that Houdini was just a New York Jew vaudeville magician. Like children all of them, who have to believe in Santa Claus....I saw Sonya [Orwell] yesterday sitting on the terrace of the Cafe de Paris and she tried to wangle an invitation from me but I decided isolation was preferable to Sonya. She told me Jane is going to Marrakech today with the Henris. I meant to call last night, but forgot. After Sonya, I saw Paul in his camel's hair coat looking sort of glamorous in the sun and like an old movie star. We pretended not to see each other. That is my social life. I keep thinking about calling David Herbert, but God, what would I do with him alone? As you know, I sent Irving the money order and the Dear Hitler letter and he has not replied. Ira says Irving is carrying on hysterically that neither he, Ira nor Ferlinghetti wants to publish his novel [*Sheeper*, later published by Grove Press]. I rather thought he was full of shit. Irving also said you were some kind of insect, I can't remember which, going from writer to writer, and you had a stinger on your belly which was poisonous. Something like that. Sounds sexy doesn't it. Did you sting him with your little old stinger?

I'm mad about Borges. I haven't been so taken with a writer since the first time I saw a Ionesco play. The story called "The Immortals," is genius, absolutely genius. I'm feeling very foggyheaded today. I've been smoking a lot of kif, mainly out of nerves waiting to get a response to my Genet. I keep feeling more and more sure they won't use it. Especially when I'm kifed. I feel as if mama's going to slap me hard for writing such mean things....Oh, by the way, my Tribune thing about breath's beloved and mushrooms. Some theater group in Wash. D.C. (like The Establishment) want to use it in their program, though God knows how. I will get about $5 a week for it as long as it runs....Edward is getting $1500 to write a movie narration....My stories are coming out, so I hear indirectly on the 10th of April....Terry Southern's novel which he wrote for Olympia is now being brought out in America by Putnam, a very respectable publishing house. So I'm thinking maybe soon I can get my old *Chariot of Flesh* published in America, the way Edward is always telling me to....I won't tell you what I'm working on. I mean I won't tell you about it. It is a book.

Norman, this may sound terribly corny, but listen. One day, sooner or later, one is going to die. One may be a long time even in the process of dying. One already is on the way from the moment of birth. And then when you are about to die, imagine the horror of never having paid attention to the truth inside. Just to find out what one really feels, however barren. Doesn't Borges say, more or less, that since everything is a lie, it doesn't matter what you say. But whatever is said, it must be said for oneself....I just reread the Genet, just this minute, it was the first time I had the nerve to since I mailed it. It's called, "Goodbye to Christendom." I like it. It is sad and uncertain. It lacks that old sure Chester touch, which means the earth is shifting under the rocks. I feel a little better now about them using it....I have been thinking a great deal these last few days. Our forms, as writers, are not ready-made for us as they once were. We must invent them, try on and perhaps reject old ones and new ones. One must not be afraid of writing bad books. One must try work after work after work. ONE MUST HAVE FUN. Write any old thing. If the final and horrible truth is that we are no one, then we must be no one triumphantly and proudly. For that's us then. It was my destiny to be no one, you perhaps can say like me.

Enough of that for now. My head is too foggy. Dris and I...ah Norman, he can be so nice, I do love him so much sometimes. When he saw me breaking my neck all day and night over Genet (I couldn't even have sex I was so worn out) he kept saying, tell me what the trouble with it is and I'll solve it for you. More or less that idea. Oh, I haven't seen Hajmi since I wrote you, though Dris did and told him I was angry at his trying to con me out of 5000. He, Hajmi, said, a *tabundimmuh* (his mother's cunt). Said Dris: Who, Warmin or Alfred. Threateningly. Hajmi, a little scared: Warmin. Okay, said Dris, then as he moved away, Hajmi shouted after, also Alfred's mother's cunt. Oh well. Hajmi told Dris that you were so madly in love with him, H., that you would not be able to stay away for more than a month. Anyway, Dris and I had a big fight the other day, I forget about what. Anyway I got very kifed the next day and walked to the beach at Merkala, you know in between the two hills, the view from my terrace. Oh, the weather has been spectacular. Mimosa is everywhere in bloom and little wild flowers are springing up in the fields. Anyway, oh Norman, I remembered again, I mean the sea, and the boulders on the cliffs, and the grass—who remembers the grass anymore, what politicians campaign for them, and I saw a baby goat being born on the road and taken away by a boy with its mother running after it bleating, with a big tit of blood hanging out of her cunt. Just the waves and the sky and the sun. They're the only things that tell the truth. Yesterday again I went and lay on the beach, your beach, and looked over at the peninsula where you had your metaphysical crisis walk. The lovely blue hills. And the waves just repeating endlessly their nonsense.... But the rain is coming, I believe. Night before last a mist like London lowered, that thick, and though it is still warm, the air is gray and the sky too.

To Edward Field   Feb. 7, 1964
Habibi,

I'm off now to the Socco Grande, which in Arabic in case you're interested is *souq i barra,* the outside market, as it is outside the walls of the medina. I can't remember why I'm going. Oh yes, because of a dream in which 15 and 41 and 56 figured and I want to buy a lottery ticket....Which reminds me I never did tell you about my insurance swindle which never came off. Another time.

Next day. I won 900 francs in the lottery on my old ticket. They didn't have anything like my dream ticket. The dream was a hideous nightmare that I was going to visit my niece, and my sister-in-law said she's your age, forty-one, and I said how silly, she was born when I was fifteen, and so I realized with great horror that I was fifty-six. And had done nothing with my life....I'm really very happy. I'm writing my novel. Would you believe it? I've only done six pages so far, but I feel right, now. It's really ridiculous and sort of endless, and the whole point is to make it go as I feel like going, so I don't have to feel responsible about art and so on. It's full of sex and monstrosity. "Now before I rambled astray I was going to make some mention of this journal. It is written for publication. It is going to be exactly one hundred fifty pages long in print even if I have to stop in the middle of a word, since I do not believe in big books and think art should have form. One hundred fifty pages is my form. I think the 19th-Century idea of a novel is ridiculous. If you can't say what you have to say in a hundred and fifty pages, then you are an ass. (If Neil's listening I'm only kidding.) Heraclitus said "a man's character is his destiny" in six words. I don't really have even six words to say. At best I have one of Heraclitus' six, which one I don't know, though I think maybe "his" is about right. Anyway, a book is supposed to entertain you. It surely isn't supposed to enlighten you. When I've entertained you one hundred fifty pages I'll stop (just like Edward said). If I feel like going on, I'll go on in another book. That is all I have to say about literature. I promise to keep you interested. If you get bored I personally promise to refund your money if you send me the unused, the unwiped, portion of the book plus a self-addressed envelope."

Doesn't that sound like fun? The six pages so far are full of fun. This volume will be called *His*, I decided after writing that bit above. The whole project which I expect to devote the next twenty years to and make a fortune out of is called *Do You Believe in Alfred Chester* and the author is Z.G. (Zavier George) Freeman. I would tell you more about it but I'm afraid you might tell someone, and the whole thing is too clever to give away. Don't even tell anyone the title. I just ran through my six pages. You would be so happy to see them. They are so crazy and so beautiful. And so surprising. I'm so happy with them. I mean it, at least I do today and yesterday, about the one hundred and fifty pages. I see the book going on in miraculous endlessness.

I have to go to the money changer's now. I got a hundred twelve-fifty from my agent on account of the Tribune. Did I tell you some Washington theater wants to put on, God knows how, my column about the beans and being poor. I would get about $5 a week.

Next day. Sunday. Ten pages done so far. The conversation between the dying father and Zavier is a panic. Zavier and his mother haven't talked to each other in fifteen years because she has a block against learning English and he has a block against Yiddish. His father speaks English but they never have a conversation until the night the father dies.

We went to see "Mutiny on the Bounty" last night. We hardly ever go out together because he thinks people will talk, but lately we do more. It was sort of a ridiculous movie, did you see it? But I thought Marlon was kind of extraordinary. I mean he was conscious that his act was a revolt against the whole of his tradition. One really felt the dazed disbelief of honest rebellion. Dris thought the whole thing was "mucho big show off," especially the movie house and the European audience. It cost 250 each to go. He always goes to the Arab VPs. He wore his djellaba which he wears in a funny way. It's sort of a camp of something that he knows is really him. Like the Hon. David Herbert on the Mountain here who camps being a nobleman and deeply is. As he was the only one in a djellaba he looks like an emperor coming down the stairs of the Roxy. With his haughty disdainful look. Part contempt and hatred for Europeans, part usual inferiority. The happiest thing in his life now I think is that he is free to despise and insult any European who flirts with him, to reject everything European because he feels his status is unquestionable.

Next day. I'm having a nervous breakdown. It's Monday, the day when the mail usually comes from America, and nothing from Commentary. Not even an acknowledgement. I wrote one little paragraph in my novel, but can't do anymore I'm so jumpy....Putnam's is publishing Terry Southern's dirty novel that Olympia first published and I'm doing an article on pornography in general for the Tribune. Naturally, I will tout *Chariot of Flesh* as the best pornographic work ever written. I guess you are right that it can be published. I've asked Girodias for a copy but I don't know if he's sending it....Nadia says in her letter that you were upset about my poor column. But that was nearly two months ago and things are okay now. I think I'm going to try the insurance thing again, though mainly because I want to get a car. The fishing season starts on the 2nd of March which means I have to go live in Arcila again. Dris says we should live on the money he earns so that we can save the money I earn for the five months of the fishing season. He earns $8 a week the first month, and between $14 and $20 a week thereafter, as he is captain, and gets a large cut of the haul when they actually start going to sea. His family however would have a fit as they are used to getting most of his money. Besides it would mean giving up the Tangier apartment and I don't want to do that. What I want to do is spend half a week here and half a week there and that's why I want a car. We'll probably live in that little house with the pretty courtyard where the dogs were, remember? It's been cleaned up and the Englishman has been forced to remove his car....Nadia says that you are serious and handsome "and I hope happy—he is discreet" which translated out of Nadiaese I take to mean that she thinks you aren't happy. Which translated into Edwardese I think means that you are bored with the Goulds lately. She says: "I feel happy or at least not resentful with my middle years." And she won't be thirtyfive until next week. She also gave me Arthur [Davis]'s news. [Israeli pianist Chester lived with throughout decade of fifties.] Last summer I realized something I'd never known before about Arthur. He was an Arab. He was the way Paul says about the Moroccans, sexually undifferentiated. Like I say in the article: The Nazarene is always either hetero, homo or bi; the Moslem is merely sexual. "Curiously enough, what feels good is very important to the Moslem. What is there is more important than what isn't there. Laughter is attractive, and liveliness. Youth is very important as are meat, cleanliness and good smells. Weddings have been cancelled because of bad breath. What is most important to the Nazarene is to find someone who looks like a statue from classical Greece and to drag him through the mud."...I've had some whiskey and am feeling calmer. I had a letter from a psychiatrist named Joseph Deuel Sullivan, 530 E. 20th St. From the Trib. It begins, Dear Scabrous Fungus Collector, and later says: I'd order you to douse the glim of your horrible light of darkness, if I had the power and if I didn't like the twisted macabre stuff....Isn't that disgusting?

Love and kisses to you both. Alfred

To Norman Glass (in Sicily)   Feb. 7, 1964 Sidi Bujari 28, Tangier

My adorable darling came back yesterday, thank God. I missed him terribly and woke up yesterday morning with a feeling of relief that he was coming back. Only a week more and Ramadan is over. Sex is costing me 300 francs a time. One hundred for the hammam and 200 for the cabs back and forth, so as not to make loveypoo walk to the medina and back during the chill postcoital nights....I spent all this morning on my book. It is such fun. I'm making it as ridiculous as possible, so I won't have to take it seriously and then maybe it will get written. I wrote a few pages of it when I first came to Arcila. They sort of slipped fartlike, when I wasn't looking. It is thanks to you I found the form, or actually remembered the form. It was of the book I wanted to write before I'd even finished *Jamie* and forgot about when I started on *I, Etc.* Actually Edward has a theory that one cannot skip any single volume in one's *oeuvre*. He says you can't go onto the third if the second isn't written. Edward you know is like Cassandra. Everything he says sounds unbelievable, but always turns out true in practice. I hope you will pray to all the bullgods that I have the force and stamina and perseverance to go through with it....By the way Ira said to me that day I visited: "What do you think will become of Norman?" I said: "Oh, nothing, he'll just go ahead and write his books when the time comes." Ira, quite astonished: "You mean you think he'll actually write books." Me: "Yes, very good ones, why not?" Ira, stunned and a little grudging: "Yeah, I guess so, I guess he's got it in him." But the thought had obviously never occurred to him. I suppose it's like Edward said to me in the Tangier youth hostel one day when I complained to him that I felt hurt because I could tell someone something and they would ignore it, and then listen to it if someone else said it, the same thing. Edward said it was because I wasn't pretentious about it, and that people only listen to you and take you seriously if you're pretentious.

Dris saw Hajmi in Arcila. He says he is fucking some girl whom you knew in Marrakech. An American. I don't believe it for a minute, not only because he's always in Arcila now, but because they (even Dris) always tell each other they're fucking girls. Dris told me he saw

Hamri the other day and told him (D. to H.) that he fucked Lucia and Rosalind....On the subject of that famous Friday night scene at Paul's, Hajmi claims Oman slept there alone and Omar claims Hajmi slept there alone. To make the story perfect, it only needs a fourth person to claim no one slept there that night, not even Paul....I dreamt last night that I was visiting my family in Brooklyn. It is a little vague. We were all going to visit my niece, and my sister-in-law said to me, she's your age, forty-one. I said nonsense I was fifteen when she was born, and so saying I realized to my horror that I was fifty-six. And had done nothing with my life. I woke up really drenched with terror.... The night before last I dreamt I was burning a corpse on a sort of fire escape, skylight affair. I'd murdered him. When I told Dris about it he said he was the corpse (not in the dream, in reality). Very hip isn't he? He went to a witch while he was in Arcila and she told him the story of Abdlkadr and the money, exactly as it happened, except she said that I was a girl, that I had lied about the amount and that it would be returned to me, in fact the thief would beg me to take the money back....Oh, the other night I went cruising on the windy palms and one of your numbers pursued me. He didn't seem to remember ever having seen me and kept insisting I was a tourist. I was sort of excited at the idea of going down to the beach with him, he wanted to, but you know, the really dead indifference on his face was too much to stomach. *Me voilà, je me trouve a la fin de cette lettre comme au début, la toute vierge, la toute pure, la toute fidèle.* I miss you very much as you surely cannot doubt.

Your devoted

Alfred

In America I was always mournful that I didn't dream. Now I go to sleep prepared to drift into some gruesome delicacy every night.

To Edward Field   Feb. 19, 1964 Sidi Bujari 28, Tangier
Mon Bien Aimé

It's done nothing but storm like hurricanes for days. Apparently it comes down again in March and comes up again in April, a little in May and then it is over. I mean the weather. But it's already spring. I mean warmish. Please forgive my talk about the weather. I have no friends, so I just notice things around me. Nature is boring to people in New York, though not you.

I'm only on page twenty of my book because I've been too nervous to work, especially when Dris went home for two days at the end of Ramadan. It's over, thank God. I was nervous because I hadn't heard from Commentary. I sent them a cable Wednesday and an answer came Friday: "Genet piece presents problems am writing today. Solotaroff." But today Monday is when the mail comes and no word from him. So I'm still shitting. My agent hasn't written me a word in weeks. She just forwards mail. Today she forwarded a letter from Epstein with Gore Vidal's quote: "AC is an extremely interesting writer, and "In Praise of Vespasian" is one of the best short stories in years." I could scratch her lukewarm well-bred eyes out. I also had a note with a boring quote from Purdy. I've written a furious letter to Random House saying please let us get together on my book. I could just see nothing happening, a big fizzle.

I wrote to Jacqueline Kennedy asking her to patronize me for the next year so I can stop writing book reviews. That was yesterday. And today came the Vidal quote which seems like a good sign. I've also written to Rex Henry, a local millionaire, who thinks I'm great. Jane will have another stroke when she hears about it, as he is her millionaire. But she has so many I don't see why it should matter. Tennessee sends them oodles of money too....If Grove publishes John Wiener's *Hotel Wentley Poems* could you get them to send me a copy. All the beatniks talk about him lovingly....Yes, we're moving into that little Arabic house that you liked in March, though I hate to. Things will just get lousy again between me and Dris in Arcila, I know it. If I can get my hands on some big cash I'll buy a car so I can go back and forth, spend half the week in Tangier. I don't know why it makes a difference, actually, as I never talk to anyone here. Though there I have to be more friendly with the Arabs....I went to Larbi's yesterday for tea and tajine. He is back with his wife. They divorced two weeks ago and got remarried the other day. Naturally I got very high on his delicious majoun I figured out the whole thing. The child is Paul's and that is how Larbi got the dough to buy such a cute young number. The child is definitely Nazarene, as white as I am, with reddish hair. I think she is really Jane's child. Anyway the wife got me very hot. She is about fifteen or sixteen and when Larbi went out to buy sugar she sat down opposite me with a big smile, pulled out her tit and started feeding the baby. The slut. I hated her but I wished she was mine. Tangier is really like Durrell's Alexandria. Dris would find it perfectly in order for me to have both a wife and him. At least he says so, and then says that everyone would know then that we don't fuck. But I notice that when we discuss this, he has nightmares afterward that I leave him and go to Europe....I know someone here who needs three boys at a time to get excited, one to fuck him, one to suck off, and one to jerk him off. The scene is very disgusting here. I tried being unfaithful again the other night, but it was too boring. I mean some very little boy. I really don't want anyone but Dris, but it's such a dull thought.

There is only one way to get to the top and that is by just being there. It is easier to be there when like me you're away from it all. You are at the top now. It is just a matter of days or weeks before everyone else finds out.

My book has nice things like Percy de la Foutre, a big black who commits all the unsolved murders in New York, maybe in America, simply because he hates humanity: he even commits the solved ones, which the police attribute to others for political reasons....My hero Zavier only falls in love with parts of people or fictional people like Tony Curtis who he says was his longest love affair except for the DeKalb Ave. men's room. (You must keep all this a secret.) "Every time I passed a movie house showing one of his pictures, I'd have to force myself to go in, no matter how many times I'd seen it before. And I'd have to force myself to daydream about him, to jerk off over him. It was like making myself believe in God or taking medicine. During the last couple of years though, his face began falling apart, to my relief, and we broke up during the third time I saw "The Great Imposter." I wrote him a Dear John letter, since I thought it was only fair to let him know the romance was over....He is going to have a love affair with VP (the people just represent moods) and with a park. And when he gets sick, the DeKalb Ave. men's room, VP, and the park come to visit him bringing him flowers....Isn't that sweet?....It makes me feel like living in a Breughel, who is really the only painter I like.

I gave Dris 500 francs to give to the witch of Arcila to put a spell on my mother.

Later. Edward, am I going mad or is it possible that people do actually write nasty things about me in newspapers? I noticed once or twice reviews digging at critics who said such and such and sounded like me. John Ciardi I think was one, or some name like that. Famous. Just now I was looking through a review of Brendan Behan's new book in the Feb. 2 Tribune and it is reviewed by someone called Jimmy Breslin who is a columnist for the Tribune and he writes: "Behan's book is a collection of newspaper columns....Behan at least tries to write for the entertainment of the reader. He is not some outlandish homosexual trying to sound off on human destiny between paragraphs about his boyfriends." I just read that and I thought that man is talking about me. And I'm feeling nauseous....The terrible thing about being so alone here, I mean, having no point of reference, is that I keep thinking I'm crazy. I mean you're not here to say what a good boy I am, and I keep thinking I am mad: I mean suddenly I think how can I write about being poor and Dris in the Herald Tribune? It is insane. *Ça ne se fait pas.* I scare myself. My life scares me. Do you know, yes you do and you don't, to suddenly put your life in public where all those horrible people like your family can see it. I mean, like I've always been surrounded by lovely people. And that really isn't how the world is at all. I'm scared. It really scares me. I mean, imagine writing a letter to Jacqueline Kennedy. Don't you think I'm crazy?

No, I'm not. Am I? That man at the theater in Washington doesn't think so. He wants to produce practically all my columns. Two anyhow, And I sent him my little play in French, remember, the one we acted for Nadia and Philip. I also told him to write you and ask to perform your poems. If he can perform my column, he can surely perform poems....Oh, I feel sick again.

Wednesday. I was physically sick all day yesterday. My cigarette stomach, remember? The rest of the mail came, delayed by storms. Six more books from Girodias (for my article on Terry Southern, but I'm just going to sell them to a bookstore here) and Rawicz' *Blood In the Sky*. Also Commentary. They want to cut all the history out of the article; I was very glad and was saying okay. You would have probably said the same thing as Solotaroff....I also heard from Harriet who says Susan won't give me a quote and that my book is already out; review copies are out; I suppose the jacket isn't prepared yet....I read Terry Southern's book yesterday and loved it. I was mad about it. It will sell a million copies....Next time I write to Epstein I will tell him we want to do an intensive reading tour in the fall. I hope you mean both of us, because I won't do it alone. We will probably be worth a good evening's pay by the fall don't you think?...I reread *Chariot of Flesh* yesterday and it bored me. I don't think I could rewrite it or publish it as it stands. I don't know why it's had such success. Girodias keeps referring to it in his articles, he is evidently proud of it. The only interesting thing about it, you should excuse me for sounding like a critic, is that it shows a change of mood in the porno; it makes fun of itself. Which was why Gid hated it at first. "We don't make fun of onanists when they're your readers," he said to me. But it turned out I was right. It is out of print again. It sold out straightaway, two years ago. *Fanny Hill* I adore....Oh, Dris has written a poem on Kennedy, several in fact, since I told him about that project. Do you want me to send it to you? They call him nowadays El Hadj Kennedy, which is an absolutely inconceivable honor. El Hadj is an honorific for a Moslem whose made the hegira to Mecca. I mean the people in the street refer to him as the Hadj. Part of Dris' poem goes: When the Hadj Kennedy woke up in the morning, he yawned and stretched and asked his wife: "Which is the poorest country in the world?" And she said: "Morocco." And he told her: "Send them some butter and flour and milk and a few dollars." After the Hadj Kennedy died, King Hassan II said to his little sister Lalla Zohra or whatever her name is (I'm still quoting): "There are a lot of gangsters in America, we better give Mrs. Kennedy a palace in Marrakech so she won't have to stay in America and be afraid."

I suppose you know about giving her the palace in Marrakech.... That's the end of the poem. The first part is about how Kennedy is killed because he wanted to free the black slaves and how the American soldiers in Kenitra used to sit on one side niggers and on one side whites at the bar. And how he [Dris] went and sat with the niggers and danced for them and sang, and a white soldier said why are you sitting there, you're white (he is actually, now his bronze has all faded; paler than you) and he said, "I have a black father and a white mother and so I have an extra cup of blood and an extra rib, etc." Did you know, or is this just local tradition, that Negroes are supposed to have one more rib than whites and an extra cup of blood?

Columbine and Skoura are well but impossible. Skoura is a thousand times better but she is still a bit feeble-minded and hasn't barked since July. She is still slightly spastic, but mostly when the weather is bad. Columbine loves Dris and he her.

You can tell Rosetta Reitz that the Golden Chalice is out of Genet. I now have more or less enough nonfiction for a book, would you believe it? But I won't publish it until I finish my novel. Emily Lambert wrote me that she hears that people are always quoting my column, but she never buys it because the Tribune is too dull. I think I have my next column in this Sunday. It is a nice one.

I feel confident of a big sale on the stories. What do you think? If I actually do sell the 20,000 I will earn something like $8000 in royalties which would be heaven. I would buy Dris a lot of sheep and a lot of cows.

Goodbye now....I have much work.

Give a big wet kiss to Neil. Could you ask him please to grow a mustache before coming to Morocco, especially if we all live together. He is the type Moroccans adore. If he has a mustache they won't like him too much.

Lots of love and kisses to you. I'm glad your movie is over. When you come to Morocco let's write a play.

xxx

Alfred

To Norman Glass in Sicily   Feb. 20, 1964 Sidi Bujari 28, Tangier

Dear Norman

I got your letter Monday but have waited until now to begin an answer in case your plans changed. About the tower I mean. It sounds scrumptious. Go see my friend Antonio who is somewhere around there. He is a very nice sad boy. Sade boy, I wrote, but he isn't that. I slept with him but I wouldn't bring that up, as he has great shame and guilt about screwing males. As well he might, since he is so bad at it. Tell him I remember him with great warmth, esteem, affection, you know the Italian story, and that I will come visit you all later in the spring when I've finished a rough draft of my book. If I have the money....The enclosed is a nasty bit of philistine bitchery I believe is aimed at me. It turns out my column is a huge success and people quote me all over the place. So now with the new one due, and it being a continuation of last month's I'm terribly self-conscious and having a hard time writing it. It's about Mailer and Genet as the last one was, except for the beginning about you. As for the Genet, Commentary edited it to pieces and I don't really care a bit. I'm bored with criticism and exposition; it is too dull. I wrote a letter to Jacqueline Kennedy asking her to send me some money. I also wrote to Rex Henry but haven't mailed the letter as I don't have his Marrekech address.

Handsome just interrupted and we fucked with the terrace doors wide open. It's like spring now or summer after a week of storm. We had a huge fight last night. Since Ramadan, *safie hamdullah*, he can't fall asleep until five in the morning so he bothers me all night. Yesterday he bought Sloan's linament for his gout and at three in the morning woke me up fooling around with my ass which was burning like all get out. He hadn't washed his hands after applying the liniment. So I blew up at him. Now I've sent him to buy sleeping pills.

Days, perhaps weeks, certainly years later. I'm in an hysterical state. My publisher and my agent are being very highhanded about my book. Edward is working at it like a dog. I've just written furious letters to everybody. They haven't told me date, budget, size of printing or anything. I said if they send me roundtrip fare I'll come back and sell the book myself. But they won't, so I'm safe.

I've sent Burroughs and Bowles letters asking for quotes. No answer yet from Paul. Burroughs I ask if he gives quotes, I'll send him over a couple of stories. You know, Norman, you never knew me. It's just become clear this week, working on the Genet and the second installment of the Mailer piece (which is great). I mean I got lost in Morocco and am just getting my wits back. Burroughs, you see, and all these palace people, they are old-fashioned. The last generation. When I left America I was about to invent a new generation. I mean that is my task: the artificial hope. That was the theme of my novel, the first one. That is still my theme. The existential choice. I never made the choice and I'm only finally beginning to now. It's all to do with my father and I haven't the energy to go into it now because I have an incipient flu and am exhausted. I realized last night, how curious that Bowles, Burroughs and I should be in the same city. One the past, the other the present, and the third, me, the future. All that dark black death. It is a fake. I am really the prophet of joy. It is true, I love life. One needs to give it a push with a little posturing and fakery at times, but the James Lange theory which I strongly believe in is if you act a way you feel it. Well, it's more or less said in my Mailer article. I also explain myself in terms of Rechy and Albee: "When I went to high school, during the war, the history books called America the melting pot. The idea was that everything Asiatic, Mediterranean, Semitic and

African (from food right on along to accents) would either be ignored or melted down into a sort of bland Englishy nothing. It was America's attempt to unify its diversities: Everything was reduced to its most common denominator: tastelessness. Dull and overwritten books like those of William Faulkner, Henry James and Herman Melville came into fashion because they seemed indigenous (i.e. English). Names like Abraham got changed to Alfred; names like Chestyapelskya or whatever it was: Russian for sixfingers—get changed to Chester. This deadening melting pot idea still pervades the middle class: in architecture, in politics, in religion (the churches talk look and act more alike as if forming a bland united front), lately in God. But it has proven an untenable concept. In a grave and austerely beautiful pamphlet called "Reflections on Kennedy," Keith Botsford writes: "The faculty of being simple, of appearing singleminded, of resolving for the right, has vanished, with civilization, from our national temperament into mythology. It is something we want but can no longer have. It is celebrated by those who praise profits and enshrine individuality but shrink before elementary discomfort." The impossibility of sustaining a unified voice is evident in Rechy and Albee. They don't know who to be from one minute to the next, what literary posture to take. They can assume, with varying degrees of authenticity, a large range of voices, none their own. As Edward Field has said, "You just stand there and somebody else's voice comes out of you like a dybbuk."...etc., etc.... Anyway it's a very good piece and has cleared me on many things including the general direction of my novel. I too have to choose a literary posture and just stick to it, come hell or high water or I will go mad.

I also put that nasty newspaper man down: "Except for a few old philistines with Romantic un-Notions about writers, like that they should be alcoholics lying in the gutter with their brains bashed in and, ideally, dead, but certainly unconscious, America has begun flirting with her intellectuals, and the intellectuals have begun flirting back. Mailer and Baldwin report on the prize fights. All hail, pop art. Intelligence is a popular commodity. The apparently American is respectable in the arts. Boredom is old-fashioned."

I haven't a bit of gossip about anyone as I haven't seen anyone....Oh, yes, I did go to supper at Larbi's. He fed me lots of kif and majoun with that special built-in evil paranoia. I don't know where he gets his sick stuff. He married his old wife again and, oh, she turned me on. So cute. Kept pulling her cute little tit out and shoving it in the baby's mouth and snailing or lowering her eyes demurely....Yes the black work is the reality, but one must ignore the temporal truth. My salvation lies in being an American and a Jew; I'm a combination of death and rebirth, that is the American mystery. I have rejected it all, now I must go through all the rubble and the rubbish and choose what I want to be. It is really a glorious time for the world. One can choose to be or allow oneself not to be. I forgot all that because I was so busy experiencing Morocco and then you. It is a conscious decision and one must keep being conscious of it, about death. Whenever I write fiction, I always get terrified of death. Why? I don't know. Because for one thing the death impulse, so strong in me and my civilization (did you hear that MY civilization, not yours or ours, MY America), is denied when I start writing and I feel guilty toward it and responsible. Also, the death is my father, the Jew, about whom I am only now beginning to write. My poor suffering father whom I was not allowed to love. Edward says in his recent letter, following my train of thought, perhaps it is your father's voice that is the dybbuk in you screaming for recognition, for you to acknowledge your heritage. He says my fight for money with my mother (like yours) is to get them to acknowledge me as one of theirs, to get my spiritual heritage....Art is going to belong to the people again Norman; don't hang back with the apes who wanted to make it a cult with those degenerates. They are on the side of death. It is all so sweetly clear to me now.

Also, we must stop thinking about God and mysticism unless we go the whole way, which I won't, and into the monastery, giving up all worldly ambition. Including art. If you can make man and nature and the things around you mean something, if you can give them life, God will come into them again. He will be happy to. He is just life.

I can't go on with this, I wrote ten business letters before getting around to you today and I must rest a little so I can start work on my novel again tomorrow.

Isak Dinesen, via Edward, to put above my work table: "When you have a great and difficult task, something perhaps almost impossible, if you only work a little at a time, every day a little, without faith and without hope, suddenly the work will finish itself."

It makes me nervous to feel happy and hopeful. It makes me feel illegal and guilty and that I am tempting fate to deal me a crushing blow. But I am feeling happy and hopeful. I had a terrible crisis just after the Genet. The dybbuks, you know. The brain inside me screaming. I'm better now. I kept telling myself, this will end up in something good, be patient.

Norman I must stop. I ache all over.

Goodbye dear boy, for now. Give me all the Sicilian chatter. I will try to do something in the real world so as to be able to tell you some gossip.

Alfred

THE MISTAKE

To Edward Field   Feb. 25, 1964 Calle Sidi Bujari 28, Tangier

Dear Edward,

It's all coming to me in a blinding but slow flash. They don't intend to do a damn thing for me, either Random House or my agent. I suddenly see the whole thing. I mean Candida writes me to tell the publisher what to do, and the publisher doesn't bother with me a bit. They're not putting any quotes on the jacket, the idiots. Candida says the jacket was printed ages ago without a word. I see the whole thing like a revelation.

I'm writing very strong letters to both of them, but I am obviously up against the same resistance you were. Please try to see that I get reviewed.

I want them to tear up the jacket or print over it. I want them to put quotes on the jacket. $15,000 worth of advertising was spent on Susan and it didn't budge a sale. I know I have got the market inside my bucket of shit, my book, she didn't.

Get hold of Bob Silvers please and ask him to help.. Please. I've written Marty Tucker c/o the Post as I don't have his address.

More later. Love,

   Alfred

I'm hysterical. I'm asking Random for return air fare.

To Edward Field   Feb. 28, 1964 Sidi Bujari 28, Tangier

Sweetheart:

I got a letter last night from Jason Epstein, so cool it only made me twice as hysterical. This crossed with my screamy letter. He says the book is out and he's airmailed me a copy. Do you have yours? Anyway, he says it's too late to put anything on jacket. The only halfway usable quote was from Gore (sic). "The book is now on its way out to a few hundred of your close friends, some of whose names I got from a list that E.F. was kind enough to give me." Plugs, says he, if we get them now will be used for ads. "Tell me where you think we should spend your advertising budget."

Upon which I nearly had a nervous breakdown. I used to be so calm about publishing. Now suddenly I'm hysterical. About everything I send out, everything about to be published. I feel like an amateur again. Edward, I did what you said, and wrote him that I would tell him where to spend the budget. Now, please do one of two things, dybbuk, either write me express what to write him or call him up and say you had a letter from me saying he should do so and so. I'll hold back until I hear you. Or try to. Though I must say, poor Dris, it's like he's living with an insane lunatic. And trying everyday to write a little without hope and without faith and with signs all over my walls. I think of course they will put a big ad in the New York Review. A big ad in Commentary. A huge ad in the Tribune. A full page in the Paris Review. A big ad in Times review. Also an ad in the Post to run the week after Marty's review (have you taken care of Marty?). Something in Partisan? As he hasn't told me his budget, which is probably a nickel, what to do? I await your word by return of post, please darling. I'm so nervous. It's like the first time I ever published anything in Botteghe Oscure, thirteen years ago. I'm old enough to be bar mitzvahed and I am not a man.

My career and criticism is drawing to a close. I know it. I'm becoming a writer again. I'll decide today or tomorrow whether to review Terry Southern's book but that is the end except for my monthly column, since I committed myself for a year. I've decided to start collecting money for my art. Since I feel like an artist again. I wrote to one of Jane's millionaires asking him to supper and adding as a p.s. would he patronize me. (He told Paul, and me, that I'm great, and I know Paul wanted me to do just what I'm doing as part of the little spite game between him and Jane.) Jacqueline never answered. I wrote Harriet to send me a hundred and also Gerry Ayres. Please hold fire on your own contribution. (Dris will have his own spending money until July so that relieves me of a little, though of course not his appetite, which has grown small lately but will be gigantic as soon as the work begins.)

I wrote Burroughs for a quote (Paul is being his kifhead playful self via correspondence about his quote). But no answer.

There is a great uproar going on here just at the moment. Ira's magazine called Gnaou published a section of Irving [Rosenthal]'s novel which has a line: "…and some of the campiest queens I've known had cocks drier than Paul Bowles' mouth caught between Tafraout and Taroudant with kif and without water." Of course Paul brings the wish to expose him out in everyone. Ira came running over the other night. At first I said no no you mustn't print that, it doesn't matter even if Paul does want to be exposed, we have no right to be judges, it is just spite and lovelessness. (After a fight with Paul, Irving had changed the line from: "drier than an Arab" to "drier than Paul.") But after eight hours of thrashing it through, I thought yes, expose him. It is what I personally feel and would do. But then the next morning, I woke up and thought, yes, even if that is what I would do, it isn't good that the world should be that way, I mean hurting people, especially when Irving's message is Love. Paul meanwhile is racing around Tangier hysterical. Burroughs caught Ira yesterday at the Socco Chico and said, *ça ne se fait pas*. (I have been seeing people the last couple of days and have caused a minor uproar by saying Burroughs is old-fashioned, that, yes, it is true the world is nothing, but we must pretend and make it better.) Irving's book is beautiful in some ways, though a bit boring with shattered drug imagery, but then there are the parts that sound like little lovehungry Irving the rat talking and that is touching. I've only read thirty pages, yesterday, while helping Ira with the proofs, but I was shocked that he could be such a worm and say so many of the things I say in my little bookie.

Also last night in the mail was three copies of my essay on Salinger. Did you ever read that? If you haven't I'll send it to you. It is important to read; I mean it is important for you and me to read, but only you and me. Because it's all about me and I didn't know this then. At first I was sick about it for an hour because it is so smart and straight and finished and I couldn't do that kind of perfect critical job now. But then after I saw that it was finished, that I didn't have to do that anymore.

What it says about me is that my spiritual hungers were in effect what had prevented me from writing all these years. Now all I say is that the whole big spiritual quest of the fifties was America's attempt to make its intellectuals religious rather than communist materialist atheists and to synthesize all the various religions into one nothing mess. Please read, if they let it through, my column which should appear about four Sundays from now....The one after this will be a demolition of Time magazine. I am going to expose it, method by method, trick by ugly loathsome trick. It is the rottenest side of America.

A little later. Just had letter from Kluger. He says you wrote him. That's good. Once, not so long ago, I would have been good for him. Now I only mean good for me. Please get your nose through the door and find out fast who he's put to reviewing me. He's being incorruptible and won't talk about it.

Love from Avrumele

The real reason I'm hysterical is that at last, like Paul Bowles, I am going to be exposed for the fake I am. But at least I have done it myself. I've just written a note to Jason and Candida saying I abdicate from all further involvement in the book, that I'm just scared, that my only self-salvation is in my novel. So that's it. Forget about advertising and whatnot.

To Norman Glass   Feb. 28, 1964 Sidi Bujari 28, Tangier

Normala:

I'm just hysterical. That's all. My book comes out five weeks from today. I wish I could calm down and be cool about it. Thank God at least I've started this other thing, some other me to believe in.

Your picture is so pretty and I will come to see you later in the spring, for a visit anyway if I have money. This letter is going to be madness, so do what you can with it.

We must go about our business of making things better now. I'm assigning you the job of bringing life back to English literature. Will send you details when I'm calmer.

On the subject of mailing you kif, Dris' comment was *Sta loco*. And I agree.

Long story now. The night before last Ira came over. That was Wednesday night. He'd gone to Paul the night before with the proofs of the magazine, as Paul had offered his help, and of course Paul spotted the line in Irving's thing, you know, "drier than P.B.'s mouth." Poor sick Paul didn't even have the guts to stand up for himself. He just started with, Jane will be violent, etc. Anyway, Ira had come to ask me what to do. I said tear it out. It's spite and lovelessness. On top of which Ira was there when, after Irving's breakup with Paul, Irving changed the original line from "drier than an Arab's mouth." Anyway Ira and I thrashed the thing out all night and finally I changed my mind and said let it stand. My reasoning was thus: Paul wants exposure. He brought the same thing out in me, didn't he? He wants it but doesn't have the courage to do it by himself. It is a drama between generations and Paul is asking to have his generation destroyed. Ira went away unresolved. I woke up the next morning and thought that is full of shit. It doesn't matter what Paul wants or what the drama is. The fact remains that it is wrong to hurt another person, and THAT IT SHOULD REMAIN SO. A writer posits love or morality not by what he says but how he behaves. How he behaves in his book, I mean. Anyway, I didn't want to think about it anymore. As I'd promised Ira to help him with the proofs, off I went yesterday at four to the [Bat] Palace. Now that I've decided to be boss again, I just dismiss them completely. I've told them Burroughs is old-fashioned nonsense, that they must stop taking drugs, they must stop the nonsensical spiritual quest, that it is all a sociological American plot and they mustn't give way to it. They're a little awed by my boldness. I told Ira he is a coward and the only reason he won't deal with Irving's thing is he's afraid of Irving. Which he sort of admits. Anyway, Ira is too far gone, he's too sick. The drugs have ruined him. He has no powers of concentration left at all. On Wednesday night I'd said, after he told me he wanted to go to India, oh enough of that, your job is to be what you are, a middleclass Jew. So yesterday he'd already effected a compromise, he would go East but to Israel. Bla bla. Anyway I tried desperately until five o'clock to keep him at the proofs but it was very difficult. I told him it was madness to print Harold Norse's bit of shit, that it was Olympia Press 1958. Ginsberg piece stinks. So does Burroughs'. McClure is an asshole. At five o'clock Ira could no longer sit still, he had to run to the P.O. to see if there was mail. I said, Ira, what mail could be more important than what we are doing right now? Yes you're right, he said, but off he ran with Billythebaconlover, who is about to go collect an inheritance in America. So Rosalind and I were left with the proofs. Ira said he'd be right back. At eight p.m. he returned, no eightthirty, and I was very pissed but I'd gone on with it, because it was, after all, the work that mattered. In the process of proofing, Rosalind and I had skipped Burroughs and McClure (I was bored) and gone onto Irving's piece (about which I will tell you presently). We were almost done with Irving when Ira came home. He'd run into Burroughs. Paul had gone rushing hysterically over to Burroughs, natch, to tell him about the wicked line. Burroughs said: you can't do that. *Point.* "The establishment is consolidating," screamed Ira. My theme to Ira has been, really, that it was not what Irving said that counted, it was what he Ira decided that counted, since the magazine is his own statement, not Irving's, that his choice would serve to define him to himself forever. But of course he is beyond all that. Anyway, suddenly he realized that Rosalind and I had not been proofing in page order (not that it matters since each page is clearly numbered) and he threw a violent tantrum, pages and objects all over the room. You know, like Paul. I seem to bring this out in people. (In a recent letter from a little old boyfriend, maybe I wrote you this, he writes: "Walter says he is mad at you but it wasn't very clear why, it wasn't a real mad, it seemed to be the kind of mad that everybody should be at you, or something like that; not a real mad, but an appropriate mad.") Anyway, he gave me orders to go on correcting, and I said no, I was done. Rosalind said, no let's go on, he's always like that. I said, I don't care, he's ungrateful. And I sat finishing reading Irving's pages. When I looked up Ira was packing a suitcase. I said what are you doing? Oh, I said this because I dug what was happening and saw that Rosalind, lying on the floor, was being too proud to say anything because I was there. Then Rosalind said, where are you going? He said: To a hotel, and then to Belgium. (I had told him he had to go to the printer, but he checked my opinion with 10,000 others.) Norman, I then did the best thing I think I have ever done in my life, the purest action I have ever made. I could hardly believe it was me. I am really SOMEBODY. At last. When I told Dris about it, his face lit up with admiration.

Listen carefully. Without kif, I reasoned. I thought first, poor Rosalind, oh God I'll have to stay to comfort her. How boring. Then I thought, how unfair of Ira to do this to me. I started putting on my shoes. I thought, Ira is using me because he is too weak to choose for himself. If I weren't there, there would be screaming and finally reconciliation. Yet if I just walk out, I will be committing a possible atrocity against Rosalind who is—surprise surprise—a human being (I had been putting her down, she loving it, the whole evening: "a woman thinks with her cunt, you should have ten children, you have no right to express an opinion, etc.). So as I put on my shoes I said: Ira, come sit down here next to me for one second. He came. I said: Now, I am going home; I'm going out that door and I want you to promise me that you won't follow me for at least ten minutes. He smiled very slightly, because he recognized my brilliant move, and slowly he agreed. I then stood up and said, I hope you'll come see me. And I left. It really wasn't until I got out into the street that I realized just how extraordinary an act it was. It all was done in a split second. I feel terribly proud of myself. Not for saving their idiotic menage, of course, (because I'm sure they saved it as soon as I was gone), but for having extricated myself. And left them slightly more conscious of their own doom.

Tu has hecho muy bien, said Dris.

I suppose you're dying for me to say something about Irving's book. Well, can I really say anything on these passages? There is probably more drama in the rest of it. Yes, he is right. Some of it is very beautiful. It is very small. It is trivial. The last bit, because this and because that inspired me. I know with gigantic conviction, and if you don't you're a fool, that I'm a thousand times more of an artist than he is. I'm just naturally bigger, is all. He is more fashionable. But I say these things on the basis of thirty pages, which is not all. I tried a little more than usual to favor it and felt I found it beautiful. But also felt I was being forced to find it beautiful. It is like something thought under kif. When you come out of it, you don't remember the thought. I remember only Irving's words where he collided with my own views, which was more often than I would have imagined, though Ira had said: Oh I know you'll think Irving's very chichi but he thinks very much the way you do....He is right. That is the important thing. For now, he is right in what he says and what he wants to do. What he actually has done, I haven't yet seen.

Flush Harold Norse, Brion Gyson, and William Burroughs out of your life, but fast, man, fast.

Out of compassion the night he was here, I said to Ira, well if you want my Tangier, here it is, and gave him the piece I had written for Show. All he will know when he reads it is that I use quotation marks, which are not hip, that I don't give any orders, that I don't make any judgments. He will never in a million years see that it would be the only lively, hopeful thing his magazine might have had. He will be too afraid to publish it, because the establishment is against it. I don't care. What they don't want is life.

To practical matters. I believe I told you I wrote to Jacqueline Kennedy asking her to support me. No answer. I then saw Jane the other day for a moment and mentioned my request for patronage, she said Oh what a good idea. Ah ha, said I to myself. I went home and looked at my unmailed letter to Rex Henry. I sealed it and went out and phoned his house here to ask for the Marrakech address. The maid said she didn't have it but that Rex might be back this weekend. I then phoned David [Herbert] and said Ho de do, la dee da, do come for dinner. Delighted old chap. Next Wednesday. Oh by the by, are the

Henrys around? No, but they'll be back on Friday. Oh, should I ask them as well? Yes, do, I adore Rex; of course she's a bore but....See you Wednesday nine-ish. So I went home and wrote a dinner invitation to Rex Henry saying I'd be delighted if Renee came too but as there would be no women present (this was to make it clear to Jane that she wasn't coming), perhaps she would be uncomfortable. Then, almost as a P.S. I said, please patronize me for one year; I am writing a novel and am turning to my expressed admirers for aid. I then also dashed off a note to David saying I'm sure you will hear about all this, so this is what I've done, but it isn't a plot and pay no attention to it, just come for dinner. Which, as you know, I mean. I showed the Rex letter to Ira and he said no no impossible, you don't ask for patronage this way, you have to hustle by being friendly first and so on. But Norman, I don't want to be Rex Henry's friend. I just want his money. So I sent off both letters yesterday and will let you know what comes of it....I believe however that nothing will come of it. Because: Paul's pretext about writing a novel I feel positive is based on Henry's patronage. That's what it's all about....I've also sent a note to Lady Eliz Montagu asking her for money which won't come....A note to my old boyfriend at Columbia Pictures; that won't come either. And a note to Harriet which may come. I am running down my list of friends, and will touch them one by one (not you, lovie, you're hopeless). I cannot go on supporting myself with essays. It is too dreary.

I received in the mail some tearsheets of my Salinger essay yesterday, printed last June in Commentary. I was shocked by its brilliance and perfection. It depressed me because I am incapable of such perfection now. Then after awhile it gladdened me. Because of course that isn't what I want to be. I would like you to see it though, because oddly enough it defines very explicitly my dilemma just before I came to Morocco. I pretend to talk about Salinger but it is me. The moral is: the spiritual quest leads nowhere. It has taken me eight months to become physically my intuition.

I must stop this letter now. And get to work. Are you now the lord mayorette of Manchester. Did I tell you I have relatives there? But I can't remember their name. I know you are English because it is so difficult for me to sign letters to English people, like Paul Bowles, love. But I will now make a great effort because of your implicit promise to be a Jew.

Love,
Alfred

To Edward Field   Feb. 29, 1964 Sidi Bujari 28, Tangier
Dear Edward
Enclosed is a photostat of a letter Paul Bowles sent to Ira Cohen. I have others and the negative, though I've given the letter back to Ira. I'm a little scared, because Paul _is_ crazy.

Just keep it and better not talk about it.

I'm feeling new and strong and resolved. I want only my novel. Love and kisses, Alfred

[The following letter enclosed]
Dear Ira:
Unfortunately, I gave the copy of the story for you to Norman, to take back to you. Whether he will or not is another question, since we just broke off diplomatic relations for all time. If he comes back here I'll throw him out. I've finally had enough of his nonsense, as well as that of his friend Alfred Chester. I'm arranging to have them both bumped off in Tangier, _incha'Allah_.

So, if you don't receive the manuscript let me know and I'll send another copy. (Of course, Norman may feel that discretion is the best part of squalor, and decide to deliver what I gave him. One can't prophesy with hystericals and schizoids.) What a shame all these people have to be born and give forth their stench to an unsuspecting world! But now that they exist, one has to do something about cleaning the place up, obviously.

Forgive my digressions. Let me know.

Best,

Paul

To Norman Glass   March 1, 1964—Sidi Bujari 28, Tangier

Dear Norman

That letter you said that Paul Bowles wrote to Ira Cohen does actually exist. Naturally I want to get out of here as fast as possible. Jane says she'll help me. I'm scared to be alone a minute now. And of course Dris is supposed to go to work at Madraba now, but I'm not letting him.

I think you'd probably be safer in America too which is where I want to go and I'll help you get there, best I can.

Send me a check for two hundred on your Swiss account. I know you can afford it. And you know you can trust me.

I enclose photostats for your own protection. Will keep you posted.

Love,

Alfred

Very nervous

To Edward Field   (Western Union telegram, March 3, 1964)

PLEASE FLY TANGIER TODAY TAKE ME HOME GET MONEY BROTHER SAUL LAMBERT ANYONE AFRAID DON'T FAIL ME AFRAID ALFRED.

To Edward Field   (Western Union telegram, March 4, 1964)

FORGET OTHER WIRE DECIDED TO BECOME A MAN ALFRED

To Edward Field   March 6, 1964 Sidi Bujari 28, Tangier

Dear Edward:

Give me a few more days and I'll try to tell you about it. I'd written to my sister before I had your letter. I've now written to my brother asking him eight questions about the family, money, etc. Not really important, but just to see if he will accept me really. I asked, for example, what I've never known, did my father have his asshole sewn up? I also asked why I never got a share in the Alfred Fur Co. I said to my brother in relation to this question: "I want to know everything, because I'm his son the way you are."

Edward, the second half of the Mailer thing, in fact both halves and the Genet (if it weren't so cut up, but even so) tell you something about my madness. It also has a lot to do with the assassination, the smooth surface over the madness and the lies, the conspiracy. I have been a Jew in an alien world here, just like my father. The trouble was between Irving and Paul (go read Saul Lambert's letter, the one I wrote to him in the middle of it all). I started taking everything, every written word literally: The *I Ching*, the threat to have me killed, etc., including your book (which arrived by the way with the beautiful inscription) and that was why I wired you: I thought you meant very literally to me, *Stand Up, Friend, With Me.* I thought my innocence was being murdered, also myself. Everything became symbols suddenly and I mistrusted all the people because I have betrayed everyone for so long.

My book came, and you know, Edward, to my surprise I feel Alfred Chester is me and that I can be Alfred Chester and my father's son. Also, I've read the book, and you know, Edward, I guess I am a great writer. Now I must write my great book, which is what I wanted you to save me from doing.

I do feel now, in my heart and very powerfully, that though you and I are not the same person, I would be lost without you. Or would have been. It is hard now I have to face it all alone.

The problem with Dris will I hope work out like this: we're going halfies on a motor scooter and he'll commute daily. I can't run in and out of worlds anymore. I have to sit here and make up my own. I hope you'll come to see me soon, both of you ...I have all your three letters, including the money, so I can start patching up my life here a little....You must not tell anyone this, because it is in the center of the madness, but when I gave Dris the 500 francs to give to the witch in Arcila to make my mother give me money, she told him that while she worked (which she has been doing) I would have to write a letter saying I loved her, and I said no, that was impossible. I'm going to do that right now. Just one lying [marginal note: line. This is the rub. I don't know to whom I'm lying, so I must make peace with the outside world and try to find the truth out in my book. But this for sure, Virgil, if you let go of my hand Dante will be lost forever in the dark wood.] saying I hope she's okay and that I send her love.

God and mankind help me now though I've done nothing but offend them....Lots of love and kisses to you both.

Alfred

You're Virgil because you can tell the difference between hypocrisy and schizophrenia. And I can't. Without you.

To Edward Field   March 10, 1964 Sidi Bujari 28, Tangier
Dear Edward:

I have written you letter after letter after letter, perhaps a total of thirty pages singlespaced, including practically the whole story of my life. All I can say is that I'm more or less all right now, in fact I feel fine. I have been too long among cripples.

I want to write my novel now and come home. First one and then the other. I don't know what it is about Morocco that forbids communication of the central truth to the outside world. But you remember the other time when I stopped writing to you in Arcila? It's been like that but much worse.

I'm okay. Only look, you can't consider Jane and Paul my friends.

The trouble with my life, with everybody's life it seems to me, is that we say the right things to the wrong people. You should never have phoned her [Jane] nor have written her. The horrible thing is that she is the only American in Tangier with a telephone. Except the consulate. I don't know which is the worse choice. There is no way of calling collect. The consulate let me phone my mother once and that was a failure as you know. After you phoned Jane, I wanted to call you but Paul wouldn't let me. We are pretending to be great friends now but I think we're scared shitless of each other. I hope to God you didn't mention either time that I'd sent you a photostat of that letter. He wrote it months ago, but my fear was real. The people here, my sweet innocent Edward, are not like the people we've ever known. Bill Burroughs, as you know, murdered his wife. Jane's best friend Libby Holman murdered her husband. You and I we live in dream worlds of sweetness and hope. I wanted to go on living in that dream. I can again when I'm away from Paul's world. I've hidden myself in this apartment for months and months. Then suddenly the world around me blew the doors open. Everything collapsed.

Paul and Jane are poison. Do you dig, man? No sweetie cootchie Jane at all to write mumsie letters to, you poor fool. [Marginal note: They won't even let me see your letter.] Not a single word from you do I have, not a single letter, and you are sending letters to Jane. Do you know that Jane would have me locked up in a loonie bin faster than you can say poor Alfred because they are terrified of exposure. Can you imagine a place where one is afraid to leave alone? Can you imagine a world, just the way America is today, where people are afraid to tell the truth? Are we so far apart, Edward, that if I say I am afraid it means I am crazy, and that if I don't phone you back it means I don't have the money and that no phone is available to me? Can you imagine being driven crazy, deliberately, calculatedly? And don't say paranoia. It isn't paranoia. Anyway I must stop this because I'll drive myself nuts.

I suppose I ought to have a telephone installed myself. Maybe I'll do that. I'm so nervous writing to you because I think everything I say you'll think I'm crazy. You know, fear was put into the body not to be removed by psychoanalysis but to inform the animal that he was in dagger. Can't your darling Alfred be afraid without being crazy? All I'm saying is that just like you always trusted me, trust me. <u>Let me be the judge of my terror and my madness, not Jane.</u> Yes, I'll get a telephone installed.

I cannot go on in terror of the Biblical God who said not to expose your father's nakedness. I hereby renounce him as my God. I've always made enemies wherever I lived, you know my landlords and stuff, threatened suicide, tried to drive myself mad just to make them love me a little, my family, I mean. Well now I'm trying to heal the damage around me, even with my landlady (whom I'm at war with of course). And for once I must go to war with the proper people. Not blackmail or lies.

Edward, that last letter, the one I was going to mail out, that was my last innocent cry. You are quite wrong. I am not my father's son. If I'd been my father's son he wouldn't have forgotten me, because fathers do not forget their sons. I am only his son in law, so to speak. I wrote to my sister that I wanted to heal my father's life; that too was a cry of innocence. No, Edward, it wasn't my father's voice crying out for recognition, it was my own. I've been my own dybbuk, hiding inside. I told Molly I wanted to heal my father's life. But I don't anymore. I only want to heal my own. Lots of love to you and Neil.

Alfred

[Note on envelope: Oh, of course, most critical of all is that in the book I started to tell the truth about my father.]

To Edward Field and Neil Derrick

March 14, 1964 Sidi Bujari 28, Tangier

Darling Sweethearts

I'm back at last.

I love you both.

I should really have a lawyer and hope you will make Si help me.

Can you ever ever ever ever forgive me?

Tell Saul Lambert to go shove it. I hate his cover [for *Behold Goliath*]. His wife wrote me two imploring letters, begging me to like it or he would collapse. [Footnote: imagine me feeling two years of guilt because that rich shithouse asked me to dedicate something to him.]

It is black like death, like his death.

I hate millions of people, millions and billions.

But I adore my Edward and Neil.

Waiting to hear from you.

How lovely it is to be Alfred.

XXXXXXXXXXXXXXX Alfred

To Norman Glass   March 17, 1964 Sidi Bujari 28, Tangier

Dear Norman

I wrote you a huge letter yesterday about the occurrences in Tangier but am not sending it since there seems no point in going into the whole thing in detail. I went mad, quite literally. Among the insane and marvelous things I did was take a photostat of Paul's letter to the Consul General. Jane gave me a long lecture yesterday, presumably about Irving's famous line "cocks so dry" but really about my having gone to the consul. The point was that it's against the rules to snitch on each other. That, she said, is criminal. I said, Oh well, writing threatening letters is criminal too. And actually she had threatened to go to the consul about Irving's line which was, I think, one of the things that made me go berserk. Well, we are pretending to love each other now, but I loathe them both, Jane perhaps more than Paul. As for you, to tell the truth, I don't trust you a bit, though I think I do understand your necessity to carry tales. It occurred to me that it was a way of preserving your personal integrity, sanity, and identity by keeping the opposing forces outside yourself. None the less, you didn't tell, and Paul has, that you are corresponding with him.

I got to know Burroughs briefly in the middle of it all, and I dislike him intensely. He is a destructive and dangerous person. You may think he has something to teach you, but my stomach told me in his presence to get out. I have too long not listened to my stomach.

I had a wire from Time magazine yesterday asking for photos and have decided to break my rule about photos and send them some. I took some in the Socco Grande yesterday, but haven't seen them yet. I don't know how things really look, but my nerves say I'm going to come out of this gigantically famous and I'm very nervous about it. I've had a copy of book and one day like it, one day hate it. You're on the free list, but it should be a month before you get yours as I can't send them all air. (I get billed for the comps.)

Paul still hasn't come through with the quote and I don't really care. Burroughs took lots of material including the column in which you're mentioned) and then left for Paris without a word. Which did nothing to improve my opinion of him.

Ira has gone to England in order to go to Belgium about the magazine. Rosalind is alone and I think wants to be looked after. I told her she could come sleep here if she got very nervous. My asshole started hurting excruciatingly in the middle of it all. (Jane had told me that Edward Roditi had cancer of the colon.) It now feels a lot better. Dris shoved a clove of garlic up last night and it seems to have worked.

I'm not going to Arcila. I'm staying put and have gotten Dris a motor scooter on the installment plan, the never-never (8800 per month), and poor thing, was delighted at first but I think is a little sad now, as it takes him two hours each way roughly (the motor being new he can only go 30 kilometers an hour). Later it will be easier, but I think I'll tell him that he'd better not come every day until he can do 60 to 70 kilometers.

Deutsch has taken the stories, offering 150 pounds which means (after agent's fee and taxes I should end up with about 70 pounds.

I think Edward is mad at me because at the worst part of my madness I wired him to come take me home: "afraid, don't fail me, afraid." Haven't heard from him since, though he phoned Jane to find out if I was crazy. I'm appalled by Jane. Truly appalled.

I don't know what happened to me these past weeks. But one very major thing is I've come out of it with less shame and less fear. I feel more [illegible] somehow than I've felt in years, perhaps ever.

I saw Hajmi coming out of the wanker's apartment one morning with W. Hajmi now whores with all those revolting queens. You see what you did, you wicked boy?

I must go wash my asshole as I'm going to the doctor today and don't want it to be too shitencrusted.

I'm not signing this letter love because I don't think there is any love between us.

Alfred

P.S. What I meant about being forced to like Irving's work, was not forced by the work, but forced by your/and Ira's esteem of it. I remember it now as a big pretentious bore. This is just on the basis of a few pages as you know. Maybe, if I ever read the whole book, I'll like it. But I'm so bored with sex writing. I wrote my porno in 1955.

To Edward Field   March 18, 1964 Sidi Bujari 28, Tangier

Darling darling

I was in the middle of a letter to Si, when your letter came, thank God. I thought you were mad at me. I'm not now going to go into the whole thing because when I do (I've written you probably 50 pages on the subject by this time, burnt along with letters written to my father and burnt) it becomes a string unwinding endlessly. In any case, I was crazy up until this past Saturday morning. I mean, when I wrote you that note on Friday saying I was back, it was only partially true, though I didn't know it. In point of fact, I came back during a dream, Friday night. I dreamt I was in bed with Arthur Miller and was pretending to be sorry about Marilyn Monroe, and then we were going to go to sleep, but to be sort of friendlyingratiating I said, how old are you, Arthur? Then suddenly, he put his hand at my throat and I knew he meant to kill me. So I started screaming the way my mother does and the way I always have, to wake from the nightmare. Usually the scream, sort of an abortive, constricted, unrealizable little wail, wakes me up into a huge terror. But this time, it didn't. Can you imagine? I just went on screaming in my dream and the scream got louder and louder and poor Arthur Miller fell back to his pillow and I was on top of him and he was afraid of me. By the time Dris (who sleeps like a stone especially now that he works) got around to hearing me and waking me up, the dream had stopped being a nightmare and turned into a victory. I woke without fear. In the morning, I remembered everything, everything, and then knew I had been mad.

I'll save all the delicious little horrors of madness for some other letter. I was very depressed for a couple of days, until about Monday I guess, and realizing that I hadn't heard from you made things worse. But then I started feeling better and better. And now feel fine except of course your letter made me excited and ecstatic, and now sort of nervous over business.

I just wrote Candida a long letter saying that between now and the first of May she was to send me twice weekly reports stating exactly what she was doing on my behalf. And that if she was doing nothing, she was to report: Nothing. Epstein, of course, has done nothing. So far as I know you are the only person to have received a copy, except Time magazine. They've been after me like a pack of wild hounds. Telegrams. And a man, huge like the FBI, was hanging around the house (Dris told me) between seven and nine p.m. yesterday. He finally caught me. And I said I'd sent the photos to Random House. They are really ridiculous pictures, but just odd enough maybe to sell copies. I'm all dressed in black with my shades on and standing in the glaring sunlight of the Socco Grande. I sent Jason four photos. The Time man scared me to death. I opened the door a crack and wouldn't let him in and Columbine was roaring and I couldn't hear what the man was saying and I just thought he was a cop and the feds had finally cornered me, public enemy number one. You know, *entre nous*, I think Time will give me a favorable review, not that I have any illusions about them, but because they like to court power, and I have a growing conviction that for some reason I am powerful. I don't know why. Perhaps only because I admit my ignorance. [Note on margin: The big mystery that now Dris, the concierge and I are trying to solve is how the Time man got into the house when the downstairs door was locked and no one opened it for him. Do you think they carry skeleton keys?]

I think I have literally been crazy for years, maybe since I was seven when my hair fell out. That's another thing. Ever since 1958, I've suspected that my ordeal was a psychological one. But I won't go into it all now, it's too complicated. I think it was the result of a betrayal by my sister. But I may be wrong. Anyway, I really and truly don't care. I mean, well that's who I am, and I'd rather be it than anyone I know. I mean I wouldn't trade places with anyone....I've bought Dris a motor bike on the installment plan so he can commute. It is killing him and I guess I'll have to give in on his coming only every other day during the season. We haven't had sex since the crisis began. (That was a big part of it. In fact it began, the whole thing, the day Jane told me that Edward Roditi had cancer of the colon.) Anyway now that I'm not crazy anymore I realize that poor Jane and Paul are terrified of me, which is good because it keeps them quieter. Paul finally came through with his quote yesterday, but it is hopeless: "Chester examines the complex perversity of human behavior; since he is a stylistic virtuoso, his reports are varied and brilliant." I'm sending it to Random. I'm also sending a note to Jason saying that thus far I have not one single shred of evidence indicating that he wishes to promote the book in any way. I'm also telling him I want twice weekly reports on his activities, vis-à-vis my book.

I think the lecture setup should be organized after the book is out, not before. And I don't want to go alone. I want to go with you. It should be a joint deal between Random and Grove and we should pull down (if [Karl] Shapiro does alone) 1000 a time together. We just have to start acting famous and powerful. It is the only way. We have to scare them to death. I've learned in my madness that America's disease is just this love confusion thing. There is no love. There is only fear and blackmail. And since I now know this, and you should, we had best start operating on these premises.

My career as a critic and a reviewer is over. I'll be damned if I do anything for that industry ever again. My only tentative agreement is with the Trib to review Terry [Southern]'s book as part of my column which I'd really wanted to use to tear apart Time magazine in relation to the whole fraudulent American handling of the Kennedy case. I can do that the month after. By that time, the whole thing however will have blown open. I suppose you've heard by this time that Oswald worked for the CIA and the FBI, that he was counter-espionage, and that he was their decoy in what was *plus ou moins un coup d'état*. I told you I thought Johnson was in on it. I still think he was. I think now it was a politically necessary move to keep the Democratic party from falling to pieces. By the way, in my madness, I began imagining I was Oswald, and sometimes Kennedy. Also I was terrified about Dris and the motor bike because of your poem "A New Cycle," me being thirtyfive and all. And Dris being my father and my son together.

I have to stop this now, because I have a huge amount of letters to write. Oh, Deutsch has offered me 150 pounds for the book. I should clear $300 if I'm lucky, after double agent fees and taxes. Also I had a note from Elizabeth Montagu who was one of the people I wrote for money (no one else answered, so they are all out of my life and good riddance—for one thing my teeth are crumbling). She says: "Listen, about money. As I explained I now live in France. If you let me know how you want it (dollars or francs) and how much and where to send it to, I'll try to organize that thing." I'm going to say that the dream figure is a thousand, but anything under is fine. (I suppose you know she is top English aristocracy.)

I mean, to tell the truth, it looks like money is going to start coming at last from all sides. I mean, somehow, I'm going to allow it to happen. Isn't that an odd thing to say? Maybe I'm still crazy. Anyway, I've spent thirtyfive years disorganizing myself and destroying myself, and I want the next thirtyfive, *insha'allah*, to go somewhat better. Now that I'm at last my own man.

Did you really write a poem for me? And if so, why didn't I ever see it?

Oh, Edward, I hope the book sells its 20,000 copies (I'm thinking it should be more now). If it does, maybe then we should publish our own books afterwards, like Ferlinghetti, and get out of this terrible rat race.

About the phone call. No, no messenger ever came. If he would have, anyway I probably would have had Columbine eat him up, thinking he was the personification of death or something. People had no individual reality for me. They were all symbols, personifications, myths.

I wrote Susan for a quote, saying, "Can't you put aside your professional opinion and remember what good friends we are?"

In case you're curious about the people who are out (not only a question of money) they are: Harriet, Susan, Irene (her name comes out of the second edition if there is one), Dennis, Gerry, Cade, the Lamberts, all editors and publishers, my agent. This leaves roughly you and Neilele, the Goulds and my cousin Marilyn. (Note: Oh I sort of accept Mrs. Schaeffer. If you want to give her a treat get hold of all the letters I wrote during those weeks and show them to her. Especially the one to my sister! And that last one to my father was a lulu. No, I don't expect you to get hold of that. "Sorry, papa, I've tried very hard to be a good boy but now I'm not going to suffer for you anymore. After I finish this letter I'm gonna go out and have fun." It scared the daylights out of me writing it. Then I burnt it. Oh, I've asked Random to send a comp To "Jacob Chester c/o S. Chester and conscience)"—that's to my father c/o the lawyer.) Maybe when I come back to New York you can introduce me to some new people.

Oh I feel so clean and love you two adorables so much.

Alfred

In the middle of everything I had: two crazy letters from Extro. And a gigantic thing from my girl in Israel who is friends with Robert Friend.

Edward, I feel so proud of myself, just in general and so loveable. I feel like a nice man.

To Edward Field   March 22, 1964 Sidi Bujari 28, Tangier
Dear Edward:

I've just made another appointment with the doctor because now Time magazine is driving me crazy. They've sent men over from Gibraltar in a flashy white car that keeps parking itself outside my house. I left a note on the door yesterday saying I was going away for the weekend, the photos were at Random and my nerves were bad so stop sending me wires. Then I sat down here yesterday and wrote my whole column on how they'd been driving me crazy, it's called "Killing Time, Part I"—and I put Luce down as having delusions of grandeur for imagining that he has rights on me. I say Time is like Pravda and so on. Better call up Kluger who'll have a nervous fit about printing it.

Anyway I had some guests over last night and I definitely saw a flash out the window on the terrace. Maybe it was lightning. And this morning I went down to get the mail and there was their car again, so I ran up the steps and they went away. They make me so afraid. They're planning some gigantic put-down of me I'm sure now or they wouldn't go through all this trouble. I started getting scared again like when I was crazy so I went to the post office and mailed my column and sent Mme. Marquis, the one who keeps wiring me, a cable saying: "Recently suffered serious nervous collapse your invasions now cause me to require further medical attention my lawyer will contact yours you may print no photos but those out of Random House." No, I left out the part about the lawyer.

In my column, I quote their second telegram: "Thanks your message however Random House says they have absolutely no pix of you therefore we are sending photographer to take pictures of you and hope you will be kind enough to receive him quickly as our review of your book closes this Saturday in New York many thanks in advance Mme. Marquis." Then I write: "Well, like, I mean: The nerve: Not even so much as a "may we?" or a "we are taking the liberty of?" just that stunning "therefore" like an imperial command. Who the hell do they think they are, Pravda? And not even eightyfive cents (return coupon) this time to say no with. Henry Luce must be having delusions of grandeur; who does he think he is, a friend of mine? I don't care how much money he's got; I don't give a youknowwhat if he's got the gold and the power to send Federallooking men all around the world to hunt out nobodies like me. No army of strange huns comes invading my tworoom castle, not for anything—not for fame, nor riches, nor rave reviews, nor anything else. Who do those people think they are? I love that littie stranglehold, 'as our review of your book closes this Saturday.' So? Am I supposed to get hysterical that Time magazine may have three inches of inexplicable emptiness in a universe with nothing—(I think I should insert 'else' here to read, 'nothing else but.' If you phone Kluger, tell him to put 'else' in please.) But? Really, Henry, someone's got to tell you to come to your senses!"

Later. I'm feeling better now but I guess I'll have to keep the appointment with Mme Roux. Skoura had what I think was an epileptic fit this morning. She'd started getting badly spastic again these past few days, then suddenly this morning she had this fit. It went on for about two minutes but after it she was better than she'd been in days. Like Jane. She chewed the rug and twitched and threw herself around.... Buchanan writes in the Express that he'd just been to Washington and the truth is coming out. It will probably be a "fixed" truth to keep the top men out. He hints they're planning to hang it on the anti-Castro people in Florida. He also says they're planning to murder Ruby as soon as he's found guilty and put it as a suicide. He also says that Ruby is the actual murderer, the one who fired from the bridge.

I don't have anything more to say. I guess I'm going to be gigantically famous soon, or do they do this to everybody? Time, I mean.

If they leave me alone now, I'll be able to start work on the book again. This thing is too much. Why did I always imagine I wanted to be written about, followed, and all that? It's too horrible.

Lots of love and kisses to both.

Alfred

To Edward Field   March 25, 1964 Sidi Bujari 28, Tangier
Habibi:

It's the most scrumptious Monday morning imaginable, with the birds going and the trees blossoming, and the terrace doors wide open to let the spring in. It's the 23rd today, I think that's spring. I'm beginning to get Time out of my system, thank God, and am going to work today. I'm really writing about business. I was just thinking that the reason Time made such a fuss is that I did something unexpected. Just because of all my personal horrors of exposure, I went about the photograph thing in the wrong way, and consequently they were ready to spend fortunes of money to have things their own way. They were even out in Arcila on Saturday, Dris told me, and he claims they didn't recognize him, but I have a vague feeling they bribed him because he went off to Arcila with a copy of my book that morning. I'll question him more closely tonight when he comes home. Anyway he says they were just taking local photos. (He carries a very respectable photo of me in his wallet, and has now forbidden me to dress badly anymore, especially on account of the recent beatnik mass deportation.) Anyhow, so I was thinking that if we go on a reading tour in the fall, what we have to do, say, is a magic show. I mean, if you really can bear becoming gigantically famous. One thing is certain, I can't, wouldn't, won't do it alone. We have plenty of time to think about it. But the idea I believe is to do the unexpected. That is the whole secret. We're both slightly exhibitionistic, you more so I think. Maybe what we have to do is theater, plays, drag shows, anything.

I read your book again yesterday, straight through. I've been reading bits here and there since it came. It gets more beautiful every time. I can hardly believe it. It's just like when you read at the Bar Nikolaus; the poems are not supposed to be read in twos or threes. They need bulk and volume. You know what I was thinking yesterday? I was thinking you should do what Whitman did. Your book is one thing and it just has to go on acquiring and growing. That is, your next book should be this book, twice as big, with your new poems comprising Section Five and maybe adding some of the old poems you left out. I mean, like, by the time you're sixty this book should be 300 pages or so. Actually for the first time I agree with you about leaving in the bad. I even theoretically agree with you about the third section of the Castro poem. I mean since it's done leave it, even though it should be cut.

Later. I've just been to the market. It's so nice now that Dris works and I have to go shopping. Seeing the food and the people and the sun is so nice. It's hot like when you were in Morocco, but deliciously newly hot. I bought three bouquets of flowers for 100 francs, one red, one white, one yellow, and put them in my clay bowls....Oh, when I got back from the market, the maid downstairs said the consul was trying, had been trying to get me all day Thursday and Friday. I expect Time got him to work for them. I'll phone him later to find out what he wants. I've never felt so unmakeableout in my life. I mean I never felt so clearly how I stun people, or anyway surprise them. That's part of my loss of innocence, I guess. I can also lie now in the coolest most professional way. I went out to Arcila the other day with Rosalyn to register at the police since we're both way overdue and are afraid of being fined in Tangier. And I just sat there making up the most marvelous story; it didn't work, but I just dazzled myself with my self-confidence. When I went to the doctor the other day after Time, she said that I had gigantic force that came from my Russian Jewish roots in the Black Sea and that if I could do a few Yoga breathings whenever I felt myself impelled to a violent reaction, it would double my force and benefit my reason. Which sounds pretty good, except when the invaders are on your doorstep who can remember about Yoga breathing. I start feeling like Samson and want to push the columns down.

Six p.m. Oh Edward I wish you were here to see this day, this afternoon. The odd looking tree in the garden that lost its leaves during the winter is blossoming. Most of the other trees just stayed green. And the bowls of flowers on the *taifour* (the little round low table we eat at sitting on the mat) are spectacular. And the sun is like honey all over me here in the living room.....You know, Edward, since I went crazy, I handle people better. I mean, I can tell them what I want and what I don't want. And they do things for me and listen to me. I had a note today from Kluger. They are so happy about my second Mailer piece. I think I was probably already completely gone when I wrote it and I don't understand it at all. It's appearing next Sunday. I remember suffering terribly when I wrote it....The piece on Time I now realize is really *un coup de genie* because it comes streaming right out of my unconsciousness and does exactly the right thing one must do in attacking Time, present them as something one must be afraid of. My second installment (keep this quiet) will be mainly an attack for concealing the truth about the Kennedy assassination and suppressing any information about the Buchanan article. I'm feeling nervous about going back to the book, though I know at last it's the right book for me. I mean, the only possible book....How was Jane's play received? She hasn't heard anything. It opened last week at some new little theater, reviving it. I expect it was a big flop since no one has notified her.... Edward, I have this profound conviction that in about a month or so I'm going to be vomitously famous. I hope so and I hope not. Do you know that *City of Night* only sold 65,000 for all its hoopla. So how can I really sell 20,000. In hard back I mean.

Next morning. Summer's gone. The valley is filled with mist. I didn't want Dris to go to work today as he was in agony. They were hauling anchors yesterday. He kept dressing and undressing and finally went. He has a conscience. I don't know where he gets it from. It is so odd for a Moslem. He brought me a beautiful yellow tarbush with a tassel and red and black trimmings. He was hurt when I asked him if Time had bribed him. It's my paranoia....I woke up this morning and thought I am working on my fifth book. *Jamie [Is My Heart's Desire]*,

Chariot of Flesh, Behold, Goliath, my essays, and now this. It begins to feel like an *oeuvre*, doesn't it? My self esteem is increasing. A boy here who once made a film recently read *Chariot of Flesh* and is dying to make a film out of it. He says it doesn't have to be porno, as it's really a psychological study, and can be handled indirectly. Can you imagine? I was so impressed.

Days later. I'm falling in love with Dris again, though now I have a rival, the motor scooter. He is in love with her. He's always rushing over to the shop on every pretext, partly to get everything repaired every minute, but really to show them that we aren't running away with the motor bike but really mean to go on making payments. I'm taking Rosalyn to the consul today to try to get our residence papers as everyone keeps getting arrested and deported. Mel was arrested yesterday. But he had the residence papers so they let him go after an hour. The Socco Chico is completely deserted. The cops came to the house next door where this Gerry Weil lives with his wife, a phony fakir (who evidently fucks them all), and a Moslem girl. Mel says it is all Interpol because northern Europe is flooded with kif that the beatniks run out of Morocco. Gerry Weil is a very successful commercial writer *Love in Paris, Naked in Rome*, etc. and he is taking his ménage to America later in the spring to present Abdulrakim, or whatever his name is, as the new savior. (G. is the only person in Tangier who evidently doesn't know that his fakir is a Portuguese carny man and not a Moslem cultist.) Anyway the situation is nerveracking. Right now an American girl is serving twenty days in the casbah dungeons for carrying a little packet of kif. Everyone is begging me to write a column about it, and I suppose I will one month or other. I'm convinced it's all due to the liquor industries. The Moroccan government is completely crazy on the kif thing. It's illegal but they really can't stop it as it's traditional. They try to turn the Moroccans onto liquor and then periodically change their minds and if a Moroccan is caught drinking in public, he gets thirty days in jail. Dris gets so confused on the liquor situation that it becomes very dreary. He puts like a half inch of wine or whiskey in a huge glass and fills it with coca cola, as he really can't bear it. But he thinks he's supposed to like it. Then he gets all mixed up about whether he's supposed to get drunk in public or not. Meanwhile everyone goes on smoking kif with intermittent arrests, and with the older Moslems, over twentyfive, not really understanding why it's wrong. The kids in school are taught it is bad. As they are taught that French is a better language than Spanish or Moghrebi. The very educated Moslems in fact pretend there is no such language as Moghrebi, that it is an idiocy based on classical Arabic. Anyway, it all adds up to that there will be a revolution soon. Chas Gallagher who is an authority says five to ten years. I give it two or three.

I'm working on my book again, nervously....I'm nervous about reviews too....I wish you could smell around and tell me what to expect....I'm becoming the old me again, to my chagrin. Partly to my chagrin. The old me loved life better. You have to take the bitter with the better, as Jane Ace used to say. My hero started an organization for a new view of the universe. His contention is that it is only 200 years old....I've changed my mind about Terry Southern's book. I mean, it is very funny and chichi, but I'm going to attack it on the grounds that a writer is not supposed to reflect his society but improve it, and all *Candy* does is be very smart and destructive. If the society doesn't offer any positive ideal like love or religion or beauty, then obviously the society has to be changed. I think, myself, that paganism and agriculturalism are the only solutions. The gods have to go back into the trees and rivers again. Shall we put them there, *paidhaiki mou*? Actually you've always been trying that, haven't you?....I'm wearing my pretty new tarboosh and the tassel is dancing in front of my eyes....I'd be a communist if it weren't so boring and just more industrialization. I suppose one really has to start praying that the atom bombs will fall and clean things up, so people can take over again instead of machines.

The mail just came and I enclose my agent's letter, just for your amusement. Can you imagine a first printing of 2500 copies? Half the copies are already sold, prepublication. It does look very good, I must say. Obviously the last thing Random House expects or wants is a success. Here are the relevant facts: She is furious and says we should break up because I treated her in a businesslike way. Jason [Epstein] is hopping mad: "He is in a state of total annoyance with you, so you can imagine how much you've helped yourself in that regard." All this because I asked for twice weekly reports. I'm broken up at the hilarity of the situation. Can you imagine, a writer asks his agent for business reports and they collapse in anger and horror. It is really too funny. I asked Candida what I was supposed to tell her if only my unreasonable requests could bring a concrete reply from her.

The Trib reviewer conked out for unspecified reasons. Shirley Jackson may do it. No word on the Times, but they will probably neither mildly like it or mildly dislike it. (That speculation is mine not Candida's.) My advertising budget is $600. (I'll bet it became $600 after my correspondence, not before.)

She writes: "Also I am now entirely out of copies, have ordered more, by messenger of course, to supply Tucker, Toffler, and whomever else you have directed me to send to, but in 48 hours I am not sure I can do. I will try to. It may take 52 hours." This now comes after instructions I sent like six weeks ago.

They're probably scampering around like scared rabbits now that the truth is out and me the biggest blabbermouth in the world. 2500 copies. Edward, would you believe it? It is really too funny. I asked my agent why she threatened to quit me every time I talked to her in a businesslike way. You're the nigger in the woodpile, of course. They probably hate you like poison. Also, I asked if something couldn't be done about that jacket, which fills me with horror. Literally. I start feeling myself going to pieces when I look at it. I asked if the black couldn't be dropped and made white, and black typography used in its place, instead of white typography and leave the drawing, I suppose.

No, I am obviously not the old me who would never have thought to be amused by all this, but to have been angered or cringed inside or something. And I would have changed my position and apologized, etc. I told Candida: "If Jason is annoyed, soothe him, but keep him hopping."

Lots of kisses to my adorable boychiks,
Love,
Alfred

To Edward Field   April 4, 1964 Sidi Bujari 28, Tangier
Habibi:

Susan is a whore. My letter was ironical of course. Since we aren't friends and since her professional opinion of me is supposed to be so high, I inverted it. Oh, who cares, anyhow? But she is really so profoundly, so thoroughly, so quintessentially Whore. Her whole mentality is whore. Really, that business about what kind of reception? To my face, she has admired and agreed with my criticism. But that is strictly her whore's cynicism.

I am feeling lousy. It's been bad weather for nearly two weeks, rain and very cold and gale winds. Equinox. There is just no point to Morocco when the weather isn't good. If I could think of somewhere to go, I'd go. I feel like I've completed my New York demolition job, begun at that farewell party where I bit everyone except Jerry Rothlein. Dris is getting on my nerves. And the people here are either completely destructive or terrified hypocrites. I haven't worked for two days, but before that I was working every day a little, without faith and without hope, like the sign says. No, actually, I was working very happily and loving my book. I was so fed up with life yesterday I went to bed at three in the afternoon and didn't get up until now, seven a.m.

I loved your little poem about Here is NeilLand. You are wise not to go away, anyway not to come here. Yes, I can hear Neil's typewriter tapping in the background? Can't you hear my teeth gnashing with envy in the foreground? Why don't you send me those poems: the octopus one, the breakfast one, and the one to me?

I had a disgusting letter from Epstein. He says they couldn't sell many books when the salesman went around last winter (only a thousand copies which makes him very discouraged) because they hadn't been able to get any comments and because I'm not known outside New York. In other words, it is all my fault, and even if the advance sale is astonishing, it is still going to add up to nothing.

I received all the Commentaries I missed except the July one so I assume your book was reviewed in July because it isn't in any of the others. There is a fancy adoration of Susan's book. I could hardly believe this was the same magazine I'd written for so much. It is so cheap and snotty, sort of a Jewish Time. I never want to write for them again. I got my Genet the other day, I mean the April issue, and it is literally onethird the size of the original. They cut very badly. Like that Freud business, they cut a full page after that, and left in the first line which is pointless now.

If you go see Yacoubi {protégé of Paul Bowles, an artist living in New York], be careful what you eat as he is *s'heur* specialist and has probably taken tons of those disgusting little beetles with him, like Spanish fly, that make you hot. Don't eat any homemade sweets he offers you, not even *majoun*. I've never met him, but he is notorious for fixing things....I've had a letter from Harriet and hate her and all women.... There is a lady who writes me from Alexandria, Virginia, named Mrs. D.C. (Mary) Jones. I think she is an agent from the narcotics squad. Not only that name, but her outlandish hip style (Sing, Allen baby, sing!). She talks of Ginsbwrg and Miller and her dead environment, the people around her, etc. At first I thought she was Jackie Kennedy (who turned down my offer, my request I mean) or some spy for her. Now I think she's narcotics....Did you see my other Mailer column in which I quote you and talk about having tea with Neil at the museum? Isn't it strange the way I suddenly drive off the road and head into the pasture, going eighty miles an hour and never even noticing? Mme. Roux is a French lady doctor who I went to a few times after, as Jane calls it now, "The Mistake." She is nice, but I can't really go as she thinks I'm a rebel and am afraid to grow up. She also doesn't think I'm queer, etc. In short, she has too many ideas. But she gave me a lot of pills which calm me down, and from my tranquillized lotus position, life is vomit.

Later. Edward, another letter from you just came. About [your reading at] Paraclete. It sounded just like your fantasy. Five-hundred people. PLEASE send me those poems. Yes, you're right you're so right, Edward. That's the whole thing. They want to pretend they're already bored with sex and literature to make the writer stop writing about sex, so they can become puritans again. I mean, you are right to go on shocking them. I'm sure—you don't know that your reading was a success. They'll wake up in three days and realize it was a great performance. (Except the Paraclete is Catholic, I forgot.)

With your letter came a huge letter from Elliot Freemont-Smith of the Times to whom I'd sent a note asking for a lot of space. *Quel con.* He likes the New Yorker story and "Vespasian." He carried on for nearly a page about "Vespasian." Then after: "Ah so. There's my opinion, and there's the reviewer's, and they don't entirely agree, and I'm afraid you will not be entirely pleased. But it is literate, and some space, and should run within the month. (And more I can't say, an awkwardness, please forgive.) I'm very glad the book is selling as it should, and will." So I don't know whether he's the reviewer, and whether "some space" means sticking me in back of the paper or what. I think he was drunk when he wrote the letter because he goes on and on. He is, I think, a latent homosexual. Or maybe an ex. Really, Edward, are reviewers going to carry on about the homosexual thing? Well, I suppose that's good for sales.

Yes, Samartino is right. But how can I go back? I mean I don't have any place to go back to, nor any money to make a place. My relatives wouldn't give me any money, you know that. I suppose if Betts Montagu came through I could, but then I'd feel terrible. I don't mind about leaving Dris. I'd leave him in a minute the way I'm feeling lately. In an hour, when I love him. Are you saying you think I should come back, right now, and in the early stages of the book? That's really my only motive and justification now for staying in this hellhole.

How awful about Nadia. I didn't know she had a lump. My sister had one and it was cancer. Burroughs says that cancer cells are beings from another planet. That we are already invaded. "We do not come to improve. We come to eat," they say. Anyway, aside from the explanation, I hope she is all right.

I thought yesterday how nice it would be to be on Sullivan St. again. Anyway I won't come back unless I've got $1000 because I'm not going to stick myself into some hole on the lower East Side. I really do need a little comfort now. I'm not so young as I was. Do you really think my book will go? I don't think now there'll be any uproar. It will just be reviewed and disappear. Shirley Jackson is too fat to get excited; the Times is too dumb; Time magazine hates me too much. Who will get excited? You? And Neilele? Oh God, I would love to come home, I really would, except it's ridiculous. And New York makes me rotten. I don't know. Lots of love.

Alfred

Edward, I just thought: what if I just appeared on my mother's doorstep, baggage and all, with a note from the doctor in my hand. She'd have to pay a lot to get rid of me. What do you think? Then I could begin suit. But will I write my book in New York?

To Edward Field   April 7, 1964 Sidi Bujari 28, Tangier

Dear Edward:

I love you, you're so smart. I've been walking around screaming with laughter all day about being Marilyn Monroe. It's like the time I told you "life is a bank where all our deposits are turned into scorpions." I was so depressed about it and then you laughed, and then I thought, Oh, it's just a number. I take myself so seriously, and everyone here is so dumb they take me seriously too. I could give you a million hugs and kisses. Isn't it funny, I never saw that in the dream. I just saw another writer strangling my voice. It seemed so serious. I never realized I was the NEW Marilyn Monroe. She wasn't in bed. I was. She was definitely dead. Oh, I'm a riot. You've made me love myself again. You see, it's so awful here. I never know who I am anyway, and having to be a very serious monster is so depressing. You're 10,000 times more of a glamor girl than I am, only you have a more fixed idea of yourself than I do, so you can see more clearly what is going on. No, I just realized, it's true. I'm natural star material. But don't worry, darling, we were meant to be billed as the Dolly sisters, and I won't let you down....The slave is here, washing the floor at my feet and distracting me....I wish you were here to hug and kiss. Edward, how can you know so much????

Gerry Weil was here now for hours. He got me a little hot. He is sort of short and fat, with a beard, a middle-aged American Jewish boy, balding and dumb. He was trying to talk me into converting to Abdulraqman again. His new idea is to involve Norman Mailer and Paul Goodman in the movement and to convert the cosmonauts. It is very grand. The truth is his wife is in love with "Abe" as Abdulraqman is called and so poor Gerry has to be his devoted disciple. Gerry has to sleep on the floor now. I finally got around to asking him about sex today and he said (because I'd been wondering how the German monster woman, his wife, got Abe to get Gerry out of fucking her): "The Master says you have to sleep with people much younger than yourself, so you get their energy." That is typical Moslem talk; the younger always feels he is giving his strength to the older. Dris is always qvetching about he's so *flojo* (weak) because he gives me all his youth. I always tell him he can keep it. But maybe it's true, who knows?

The guy from the Times says: "Do you really mean that Norman Mailer's piece in Esquire was even partially (beyond, say, six votes) responsible for JFK's election???? Swayed votes? Established a climate? I know Mailer believes it, or must assume he does; but to believe what Mailer believes about his real effect is, well, astounding. Especially his political effect. I suspect his political effect is about as considerable as my own." What an ass. It is that kind of mentality that allows politics to belong to the politicians and breeds mouldy cucumbers and horseflies. He's right in what he says, in that people only allow themselves to listen to politicians on politics. They are the professionals, the authorities. Have I changed things a little teentsy bit in my article? I just read that Brendan Behan died. I made reference to that idiotic columnist's reference to him, about alcoholics lying in the gutter and ideally dead.

I just realized what he means, the Times guy, Elliot. About his opinion and the reviewers'. It follows a long paragraph on how wonderful my homosexual writing is. He means the critic is going to attack me for it. I think. Very good if so....I wish I could think of something for Leonard Lyons. How about: Francoise Sagan and Alfred Chester drinking martinis (dry) in the Minzah swimming pool (wet) in Tangier....She's here now, though I haven't seen her....Or: Alfred Chester put on his favorite djellaba and thus managed not to get run out of Tangier in the recent beatnik deportation. But then everyone will think I'm a beatnik which is bad. No, I can't think of things. I hate Leonard Lyons anyway, and the people who read his column don't buy books I'm sure.

Jane just came over to invite me to supper tomorrow night. She wants to have a book party for me but I don't want it. As her reviews were mixed, she's having mixed feelings. She brought over a big ad from the Times. Maybe it's better to have a quote from her than from Paul. I told her you'd said I was Marilyn Monroe and she screamed with laughter. She took your book of poems (which I'm going to have bound in Marrakech; if you want yours bound, send it) and said to tell you she would write. We talked about The Mistake. She said the totality thing was classical, where everything fits together. She said she thought I was really going to go over and that if I managed to spring back this time I'll never go crazy. But of course madness is just another role, which she doesn't see.

Lots of love,

Alfred

Written Second, But Read First. I was at Paul's last night and he told me again what I'd forgotten which is that Allen Ginsberg loved "Vespasian." He said I could reach G. c/o Ted Wilentz at the 8th St. Bookstore and I was going to write today, but then thought maybe you could as maybe it is better indirectly. Maybe you could ask W.

118

where G. is and write him for a quote from me, and if he doesn't have a book I'll have one sent. Ask him maybe if he would review my book for Kulchur which seems to have become very chic lately. It's all a union that whole bunch. Only Susan could whore her way in and get away with it (as I understand she has)....There was also a copy of Time at Paul's with a review of *Radcliffe* an English queer novel and I thought I'd throw a fit thinking how they would tear me apart in just two weeks. Will they dare attack homosexuality twice in one month? Paul says, oh yes, they love to attack homosexuality in every issue if they get a chance. Edward, we must write dirtier and dirtier until they show their real horrorstricken faces, until we break through their bored pose....Also lying around at Paul's were two faggots who saw you a few weeks ago at a party for Howard Griffin. One was called Roy. One paints. One talks and looks like Jason Epstein. They are sort of typical dreary queens in that Edwin Denby/James Schuyler/Art News set. Anyway I was so happy to see them and was dying to hear all the latest in New York, and it was just like expecting two muffins to gossip with you....Dris didn't go to work today. He's in bed being sick and unhappy because, in our idiotic lingo, he thinks I'm rejecting him. He usually stays overnight in Arcila on Sundays, so I never bothered telling him I was going out last night. And he came home and waited and waited, and didn't know where I was. It is nice the way he can be so direct. Once he smelled my crotch when I came home to see if I'd been unfaithful. I, of course, am much too dignified to do things like that, aren't you, even if I want to....It's Monday and most mail comes today and I'm sitting waiting being horrified with whatever hideous news is in the mail. I tried to work a little but I really can't concentrate with Goliath on the verge....Oh, Paul said that he saw Burroughs last week who said he would give me a quote, that he'd read my things. But I can't bear to get in touch with him, I mean go see him, because I can't really talk to him and he's always "experimenting with consciousness," meaning drugged on something or other, which gives him the advantage of being detached. Maybe I'll just get very high one day this week and go over with Dris on the motor bike....Oh, tell me where to get peyote. Paul has some mescalin that he keeps wanting us to take together, but I don't know if I want to get high with him, and we don't usually stay friends for a very long time. I mean between a decision to take and the taking....Those nitwit muffins said it had never occurred to them that the assassination was anything but like the papers said.... Jane said she read your poems and loves them. She always loves the winner.....I read Sorrentino on Hubert Selby. Am I wrong not to think Selby is anything special? Am I very square? I read a queer story of his ("A Fairy Tale") that I thought horrendously bad. And "Tralala." Who cares? I was thinking now that I'm really very unfashionable because my main concern has always been language, the sentence. That is out of date. But I suppose there'll be a revival before the ultimate silence takes over....Mail came. Nothing exciting except a curious letter from Harriet saying she read my Genet essay and cried it was so beautiful.

Love Alfred

I'm feeling like a great writer again. But they're going to hate me (the critics) for not being a sociologist.

To Harriet Zwerling   7 April, 1964

Dear Harriet: I was expecting the usual horror in my mailbox this morning, so imagine my happiness finding your letter. You are really hopelessly old-fashioned noticing something because it's beautiful. They cut the [Genet] piece down to one third its original size (because the real point of the article was an attack on Christianity) and then shoved it in the back to hide it. But I too was moved by it when I read it the other day.

You must have forgotten me a lot if you have the idea that your role for me was the nice absurd yenta. Can you really believe that, or are you just feeling sorry for yourself eating that gorgeous *veau à la crème* all alone?

By the way, if you are still seeing that whore friend of yours, tell her that if she says one more word about me to anyone, I will break every tooth in her head when I get back to New York. She would love it, wouldn't she, since it would be in accordance with her own estimation of herself. Did she really not know my letter was ironical? What has become of her devotion to my art? I also understand she, who pretended to admire and agree with my criticism, is now, true to her destiny of cynical whore, saying, What kind of reception can he expect after attacking everyone? Well, she whored her way into academia, bohemia and the establishment graveyard, so that is her vision of the world. Some Americans who were at the Bowleses last night were saying she is evidently whoring her way in among the beatniks now. Is that so? Yes, you can read this paragraph to her.

I've been having a terrible time with Random House. They just won't do anything for me. The whole burden of my book seems to have fallen on Edward. I'm apparently getting put down in the Times, and I suppose in Time Magazine. (The latter chased me around for a week, to my terror, and I couldn't believe their anxiety boded well.) Shirley Jackson is doing the review for the Tribune, and I don't know what her taste is. That's all I know. Burroughs says he is coming through with a blurb, but who knows? As there aren't going to be any ads except over Cerf's dead body, the quotes don't really seem to matter. But I keep acting like they care. I have finally used my trump card with Epstein, and very subtly told him if he doesn't cooperate he can forget about anything more from me. Oh, I'm working on a book of all things. Not for the past few days, because I'm so nervous. It's called *The Maniac* and it is filthy and dark and out of date and beautiful. I hope Goliath makes some money, so I can publish the book by myself. I don't want to have anything to do with that poisonous rotten industry. *A part de tout cela*, I'm all right. I didn't like your reference to Dris as that big cock....How is Milo? Bill? Louis? You? Me? I hope you will write; I mean prose. Maybe now with Milo you can stop noticing the scene and write out of your self. That "nice absurd yenta" is really too much. What put that into your head I wonder. Or who? Yes, Who?....Yes, I wish I was there too.....Love and kisses, Alfred

To Edward Field   April 9, 1964 Sidi Bujari 28, Tangier
Paidhaiki mou

I had a letter from my brother yesterday saying my mother wants to give her children certain bank accounts in their name. The sum comes to "several thousand dollars." I've written back asking for more detail. I'm supposed to decide on how I want it.

Kluger is printing my Time piece. I like him more and more. He is a good and loyal person, even if a little dull. Apparently John Hawkes is coming out in grand style the same week I am, so he will steal all the glory, and I'll be drowned away. I don't really believe anymore that I'll sell 20,000, do you? But I believed it up to the last utilitarian moment. Now it's out of my hands. *Insha'allah.*

Next day. Today is Thursday the ninth. My book is officially published in two days. How nervous-making. Don't feel too bad if my book doesn't sell too many copies.

Dris quit his job as of today. I mean he just went on sleeping this morning, so they will fire him. I didn't try to get him out of the house because I'm glad. I'm happier when he's around. But his family will be in an uproar about it. He says it doesn't matter, he'll fish here in Tangier and give them money. He has this gigantic vanity about me; that is, that nobody has the right, or even less right than they used to, to push him around because he lives with an American. Also he created an uproar recently (did I tell you this?) when the company (Spanish) tried to cheat the men out of the Good Friday wages, giving them the day as a holiday and then claiming they had to work it off in extra hours since Moslems are not entitled to Christian holidays. So he rioted and got one boy and one old man on his side. All the others (about 200) just sat there being afraid of the Spanish masters. He won, but the company started stamping his paycheck "*rojo*" (can you imagine?) and told him he couldn't be vessel captain anymore. They called him into the office and said they'd continue his salary (that is, a captain's salary) and offered him certain other benefits providing he didn't try to provoke the men anymore, but that if he was dissatisfied he should come to them, the Spanish bosses, and they would make him happy. Just to shut up. They'd already done this with his friend Mohamed (the one in the photo with us) and Dris hasn't spoken to him in a month. Anyway, Dris actually considered their offer, saying that the men were chicken not to have stood up with him and deserved to be slaves. But of course I blew my top, just out of conditioning as Extro would say; having been born in 1928, I just go on believing in unions and fairness, even though I think mankind stinks. Especially Arabs. But anyway it doesn't really matter what he says because all the men think he can say what he wants because he has his American and won't starve to death, so he can act like a big shot. Anyhow, three unexcused absences is automatic expulsion. Today is the third, so that is that. I shouldn't be glad but I am. It is so nice to hear him snoring in the other room. And the weather is warm again. Flowers everywhere. Yesterday, I walked into the living room and looked across my bowls of flowers and through the open terrace doors and saw the mountain and the sky, and I was stunned. I lay naked on the terrace taking the sun. The terrace is about twice as big as your apartment and faces north, south and west.

Paul Bowles thinks your poetry is marvelous. He thinks the personal ones are terrible though. Perhaps he will write and tell you. I told him to. (It is always good to have some extra quotes lying around.)....I happened to see Newsweek this week with the big story on the "plot theory." It looks like a prepared government story, but I don't know what it means. Is some sort of truth going to come out? Why don't they let Lane sit in on the Warren investigation? Since he is Oswald's lawyer, they can't keep him out. Can't he get some sort of writ? And why isn't Oswald's mother bringing suit against all those papers, like the Luce publications, that keep referring to Oswald as the assassin. That's against the law. The burden of proof would then be on the papers.

I'm trying to do a little work, but it's hard because I'm nervous. I can't even concentrate on the *Candy* review. I loved it when I read it. And now I hate it. It irritates me because the one thing Southern and Hoffenberg leave out is the drug scene which would be the natural

123

conclusion. They only leave it out because Hoffenberg is a junkie and Southern fooled around with it. In other words they ridicule everything but they really believe in something, though they don't admit to believing in it. Of course, it is hard to attack them in this way. It's very easy to dismiss and ridicule with the drug religion. Ooooooh, I want some peyote. Where should I write for it?

Dris bought an insurance thing on the motor weeks ago, paid for it himself and just finally showed me the policy. He can't read and they swindled him, so now I have to go scream at the insurance company. It's only a matter of $2, but they also swindled him on time. With literate people, swindling is subtler and greater, but it feels worse here over little bits, because it's like cheating the blind. Maybe it's always cheating the blind. Maybe it's only the blind who ever get cheated. We're now talking about going camping every week in the good weather. What fun. Oh, I'm so glad he's not working.

Do you think it could have been the witch in Arcila?

Two more days. Keep your fingers, balls, legs, kisses, crossed.

Love,

    Alfred

To Dennis Selby   13 April 1964, Tangier

Dear Dennis:

Humph and grumble. I am high and your letter is making me feel humph and grumble like an old uncle you're humoring so he won't cut you out of his will. When the letter came earlier I felt like Gerry Ayres. I felt like hissing and spitting in that butch way because in my heart I am a loving girl. Fuck you. SSSSS. Hisssssss.

If that faggot you live with reads my letters to you then he should tell you to keep up your correspondence more regularly so then I will know that you hadn't fallen asleep on me and actually heard but couldn't do anything. O, man, I'm letting go. Can't I have some peyote? I want some peyote. How do I get it? You've got the idea now, baby. Keep 'em drugged's the way, that's the way....Thank you for all your literary criticism. Hmph. Who the hell does he think he is telling Alfred the Great where to get off? Who the hell do you think you are? Tweeter tweet. I suddenly feel like my old faggot self again. I started getting high to go to William Burroughs. You know, how with some newfangled movies you have to put on special glasses in order to see the film the right way? Well, with Burroughs and Bowles I find I have to put on my kif in order to get into focus with them. Anyway, he wasn't home. I was glad. I only went to get my quote. Maybe he was boiling one up in the cellar and didn't hear me knocking. Oh yes, you're right, the letter was from the Nation. And they want me to write for them. I said in principle all right but no reviews. That career is over and done with as soon as I finish this one on *Candy*. No support for the Industry from me, no sir. Wait till you read next month's installment [in Book Week] about Time trying to break my door down. I take what God gives me, as Edward says....How dare you? S. Sontag an inferior Alfred Chester? Where, how, splutter splutter. (I knew suddenly what all the splutter and the humph is about. It's about your line saying...shurg. I feel like I'm in a comic strip.)

You asked me to write about my personal life. I no longer have one. I am a celebrity. Everything I do is in the public eye. Thank you for the ad; I was surprised. I wrote that blurb myself when I was Not Myself and said they should use it in the ads. Now I don't know what it means....I understand you were under the illusion that I would let you become an American citizen? Tommyrot. Who do you think runs things around here? Tweeter me again. Listen, Dennis, you wrote me you were becoming an American because you had a plot a-foot. I knew you couldn't mean well for the empire. Was it money, or love? (Do you spell a-foot with one "f" or two?) I wonder if I'll find this letter the laugh sensation I think it is now when I read it sober....Honeyboy just slunk his ass in. With stories of the outer world. I suppose he is my personal life, in a way. He's a real cute cutthroat little bugger, lawdy don' ah know it. No, he's a nice Jewish boy. Mama couldn't be happier.

If he was a nigger it would be something else again. He is a cuddly darling. Is yours? Yours is so *shkutz* though. That's the adjectival use of *shaygitz*. I guess being Welsh is just like being Jewish or a nigger. Under the English boot too. As I say in this book I'm writing, there's nothing like the middle class for frenzied and ferocious cocksucking.

Next day. An African morning, roaring with silence, the sea glassy. Such strange rrtitichi sounds. But silent. Heavy. It is hot now....I'm a little headachy from too much kif last night....You should write some plays. Isn't marriage conducive to writing? I mean, you don't have to go out so much and all. One of your next two plays is bound to be successful.

I would love to write a musical comedy called "Moroccan Follies" about life in Tangier. Most of the beatniks have been rounded up and deported. Kif. Interpol is making a fuss. The Moroccan police told them as they got on the boat to Algeciras: Just shave, wash and came back. They haven't, though. Now, apparently, they've cleaned out Marrakech as well....I really don't have a personal life. I mean I have a number of acquaintances but they are all fraudulent relationships. It may be my fault. I can't give myself to these people here the way you know me to have. Because they are too sick. So there is my work and Dris and New York. Dris quit his job. He created a big fuss and they got scared, the Spanish bosses, and then he missed three days of work which is automatic firing. So he went and they were too scared to fire him even, that he would make an uproar. He quit. I pushed him very hard to. He used to leave at five in the morning, come back at seven or eight at night, too tired to eat and just fall asleep. Now he is skinny as a rail but life is all kisses and hugs again. His family will start screaming soon as he used to give them most of his salary....Did you hear Edward's poem "Letter to Alfred?" He said he read it, but he doesn't send it to me. That line you quote must be from that one he told me about called "Breakfast." Yes, it brought tears to my eyes too. It is such a sweet lie. He said his reading was a big fiasco, but I knew it wasn't.

Actually I thought the Mailer column was so crazy, it wouldn't make sense to anybody. It was the same thing with that Burroughs review. I didn't understand it and everybody loved it.

126

Yes, I'm writing a book. I hope it won't be long. The hero says it's to be 150 pages. He also says a lot of other things. He makes fun of me. I don't have to pay attention to him though. He is sick. But I think he's quite right about 150 pages. That is enough length.

The weather is very sexy making. Africa screams. The cock expands and the asshole twitches with rapture. A big wet kiss to you, o torrid one.

Alfred

To Edward Field   April 17, 1964 Sidi Bujari 28, Tangier
Coochie,

Are you back from Florida? Dennis says, as I knew anyhow, that your reading was a fabulous success. He also said your sister was beautiful and chic. Oh, and that your public manner is marvelous, devilishly handsome, etc. etc. etc. Like he was in love with you. Hmph. Maybe I don't want to go on tour with you after all.

Listen, I just got the Times review [of *Behold Goliath*], so don't worry I saw it. And I also loved it. Obviously he [the reviewer Saul Maloff] is out there gunning for me which gives it lots of pep. I think he must be the guy who asked Kluger ages ago to please let him put me down. I judge from the things he says that he has followed my criticism closely and is jealous of my reputation. Naturally, I've written a shocked and indignant letter to Fremont-Smith correcting the falsehoods, that only three stories are queer, just as three stories are heterosexual; and that all the stories were written after Jamie not before. I've also written the critic a letter. Oh, I decided last week that I am not going along with the conventional absurdity of an author being silent about his reviews, and I am going to answer noisily those bullshitters. To Maloff I write: Dear malice: It's my criticism you're really after, isn't it? But here's a word of advice from a master: Don't discredit yourself with lies. Always tell the truth about a writer, even if it hurts, and then make it perfectly clear that your anger is personal. Don't disguise it with all that phoney academic garbage to make it look like you've got tradition on your side. Tradition is fickle and always runs away with the most brilliant. Anyone who reads my book will know you haven't told the truth. That's bad politics. A first-rate critic never puts himself in the position of being discredited by a simple reading of the work. Best, Callous. P.S. Also, you should always make it look as if you've been driven to anger in spite of yourself, not as if you're out there gunning for the guy from the very beginning.

I feel somehow in control of the scene. The review in the New York Review is marvelous but who will see it? Everyone here is mad about Goliath which makes me feel hopeful. Even people who hate me are mad about it. One bookstore has been selling, another taking orders. He's (Jason) already getting on with the second edition, but is obviously unhappy about changing the cover, and since he's being such a good boy, I'm saying all right let the cover go.

Oh I am so busy feeling like King Shit I forgot to tell you. Another letter from my brother, loviedovie. The sum, hold your breath, is $7600. Oh I'll pay you back now: $250, okay? I want to buy you something wonderful. But what? Tell me. I'm rich and can send you something nice. But what would you adore from Morocco?

Don't giggle or be mad at me, but now that I have money, and if things go on honkydory with Dris, I'm going to take him in on a tourist visa. Six months. So if he gets married he gets married, I don't care. I'm not going to dump him back into his poverty after having shown him what three squares a day is like. Not that there's been three squares a day all the time. You know, those bastards didn't fire him. The fishing company. They were afraid to lest he raise a fuss, so he withdrew voluntarily, which puts him in a good position. You know what, I felt terribly rejected by his job, in spite of all my bullshit. I thought if he had his own steady salary he wouldn't love me. Anyway it is all scrumptious lovie lovie now. Oh here is something awful though. He wants me to fuck him and I can't. I keep making excuses, but the truth is it isn't what I want. Isn't that loathsome?

Philip Lamantia was here forever last night and didn't shut up for a minute and ate most of our supper. Dris left in a huff and went to the movies because Philip consistantly refused to acknowledge his existence. Usually, Dris is very retiring with Nazarenes and is happy sitting and learning English, but he likes to be acknowledged occasionally, if only by me, and Philip wouldn't let me say one word to him without interrupting. He lectured on Pharaonic thought to me. There is something in it I like. It's emphasis on geometry appeals to me, oddly enough, and he showed me the first step which is dilemma.

I feel I haven't expressed sufficient love to Neil lately, and tell him I really do love him. Actually I'm beginning to like everybody again, to my chagrin. Anyway, just in case Neil feels I'm ignoring him, I'm not. And my letters are to him too of course, even the crazy ones.

Did you see the Resnais film "Muriel?" Jean Cayrol wrote it and I knew him in Paris, he worked for Seuil, and he was the first NewWaver before the new wave was invented. In the late 40s. I liked it better than "Marienbad" which I'd liked better than "Hiroshima." It's warm and sad and human just like old Cayrol. But really that camera work and pretention of Resnais! *Il exaggère.*

Oh, the Nation wrote me red hot with admiration about the Mailer piece and they want me to write for them. I said okay, let's correspond about it, but first see that my book is reviewed. Marty wrote that the Post isn't doing it because they only do "big" books. If you're still feeling brave, you should call up the woman editor and tell her she is an idiot....The Time review will come next week I guess. I keep vacillating in my thoughts about whether it will be good or bad. Now I tend to think it will be bad just out of general apprehension. But yesterday I thought it would be good because the queer stories are unhappy....Just imagine if all the reviews are bad. Except the New York Review. Could that be? Maybe I am a failure. Oh, bullshit. I feel great.

Dris got a rabbit on the way home from fun-fishing yesterday. He skinned it and cooked it up in tajine and we're eating it tonight with peas. Morocco has the greatest fresh peas I've ever eaten....I just reread the Saul Maloff. It is really exhilarating and so transparent. Somebody should write defending me. Not you. NOT YOU. Because of the dedication.

Oh, who cares? It's probably what Mel Clay calls a Box Office review, which is all that matters....

Lots of love and kisses to both my darlings,

Alfred

To Edward Field   April 20, 1964 Sidi Bujari 28, Tangier

Habibi:

Yes, I'm sane, isn't it ghastly? I suppose that Marilyn Monroe thing helped. It gave me a new way to look at it. I'm generally happy these days, though I've got my usual nicotine poisoning and everything like kif, cigarettes and coffee makes me feel lousy. But Dris is being like the juiciest fig in the juiciest oasis. I woke up this morning feeling nasty about that Times review. I mean, I simply don't understand how that man could just lie like that. What is his motive? Envy? Hatred? Fear? It is so strange and upset me. Anyway, Burroughs is coming to supper tonight and promised to bring me his fucking quote. If he doesn't, I will invite him to leave before supper.

I'm going to have to take the bull by the horns and write my brother today to put the money in a bank account. Gerry Weil wants me to buy his car in Gibraltar next week, but I doubt if I can arrange my money affairs that fast. (I'm having a sandwich of black and green olives and onions and butter on French bread, yum.) Jane says she will fix me up with Libby Holman's lawyer.

With your letter came a letter from my girlfriend. I think the affair is over, thank God. Also a letter from a lady in California complaining about how sick I was to call Mailer a writer. "I wonder if you saw him get verbally flattened on Channel 9 by Mr. Buckley? It was the funniest spectacle we ever saw. Mr. Buckley is a marvelous writer and speaker. The English language flows like poetry from his lips. He is head and

130

shoulders over any of the socalled writers you have mentioned so far. You book reviewers like the sick sick sick writers. If they do not deal with homosexuals, or insanity, or incest, etc., you consider them not worth mentioning. No wonder we have a doomed western civilization. Even worse than you is Stanley Eichelbaum, etc. etc. etc." She ends thus: "Oh well, no doubt when Rome fell, the man in the street shrugged his shoulders in despair and knew he was being sold into bondage by the writers, liberals, philosophers and intelligentsia of his time." By the way I've written a letter to the New York Review to publish in answer to the question that Adams asks at the end of his review. The question why are faggots always represented in a poignant quest of love and the normal doing the same things as clods? My answer: It is a consequence of the fact that human love has degenerated into a sentiment credible only in the very stupid or the completely depraved.

Gerry Weil says some mescalin is coming to Tangier, so don't bother sending me the peyote. It can wait until I come back. One of the things since any crisis is that my memory is very bad. Also I am so hard, HARD. People have always said I was hard, but I never felt it. Now I feel it.

Tell me what I should buy for you and Neil. I mean for your home or something nice you would like that seems Moroccan. Some sheepskins? They are lovely for cooching on or under....Will everyone except you be secretly glad about that review in the Times? I imagine people saying poor Alfred and giggling. Isn't that how people are? Burroughs and Bowles said it would be good for sales. But such malice. Oh, I'm not sending him a letter but a picture postcard of Tangier with X's all over the town, and the message says: Dear Jealous, see over for your added conveniences. xxxxx Baedeker." [Note: Oh, I'm not sending him anything. He doesn't deserve it.] Is there no recourse when a book is misrepresented? I'm feeling again like it's not going to sell. And am trembling at the thought of what Time will do to me.

I don't have anything more say. Except lots of love and kisses.
Alfred

To Norman Glass   April 20, 1964 Sidi Bujari, 28, Tangier

My dear dear Norman:

Your letter arrived only this afternoon, thus taking sixteen days to get here. I've been thinking you were mad at me and/or disgusted, faintly believing you and Paul were having a great bitch correspondence over me. I've been wanting to write you again and didn't know what to do, wondering if you'd moved, etc.

It's been such a gigantic month that I don't know where to begin. What you must understand is that I went crazy, quite literally mad, insane, crazy. Why? God knows. I haven't really talked about it with anyone, and just now, I'm still a little too delicate to go into the whole thing. Yes, it was partly kif of course. But it was many other things. You may not believe this, but I believe it has a lot to do with the witch in Arcila to whom I gave a thousand francs to get my family to give me money. I made havoc on two continents, but I am getting money from my family. An allowance probably. I hope to have some end of next week and will send you what I can. I was going to say I'll send 50, but I have no idea how much it will be. Fifty dollars I mean. Let me know *par retour du courier* if you want it. Or less. Later more. Or whatever. Or your financial setup.....I knew perfectly well you hadn't a bean. I was meaning to cash your invalid check at Italica while fleeing the country. There was a gigantic blackmail thing involved, didn't I write you all this?

I've just come back from Visiting With Burroughs in his hotel room. He's at the Atlas until he finds a new place. It was nice until snotty little Ian came. Ian came to dinner last night; it was dinner for Bill, but Bill didn't show. He's been sick. This is the quote he wrote for my book: "One voice speaks through these pages like an electric scalpel; Mr. Alfred Chester writes like White Lightning." Is there something wrong with that? Excuse my paranoia. But I keep thinking there's something truly rotten in him....Paul gave me a quote too, but don't remember it. Very dreary one, of course. I've had two reviews so far. The New York Times (a teacher named Saul Maloff) wrote what surely is the most vicious attack I've ever seen in their pages; it was

132

an attack on homosexuality, and completely disregarded the fact that eight of the eleven stories had nothing (or practically nothing) to do with faggotry. He said I presented two worlds, the square world (cold and frigid) and the passionate deviate world of bars and pissotières. All garbage. He also attacked me—this will kill you—for a unity of style, a too-repetitious style. All my voices! The other review in the New York Review was a rave. "They deal, in a style of great inwardness, with consistently deranged sensibilities; characteristically, it is by following out a thin but always visible thread of logic that these agents reach their ultimate perversities. They are not verbal tricks, cut-outs, or wistful after-dinner companions; instead they strike directly at the roots of their cluttered and hopeless, yet still imaginative, existence." Then he describes the stories, and after: "The crisis of mere existence is caught beautifully, because authentically in these stories: without self-indulgence, without theatrical self-flattery, Mr. Chester presents a group of individuals trapped, in effect, in Sartre's cafeteriatype hell.... strong, inventive stories, and exhilarating as all writing must be which exhibits a free, unstudied craftsmanship." Oh, and he says at the beginning: "And now at last *Behold Goliath*, the jubilant title of which, by a happy happen-stance, heralds the appearance not only of a writer but of a story teller."

The Tribune received a terrible review from Shirley Jackson who hadn't the faintest idea what was going on in them, in the stories. She thought they were ghost stories like she writes. So because of this and considering the absurd attack in the Times, the editor threw her review out and asked Ted Solotaroff of Commentary to review it. I haven't heard from S. ages so I don't know what is up, and of course the Trib guy doesn't say, but they are planning a Major Essay on some subject or other, using me as the pivotal thing. I doubt if faggotry, and having read some of S.'s criticism I believe it will be either on the assumption by a Jew of western culture or on fiction as art rather than sociology. Anyway, it will cause a storm, as the Times piece probably has. Random House is starting to advertise and it looks like it will go, though later in the spring. Burroughs' quote will help to confuse the beatniks who would be against me. It is all political as you know. Like the beats love Edward's poetry but now that he's gotten that prize they consider him academic....Also my last Mailer piece helped. I'll enclose that if I can find a copy, along with the first piece. The second piece has gotten all sorts of people hysterical, especially the right wing. You should read my correspondence....Burroughs told me some woman had written asking about me. She'd already written to me in ecstasy asking me to write for the Nation....Time magazine is a mystery. They invaded me for nearly a week just as I was recovering my sanity and I got so scared by them that I hid and everything. Finally I wrote my column about what pests they were and I heard from my Trib editor today saying they (Time) may not even run the review. They are just waiting to see if I get much attention and then if I do they will write one of their yawn-how-boring-another-faggot, articles. My next column is an analysis of Time as a totalitarian instrument in American life. Oh, I've given up reviews and articles except for a last one, *Candy* (*Lollypop* in the Olympia edition) by Terry Southern and Mason Hoffenberg (Maxwell Kenton in the Olympia edition). I've really done it only because Girodias was sentenced to jail and I wanted to defend him. Putnam is publishing it in America.

I talk about Olympia books being erography rather than pornography, which is probably splitting hairs but words change people's minds. "Erography is dangerous only in sex repressed societies. Among people for whom sex is of the flesh, that is, a natural and free expression of the animal, rather than of the mind, for whom the act is more delicious than the fantasy, for whom the literal partner takes precedence over the cultural dream, sexual literature is as harmless as books about geography or motors and certainly more instructive than the pseudo-scientific garbage that kids find hidden in parents' dressers. Erography should not be feared; to fear it, is to fear oneself. What the reader should be on guard against is that posture now being assumed in some dubious American circles (Time magazine is a case in point) which, pretends very noisily and very frequently to be already bored with sex in literature. This pretense at boredom is, in fact, a concealment of outrage, for a sexually free people, free to accept or reject the act or the art, are automatically disencumbered of numerous guilts and thus harder to control, to manipulate, to indoctrinate, to own." I know this is all old hat to you, but this is written to two million squares. I'm becoming quite adept at propaganda.

Well, as you see, I'm all wrapped up in my career. I wish you were here. I mean, I miss you and though my social life has broadened you are the only friend I've had here. I think, though, we are a little harmful for each other because too much alike. Perhaps best not to talk about this now....Jane is a monster. They are in terror of me, and so polite. David Herbert keeps away. She tries her best to screen my visitors and keep her hand in everything. The Wanker was in town yesterday; he came to see me. I was not friendly but asked him in. He bought a house in Marrakech for $4300....Paul is Paul. He really hates me but conceals it carefully. Lamantia is back, having had a devastating experience with pharaonic thought. So dreary. The man next door, an American writer named Gerry Weil, has a wife and a fakir. Another devastating mystic. Their scene is just like "Laughter in the Dark." Ira fled Tangier suddenly to go print his magazine in Belgium when the cops started rounding up the beatniks. So he left Rosalind on my head, hands and money. She sickens me more and more. Poor broke Rosalind. It turned out she had a hundred dollars, and then suddenly he wired her a hundred fifty more to come meet him and make the grand tour of Europe....Irving and Peter are back, I hear from Ian, but of course haven't seen them. Apparently they are returning to Marrakech. Ian spoke mysteriously of Irving being "bad news" now, some police complication; he was very vague and mysterious.

Dris *est toujours mon adorable, plus que jamais.* He worked for a month but then quit, partly because it was really ruining things between us. (Worked at the Madraba.) Listen, Random House is fixing up a lecture tour for me around America next fall. Why don't you try to organize your visa for about then. Then I could help you get installed in New York and introduce you to everyone. Surely you'll have had enough solitude by fall. Even solitude with Mario, whose picture I admit is delicious, though his cock is rather small and I don't know whether Bronze feels nice in bed. Have you seen my friend Antonio? I wish you would.

It's so nice to be writing to you. I thought I'd probably lost you forever. Oh, you should know one thing about me. I always make huge parting scenes like forever and ever. People who know me well don't take them seriously.

Dris is bringing a friend from Arcila to dinner tonight and to sleep here. A Jew, of all things. He was sort of hesitant about it until I reminded him that I was a Jew. He dropped the whole subject then but I'm wondering if he'll actually bring the boy here.

Day after tomorrow is Aid Kbir, when every family slaughters a sheep, a ram, in commemoration of Sidi Ibrahim who was about to sacrifice his son Sidi Isaac when God gave him a ram instead. Surely you remember your Koran.

Love (we act like a pair of lovers). Yes I said *O*V*

Love

Alfred

To Edward Field   April 22, 1964—Sidi Bujari 28, Tangier

Dear Edward Fieldinsky:

You sounded already high at the beginning of the letter. But the end was as lovely. It must have been a lovely high. I guess you like it better than kif, or was Morocco and traveling just exhausting you too much to enjoy anything then? But this one seems very sunny, I mean the peyote. The mescalin is in Tangier, and Gerry Weil is being the middleman so it is costing me $5. Can you please check up with some reliable user and find out how much I should take and also if it is safe considering my recent state. I think my *crise* was paranoid and mescalin tends to schizophrenia (which was my *crise* during the 50s) so probably it is okay. I don't trust anyone's opinion here, since they are all confirmed drug addicts.

Can you please send me Kulchur with you in it? I would like to write an answer. I'm just fed up with their club rules. America just isn't going to have one kind of art, much as Kulchur and Time would have it. Paul says, and he is right, they are just dislocated Madison Ave. boys...Isn't Lincoln Kirstein a soprano? I'm only joking. The name is familiar....Bill Burroughs is also being nice these days and doesn't upset my stomach too much. I sent Jason an express letter with his quote yesterday. It is: "One voice speaks through these pages like an electric scalpel. Mr. Alfred Chester writes like a streak of White Lightning." Or something like that. It sounds good, but I'm so suspicious that I imagine it refers to something in *The Naked Lunch* that I don't remember and is a sneaky putdown. Rosalind calls him The Green Slime Man.

I was born in New York on the 7th of Sept. 1928, but I don't know what hour. I think just past midnight. D.H. Lawrence has my same birthday. Isn't that flattering?

Where is Neil while you do all the peyote cooking? Sexy is in the other room asleep. Oooh, I'm so hot for him these days. The weather partly, also he is so gorgeous and lazy now and cuddly and sexy. He brought a Jewish boy from Arcila last night to eat with us and sleep here. A *gruber jung*, as mama would say. Seventeen and sexy, but so coarse and spoiled. I made the mistake of telling him I was Jewish and he chewed my ear off about it. All he thinks about is that communism is dangerous. Dris kept denying I was Jewish to him, probably because he thinks the boy will tell the town and then everybody will be contemptuous of him. By this time he's already repressed it. He forgets I'm Jewish so fast, it's incredible.

I had a letter from Susan Sontag yesterday. It is due to my violent denunciation of her to Harriet; Susan says she wouldn't let Harriet read it to her. The thing is she wants to be treated like shit because she knows that is what she is, and now that I have done it, she's ready to love me again. She disgusts me, but I'm going to write her a warm and affectionate letter, like the hypocrite I have now learned how to be, so she will work for me. Maybe you should ask her, if you see her, to write to the Times about that review.

It's very good about Burroughs, my quote I mean. It will make all the beats very confused. They will have to say about me the opposite of what they say about you: Well, he seems academic, but now we must deal with the fact that Burroughs has said something nice. Then they will reluctantly love me, as if they discovered me all by themselves. Life is really unbelievable, isn't it, Edward? I never knew it was all like this. Never before so clearly. I've lost every shred of innocence. And I realize that you haven't been innocent for a long long time. Have you known I was?

Was the play "The Machine," Irene's play? About Isidore? That's me of course. She told me so. I also had a feeling I was Jean-Jacques in Susan's book, though he was too boring to follow close enough to find out. Susan is really no writer at all; you can see this even from the absurd letter she wrote me. But I just took a shit and realized that her function in life is to help US. Do you realize this? You must invite her for dinner again and make her adore you.

Gerry Weil says it would be very easy to take Dris in as a tourist to America for six months. I don't know if he could bear it without other Arabs, but for awhile he will love it anyway. I'm wondering what's going to happen when he realizes he can fuck everyone, thing, sex, in sight, and him with his unlimited supply of gism. He is a little shocked by the idea that people who don't know each other sleep together without gifts or money changing hands. I'm really mad about him these days....Norman has written to me after a month to tell me my letters were crazy and that I must have consumed huge quantities of kif to bring on such paranoia. Oddly enough, kif hardly affects me now. It doesn't make me inner, or bring on my father (remember?). Love and kisses to you.

Alfred

To Edward Field   April 25, 1964 Sidi Bujari 28, Tangier

Aoulidi:

I was about to write dearest cocksucker which oddly enough has become a term of endearment in my castle of depravity. "You cocksuckuh!"

I have now read that magazine [Kulchur] thoroughly and it is poison. Irving agrees and says though that it represents a whole new movement in American writing, antihuman, etc. Maybe he is right. These kids could vote for Goldwater, with all their nasty narrow-mindedness.

Not that Irving isn't prone to the same thing. He's back, anyway for awhile, and it's such a relief having someone I can feel reasonably free to talk to. He said all manner of flattering things about your book. He says to tell you he can't write now. He's had a lot of trouble, including being arrested on a trumped up counterfeit money charge. (Revenge by an Arab.) And also breaking up with his American (Jerman-Gewish [stet]) boyfriend [Mark Schleifer]. He is better off without him but doesn't know this yet.

I'm happily back in my book. Everytime I'm back in it, I'm happily back.

It was *Ahyed Kbir* (lit. Big Feast) when every family slaughters a ram in commemoration of Sidi Abraham and Sidi Isaac when Allah gave Abe the ram. I had a ghastly moment there. Twenty-million rams or something like that, all killed in homes at the very same moment. The Medina was running with tripe, blood, horns. Then suddenly everything was mutton. Dris brought a leg back from Arcila and two loaves of bread shaped like mosques that *yimma* baked with hardboiled eggs in the minarets....For days before it was all these rams being dragged through the city and unhappy bleating. I really felt terrible. I mean baa baa, and who was listening? And then getting your throat cut because of some ancient tradition, by strangers who hold your head while the blood leaks into a pot. But then I thought at least the Arabs face the murder that must be committed to eat flesh. Not just nice cuts of beef in cellophane like they came out of factories. There should be muzak in every supermarket with the sounds and cries of the slaughtered.

Dris brought a tiny turtle home and it's now living in the bathtub after disappearing for awhile. (Columbine was wrongly accused of murder.) Have you studied a turtle lately? It is fascinating, like a prehistoric machine. It steers and goes into reverse, and it walks on its claws. Among my other naturalia are: a purple cactus flower, two Japanesey stalks with yellow Japanesy flowers that don't die, a little tree that looks like a miniature palm but is a cactus, and a little pot of mint. I have a black thumb. All my plants die....Oh, and two bouquets of sexy calla lillies that Dris just got at the market. The place, I mean Tangier, is crazy with flowers. Everywhere. And trees full of strange blossoms. The Japanesy flowers look like tiny yellow birds with big wings and a big peacock like tail. All yellow. I would have a pair of peacocks now from David Herbert except Jane is very aciduously screening my visitors. One American got through the other day only because he practically fell in love with me and Paul had to keep taking him here and finally I arranged for him to get over alone, not without virtual hysteria on Jane's part....I like Paul better now since The Mistake, because he is careful what he says to me. All my life I've always had to be the careful one with people, not to tread on their dreams.... And also birds. The place is wild with birds. All over my terrace. And they fight divinely, fluttering and graceful....My slave just came. She is really very sweet. Maybe I'll have to take her to New York too. How can I let her down? Every now and then I give her some extra money and she goes into a corner and cries. She kisses my hand and stuff. For the feast she brought me a gigantic pot of saffron couscous with lamb roasted with olives and raisins....Edward, are you as neurotic as I am? I had a huge fight with Dris today, presumably over a razor blade but really because Irving's stories about his romantic whorings in the south had made me envious and were working in me and because Dris came back from Arcila with a bad cold and he went to bed and I felt rejected. Does all this ever ever ever ever ever stop? An American girl is hot for Dris and I said he could fuck her if he wants to. (I think he's fucked girls about twice in his life.) But he said he was afraid someone would see him with her and they would think he was betraying me; i.e. I would be dishonored. I wonder if I really wouldn't mind though. It would be nice if I wouldn't, didn't. You know why infidelity seems so terrible in America? Because it implies a whole area of fantasy in the unfaithful lover's mind. But here there is no fantasy; there is only the real partner or the real object. They don't hunger after a dream. They only get hot for the available. And for us, settling for the available has to be accompanied with great bass chords of disillusion, etc. God, what bullshit, that Europe.

I hope you've written me what you and Neilele want, because I'll go to Gib for the car in a week or so (as soon as the money comes) and will mail things from there as it's faster and cheaper. I'm dying to send Harriet a caftan if I can find a good second-hand one. They're gorgeous and she'll look like a whole opera in one. I'm going to buy a tent in Gib, and a tape recorder. When I borrowed Irving's last fall, I had great fun with it and even wrote with it. Dris also invented plays, very remarkable, with sound effects and he used five or six different voices in them. In Spanish.

I have to go to the dentist. I still have seventeen cavities. They have become caves

xxxxx and love,

Alfred

Monday. I waited to see if I'd hear from you today, but no, so sending this. Letter from Elliot Freemont-Smith of the Times being full of shit. Justifying his heroism as editor.

To Norman Glass   Seedy B, 3 May 1964
Precioso:

Yes, you are quite right in some of the things you say, about me. About having been caught up in the contemporary mud in NY for the last couple of years. But what you should remember, forgive me for being humble, is that my stories were written in virtual isolation, after years of living alone with Arthur, and concentrating only on this formless mass of matter called I. When I went back to NY in 1959, age 30, I brought with me a consciousness I hadn't left America with but also my eternal innocence, which only my recent madness has finally, if not completely, withered in me. I don't really understand your comments on "As I Was Going Up The Stairs," but this story was written in 1955. It took a year to write, as I think I've told you, and the story that immediately precedes it chronologically is "The Head of A Sad Angel," so you will, when you read "Sad Angel" (which Paul loves but I despise, but put in the collection because it has been popular for ten years) see what that year did to me. Now that I think about these things, and you know this is the kind of thing I hate to think about, all my personal evolution has depended upon my writing. I've grown through my writing, and by the accidental facts of my life. If I give you the dates of the stories, you can get an idea of what was happening in me. "Rapunzel" ('53), "Angel" ('54), "Frog ('54), "Up the Stairs" ('55), "Cradle Song (Berceuse)" ("56), "Victory" ('56) , "Behold Goliath" ('58), "Vespasian", ('60), "Ismael" ('60), "Phoenix" ('61), "Beds and Boards" ('62). The last story was written for money but it also represents the mud I was stuck in from about '61 which made me virtually give up fiction. "Goliath", as you know it, was rewritten in '61 and given the present form it has. When I first wrote it it was part of that interminable monster novel that I burned and was embedded in an episode seventy pages long, most of which was a conversation in a living room, marvelous, brilliant, endless, pointless. All gone up in smoke at the very same moment that the fish and chips shop on Sullivan Street next door burnt down; I heard the fire engines screaming as the manuscript went up in flames and I thought, how weird, they are coming to stop me. But it was Harvey's shop, and Harvey is the Ben of "Beds and Boards." He was also out in the street with me that night a year and a half earlier (me with dogs and cats), him with his wife and two kids, that night that Arthur didn't come home but a fire broke out in the cellar of the theater underneath me (Harvey had the apartment under mine and a shop next door), mentioned in "The Phoenix." In "Beds and Boards," though I never realized this before, Harvey burns his furniture (as in fact he did) to get rid of the old life, just as I burned the manuscript. "Ismael" came out of my diary, and the frame it now has was written here last fall (and is costing me $300 in printers' charges, so you'd better like it). "The Phoenix" came from a bunch of notes written the first week or so after Arthur left me, January '60, and were written just because someone said, write so you won't think about it. Or won't suffer.... Why am I telling you all this, I don't know. All I'm saying is yes, I have sinned. When I was in Europe, literature for me was Lawrence and Shakespeare and one or two contemporaries (friends) whom I didn't like. I made the mistake of reading Justine which shoved me into the wrong direction for a year with my novel. (Durrell). When I came back to America and became a critic, I was out to destroy literature because I was sick of it and blocked in everything else. It doesn't matter all this, but yes you are right, I haven't seen the forest for the trees....Anyway, here is feeling right now if you want it: That new minds, my mystical leanings, sociological earnestness (such as in Burroughs and even in Irving), does not interest me. What interests me is creating something beautiful best I can. Art, ugh. But that's the long and the short of it: I hate Art, but it is the only way. For me. I feel this morning that I have never been a brave man, just full of bravado. (Beware of people who ask, when you haven't said anything: "How is the work getting along?" They are the truly destructive people. Anyway, my book of stories, if it has any value, has this: that it shows an inevitable rejection of tradition. Forgive me now for banging my own drum, as I have been humble, but when you look at two stories like "Beds And Boards" and "Sad Angel" you know I could have become early a celebrated traditional writer. I can probably still do good realistic stories, better than Updike and that crew. There is something in me that holds me back from going the whole hog in madness. Suddenly: Enough of this. Here: To be innocent too long is dangerous; it becomes a blindness, an unwillingness to see; you can become a victim of your own destructive impulses, you own inner corruption.

Has any of the above made sense? It is in some way an answer to what you say about me. Not a contradiction, a humble explanation, an apology....As for Mailer. He is garbage. What excited me about him recently was the existential hero idea. This jives with something I've always felt, that by posturing at something you make it become possible. The idea first. In the beginning was the word. That's why I mean by taking the visionary position. He knows he isn't IT, but he poses at it. By posing at it, it takes a form which other men can become and believe in. It is, I suppose, by me an admission that anything man thinks he is is an illusion invented by other men. Burroughs would agree, I suppose....I should be writing my column now. On Time. But it seems very trivial and I don't care whether Time lives or dies or destroys. Anyway, I need the $90 so I will pretend to care. I haven't heard a word about money since I last wrote you, and don't know what is up with my family. Maybe tomorrow. Most mail comes on Monday. Haven't heard a word from agent or publisher either and don't know what my book is doing. I can't understand why you haven't yet received your copy.

Irving was over yesterday. We are friends now and he is lending me his book. He read my stories and came over and said "If you give me a copy of your book I'll tell you what I liked and didn't like." Then he told me, but it wasn't too interesting and was predicable. He liked the queer things and things which made the writer out a fool or shameful, etc. You know. Allen Ginsberg has gotten him a $250 option from Grove on condition he does all sorts of editing, which apparently he will. His purity is most extreme when applied to other people, like most of us. He is not against compromising on his own behalf. This isn't meant as bitchery because I'm now very fond of him. I'd heard he was in prison and went over to the palace to see Peter to see if I could be of any help. Paul was delighted about the prison bit; Philip Lamantia giggled about it; Ian said "Irving's bad news these days" which I assumed reflected Burroughs' opinion. So I thought, Oh, no one's going to do a damn thing. So I went to see if I could. But he was out of prison. He'd been in for a day on some phoney counterfeit money charge. Then he and Peter broke up and P went to Casa, and Irving's alone and distraught but sweet as he can sometimes be. It's nice that he's here because I feel more relaxed with him than anyone else here....After prison, he wanted to run away from Morocco and I suggested he go see you. Probably he will write to you....No, I will not ask Burroughs for anything for you. He's moved out of the Atlas and now has an apartment but I don't know where. You can write to him at 4 Larache and I expect they'll forward. Though I don't know if he'll get around to sending. Oh, maybe I will go over. You could write express to Evergreen, Grove Press, NY (Greenwich Village). I told Paul what Burroughs had written for me and he said: "Oh, White Lightning is his name for you." But Irving says I should feel very complimented. Paul says it isn't a sneaky bitchy thing to do, but am I wrong to feel that if there is a private joke involved (it is a name for me Burroughs shares with Flopsy and Mopsy, whom he evidently sees often), and I'm unaware of it, that there is green slime intended. I think I will ask him about it. Norman, do you really think that is the way to make things better In Here or Out of Here? Perhaps I am unredeemably square, but this seems to me just vicious faggotry. And what does it accomplish except reaffirm my feelings of suspicion and mistrust which can no longer be considered paranoia? I mean, so I was right when I said to you in the other letter that I thought it meant something else. My considered opinion of Burroughs is that personally he is a fake, a sick fraud. And there is no point raising this to a transcendental moral or mystical level. My review of *Naked Lunch* is true. I looked through the book at Paul's the other day. I also listened to some taped cut-ups (boring) and that speech he made to the heretic society; this latter I find boring but intermittently brilliant. I just can't stand listening to the same thing over again whatever relevence it may have to MEANING. He is a bore. And I don't like his easy assimilation of the vocabulary of Industry and Wall Street. Remember, remember, he is the Burroughs Adding Machine. With them, of them, against them. He is the world of science and mechanics. He is the modern world, and I'm afraid I profoundly reject that world. Machines make me nervous and suspicious. He obviously believes in assimilating the machine and using it to personal advantage. Anyway, it suddenly occurred to me never mind....Why don't you send your piece on him to Commentary or Partisan or one of the American reviews? Oh by the way, Esquire finally chose him to do the famous Tangier piece that both Paul and I had been queried about. Remember that photographer and all. It is a seven page spread of photographs of Burroughs, Paul, Jane, Wanker, the Mountain Gods, Annette Wilcox, Flopsy&Mopsy and other non-entities. Burroughs wrote a thousand words. I heard this from Paul. Plus captions for the photographs. Part of the piece is in cut up.

Now to make you a little envious. I had some delicious *kullshi* last night. Gorgeous is strutting around the house; up early this morning. We don't make it as often as we used to, every other day now. Ever since my crises when my asshole started aching like crazy. (It still isn't too good but better.) But it's more fun for a middle-aged man like me doing it less often.

How odd I didn't tell you about the blackmail. Oh well, I'd written to Rex Henry finally for patronage. (Also Jackie Kennedy, and I'm not at all sure those columns on Mailer were not a definite public courting of Jackie. I think I was quite mad when I wrote those columns. In fact I'm not at all sure you've ever known me sane.) And I decided to take advantage of Irving's line about Paul, which had thrown them into a tizzy, by saying I could get the line out of the mag if Jane would help me get Henry's money. But then Rosalind (they were in on it of course like with your insurance but naturally hiding in the background with me doing all the bloody work like you, except I am braver than you and can do it with people, not just corporations) said, Oh it's blackmail. I hadn't wanted her in on it, but Ira insisted. We would share the money. $10,000 or whatever it was. So I said if it's blackmail give me the letter. I can't remember actually when I started taking the letter literally, but I think I had to take it literally as my guilt was unbearable. So then I had a showdown with Jane. She said: "Oh I love you, Alfred" in the middle of the blackmail, and I lost my respect for her forever. (Ira's famous line: "I know Paul is guilty but I don't know what his crime is." After that it all got madness. I wired Edward to come take me home, wrote insane letters everywhere. I can't go into it, partly because I don't really remember what it felt like. As my English friend Peter Everett wrote: The trouble with madness is you can't make capital out of it. I suppose if you stay mad you can. Anyway, so now Jane is very cautious about me, natch. And tries to win me into being one of those eunuchs surrounding her like David and Wanker and Chas. Gallagher. But I just sort of ignore her. If she tries to become helpless and needs my help I change the conversation. Her play was a flop though she had a couple of good important reviews. I believe I wrote you there was an off-Broadway revival.

I just thought. Burroughs is really very irritated about my review of *The Naked Lunch*. I told him when I was nuts that I'd put it down, though he probably knew before. And this is his way of backbiting..... Irving said, an extraordinarily irrelevant criticism, that "As I Was Going Up The Stair" reminded him of Salinger. Salinger, you know, is not on OUR SIDE.

Monday.

Still no mail from my family. So.

Love, Alfred

To Edward Field   4 May, 1964

Lovest:

I'm busy working on my second antiTime column. My style is changed since The Mistake. I am more ponderous and serious and impersonal and boring. I accuse Time of being subversive, trying to subvert the very morality it claims to be upholding. My usual perverse approach....Allen Ginsberg got Irving a $250 option on his novel. They operate very smoothly, those beats. No trouble at all. Just like

Burroughs writing *Naked Lunch* in a trance, throwing papers on the floor with Ginsberg waiting to pick them up and peddle them. By the way, I was right, did I tell you this, that Burroughs' comment had a double meaning. I knew he was rotten. White Lightning is his name for me behind my back....I am fed up with Candida and Epstein. They haven't done a thing for me. Sorin Agenou writes me that he's reviewing my book and loves it. The Voice. Marty [Tucker] has done reviews for Epoch and Lousiville Courier. All these reviews I got on my own. Not one did they get me, those bastards. I feel sure my book will take off in a little while, maybe in June.....Could you ask Lincoln Kirstein to get the Nation to review me? That woman never replied. Paul told me all about Kirstein.

I think I won't buy Gerry's car as you can get perfectly good cars in Gibraltar for $100 or $150 without taxes and stuff. And his, though it is a station wagon, is $300 and on top will be taxes and everything. Isn't it lovely to have a car? I'm dying to try mescalin from what you say. I've been quite sick in the stomach lately and Mel says it is from too much beef. I've been smoking heavily and don't much like it anymore, since it just fogs me up but doesn't do anything interesting. Except in the country. Lights and colors and patterns get more intense. It's just escape from boredom. We're still you and me just like on the telephone at that typing job you had.

I'm feeling dull about my novel too. I'm giving up on trying any sort of form and will just throw everything in. First person, third person, outside characters, dreams. Maybe it will add up to a book. You see, we never became professional. Did we? I'm hating Dris lately. Which makes me feel very sexy. I wanted to go with him out to a faraway beach yesterday on the motorbike and he wouldn't because a lot of people would see us together. So now I've hidden the keys and said he can't use the bike for a week. That made him happy. Oddly, he loves it when I punish him. But he only loves it for a day....I wish there was some excitement about my book. I haven't anything more to say now. Except love. Alfred.

I just suddenly got a rush of energy, so I'm adding some more.

It frightens me to think of a sweet Swiss boyfriend of [painter] Avel [de Knight]'s coming to see me. It makes me feel ugly and unglamorous. That smart elegant gorgeous faggot set I never made and can never make. All I really want to do is find somewhere in the jungle away from anywhere and live there. That is my recurring fantasy. I keep thinking of moving to West Africa, you know the underside of the lump, on the Atlantic.

I am virgo, stable, practical, and useful. I don't know the hour and it isn't the kind of thing I can ask my family anymore. Marilyn can't ask them either.

Dris wants me to shave the hair on my chest. Should I? It makes me feel hot to think about it. I'm convinced I have syphilis in the ass and I temonstrate about it constantly. Oh, who cares? I am so tired of myself. It is just exhausting getting up every morning and thinking: oh God, I have to be him again all day.

Harriet says that she agrees with Walter that "Ismael" is now vicious and that I ruined the story. I dreamt about a woman with strange shoes and then I realized she had no feet and then she toppled over. What does that mean?

Now I'm not dull or exhausted, but depressed. I suppose it is getting used to the hot weather.....dear Edward, I love you very much. Your Alfred

To Edward Field   6 May 1964
Dear *habib:*
I just sent you a letter yesterday and here I am again. Depressed. Partly because of last night that elegant dinner with Cecil Beaton. He is nice and witty and gentle and kind, and the dinner was stupendous, and the evening was like paradise, and the garden was starry and full of flowers and huge trees. And on the table were huge overblown roses in that elegant English aristocracy house. And I said, smelling the

roses, "They don't smell." And the Hon. David Herbert said: "Oh, yes, they do. And I said (knowing that Cecil would love it): "Oh, bit pissy, like not quite clean diapers." A moment of stunned silence. Then Cecil cued in with a huge guffaw, and then David roared with laughter, and then Jane and Paul came in with a nervous titter (they were identifying with me), and at last Margarite McKay (Loeb of Leopold and Loeb, Inc.), and I was the star. I don't really feel sick about it like after Hortense Calisher, but I'm a little depressed at even bothering. During coffee and cognac in the living room that is practically a museum, we talked about how boring people were who tried to impress other people. And everyone was trying to impress everyone else. Cecil wore a tan suit and a pink sort of gown shirt with rose embroidery (I'm not joking) over his pants with sort of flower pots. And a deep pink chiffon ascot. And black patent leather pumps with bows on them and beige socks. He is a big old bald Englishman. He really just wanted to get me in a corner to tell him about Dris. It seemed a little dull talking about Dris. (We don't take our Moslems along to dinner.) No magic. An evening in the past. Afterwards I liked Paul better because I could see his reservations about that world and I was surprised and pleased. Is there something to be successful for? I saw an ad in Time magazine for Rolex watches. Something like: the men who make your destiny wear Rolex. And I thought about my little thatched hut in the jungle away from where people made each other's destiny. Then I get driven home in a Mercedes and Dris was just going up the stoop of the house and my heart actually moved. Oh it was so nice being back with my dumb illiterate Moslem who always knows why he wants to impress people and exactly what they are up to.

Your letter came this morning. I haven't heard a word from my brother about the money, and I wonder what is up. Yes, I'll buy the blanket and the hassock. I will get you a measure of djellaba cloth which is thick and handwoven and the size of a double bed. Black and white, like salt and pepper. Very cheap too. I can't think what kind of hassock to buy. They are so vulgar. I'll try to find one plain and pretty....I don't know what to say about cock. I've discovered that the whole point of them if you're queer is to have them up your ass. All the other, the rest, is just fooling around, not knowing where to put them. I have fantasies lately about fucking little boys in the woods. Just making them drop their pants and shoving it in, fast, and giving them a hundred francs.

I'm off kif for awhile because of my stomach. I'm doing exercises again, having gotten fat. Not fat really. But I've gained ten pounds or so. I know you have a thing about the vegetable kingdom, but it likes you back. It only wants to die around me, though I think I really love it. I gathered some nasturtiums on the road while a French lady screamed at me (in the house next door to Lawrence Durrell's motherinlaw), because they were opposite her gate. First I went away. Then I changed my mind and spent a long time choosing while she roared. And finally, I found a nice root to replant and I said to her: Don't you want to share a little beauty with me? I felt the undercurrents of a revolution when I spoke. She humphed. Did I tell you this?

Next day. I got the money today, but am not feeling the least happy about it.

I also had a letter from Susan saying that she wrote to the Times, but that Jason told her it was fifty to one they would print it. Against printing it. I am feeling like a failure. And what you say about my book makes me even more depressed.

From just the few tearsheets the woman sent me from the Nation, I could see the whole configuration of coming events in America. The left is getting a voice again and will be more clearly defined. So the right too will grow stronger and people will have to start choosing sides. The beats will all become leftists. There was a piece by Susan about the new movies and I felt sorry for Susan in NY trying to be on everyone's side at once and having to explain all her positions. It is quite a moving piece because of that. Suddenly she didn't seem like a whore; she seemed like an extreme case of Alfredism. I feel sorry for her. But she is still a whore.

I realized why people used to like me so much. Because I always helped them believe in their illusions. It was like a bargain: I'll believe

151

in yours if you'll believe in mine. I loathe myself.

I'm going crazy with this column. Too depressed to write. And hating everyone, especially me. Love (out of habit), Alfred.

To Edward Field   Sidi Bujari 28, Tangier—18 May 1964

Dear Edward,

I just fired Candida. The immediate reason is a review in The Kansas City Star, long and very good, by an old fan of mine. Apparently he had to buy the book himself, which explains why there haven't been any reviews. Copies of the book weren't sent.

The reason we don't get anywhere is because we waste our time and energy on our nervous disorders and our boyfriends. Even this wouldn't be too much of an obstacle if we had any real sense of loyalty to each other, but we don't. [marginal note: I just read this over and it sounds mean. I don't mean it to be mean.]

I went up in flames yesterday afternoon like a human torch alone in the kitchen. My wig is now a charred heap lying in the fireplace; so destiny took the decision out of my hands, thank God. Now I have to face the world as I am which is a little frightening and embarrassing. But I wouldn't have it any other way for a million dollars. Now I keep thinking I better go change my passport picture, and I imagine they'll arrest me at the consulate. Aside from the wig and a little melting of my plastic shirt, the fire caused no damage except slight blistering on one finger. I had the presence of mind to put my arms under cold water as soon as the fire went out. The whole kitchen was ablaze for a few seconds. Dris is feeling a little nervous—change is very hard for an Arab—which is good because it makes me feel stronger.

It is summer and hot. I don't have anything else to say.

Love, Alfred

Later. Your letter came. Irving was here all day and we made potato salad. Allen Ginsberg is handling him like a promotion agency.

Irving says the only thing you and I have in common is that we're both Jews with goy names. I told him that we've known each other for so long it didn't matter whether we had anything in common or not. Lots of love, Alfred.

To Edward Field   Sid May something (1964)
Dear Edward:

Now that I'm my own agent, I have more energy. I wrote Epstein yesterday bawling him out. Now your other letter came and I've sent him another letter telling him to send a salesman to 42nd St. to put the book in the window. I said my spies would check to see if he'd sent a salesman. I told him he was a disgrace and the whole thing was a scandal. I also warned him if he didn't behave I was going to start writing letters to [Bennett] Cerf, which I will. I also told him to run ads in those places you mentioned yesterday and to put Burroughs' quote in. Candida recently tried to warn me there would be no second edition.

He [Robert Duncan] did not marry Jess Collins in 1960, that's so silly. Did he say that? Duncan? I met them in 1954 and they had that worn out look from too much marriage and Duncan couldn't think of anything but what he called the cosy little pissers. (Pissoirs). Jess Collins used to just sit in utter silence like a discontinuous form in spatial composition. Yes, that filthy slob [Robert Creeley] put his finger in my ass. I was terribly sick from pot, cognac, Walter and Arthur at Lynn's Xmas party.

Please tell [Lincoln] Kirstein to make that stupid woman get me a good big review. Burroughs warned me against her and against writing for the Nation. He is really such a goy. I've been thinking over about Irving. He always cows me, like Arthur; he's sort of a little strutting Napoleon and he really hates my writing. Then I think over the next day what he said and it is such balls. He has very strong opinions like

Arthur used to have. And really you have to be one of his ingroup friends to be approved of as a writer. So he likes all sorts of awful writers like Kerouac.

I was all set to go to Gib when a form came from the embassy saying that American residents must get reentry visas now if they want to leave Morocco and return. (It is just another way to get money, I suppose.) And the visa may take weeks. So now I don't know whether I'm stuck or whether I can just leave and come back the next day as a tourist not a resident. The idiots don't make that clear. Probably the law isn't even clear. They really don't care what you do so long as you pay some tax or other. It may also be a plot to get foreigners to bank in Morocco.

Skoura is better physically but her brain is practically gone, it seems. She almost jumps in the air when I mention her name, like something hit her, a memory, but she doesn't respond to me at all. Just the name. Then she ignores me. She stopped wagging her tail again. I think she's had a relapse. When she gets like this, I stop caring about her. It is like she is a stranger hanging around.

Do you remember in your letter you said you got your pronouns mixed up? Well I've noticed that a lot of the things I tell people I'm really telling to myself. In letters. I give myself advice.

I've been thinking of buying a little land on the way to Arcila; it is very cheap, one hundred francs a meter. The best, woodiest stretch is American, an abandoned radio setup, *forêt diplomatique* it's called. And then Dris could find a bunch of boys to build a little house. And then he can raise chickens or sheep or something and have something to do with himself and I can have like my thatched hut in the jungle. He brought three little tiny orange rabbits home the other day and was going to raise them in the extra toilet. But it didn't really work; I was terrified that Columbine would eat them and their shit began to stink because the slave didn't seem to think of cleaning the place. (The slave is very old by the way. So he brought them to his father in Arcila.

The slave has worked for me since October and I still don't know her name. Maybe I'll call her Edwina.

My head hasn't caused much of a sensation, but mostly I've been wearing a *tageeya*, those knitted yarmulkas they all wear. My money changer I think was stunned. Pepita, the dyke concierge, generously said it was a good idea to have cut my hair off. Irving said only, so what's changed, and I felt hurt. Suddenly the whole thing is so predictable it's boring. Jane will want to burrow into my confidence because of it.... The thing is I don't really give a shit about it myself.

I promised the witch in Arcila five thousand francs if I got money from my family. And since her work was so efficient I've now given her a commission to make my book sell. Do you want anything taken care of?

Next day. You are going to be forty in practically no time. Is that right? Happy birthday, dearest Edward.

I just phoned the consul and he said no, don't go buy a car in Gib because the Moroccans will catch me for at least fifty percent tax and my whole residence thing might be problematical. He said (as Dris has kept telling me) to go to Rabat or Casablanca where, though not as cheap as Gib, they are cheaper than Tangier where cars are always in demand at high prices; then I could sell it here for more. So I'm not going to Gib.

Dris is so beautiful these days, really so stunning. We had a terrific fight during supper and he flung his steak to the floor—really a tragic thing for him, considering his feeling about food. He says God brought me to Morocco to find the other craziest person in the world. Wasn't that nice of God? Love and kisses, Alfred

To Norman Glass   May 22, 1964
Dear Norman:

I haven't written sooner because I haven't had anything to say. I still don't have, but I will try.

I'll tell my publisher you haven't received the book yet. I've been very depressed about the whole thing. In fact, I fired my agent. They simply won't distribute the book and I don't know why.

I got high last night and hated my book, the thought of it. I thought: I'm just a gigantic fake and can't stand myself or anything I write.

I've been doing nothing except reading a little. I now have a thousand dollars in Gib. I'm buying a car, I hope. I'll go to Casa next week unless Dris comes through on a Morris in Arcila for $300.

I saw Paul last week. We went up the Mountain to look for a place as I'm dying to get out of here and go to the country. Of course, the place he had in mind for me was the dreariest bungalow colony where Tennessee and Truman and Paul and Jane had once stayed. I saw the house he's rented (forty-two thousand per month). He is always looking for decor, isn't he? "Is this the kind of place that Paul Bowles should be living in?" he asks himself. Anyway it is spectacular. In fact, its very spectacularity makes it dreary. Panavision; the Straits. Great forests surrounding the house. Little pools. Broken marble benches. I'll bet he answered your letter finally because he wants you to come stay with him up there. He said he was afraid to sleep there alone. On the way down, he antagonized a bunch of kids into throwing rocks at him. I think he is planning to end up like "Suddenly Last Summer." *J'ai marre de ces vies à la littérature.*

I also saw Irving. He came over and I made him potato salad and we had quite a nice time. But I've been disgusted with him since. He is destructive. Oh, Ira's magazine has materialized. In mauve. Or fuschia. It is boring. But it exists. Irving's thing is pretty and well written, but who cares? Peter has gone to sea as a merchant mariner on a German ship I believe. Allen Ginsberg is taking charge of Irving's career. Grove is publishing a book, pieces are being printed in Evergreen and Paris Review, etc. Money is coming in, etc. Their scene. Irving will be hailed, etc. Dull. etc.

I just reread up above. No, I'm not disgusted with myself. Something odd has been happening to me. It is difficult or impossible to unravel and I'm not even going to try. I am another person. Or finally no one. My sense of waiting, of expectation is over. My past belongs to someone else, some romantic madman. Who am I now? The question doesn't exist. I am what happens.

I didn't too much like the quote you sent me from your article on Burroughs. The generalization about the Beat Scene is no longer true. Even while I was in America, the beatniks were mixing social consciousness with zen. You know, the peace marchers, etc. Well now I believe they've gone full cycle. I think, as I suspected when I was in Greece, that the whole religious bit (as a mass phenomenon) was a result of being politically squelched. Liberals and radicals and revolutionaries in the west were afraid to find their polticial destinies. Also, as I've probably told you, when I left America in January, 1951, all the intellectuals were snotty about America and didn't believe in God. The subway posters and the newspapers and all propaganda was geared at making people love America and be devout (not like the Communists). When I came back in March, 1959, I found that all the new intellectuals (myself included) had been turned on by God and pop culture. The posters had worked. Norman, 'evolution' is a theory. Don't pay attention to it. It is a belief. The way out is the way out of the mind. Even identity, non-identity, who-am-I, the I's, the voices, are tricks of the mind. Observe, see and see through, but don't explain. Explanations prevent truth from coming through. The new man is a hypothesis; the old man is intolerable. When Irving was here the other day, he went on at length about Peter's weaknesses and bad qualities; "Could Peter change?" he wondered. I said it was not Irving's job to improve Peter, that if he was looking for a good man, he himself must be it.

Oh all this is garbage and makes me impatient.

Irving, on Burroughs: "I think he is the most evolved man I know. I think he is even more evolved than I am."

I am so sick of people who have found the right way. "His vocabulary changed radically, as did his *weltanschauung*, and, since any change of ideas makes a thinker feel he has come closer to the truth (even when the new idea serves to negate that very feeling), he became even more smug, even more complacent, even more patronizing." Three cheers for Alfred Chester. Avoid like the plague anyone who has found the right way.

I just opened my book to quote that line above and started reading in the middle of "Rapunzel."

Now I've spent the last hour reading my book and I'm feeling grateful for it mostly. Its spirit is so large and open. It is like fresh air. How humble and idiotic of me to take Irving's small-minded pettiness (his writing) seriously. He sat here the other day talking about how he'd tried to make his book spacious. No wonder, he is all tightassed, closed in bitterness and hatred. Like Burroughs. Meaness and pettiness. Self indulgence. Joyless. Life, Norman, is joy. Art is joy. It is true what Edward says about my book: "Nobody has testified like you, with such responsibility, with such a chorus of voices, and the ringing of bells. Everybody else writes like smearing a thin layer of goo over the mess of our world."

Why do I pay attention to people—even to myself?

Love, Alfred.

To Edward Field   May 29, 1964

Dear Edward,

I was standing with my new volkswagen at the garage when the mailman passed and gave me your letter. (Isn't that a casual way of saying "I bought a car?" It cost $300 and there's plenty wrong with it, and will probably go up to an initial cost of $500 by the time I can go to Fez. But as my cousin Lennie said, "better spend a little on an old junkheap and know what you're putting into it." I've already spent nearly $20 today on new brakes, the horn, etc. There's something wrong with the transmission or gear in third; when I take my foot off the gas pedal it makes a noise. But the VW mechanic said it would hold out awhile. And also he said the steering apparatus is fucked up, but that can hold too. I would like it to hold anyway until I can find an honest mechanic. Dris' friend the cop down the street who wanted me to buy his huge Citroen has a good mechanic. Well, anyway. It's about 1950 or '52 model, a cream-colored convertible, adorable looking. With bucket seats of leather. Old and used and lovely. I'm going to buy two rubber things like what you slept on at Paul's so we can camp out on our trips. Oh, speaking of trips, I think you should come to Morocco in September, both of you, and then we'll go across to Egypt and see the temples before they disappear. Is it part of your childhood as it is mine? Yes, you can buy land too. Are you really interested? If you're just thinking of an investment, it's pretty touch-and-go, let me tell you, because Arcila is not getting too popular; it will be more than a couple of years before it gets discovered. And by that time the Government may be out and the land seized. You know about the world. Actually there may be a break in all this as the king will probably turn himself into the president or prime minister like Prince Sihanouk did. (Did I tell you I wrote Sihanouk a fan letter?) The students want a republic and they will be satisfied for years if the king calls himself president...A house in Arcila can be anywhere from $200 up, depending. The seafront properties are expensive, of course. But really you couldn't mean Arcila as a holiday place, only as a speculation, no? Well, who knows, postwig me, I'll have to start seeing the world all over again. Maybe it will be different. I doubt it.

I'm not exactly peaceful. I've been feeling unhappy. The thing was, before there was always something to look forward to. (I did it in Greece but that was not really public). Oh, now, what am I saying? After I wrote you, I lost some of my bravado and didn't go out of the house for practically a week. As a matter of fact I haven't really seen anyone since writing to you. I feel embarrassed about going to people this way. I feel they have to come on me. Paul was over the other day, but I missed him and I'll call back soon. To tell the truth I feel sort of sore and dead inside. And when I get kifed I start going crazy again. I mean, I become panicky and think, are you mad, how can you go into the world like this? *Comment ose-t-il sortir, un tel garcon dans le monde?* You know, my family's shame and stuff. I really have to get used to it. Adjust. (By the way, I've been thinking about old and new words for the same thing and how the older ones were somehow more honest, like "reputation" for "image" and "get used to" for "adjust.") Dris keeps calling me Marlon Brando now, meaning so butch. Actually he's right. You can't be a faggot with a great big bald head, it's too ridiculous. It really and truly is. I'll buy a camera and take a picture and send it to you. Oh, Edward, but it isn't so simple not changing the passport. I know you're thinking I won't be able to bear it too long. But I mean what if a cop stops me and asks for my passport? Edward, I really want to make this irrevocable. I'll talk to Dris about it and get him to discuss it with his cop friend. Anyway, I don't run around the streets bare headed, I wear a *tageeya*. You know, like Larbi, remember? In Greece I tried going around with nothing on and all I heard was Yul Brynner for miles around until I couldn't stand it.

Oh, I had a letter from Girodias yesterday, ecstatic and grateful over my review. He says his friend Barney Rosset [of Grove Press] was visiting him and they are compiling an anthology of Olympia books and including some of *Chariot*. I must rewrite it....I'm not a writer anymore, *Je suis la cantatrice chauve maintenant*. Actually I have been piddling around with some writing and also reading a lot. I read *Behold Goliath* and agreed with you, but now I don't. Now it embarrasses me. Edward, why does everything embarrass me? When I think back over my columns in the Tribune, over my reviews and essays, my stories, my novel, my porno, my loves, my life, my everything—I feel so ashamed. Why do I feel so ashamed?

I had a letter from Candida saying one day I would realize how much she has done for my book. I wish I knew what. Edward. How could *Behold Goliath* have upset anyone, the literary scene? I'm very irritated with Irving Rosenthal. So self-righteous and superior. No, we don't have to be more loyal to each other: The thing is really, we aren't career people somehow....Dris told me the highway cops came into the cafe down the road where he plays cards and took away all the kif and wrote down the names of the people. Can you imagine? Those poor old Arabs. It would be like writing people's names down for drinking beer in America.

I suppose you realize I'm changing, or that something's happening. I don't really know what's going on. The master control seems to have gone. That which organized my experience has withered. I just go from event to event now without putting it into some pattern. My memory has gotten bad, just like an Arab. In fact, I have an Arab mind. Sometimes I get a little frightened by it, but mostly I don't mind. I have really got to start accepting the Now. I was always postponing Now by imagining how things would be different. Everything is just sort of jammed into my mind helterskelter; it doesn't get neatly filed away. The filer is gone. There is only the cabinet. Is this insanity or what? Even my little diddlings in writing reveal this. I really haven't been able to write for years because My Filer didn't know how to organize and just stood there watching. Now even he's gone. Things, though, get a little clearer when I take benzedrine (a little and rarely). It's like my business with Harriet. I forget to be careful and keep all my guards up; I sort of let things slip, like what a whore and shit I really am. I would write to her nicely but to tell the truth I can't get the interest up.

Later. I've been trying for hours to write another letter to Epstein, but I don't know what to say anymore. I should have had an agent to fight with him but don't.

My burnt finger became quite infected and now seems somewhat better but a little bizarre. I was terrified of leprosy or something. Like Dris' brother, Hamid. Two or three years ago he spilled some boiling water on his foot and it just rots. Could it be leprosy? Dris says he goes to doctors but never comes back with a name for the disease, only medicines that don't help. When the car is ready I'll take him from Arcila here to a doctor and find out a name....The Great Fire of Tangier. Actually it wasn't altogether accidental. But it wasn't altogether planned either, so that's why I made it sound like an accident, as I didn't think I could take the credit. I just sort of blocked off on a connection between benzine and a lighted fire. Bazoom! as Time magazine likes to say now that it's getting poparty. The wig was in my hands, not on my head, like a sacrificial victim.

How is that teapot? If you rub it three times and say, as Dris puts it, *Abre, O Sisamo!* I will come flying out of the nozzle.

I know your name is Edwina, that's why I said I'd call the maid Edwina, because that's your maid name, isn't it? Listen, tell Miss Baddie Oneshoe sitting at her machine there that she should tell all the ladies at the museum [of Modern Art] to give her their old clothes and especially shoes and make a package or a lot of packages and send them to me so I can distribute. It is too bad the way people go shoeless and clothesless in the winter. That can be the present to send me if you want. THAT and your POEMS.

Edward, please think hard what I should do about Epstein. I have had three reviews in the whole country.

Lots of love and kisses to you both.

To Norman Glass   June 2, 1964

Dear Norman: I just got back from the police where I registered my new car and found your big Harold Norse-looking envelope. I haven't read the piece yet and won't until my mind clears a bit. I'm not smoking kif, but the weather has been very bad for days rain, stormy, very low pressure—and that clogs me up. Among other things which I will get to presently, first, my car. It's a bright red '61 Dauphine in very good condition. Cost $300 which is a steal. I'd put a deposit on an old VW, but then a very cute mechanic came and told me it was ridiculous to buy it. Until he came along, a price like $300 was unthinkable for a car newer than 1953. I was almost decided to go to Gib and pay import duty into Morocco. (As I've got my residence now, I can't bring things in free.) I could sell the Dauphine tomorrow for twice as much and soon, the mechanic says, it will be more valuable, for gasoline (petrol to you) is going up and the Dauphine uses practically none. Anway, we're going to take a trip to Fez, insha'allah, within a few days.

I hope you haven't yet written to Paul asking directly if you can stay. I think that is very bad politics with him. My brain is too numb to think of a clever approach. But you are pretty ingenious. Actually, maybe you're right. Maybe a direct approach is right. I haven't seen Paul in three weeks. The real reason for this is that I've stopped wearing my wig and am very shy about going out. My hair fell out when I was seven and it's something I have never gotten used to, thanks to my shithole family. So the only people who've seen the new (old) me are the people in the house and Irving who's been over a couple of times. I somehow am too shy to make the initial step, as if I'm a new person. He was over a few days ago (P.) and left a note (I was out) and I haven't gotten in touch with him, though I've wanted to. I will try. My impulse is really to run and hide. New people don't bother me too much but facing old people seems horrible. Dris has been remarkably understanding in his limited way. He is of course pragmatic about it. Anyway I'm thirty-five and the whole thing is too silly, behaving like a child about it. Ugh. Anyway, this is also one of the reasons my brain is off. I wear a *tageeya* in the street, a ridiculous yellow one that was lying around the house.

I just read about two-thirds of your piece and found it stimulating. After that I had to awake my breath's beloved up....So you are sucking off the gentiles, are you? Do be a bit careful, as you say Porticello is only a mile from where you live. What do you neighbors think of you anyway? When I lived in Italy they sort of accepted us. (Me and Arthur). Your conversations with those little boys strike me as somewhat mad. You should never blow them or anything when they're in a gang. One at a time. When they're just like people. The shock of my opinion of Italians came through Antonio who was, and perhaps still is, undergoing an existential crisis. A Sicilian peasant. Democracy really makes things go too far.

I'm reading *Steppenwolf*. I never wanted to before because I knew it was one of those books that defined me to a certain extent. I like that "self hate is really the same thing as sheer egotism." I have lately come to that one by myself. It makes my self-contempt less noble, doesn't it?

I've now taken some dex to wake up. I haven't any of that so called creative energy. If you saw my pissings you'd be shocked I've given up writing. Now I sort of piss. Yes, Irving is destructive. I imagine him sitting in the chair here with his feet not touching the floor. He keeps promising to let me read his book, but still hasn't. Which makes me secretly glad, because it means he is worried when not surrounded by his own crew. Scene: Rosalind, Ira and me during the blackmail era. They unearth Irving's ms and seek out a passage to read me. He sits, she leans over his shoulder; he reads passages here and there. They chuckle with pleasure. Our little boy.

If I can get Dris a passport I would love to drive to Sicily and call for you. I think he'd have a fit if I went alone. Did I tell you I nearly fucked a boy down on your windy palms street. In some dark corner on the way to the port. A dirty little wretch. Sweet though and humble, no male arrogance. He pulled out his cock and then I turned him around and pulled his pants down. But two cops on bicycles appeared and that was the end of my potency.

Please tell me about Irving and the boy in Marrakech. The stories he's told me are very romantic and naive. You know, I like very much being with him, but as soon as he leaves I realize all the nasty destructive things he's said. Like, that neither I nor you should write.... There is a white bird, an albino lark maybe (?), outside now with a harsh twanging voice like a Jew's harp. The storm has been hard on the birds. The fledglings have had a time fighting with the gale and the mother birds scream unhappily. They're nested all around the house. I get up at six a.m. to smell the morning.

Later. I think you're romanticizing Paul a little. Beware. Did I tell you he's turned Boulaich into a painter, and quite an extraordinary one at that. I wanted to buy one of his pictures for one thousand francs but hesitated because of my own little Michelangelo. I read in the paper yesterday that there is a new gallery and that Boulaich showed his pictures there (catalogued by the famous writer Paul Bowles) and they are wonderful, promising future, etc.

I've decided that Solotaroff's review [of *Behold Goliath*] is really very bitchy. The realisation has come via Steppenwolf who is, so far at least, the underside of the bourgeois normal world. Apparently, my stories (someone once told me this) exalt the underside and make it the right, the normal and the good. So Solotaroff is reacting against it. He hates me but is too sophisticated to say so and puts me down the way Time would. I'm going to write him and tell him so.

Thursday now. Going out of my mind with the car. Who to trust? Anyway, Dris is being an angel. I've been treating him like hell because of my nerves about the whole thing. I don't even want to talk about the car now. It is already eating up all my money and time.

I've now read your piece which I enjoyed very much. I do think it could use a couple more rewritings and be filled out a bit more. It feels sketchy. You take too many things for granted (that the reader can follow you) and I get a little lost sometimes. Also, the syntax is sometimes confusing, i.e. p. 16, the sentence beginning "Where Burroughs wields words." Does a forcep wield words? And the rest of the sentence gets lost: You seem to be saying he fails to achieve the anarchy which burns through the book. Can this be? Anyway, you'd better look it over again, even if Evergreen takes it. If you want a more careful criticism from me let me know. I love that quote from Carlton Coon. I never heard of him....Can I put a thought to you? That Burroughs hatred of sex is Puritanism.

I wrote, excuse me, pissed a paragraph this morning about Thomas Ferguson Sawyer who is he with whom everyone must fall in love. Where will all these pissings lead to I don't know. But I'm following because I can no longer lead.

I'm enclosing Times' bitchy review of Larbi [*A Life Full Of Holes*, tr. by Paul Bowles], or rather Paul. I ran into Paul yesterday while he was standing talking to Stuart Church off the boulevard. I was on my way to the police as I'd gotten hysterical about being cheated with the car. (It was really Dris who'd gotten hysterical because of some new mechanic and he, D., said I'd better get my money back, they were all crooks.) On top of this hysteria I was of course embarrassed about my head, but Paul was very cool. I just stood there being hysterical for ten seconds and fled. I figured the news must have been all over town already, which is a relief.

Dris and I got drunk last night to unwind from all the tension y

Alfred Chester against the ramparts of Arcila

ABOVE: Chester pacing on Tangier balcony
BELOW: Neil Derrick and Edward Field in bernoose with Chester on Tangier balcony

ABOVE: Chester with Dris
BELOW: Dris in pool

ABOVE: CHESTER WITH NEIL DERRICK
BELOW: CHESTER IN CAPE

PENCIL SKETCH OF CHESTER AS FAUN
BY HERMON ROSE
USED FOR ROSE'S *ORPHEUS, HOMAGE TO POET EDWARD FIELD, 1962*

CHESTER WITH EDWARD FIELD

Dear Dennis:

Your, I mean Edward's letters, were brought to my cabin
only last night. Five days after sailing. So you came.
The reason I wasn't in my cabin is that I wasn't on the
ship until practically the last minute. In fact I wasn't
going to sail until nearly the last minute because of the
dogs. When I got on board I found to my horror that there
was absolutely no place to put the dogs, and they sort of
expected me to leave them on deck all the time. I got off
the ship and spent two hours on the phone with the travel
agents and the zim lines, threatening to sue, demanding
first class passage on the next available ship, etc. Fi=
nally they got this brainstorm and put me into the isolation
cabin (generally for maniacs, criminals and people with con=
tagious diseases) which is just grand. I'm all to myself.
It is large and all the way aft on a deck of its almost own
with private bath and toilet. I'm out on my deck now with
my little moroccan number all agog at the typewriter (which
I borrowed from some girl). The ship's crew is almost all
jewish expatriates from morocco who are now israeli but continue to say that m. is the greatest country in the world.
(My steward has just come to get the bowls to fill for the dogs
What a life!) The passengers are rather dreary. They are so
intellectual! Hundreds of students going to Israel for a year.
Lots of idiotic isreali savages. Middle class vulgar stupid
Jews. It is like travelling with my family. Naturally everyone
adores me, and I have little girlfriend, a blonde from Boston,
nineteen who looks fourteen. I finally necked with her last
night and she obviously wanted to come to the cabin but I was
scared shitless and couldn't get it up so i acted paternal and
took her back to her cabin. But it was sort of romantic late
at night on the deck under the stars, etc. And there are still
four more days, though I've been avoiding her all morning. It
was all so natural and easy (except pour ma bite pour qui
ce n'était ni naturel ni facile). She looks fourteen. There
are a couple of others who are interested. (Us mature men
are scarce on the ship. Just boys -- adorable ones-- and
older men, and the delicious moroccan crew)

Edward said in the letter that he would be waiting for me in
Gibraltar. I expect this will annoy Paul, but I am glad as
can be. Dennis, I miss you. And also I miss Harriet. But
everyone else I think of with anger and distaste. Isn't that
awful? Even Walter. I think of New York with horror. Maybe
because this voyage has been so pleasant. The sea is almost
always calm, blue as the mediterannean, and the weather is
hot really. I am sunburnt. The food is tasteless but good.
I have had the number of quarrels that is par for the course,
and made a considerable number of people angry, hurt and insulted, while preaching to everyone morality and love. There
are really quite an extraordinarily large number of people
one wouldn't mind seeing even in New York except they are too
intellectual. Iv

I've been trying every day to do the article for partisan
but can't. It just seems such a silly thing to do. I mean,
why? Who cares? What the fuck do I have to say about the
theater, and I just can't see any point being a smarty-pants
and showing off now. And it doesn't matter. It is so nice
to be out of New York and not to need a career.

We call at Madeira on Friday for four hours, but this letter
will probably be posted from Gibraltar.

I think of Extro sometimes and get confused. It isn't
possible with men the way it is with women. Even just last
night told me this again. Did you fuck that girl? I hope
so. Maybe that's why you didn't answer the phone?

Dennis, sweetie-pie, I'm grateful to you for the last months.

Next day. I woke up this morning thinking I wasn't going to
do the drama thing & it's such a relief to allow myself
the rest of the trip the indulence I've allowed myself so far.
My little girlfriend is beginning to bore me! But it is
Thursday today & there is half a day in Madeira tomorrow
& then Saturday night Gibraltar.

Write me.

Love from
alfred

LETTER FROM ALFRED CHESTER TO DENNIS SELBY, 1968

HARRIET SOHMERS WITH SUSAN SONTAG
IN FRANCE IN THE 1950S

HARRIET SOHMERS
WITH SON MILO

אברהם יצחק ל'יב בר יעקב
ה'ג'צ'ב'ה

ALFRED I. CHESTER
SEPT. 7, 1928
JULY 26, 1971

BROTHER

GRAVESTONE AT BARON HIRSCH CEMETERY, STATEN ISLAND

compris my head psychosis which though I barely mention to him he is very aware of and it evidently makes him suffer. Anyway, he said how much I had hurt him by the way I'd been treating him about the car and that I really didn't realize how much he loved me. He says that since that breakup (remember? In Arcila?) he hasn't slept with a faggot, boy or girl, but that he knew I wouldn't believe him. I both do and don't believe him. The thing is that I've become so used to the idea that there is no fidelity here, it hasn't mattered whether he did or not.

Norman, I'm feeling very revolted by America these days and I really don't want to go back. Since my insanity, I've changed a great deal and become alienated from most of my friends. In fact you and Edward are the only people I write to, or who write to me, rather. And I've been hurt and disgusted by the way my book has been treated. Anyway, we can talk about this more when and if you come here. What I want now really is to find a place in the country and get out of this apartment.

I have to go now and fix the lights in the car and do something about the shift. So I'll mail this rather than wait. Write soon. Love from Alfred.

To Edward Field   June 3, 1964
Dear Edward:

I got a proof of the Solotaroff review the other day and actually took it seriously. I wrote him a sort of humble failure letter. But then yesterday I suddenly realized what it was all about. It's just that new game that Time invented and I perfected of being hipper than thou, the critic always trying to outsmart the writer. So I wrote him telling him he was a bitch. Imagine throwing in that Grace Metalious thing, and he's supposed to be a friend. Anyway I do think it will sell copies because it makes me seem exotic. Just after I mailed the letter to him your letters came and you say the same thing. Thanks for writing them. What did Harper's say or can I guess: "another homosexual, yawn, yawn." Well, it is all Epstein's fault. If he had pushed it a little and declared himself personally responsible by writing letters to the editors, they wouldn't have dared to be so snide. It's just that the book looks like it has no father so the kids are showing off how brave they are. He [Epstein] hasn't sent me the list of newspapers, and as of now I don't care. I'm not going to bother about the book anymore. I woke up this morning (it has been storming for days) and it was clear at last and Skoura wagged her tail (she gets bad in bad weather; had four fits in two days) and the birds were singing again, though I think a lot of the fledglings died in the storm, were blown away by the gale; anyway, I thought, really am I going to spend my life being in anguish over this or that, my writing blocks, my head, everything. There is enough real suffering and one must have joy. Well, you are right. They still hate sex in America.

I got my money back on the Volkswagen, and for the same price bought a bright red 1961 Dauphine which seems to be in perfect condition. It transpired on account of a mechanic who suddenly opened a new world of car prices for me: I want to get your things today or tomorrow so we can go to Fez, maybe on Saturday or Sunday.

The little wood on the edge of Arcila where the boys go to fuck is being turned into an international camping center, so I was wrong about the delay in tourism and you and Neil were right. Maybe I'll drive out today and tomorrow and see what I like. Dris says there is a large tract of land with a house on it, asking price $800, meaning it could go for five or six. The land I like best, aside from the American Forest, is the upper part rather than the beach because I like woody land. Anyway I'll tell you what there is if you're interested.

Kluger doesn't want to print my Time thing. He says it's already been done, but I think he is probably afraid. But he's paying me for it and I told him to send the manuscript to you. Just for you to read it. Then throw it away. I don't especially want to publish it....No, I didn't know about Irene [Fornes]. I guess she got hooked up to Spoleto through Beni Montresor, that wop whose boyfriend looked like a big Arthur.

She's in that glamorous queer set sort of tangentially. I once went to a party where they all had elegantiasis, and got drunk and went to the john, and when I looked in the mirror after all those people I looked to myself just like a frog....No one writes to me except you and Norman. I didn't break up with Harriet. God, women are impossible. She's really angry because I said her letters were dull. That's the whole thing. As for Susan. The reconciliation wouldn't have taken place except Harriet kept pushing it. Anyway I sent her a card. I expect the Times is never going to publish the letters.....Did you see that cruel review of Larbi's book in Time? They are really and truly insane.

I don't know whether that party means you're in with Grove. I was invited to that Partisan [Review] party last year with all the old fashioned smarties like Lowell and Spender. But I never got asked again. They know who belongs like the National Book Award knows who to give the prizes to.

I've given up smoking for awhile. Dris got me a quart of contraband scotch (Johnny Walker) and a quart of Gordon's Gin for $3 each. So I'm drinking a little and that's fun.

Lots of love and kisses to you and Neilele. Alfred

To Edward Field   June 8, 1964
Dear Edward:
The reason Epstein put the ad in the Voice is that I wrote him saying what happened to those ads he promised in the Tribune, Commentary, etc. He sent me back all my letters the other day and said if I wanted to quit Random House I could. There is no use fighting.

My car has been a problem of course, and Dris and I haven't stopped fighting since it arrived. Now it's in the garage again because the motor overheats. But the mechanic says it's nothing. I know the car feels I don't love it, and it's true I don't, because it's French and sort of all plastic and junky.

Peter Everett came on Friday with his woman and their little boy, five months. They'll be here for three weeks. His agent is very up and coming, and good on European rights, and knows of me and says he wants to handle me, so I'll send a book back with Peter and see. Peter will also try to make him handle your book. We had a big fight last night. He says the reason all writers are stuck is that they're in the cul de sac of humanism and reject science, which is the way. Like Burroughs. You know, the scientist-priest bit, really. The mechanistic god is coming into his own. I couldn't fall asleep for hours imagining about it. His notion is that the way it is now is the right way, leading somewhere. I see all the world paved with concrete and iron and turning into a machine. So I asked him what about the trees in the forest. But all that doesn't matter, because that is the past phase of the earth. He makes me feel old fashioned like worshipping dead gods. The new god will come out of the machine. He isn't as coherent on this as I am. He just feels that wave of energy and wants to join it because literature seems so dead. Suddenly it becomes a world where Hitler could be a saint, since he produced Von Braun. It seems so callous to life. Yet it's sort of hopeful. He says you can't stop it anyway so you might as well join it. And it also makes the communist-capitalist struggle irrelevant, which I think is true. They are both the same now. But his idea is all linked really with a re-emerging Europe as against America. Like DeGaulle. What it all adds up to finally, I think, is just the same old ignoring of people so the aristocracy can go on. All the deadness doesn't matter because the scientists are on their way to the miraculous new world.

Was that paragraph readable? I know [Barney] Rosset and Epstein love each other; that's why Epstein was so unhappy about my review of *City of Night*....It's a good thing you're busy in October because I don't think my Dauphine would make it to Egypt anyway. I haven't done a thing about the land in Arcila since it's been car and Peter keeping me busy. But I will do it this week and tell you what the prices are. Things are cheap enough not to have to worry about Stanley Moss. Tell him if he's really interested to write to me directly and confirm because

Arabs become difficult to deal with if you say you want huge tracts and then start backing out. As for a house. If you don't live in it, you rent it....I still haven't bought your things. I've looked at hassocks, however, and they really are awful. They aren't Arabic tent vulgar but Alhambra movie palace vulgar. Maybe I should start an export business....I had decided never to buy Time again after the way they talked about Paul, but I'll buy it today to see about your [documentary] movie ["To Be Alive"].

May [Swenson]'s, quote was sent to me by Epstein and it's beautiful, so much so that I haven't been able to write and thank her because I think maybe she is just being nice and she will think I'm silly. She must really be a very good person. Because it sounds like what she's saying is what she's saying. After a year in this hole, nobody seems to be saying what they're saying anymore. There always seems to be some rotten, bitchy context. Like Burroughs. And Paul. Some other relationship that you're not aware of is always going on under the surface. People aren't saying what they think. And they aren't thinking what they say. Anyway, tell May thank you very much and that I'll write soon. Epstein sent me a few reviews. A good one in Houston and a bad one in Chicago (Francis Coughlin; no one with a name like that could like me—he does the super-sophisticated number, no mature person will be shocked, etc.). Maloff's reply to Susan is irrelevant. He is just altering his position to defend himself. What a slimepot. But they didn't print my letter or Nadia's. Do you think letters sell copies? Since it's always worked in my life that I get what I want when I don't want it anymore, I can just see the book taking off over the summer when the thought of it makes me nauseous.

Edward, I don't want to write my column anymore. My next deadline is 25th of June and I was thinking of saying something about Caetani [Princess Marguerite Caetani, publisher of Botteghe Oscure] whose death has been overlooked. Will you please advise me? Do you think I should go on with the column? I am another person from him who wrote the column....Peter came with a copy of Esquire and I read it and felt dejected about the whole world. They advertise falsy baskets for men, can you imagine? And latex rubber clothing. That's what the whole thing is, and Peter's idea: it is all the world of the mind. It is the triumph of the mind, the intellect. It's the world of idea.

Yes, Joan Michaelson is my girlfriend, but I have stopped writing her. She is so literary it makes me sick. I told her to ask Robert Friend to teach her how to write. I don't flatter myself that she is trying to get to me through you. I imagine she is just looking for another literary figure to try to sink her teeth into.

What was in Evergreen that the DA seized it?

Edward, I can't do a thing about my book anymore. Really, not a thing. It is gone. It's really over.

Maybe Peter is right and we are just flotsam from a dead world. I lay around in bed feeling like flotsam, God's outcast.

I just wish I could believe in writing enough and had energy enough to write a book, old-fashioned or stink-fashioned or no-fashioned. I will go back on dex.

Alfred

To Norman Glass   June 13, 1964
Dear Norman:

I think today is my brother's birthday. He must be forty-five. My sister is forty-seven.

I'm glad you're coming, but I have messages for you from Irving and Jane, both of whom I told. Irving said, well, have you written him about what's going on here? And Jane said, Oh well, you should tell him; I love Norman but you should tell him. Har, as you would say... Anyway, I'll tell you what's going on here; though it isn't going on for me, touch wood, so far. A couple of American Negroes were arrested for making (and evidently pushing) hash. They were caught with something like sixty pounds of kif. According to Ira, Irving, Paul, etc., they were hung by their wrists and tortured. The police

181

connected them with Philip Lamantia and they broke into his room at the Atlas and found a tiny bit of hash. He was in jail for six days and was fined sixty dollars. Tke other thing that's going on is that an Englishman came over and took nude (or porno, no one is quite certain) photographs of some boys. One of the boys squealed and now he is coming up on trial. Irving sees this as a moral purge. Irving says Jane and Paul won't see Philip. Jane says she agreed to see him and even give him money to get out (evidently she was anxious to get rid of him). Irving says Burroughs is leaving because of the purge, though he later said Burroughs was leaving because the life he is leading could be led anywhere, apartment, view, prices, etc. Anyway, Norman, I've told you what I've heard. Apparently this information is supposed to throw you into a state of paranoia and to prevent you from coming.

I'll include a list of things you should get me in Gib. Will you please bring your tape recorder? I'm dying for one, and nearly bought Irving's except it's so big. And I'd really prefer a portable. But the Japanese things here are worthless, according to the mechanic. If you want I'll buy yours from you. Or you can lend it to me or rent it to me. Or else I'll buy one of these junk ones, very cheap and it'll last as long as it lasts.

As you can judge from the above big paragraph I've been invaded by various and sundry. My old English friend Peter Everett is here with wife and child, but I find him rather intolerable now. I always did, I remember now, but forgave him on the grounds of youth. (When I was twenty-five, twenty-three seemed much younger.) But now he is thirty-three and the same sort of smart aleck and I find him intolerable. He's full of money, and I've spent scads on him now and he never thinks to invite me out. And for the first few days he was like a cranky child wanting to be entertained all the time. Now I've sort of left him to his own resources as I'm very busy with the car. We've also had a discord of principle about the machine age....When I mentioned to Paul and Jane that you were coming, and this only two or three days ago, they didn't seem surprised but they did represent themselves as being unaware of your coming. But from your letter, it would seem they must have known. Anyway, Larbi is staying with Paul for the summer. He has his passport and wanted to go to Belgium, but Paul says he refused to lend him the money, I suppose to keep him here over the summer.

It never occurred to me you didn't know I wore a wig. Actually, I've surprised more people than I thought, because I never thought I deceived anyone. That was part of the psychology which is boring. I knew Hajmi knew when he came back from Matrakech, but I supposed you'd told him. I could just tell.

Oh, I was sitting at a cafe on the beach the other day with Peter and Hajmi walked by, but I pretended not to see him. He kept circling, but I kept pretending. Finally he gave up....I found a great mechanic and the car is doing splendidly. That other horse's ass was just a big crook....I think it's fine you're going first class and you should tell Irving so. I'm so bored with people being afraid to say and be what they are. Irving can go to hell. Odd your sending that photo of Brecht. It's been on the tip of my tongue everytime I've seen Irving lately to say how much he looks like Brecht, but I forbore out of fear of hurting him. Am I the only person around who tries not to hurt other people? All those—dashes—in your letter—make me think you've seen Burroughs' piece—in Gnaoua. Darling—I'm not going to show your essay to Paul as I don't want to have to discuss it with him and listen to him put you down, as I'm sure you know he would, just because he does. I mentioned the piece to Ira and he asked to see it so I showed it to him. He kept connecting the ideas and quotes with himself and Irving, and his final opinion was that it was like a college paper by a very hip student.

Later. Peter and his family were here and I had to get high to endure it. For some reason it's made me sickish....Aside from the Solotaroff review, the Times had a correspondence about me and then the Times mentioned me in a roundup of books (few books mentioned, few praised, mine was). So maybe things will pick up. Epstein swears he sent you the book, but I don't believe him.

I have to go to the garage now. If the car works we're going with the Peters to Arcila tomorrow and to the souks. We'll have fun with the car. I'm dreaming of picking up a boy and fucking him in it. I don't know why though, sex with Dris is more scrumptious than ever. He said the other day that sex was the only thing we didn't get mad at each other over. Of course there are moments even out of bed though.

Goodbye for now, ducks. Shall I get you a room just in case or what? Maybe we should both take insurance policies out and have the things robbed from the car?

Love, Alfred

To Edward Field   June 23, 1964

Paidhaiki mou:

Your letter just came and I've had to take an equanil, it made me so nervous; so full of activity it is. I've been lying around trying to think of something to write my column about. I was going to write about [Marguerite] Caetani for the tenth time, but what is there to say about her? Dris is in Arcila and I'm dying to go down to the beach in my car and cruise in it for fun. There is one thing wrong with the car (so far) and nobody seems to know what it is. After twenty kilometers, it suddenly gets hot and uses up all the water. They said it was the radiator, but that's been cleaned. So now they say he didn't clean it well. It's been costing me a fortune getting things fixed that weren't broken. Anyway, it takes me out nearly every day to the grotto of Hercules or Cap Spartel and I swim and do exercise and lie in the sand. It also took us out to Arcila one day and I couldn't see any land I liked, but Dris says he'll talk to his brother-in-law who is smart about those things. So we'll see. I'm not feeling like buying now anyhow, on account of the car. The horrible thing is I could sell it at a profit but what good would that do. Dris says we should just take lots of water and go to Fez as is. If the new mechanic (tomorrow), who says the *culatta* needs to be cleaned, doesn't fix it, we'll go as is next week.

I have your things. The blanket and the puff or poof. I couldn't stand the poof problem anymore, so I told Dris to go out and buy one. I thought maybe he might get something Arab rather than the bazaar kind of things I've seen. I forgot to mention it was for someone else, he thought it was for us, and he was very relieved it wasn't. Tell Elia it's all camel skin and it's the nicest one an Arab could find. I hate it myself. I'll stick a few kif seeds in the blanket and send them this week. As the blanket is stitched closed, if the Feds catch us, I can always claim I never opened it. (The seeds can be slid in through the sides.)

Norman is coming back tomorrow. Peter is still here. I didn't see him for a week, he is a bad, mean person. But as he leaves on Saturday, I'm making the best of things. I think it must be a dull season for everyone....I do a little piddling every morning. When I think about them [the characters], I get quite excited, but when I sit down to write I sort of go dead. It is full of characters that don't have anything to do with each other. The whole thing is disconnected. Tony Curtis may be in it....Peter told me yesterday that Andre Deutsch gave Norman Mailer twentyfive thousand pounds as an advance on his new novel. (I got a hundred fifty after some bargaining. And after taxes, it came to two hundred eighteen dollars and fourteen cents.) I read a chapter of it in Esquire. Ghastly....Oh, I got a telegram the other day from a German publisher interested in rights. It made me feel good. And also I had a letter from Norman who finally got my book (Norman Glass, not Mailer) and he says at least three of the stories are immortal. I felt glad....Yes, I had seen that Boroff thing, but it didn't make me rejoice. I mean, how good can I feel about him after he begins by saying Updike, Salinger, Bellow, Styron, etc, are rightfully taking their place in the pantheon? No, I haven't seen Marty [Tucker]'s review. Please send it. ALSO GODDAMMIT SEND ME YOUR POEMS. I'M NOT GOING TO ASK YOU AGAIN. AND I'LL BE HURT.....I also heard from Susan who didn't get a Gug but got a $6500 Rockefeller grant, she didn't say what for. The whole letter was sort of German romantic suffering... I've been reading *Ulysses* by James Joyce. I never could bear to read it straight through, but I'm trying again. I keep feeling sorry for him, working so hard and feeling so little, and just building and building.

And sometimes those nice romantic sentences that he really enjoyed writing. He got trapped by his time and his brilliance, poor man. I also read *Steppenwolf* which I didn't like. I already had all that information about *I etcetera* and it is another construction.

Am I still feeling calm? I don't feel so shy about my head now. All my anger is going into the car. I named her yesterday. Aisha Kandeesha. She's the lady with goat's feet, beautiful hair and lots of gold who calls out to men alongside streams with their mother's voices and then they go mad if they listen.

I want to do a tape for WBAI. Maybe Norman will bring his recorder and I'll do one. I want to tell a spontaneous story. I started a lovely one about Extro when I had Irving's. It begins: There is good and there is weakness; there is evil and there is madness. And then it goes on about sex.

I hope you will direct Elia [Braca] when she reads my story [on WBAI], because she won't know when the girl is being fake and when she's being real.

Next morning. I have made a decision about the car. If the guy this morning doesn't know what is the matter with it, I will take the ferry to Gibraltar where Norman will be this afternoon and buy a car in his name and sell this one when I get back. Just writing this down makes me feel it is crazy. The reason I made this decision is that I woke up this morning thinking that the first mechanic had already cleaned the *culatta*, so I was back where I started and couldn't go through the whole thing again. Anyway I'm off now.

Lots of love, also kisses. Alfred

To Edward Field   28 June, 1964

Habibi: I'm sitting here with a million letters to answer and I can't get up the interest, and then yours comes and I want to talk to you right away. O God, it would be so nice to have fried matzoh together and kvetch.

Dris may be in jail for all I know but I doubt it. Anyway, somehow I'm feeling Moroccan about it and it can wait. He knocked over a woman with his motor a couple of months ago in Arcila (the whore who was slipping out of the gardens late at night). He thought she'd never sue, so he didn't tell the insurance company, and now she is suing and the company said it wasn't their affair as it was so late. I wanted to go with him to the trial yesterday, but he said they'd want more money if they saw me. We also had a big fight as he was leaving and he packed his things, then said he'd come back for them in the evening. Which I thought was his way of saying he wouldn't spend the night at home (Arcila). Anyway he didn't come back last night. So either he is in jail (do people go to jail in civil actions?) which he had said was a possibility, or else he is trying to worry me because I didn't phone to find out the verdict, as I said I would (before the fight). These details are getting involved and boring. Anyway I'll go to the PO and phone as soon as the slave comes. I'll also take your things and mail them finally. There are about six kif seeds in the blanket, even though you don't need them now, and I hope they don't sprout on the way over. Kif likes wool according to Dris. His father keeps a year's supply wrapped in wool in the house.

We fought because I was angry about the car again. Now it's up on the Mountain at Mr. Caneday's, a former missionary from Minnesota, who has been here thirty-seven years. I didn't go to Gib. Even Caneday has turned into a Moroccan, and for the first two days the car was there all he could do was think how he would buy the car from me after the summer. (He was convinced I was just passing through.) So he wasn't taking it seriously. Yesterday I grew angry with him and explained that how long I intended to own the car was not a consideration in his discovery of the water problem. I think he will be more serious now, because he said: You're an American and I'm an American. He is about sixty-five. No, there is no leak. Mr. Caneday lent me a big auto book and I'm reading it, though I can't understand too much. I think if someone is interested in mechanics or science, life must be very full. Anyway, according to the book, there could be any of ten thousand things wrong with the car, or all of them.

I told Kluger I couldn't do any work for him over the summer, so the Caetani thing will have to wait. I really have to put myself into a different mind for essays or journalism, and my fiction mind is fragile now. I work almost every day. "It is the same with me as it is with you, my friend. I am not going anywhere. I am only on the way. I am making a pilgrimage." That's from *Siddhartha* by Hesse which I read last night kifed and finished this morning sober. It's an unbearably beautiful book. It is so wise, so wise, so wise. Please read it, Edward. With kif it was jewellike, and sober it made me cry....I know which parts you cut from "Berceuse," the metaphysical parts. No, you shouldn't have changed the baby's name to Goliath because it was Calvin at the beginning. "So I named him Calvin after Calvary," the girl says. In 1957. But then I thought Calvin meant bald and I got self conscious. And I changed it To "So I named him Goliath after Golgotha." And that's how Goliath got born....Walter Minton wants to punch me in the nose because of my *Candy* review. I said it was a pot boiler, but that I didn't have anything against pot boilers, so I loved it. But I said it was immoral because it made fun of crackpots rather than squares, but I also said "Dr. Strangelove" was immoral for making the atom bomb a laughing matter.

What is this about Oswald's diary? The paper says "new revelations" that caused the Warren Commission to go on working?

Norman just came and the slave is here, so I'm going to the post office. I'm very tired of Norman, he is here a week. I dropped Peter at the end. I gave him a piece of my mind, strengthened by your letter, and said I wasn't interested in the names he gave things and that he ought to have a little self-awareness. Only I said it very strongly. Afterwards I asked if he'd minded and he said "Not if it helps you....Those terms just don't apply to me." So then I felt all further discourse would be futile.

Later. I called Arcila and Dris isn't in jail. They wouldn't take your package at the PO as they say it is badly wrapped. That was Dris's touch. He spent two days wrapping it, claiming he worked at the PO when he was fourteen and knew how packages should be made. Now I have to get brown paper which is hard to find and start again. You have been waiting a long time, *paidhaiki mou*. Forgive me. You still haven't said anything about the teapot and your silence makes me feel like the time I made the chicken and tuna salad and you wouldn't eat it. If you don't send me those poems I will ask the witch in Arcila to put a spell on you. Don't you have copies?

Norman went to the post with me and then came back and I said if he didn't change he couldn't be my friend. He is just unbearably selfish and I used to find that attractive in people (cf. old lovers), and in fact it has been a little like a love affair. Though I don't really find any charm at all now in people who just take take take. So he got very dramatic and poetical about the ungiving blackness in his soul, etc. And I said well, stow that, that's your problem, I just want to know if you can change. And he thought a long time (suffering a black metaphysic) and said he saw no possibility of change. And I said well, then I couldn't be his friend, except on a formal basis, exchange of dinner invitations. God, ritual and formality is terribly important; it keeps the black metaphysicians from getting on each other's nerves. Anyway, it is quite a remarkable change in me, getting rid of these people. Instead of falling in love with them. I have now had two cold-blooded, unhysterical scenes in a week, telling people to be nicer to me or get out of my life. It is interesting that they went without a murmur. Largely, it's my own fault. I have to stop giving the impression of being a boundless giver. Because I don't think I am anymore. I need reciprocity now....Did I tell you I think the title *Sex Stories* is the best title I've ever heard? It is a *coup de génie*. Your next book, or section of main book, should have that title....Norman told me that someone told him a secondhand copy of *Goliath* was in the English bookstore for four hundred francs. Awfully cheap. I felt terribly offended.

I enclose the Epstein letter, but I had cooled before that actually. I heard from Solotaroff: "I've been sitting on your two letters until I found I could make some level headed reply to them. Not that I was particularly sore. Maybe somewhere in between lies the way you really feel about the review. I didn't write it though to put you down for asserting your superiority to me. I think I wrote it mainly to give you at least one fair hearing. I didn't like most of the stories as much as I thought I would and had to be honest about that and try to explain my grounds. Perhaps when you're back in NY, we can talk about the review." Did you ever? He begins by oneupmanship, his calm detachment against my hysteria. Then goes on to say he reviews a book he doesn't like to give it a fair hearing, a book by presumably a friend. Then *culot* and arrogance talk about HIS REVIEW in NY, not my book. Then he goes on to describe how he is divorcing his wife as he is having "an immensely satisfying love affair"—that's to put me down for my stories of romantic suffering. "I think that I'm heading for another marriage, which along with being so unusually happy, makes me a little nervous. Like most of the squares, I trained for deprivation, not for abundance." Edward lovely, what is it with me that makes people feel my existence is a threat to them? Irving attacks me for writing for squares, Solotaroff for writing against them. My family always felt that just doing what I wanted to do couldn't be. Why do these people think I threaten them? I don't. Just living my own nonliving way bothers people. It really does. Please answer this or these questions. You know the answer.

I tried answering Susan but had to give it up. Harriet loves me again and I love her, but I find it difficult writing to her....I like your little thing about Caetani. You could probably do it better than I could because you never met her. Finally it all becomes money when I think of her....Today it is one year that you left Morocco and yesterday was one year since I looked on the shining faces of my boyeles. (Yours wasn't too shiny though, and Neil's looked like he put, applied, the shine before going out. You looked tired....Yes, you can publish my letters. I don't feel like writing a book about Morocco. I try to keep a diary occasionally, but my heart isn't in it. And besides I don't have any adventures with Moroccans except Dris. I met the most delicious sexy one on the Mountain last week when I was looking for a place in the country. You know, I'm always sort of dropping hints to Dris about boys I talk to and he never gets jealous, but when I just mentioned this Mustapha quite casually as having shown me the house, he was upset for twenty-four hours. He is a genius at instinct. I mean he is so real. He saw a photo of Jackie Kennedy in evening dress and he said, "Oh she's out looking for cock again." That Mustapha had a little butch build and no shirt and his pants kept threatening to fall down any minute. I was almost swooning. And round delicious buttocks.... Another interesting thing of Dris (for your collection). He went fishing down at the port the other day and I asked if I could go, and he told me no, they'd (the fishermen) think we fucked. I said, well what about all your friends here in the neighborhood when they see us together, what do they think? He said: Oh these people here can read and write and they've studied and they have their heads full of things, they're smart, so they don't think we sleep together; but the fishermen are stupid and uneducated and have nothing in their minds, so they think we do. I said: But it's the fishermen who think the truth. He was quite surprised at that.

It is so strange up there on the Mountain. All the Europeans live fantasy lives here. Caneday has turned his property into an American tumbledown farm wth old cars all over, just like New England or the midwest; David Herbert's grounds could be Cornwall or Dorset; the Henrys are haute bourgeoisie, gardens, formal, boring; etc. I like Caneday's best. I picked an old wop up in my car and he invited me out to a cafe he owns at Cap Spartel and it was just like Italy, grape arbors, and another old Italian with a thing around his middle (a cloth belt) and a wide brimmed hat and a long white beard, and lots of scruffy land. I liked that too. And the crazy shack....A man came up to me and sold me a flower, the most beautiful flower I ever saw. It was big, white and closed and smelled like lemon with a little anise. And big shiny green leaves, brown on the underside. Dris never saw one like it. It looked tropical. In the night it opened and smelled powerfully. Then in the morning it turned brown and all the leaves fell off; the petals I mean, the leaves are okay....I must stop this now, it is going on too long....I give you and boychikele a thousand kisses and love.

To Edward Field   July 15, 1964

Dear heart:

I've been going through another little crisis. It's really about writing, but it's affected everything else in my life. I've been through a week or ten days of despair, mainly I think because I can't connect all the material in my—I'm too humble to say book—piddlings. I'm feeling a little better now because I've made a couple of decisions in my mind. All connections are artificial anyway, and I'm not looking for a semblance of so-called reality. So I'm going to make the connections as artificial as possible. I don't understand what I'm doing. I must just learn quietly to accept. I'm too diffuse myself, and there is really something profoundly wrong with me that refuses to let me have my own unified voice (cf. *Siddhartha*). I must accept this at last because I'm nearly thirty-six now and it's not likely my voice will descend from heaven if I haven't yet found it. I'm just a lot of voices, none my own. I just don't exist. And the existential crisis is old fashioned, but there you are; I mean, there I am.

I got all your letters and tearsheets and the poems. And there you are, so simple and sweet and beautiful and honest. I like "The Octopus" best of all. I wish you would drop the article in the title; just "Giant Pacific Octopus" like you called it in your letters. Also, "Curse of the Cat Woman," without "the." The movie poems are perfect and they are you. Maybe you think they are funny, but I don't think they are funny. They are tragic. I don't like "that the mob shall" rather than "will" in Frankenstein. I kept thinking that "SHE" is really about you and Neil.

Speaking of Neil. You are right. You must do something fast because your successes are beginning to make me feel inferior and envious; I can imagine what they are doing to him. I'll do anything I can to help; you know that. The thing is I'm sure he can get an option or an advance on his novel even in the state it's in now. Would that help? You know all my connections and stuff, and you are finally much sharper at knowing who will publish what than I am, so let me know what you think, if I can do

Paidhaiki mou, I can't do anything more about *Behold Goliath*. I can't fight with Epstein anymore. It eats me up and he just doesn't listen. I think he doesn't put me in the ads to keep the book from running over into another edition, more expense, and getting stuck with copies. Obviously if he wanted the book to sell, he has damn good quotes now, which he refuses to use and he has backed out of the ads he promised in the Trib and Commentary; also it would now be an ideal time to run a small ad in the New Yorker. (That woman was sort of irritating, but she mentioned me a lot anyhow.) I've had a new letter from him which says that the book is selling twenty to thirty copies a week, but returns of the same amount are coming in, meaning I suppose the advance sale. I think also Cerf may have been a little disturbed by the reviews; he is very anti-queer. To comfort me, Epstein says Terry Southern's *Magic Christian* sold as badly as *Goliath* and now look where he is. Also, he says now that it's my fault for not being in NY for publication.

I had a letter from Harriet telling me to get in touch with Norman Mailer if I want to be rich, that he would fix me up with his agent [Scott Meredith] so I sent him a note, but have heard nothing. I just thought I'll enclose with this my piece on Tangier, though when I read it now, it seems superficial, untrue and a vision imposed on me by Paul Bowles.

Dris and I had another huge fight yesterday, the worst. We almost started hitting each other. He packed and left. It was mostly my fault because I've been treating him very badly on account of my crisis. Also I've been feeling I hated Morocco so much that if it weren't for him I would get out and go home. After he left, I thought, well, nothing is changed. I'm too old to deceive myself. All my problems were still the same, Dris or no Dris. My book, etc. Also, really, this place is too small. When he wakes up in the morning he wants the radio on and I want to work and there's just a big archway between the main room (where I pretend to work) and the bedroom.

The car has also been a gigantic problem. You were right of course. Six mechanics couldn't find the leak but I finally did. Only now I hate the car so much that I'm selling it to an Arab boy down the street for the same price I paid. If I buy another car, I'll spend more and get a guaranteed one. There's a nice DKW for $600 which the Renault company is selling.

Oh, your package has gone with the seeds and all. I rewrapped it and the post office rejected it again. Then I rewrapped it a third time and it is gone. Thank God. Tell Elia [Braca] the hassock is a present for her performance....Yes, I did feel creepy with the flower. Afterwards, two buds started appearing (I left the thing in a glass of water) so I put it out on the terrace in the sun and it dried up in about a minute, all the big green leaves. I brought it in and it is here on the desk growing drier by the day. Where should I look for a seed? Yes, I don't trust it too much. It is strange....I read the Oswald Diary in España but it doesn't say anything except how boring Russia was and how he wanted to go. What's to make a fuss about that?

For your collection of Moroccania: After Dris left yesterday, I drove out to the beach at Cap Spartel and left the car on a hill. (I didn't want to leave it with the Italians as they follow me out to the beach to try to sell me a share of their bar.) There was another car alongside with two Arabs in shorts with underwater equipment, very evil-looking they were. But there was a guardian down below with some other cars and he said he would look after mine, and started up the hill. I went to the beach but there's a *sherkie* (or whatever it's called, a big wind) on, so it was impossible. I hadn't been away five minutes, and when I got back the Arab car was gone and I saw the trunk of my car open. The spare tire (and wheel) were gone. I raged at the guardian but he said it couldn't have been those men who stole it; they were cops. So I drove off to the grotto of Hercules and brought another cop back and berated both him and the guardian. I said cops were the biggest thieves in the world, that I worked for the Tribune, that this was a fine way to treat tourists when Morocco needed them so badly. They told me the cops who I believed had taken the wheel worked in the Socco Chico and that I should go there. Of course I didn't dare because there's a big kif investigation there and I was afraid to show up. Anyway, I went home not knowing what to do. And about seven o'clock, a knock at the door.

An Arab: Didn't you have something stolen today? It turns out this was one of the two cops. He said he'd seen a boy steal my tire and he chased him (which is why he disappeared) and he caught the boy and got the tire back. A real hero. I pretended to believe him. He was quite scared shitless. He hunted all over Tangier to locate me. End of story.

Another story. On my way back from the beach to Tangier a shepherd boy made a sexual signal at me (as they all do). I usually ignore them; I mean, I always ignore them. But this time I stopped. He was about eight years old, sort of funny-looking and wild. I got terribly hot though and felt like a pervert when a line of big black Bland Line (Cooks Tour) limousines went by. Anyway I took my cock out, but then so did he. He took his little pink thing out and said he wanted to fuck me. Can you imagine? So I laughed and took him for a little drive, then dumped him.

The slave is here, so I'm going out. Lots of love and kisses to you. Alfred

I keep meaning to tell you—or maybe have told you and forgot—that Norman came from Naples on the ship with Edward Albee. Met him on the ship. They talked about me and Albee said I had no right to accuse Rechy of being sentimental (which I never did) when I myself was. He then denied having read anything of mine. He said that my reviews were destructive—typical of young people. When Norman said I was almost as old as Albee, he grabbed his boyfriend away and said lets go have martinis, and didn't talk to Norman again.

I am being hot for little boys.

No sign of Dris.

To Edward Field   July 26, 1964
Dear Heart:

It isn't even seven a.m. and I should be writing my book but my head isn't with it. I have a lot more pages now, including a oneline chapter and a chapter about Richard Burton and Elizabeth Taylor. At the end of it she commits suicide in the bathtub by clutching an electric razor like an asp to her breast. Just before that, he says to her: "Go take your bath. The insides of your thighs are glistening rather vulgarly like jewels." I'm writing a difficult chapter now about Walter. After I decided about artificial connections I felt free not to worry about connections. I was thinking that you are the only person in the world who will like my book, isn't that nice? I keep thinking how everyone will hate it and I feel glad. Oh, in my chapter about the Comet [theater], called the Rocket, I said it smells worse than Pandora's box. Norman suddenly started talking about literary theories the other day, and I said that to judge from my book mine must be that there mustn't be one memorable line in a work. I mean, like wisdom. I just want things to happen.

I bought a new car yesterday. An Austin from, I think, '56 or '57. It was love at first sight. Did I tell you I sold the Dauphine and good riddance? The leak was in the radiator itself, I think, although I hated the sight of it too much then to dismount it and see. I never want a small car again and my instincts were right about those crappy French cars. The Austin is a dream, though it's older than the Dauphine. It is passport blue with sky-blue leather inside, real leather. The original upholstery barely worn. The outside is also the original paint job and the car has obviously been loved. We drove straight out to Arcila and it was like driving a Rolls or a truck. Dris said it made his asshole open to see how happy I was. (His image for happiness is always that the asshole opens.) It cost $500. Mr. Caneday tested it and approved glowingly, though he says that after 30,000 kilometers I would have to have the motor rebored which is why it was cheap. It's done 77,000 kilometers. I have to rebuild my personality around the car now; it was like suddenly becoming a person who travels first class on a liner. But even before I got your letter I had decided that very thing: I don't have to suffer anymore. It's very strange suddenly seeing that.

Oh, I heard from Norman Mailer who says Scott Meredith will get in touch with me and make a lot of money for me. He says also that Epstein never sent him galleys for a quote. Isn't that too much? Burroughs quote is: "Alfred Chester writes like white lightning." There is more to it, but that's enough. May Swenson's quote is long but begins: "Alfred Chester is an American Genet. He writes with satanic brilliance." Later she says: "It must have been even more terrifying to write these stories than it is to read them."

Listen, lovey, the blanket and thing should be arriving soon. Be careful when opening the blanket. It is stitched closed and the seeds are stuck into the folds. You should feel around in each fold for the seeds before opening. About six I think. I hope Interpol isn't going to arrest us.

Edward I keep reading these horrible things in the papers about riots in NY. Is it true? Also, it occured to me the other day when I was high that Goldwater might actually win. I mean, there is something in me that finds him appealing, his novelty and the excitement around him. He could be elected just because things would be more interesting if he was.

Yes, I'll send you some photos soon. Wednesday is circumcision day and Dris is borrowing a camera for the festivities in Arcila. He is carrying three children to be cut. I hope after that we can take our camping trip and go to Fez. Arcila is filled with tourists. Dris says, and he is probably right, we should spend a hundred dollars buying things in Fez and put them on sale in Arcila where there is no bazaar at three times the price....My in-laws were snowed by the car. They weren't impressed by the Dauphine. Norman (who came with us yesterday) and I stopped and had lunch at the family pinchito stall while D. ran around to see his friends. Abdeslam (pronounced like you would say Absolom by everyone in Morocco except Paul Bowles) was tending the stall; he loves me; he is D.'s little brother about fifteen or fourteen, though he thinks he's eighteen. Suddenly he brought three vials of penicillin to the table and said that five faggots (Englishmen) came to Arcila last month and he fucked one of them and got the clap and D. told him what to take. I was horrified. Really, all my middleclassness rose in a rage; I felt like my little sister had been raped by some smart city slicker. So I shouted at Abdeslam, *mandekshi hashuma*, aren't you ashamed, and he said he wouldn't do it again. Then Dris appeared and I yelled at him for being so casual and modern about the whole thing, but it was the first he had heard about it and then he started beating up Abdeslam. And then it turned out the vials belonged to the boy in the shop next door and Abdeslam had made the story up to impress me. Norman was reduced to his hysterical queen number and shrieked: Oh, I hate them all, I hate them. Of course, I'm such a hypocrite. While D was away (he came back after three days complaining that it was my place to go after him when he left, not wait for him to come back; but we've been lovey ever since), I fucked a boy who Norman said was twelve. Norman has been fucking him ever since. Norman by himself, like Paul, never finds boys who like to hug and kiss and fondle. Or if he does, like Paul, he turns them into the kind who don't. Oh, I told Dris about the boy and he was angry and said we should do those things together. Like you said.

Later. We just washed the car and I gave Dris a driving lesson which I never would do with the Dauphine because it all looked like plastic and I thought it would snap. (His last driving lesson, two years ago, he told me he stripped the gears on a Jaguar.) He is difficult to teach because he immediately gets into the posture of an experienced driver and starts dreaming and goes into any old gear and turns the wheel any old way. All of which he does acting like he's casually doing one hundred on a super highway....He is going on trial on Thursday for knocking a boy down on his motor in Msallah, an Arab quarter here. The other victim, the woman, has been postponed for awhile.

Monday. I have a splitting headache. *Paidhaiki*, you won't believe this, it is too grotesque, but the Austin sprung a leak in the water system yesterday, a great big one that I could locate. It's in the connection between the radiator and the pipe that brings the water back from the engine to the radiator. I'm not too upset about it because I could spot it. Except now I have to do something about it. Do you think this can just be a coincidence?

Later. I went to the Inimex garage, the Austin outlet where I bought the car, and guess what, they put a new tube in for nothing. What do you think of that?

Later still. Everytime my piddlings start getting realistic like in the present chapter or in the story about Ismael and Tommy I get a little bored. The psychology starts making me tired. I like the fairy tale and silly parts and poparty parts best. But you are so smart; it has taken me thirty-six years to relax.

We're going to drive out now to a river on the Arcila road to go fishing and swimming.

Evening. Dris caught a lot of fish including a big fancy yellow one that made a burping sound as it suffered. It isn't a river really but a basin with tides like a gigantic salt water lake with water like the Aegean. It was the best swimming since Greece and the car was divine again....Speaking of Greece I found now a letter mailed in Piraeus from my girlfriend on the ship who thinks she is coming to visit me. She's also going to visit you, she says. I hope she has better luck with you than with me, because I'm going to be in Fez.

xxxxxxxx and love to both of you. Alfred

To Edward Field   August (?), 1964—Sidi Bujari 28, Tangier

Qelbi:

I have diarrhea today. I've been sick on and off since the trip to Fez. But I've been feeling better lately. I had a letter from Kluger yesterday that depressed me terribly; the spies told him that my book has sold 1090 copies. It made me practically cry I felt so unhappy about it.

A letter from Paul came the other day full of the usual kif subtext and I've answered it in kind.

Among my more recent chapters is one in which Major General Finn and his wife got to dinner at Mr. and Mrs. Thos. Ferguson Sawyer's. They are planning a war of liberation. Other chapters include the following (complete)

M

No, Maybe it was N

M or N. Nothing else.

Or perhaps Nothing else.

That's why I call it piddling.

I will be thirty-six next month.

I went out to Cap Spartel alone yesterday and had a fine alone time at the fine alone beach. And I saw *Andi Kbira* (I have a big one). He followed me down the road once wailing: *Ya, nisrani* (Nazarine), *aji, aji,* (come) I have a big one. (Indeed, he has this gigantic basket.) He's a ragged shepherd about eighteen and so handsome that I don't know how it is he's not being kept on the Mountain by a rich Englishman. Too rough looking, I guess. So sexy. He wears a big straw country hat and Arab clothes with blue jeans, very dark. Anyway he was with a friend so I didn't stop. About twelve-year-old assholes, well, you know how it is here. They start having sex very young. The six-year-old fucks the four-year-old for ten francs, the eight-year-old the sixyearold for twenty, etc. Anyway their nervous system is different. And everything is sexy to them. Dris sticks his finger in Columbine's cunt and gets a hardon. Once he started kissing me when I was reading Time and he was sort of kissing me all over and even kissing Time out of his exultation. Moslems never remember when they were virgins. I seem to have strayed from the point. Anyway, there are lots of men who like very young boys, little boys, so that's how they get stretched.

D's brother Hamid has gone to some holy place to water his foot. But I'll take him to the doctor when he comes back, Mr. Caneday says it is surely leprosy. But I thought there were new ways of arresting it. I must do something about it if anything can be done because it's horrible.

Yes, I more or less speak Arabic.

Do you know what my change really is? I never minded being me, but I always thought others minded, so I pretended not to be me. And then everytime I confronted me I felt bad and suffered. Now I refuse to be an object. I mean like if someone tries to insult me I think what's wrong with him that he thinks there's something wrong with me? And then I don't suffer. If this interests you we can go into it more fully another time. It really doesn't interest me too much.

Lots of love and kisses,

Alfred

To Edward Field   August 6, 1964

Lovely:

I heard from Scott Meredith, Norman Mailer's agent, and have now written him to get busy. I told him to phone you if he wanted to know anything about how Random dealt with *Goliath*. O.K.? I don't think Rosset would publish my Tangier piece [in Evergreen Review], but you can show it to him. If he wants to use it, tell him I want to change some of it.

We went to Fez. Trip only lasted five days because of the heat. It practically turned into a pilgrimage to watering holes, rivers, etc. I've never known such intense heat in my life. The evening we got to Fez it was 45 degrees centigrade. (37.5 is 98.6 fahrenheit.) And when we were out in the plains during the afternoon I will bet you it was over 120 F. We literally were gasping air in the shade by a river. That afternoon the car started boiling every ten kilometers but stayed at normal when we got to Fez, so you can imagine how much hotter it was. We took a lot of photos and will send them when they're developed. Also we quarrelled the whole time, not being able to agree on stopping, starting, speed, direction, dogs or anything. Columbine killed a farmer's chicken the minute we started camping out near Ceuta on the Mediterranean, and Skoura kept getting lost as she is really quite crazy now and doesn't know who or what or where. I was mad about Chauen; it is stunning.I saw Fez only at dawn because it was too hot to hang around and I was quite dazed by the heat. Thank God all these Moroccan cities are built around sources of water. *Ras el ma,* they're called, meaning head of water—*rosh ha'mayim* in Hebrew. (Dris says I have ten tongues: Nine from the countries I've been to and his). The one near Fez is a dream with eucalyptus and a freezing natural pool. Once you get about a hundred kilometers to the south of Tangier, it really becomes Africa here with mud and dung villages. Do you know, I didn't feel the least bit sad for those people; I thought how much better off they were than people in New York or Paris. Outside of Fez we went to Moullay Yacoub which is a holy watering place. You go through about ten kilometers of the most extraordinary hills. Yellow, barren, crumpled, cracked into pieces from extremes of heat and cold. Like the moon. But the place has been turned into a tourist trap. Dris was shocked because his father had gone last year and it was still just a street and a mosque with a few houses. Now it was jammed with hotels and two elegant bathing establishments, one for Moslems and the other for Europeans (Nazarenes). 250 francs for a second-quality bath in holy water. Prices ranging on up to 4000 francs....The nicest part of the trip was just hanging around rivers and streams and looking at the naked boys. At Sidi Kacem we sat in a quicksand river, under a bridge. A worm got into Dris' cock but he managed to pull it out. There were about a dozen boys sitting in that shallow river up to their chins. They sit there for hours every day during the most intense heat. It is like a warm bath and your head boils in the hot wind. The last night we camped in a thatched hut near Larache. It turned out the cop there had known Dris as a little boy so he lent us the hut. It was like my fantasy, but I hated it finally because of the mosquitos. Wherever we went Dris was also whipping up stews and paellas and being very serious about meals. We took all the blankets and sheepskins and in about three seconds he would create a little Arab home....We went to Meknes but it was too hot to stop. The next trip will have to be when it's cooler, and also I'll leave the dogs with Larbi or someone like when we went to Marrakech....Anyhow it's good to be back, though I wish I had a bigger place.

Dris fired the slave because five of our pretty tea glasses had disappeared, so I've been Alfreda the maid ever since. I don't mind it. In fact, I quite enjoy it, washing the floors and doing the laundry. It keeps me busy. But I think we're getting a new one tomorrow.... Norman said yesterday (he is only 26, so very concerned with family and Them, the others): We actually live the lives they dream about. He meant sex mainly; he says they are all obsessed with sex but don't dare admit it....Yes, kif makes one crazy. I'm giving it up for a time, mainly because it is affecting me muddily. When I get high I have a whole muddy day the next day. It doesn't sharpen my mind except during the high, and then I start getting intellectual....A little American named Charles Wright faggot came by leaving a message that Candida was his agent and sends me much love. Norman went to the door and I told him to send him away. When Charles Wight said: Candida loves him very much, Norman said: Those are the people we trust least.... Would you do me a favor? Call up Jean Ennis at Random House and ask her what happened to my lecture tour? I think even that was just a big lie....I told Scott Meredith to try to get my porno published and a book of my nonfiction, paperback rights and European rights and everything. Potentially, I'm sitting on a fortune...When I think about my piddlings being published, I think how irrelevant anyone's reaction to them would be. It makes me feel good.

I just figured out that 45 degrees centigrade equals 118 degrees Fahrenheit, which it was in Fez, so it was probably closer to 130 in the plains where the water kept boiling....The car was divine except for that afternoon.

Friday.I wrote a bunch of con letters for Norman a couple of weeks ago, and the first one came through yesterday with a check for $750. So we went and celebrated up in some stunning little Arab teahouse in the Marshan which we recently discovered. Afterwards we went and had martinis at the Fat Black Pussy Cat and it gave me cramps because I remembered sitting there waiting for you to land when I was crazy. Also, because it was just like America with blondes and niggers all over the place. Charles Wright was there and I fell in love with him. I don't know if I would have if I hadn't been drunk. (It was glorious getting drunk again instead of stoned.) Only he was so pure, innocent the way

Americans are—not sitting there like everyone else in this country thinking what you are thinking and trying to destroy. He wrote that book called *The Messenger*; I remembered seeing the ads, you know he wrapped everything up in one package—nigger, junk and faggotry, the whole lot. It sold a lot of copies and he earned $7000, he said. So then I took them both home and I think I got a bit bored with him, but I'm not sure.

I heard from Kluger yesterday who is so anxious now for me to go on with my column that he offers me 150 a time. So I've agreed. He says that girl who wrote the thing in the New Yorker is bitter because she wishes she could be in the New York Review crowd and can't make it. Can you imagine? I really got away just in time.

Saturday. The Hamacha, Dris's father's cult, put on their annual saints' day song-and-dance in the big square of the medina in Arcila yesterday. We went. It was pretty good, though no boiling water drinkers like last year. And I wasn't convinced by all the trances. One older man did marvelous kabuki sort of dances and I think there were moments when he went off and started howling and barking for real. Exorcism. The music was good though. D.'s father who is about eighty went home early as he doesn't like the public rites, and I think he's right. The government is trying to get rid of the whole thing as it is pre-Islamic and like the jungle. It frightened me a little when they take the children and start throwing them around. They break their heads open with axes (not the kids, their own) and stones, but D. says they heal in the mosque overnight. Afterwards we went and had tea with his family. I have got to do something about the brother with the foot. His whole toe is gone now and the foot is black in spots. I think it must be leprosy.

On the way back from Arcila there was a gigantic fire. It lit up the whole night. A farm. Two mountains of wheat, stacks. And it was spreading. Two little fire engines came, but there was no water for miles around and they had to go refill at pumps far away. None of the engines came from Tangier. It was midnight. The Time correspondent was there. Dris recognized him from when he was hanging around the house.

I think I'll stop this letter now. My piddlings aren't getting anywhere But I won't abandon them. What else would I have?

XXXXXXX and love. Alfred

To Paul Bowles   Monte Viejo 288, Tangier   August 14, 1964

Dear Paul:

Surprised to find your letter, and delighted, naturally. One hears such stories in Tangier!

Yes, the last few months have been very pleasant for me too, perhaps the most relaxed since I came to Morocco. Martin Tucker is here for the week and Dennis Selby will be coming next month.

Oddly enough, I was just thinking about you because I'd come across a postcard you'd sent me from Essaouira. Ages ago, of course. In any case, my address is 28 Sidi Bujari.

Ah yes, I think I do remember being shown your house by some rather terrifying-looking agent. I thought it best not to deal with him. People warned me he was a bit loco with kif. Ah, Tangier!

I'd heard that Norman was staying with you, but of course I never dreamed it was true. Glad you find him improved.

Anxious to get together,

Alfred

To Edward Field   September 11, 1964—Sidi Bujari 28, Tangier

Habibi:

I just put the car into the driveway and there, lurking in a navy blue overcoat in a sort of angle of Miss Muriel Mitchell-Henry's green lattice fence, was a man with the most horrible face I ever saw. It looked like it had all been burnt but only it didn't look burnt. It was all gone really except for one eye, but the ears were perfect and his hair was thick . He had delicate white hands. I thought he must be Spanish but he talked Arabic. He was begging. I brought down my black cowdens and 200 francs. It was especially strange because in my novel, Ismael smashes up his Jaguar (I think Tommy maybe fiddles with the wires, but I'm not sure as I haven't written that part yet) and his head bursts into flame. He ends up looking like a toasted marshmallow. Except for his bright green eyes. It happens because of Tommy's operation which makes his face twisted, and Ismael gets cool and Tommy finally gives him all his money and runs away. (There are about six characters called Tom or Tommy or TomTom. This Tommy was an advertising queen who dressed in black leather and rode a motorcycle in his spare time.) So Ismael buys a Jaguar convertible but then falls in love with Tommy. You know, the withdrawal syndrome, as Harriet calls it. Well, Tommy often sleeps away the days at the Rocket (Comet) [theater] because he is a bum, and one day he wakes up and finds Ismael stroking him and loving him. He runs away. But what he does is he gets John Anthony Devine to make him a masque like his old face. And he goes courting Ismael, but Ismael won't have him because he says that isn't Tommy's face. And either Ismael drives away and crashes or Tommy fixes the wires. It goes on and on after that and gets more elaborate about masques, etc. Sometimes, Ismael goes out with his toasted marshmellow head to torture people. So when I saw the man downstairs, although I felt terrible at first, I thought maybe inside he is whole and sound, like being inside a robot. Like last year in Arcila when I used to see Paul's emaciated parched chest. I thought he was exposing it out of a kind of spite and laughing inside the whole time, saying to himself of him: "He thinks it's me."

I didn't mean to say all that. It just slipped out. I'm sick. I've been sick on and off ever since Fez. But then last week on the beach I thought I was going to die, everything started swimming. And it continued. It became so bad I couldn't turn my head without the whole ship rocking. Nausea and general debilitation. I've seen two doctors, a Spaniard and an Englishman, and both agree it is liver. Probably from too much kif and too much oily food (Dris's tajines). I'm on a strict diet now and pills and feel better, or somewhat better. I miss the kif and so does my book. But the thing scared me terribly....Does Susan have a TV show? How can that be? I had a letter from Helen DeMott recently and she said something about the Susan Sontag story on TV, but I thought it was some kind of joke. It is depressing that all my friends are famous and I am not. I heard that Peter Everett sold his novel to the movies for lots of money.

The "Bride of Frankenstein" is very good. I think actually it's the best of the movie poems. The ending though is horrifying and very unlike you. What do you mean by it? Could I make a suggestion? Could the line reading "and the equipment really goes crazy" be changed To "and the equipment goes stark raving mad"? It makes the next line much more powerful and funny.

Lately I've been occasionally feeling that my novel is a masterpiece. I've brought Extro into it now. Zavier. I was hoping to have the rough done by the end of this month, but this past week has thrown my calculations out. You must give me a title that will sell. Probably no one will want to publish it. And I've gone past the stage of just being grateful to God for giving me a book to write and am feeling ambitious again. The early parts seem like shit now, but I'm afraid if I start with trying to fix it up I'll fall into some endless trap. I have about a hundred pages I guess. Anyway, I know exactly what has to happen. Mary PoorPoor and TomTom Jim forget they are looking for fairyland and all they know is that they are looking and they keep having more children but Baby never grows up. The other Mary PoorPoor (she is two separate characters) keeps getting thrown out by Emily who keeps discovering that Baby PoorPoor is a changeling, a kind of vampire. But they keep meeting again and failing to recognize each other and remarrying. And James Madison (Baby PoorPoor) and John Doe (Tom Sawyer) just go on with their dreary fantasies. There is lots more, of course, since the chapters are only about two pages each. I'm trying very hard for it not to meet anything and to keep the chapters from ending on a climax.

Saturday a.m. I'm feeling rather shitty this morning, floaty, dizzy and weak, and my piss was rather red. It's hard for me to concentrate. Actually my piss may be dark from all that liver I ate yesterday. A pound of it, because Dris went to Arcila, so that was all I ate, and beets....Oh, I understand now about the ending of your poem. I think I wish you wouldn't keep using that word equipment; it is so vague. Couldn't you say bottles or some thing?....Did you see the Tangier photos in Esquire? Charles brought them over....My birthday was last Monday, Labor Day, and I think the Jewish New Year too. Norman and Charles came and they drank a lot and Dris did too, but of course I couldn't. The odd thing with this sickness is that I feel better as the day progresses. I can't really clear until about noon....I know just how Neil feels about New York. I feel the same way. I miss it terribly, though only in a kind of fantasy way. I wasn't thinking of wearing a wig when I went back. Should I? I suppose I look sort of ridiculous without one. The photos from the trip came out lousy....The day before I got sick I finally had an encounter with Paul. Here. I invited Charles to act as a buffer. It was all subtext, innuendo, sort of horrible. I smoked pipe after pipe of kif, even after he'd gone. And the next day on the beach alone the sickness began in the middle of a cigarette. While I was high I went crazy again just the way I had last winter only less severe. I started imagining that Paul had invented the mountains and the sky and the sand and the ocean. Or that I was imagining it all through a kind of hypnotism....My new agent is really a washout. He writes me that he talked to Epstein and swallowed all Epstein's lies. I've written him now to get cracking with paperback and foreign rights, but I think I will be firing him soon....Oh, I've quit the Tribune. I was planning to do my column the day I got sick. But anyway I'm not that person anymore. I can't be smart and elegant and witty. And bitchy. It makes me want to cry and to vomit....It's funny, Charles told me this past week that Adlai Stevenson was queer. I'd never heard it before. How can he get away with it? Beating little boys and all? Don't they tell? I am all confused about Bobby Kennedy. I was all for him but I can't stand him running for the Senate from New York. It seems so cold blooded. I mean he doesn't have any justification for trying to throw Keating out....My head is clearing, so maybe I can work now. God, how much I long to see you.

Sunday. Dear Diary. My piss cleared up as the day progressed and today it seems all right. God be praised. I hate being sick....What I meant about that man with the horrible face at the beginning and Ismael and Paul is that the man acted as if he were consious of how loathesome he was, he crouched and cringed. But perhaps he—oh skip it....I wrote a four page chapter about piss yesterday. Actually it is based on something in *I, Etc.* Do you know this book is among other things *I, Etc.*?...Norman is married to Hajmi again. I insisted he get married because he gets so dependent on me, so he married a whore from the Socco Chico, but it only lasted a couple of days. After which he wired H. to come from Arcila. But H. has changed and wants to go to queer bars at night, etc. So N. is having trouble, but he is much better and easier for me to be with....We're going to Arcila today with Charles. I'm thinking of renting the consul's house, where Paul was last summer, for $40 a month and letting Charles have this apartment for a few months. I need a change. This place is really too small with dogs, slaves and Drises everywhere, and Alfreds. N. and I went to the medina looking for the perfume shop last night but couldn't find it. I hadn't been in the medina easily for six months and it was terribly exciting....Marty Tucker went to see all the celebrities before he left, I mean Paul and Bill Burroughs. He got up some pretext as I refused to introduce him. He is like Uriah Heep. The last night he was here Dris and I boiled pot after pot of tea full of kif trying to get him high but it didn't work. He even managed to meet Charles at the end, though that was my fault. I think he is the most loathesome person I have ever known. I insulted him thoroughly, told him to get rid of his cuntlike giggle, etc. He blamed my health. I had a letter from him the other day thanking me for my hospitality and being glad that we had talked like old friends. Is he joking? Now he is yours again. Hurrah!

Norman said to me last night, how does it feel to be the most popular man in Tangier? And it is really true, everyone loves me, I mean all the Arabs. It is very exhausting....Ted Woodham, the Englishman in Arcila, has broken up with his boy and he is shutting his houses and his fishing boat and going to England. I can hardly believe it....I was looking at myself in the mirror and imagining how I would frighten people to death on the TV. Doesn't Susan realize that she has got to be a little stingy with herself if the world is to set a value on her? People will get bored with her. I think she will probably marry a movie star or a celebrity next and maybe become a movie star herself, although her legs are a problem. In that last letter of hers she said that only her son had prevented her from suicide this past year. What balls. All she cares about is glory.

Norman has discovered they sell Eubispasme here at the drug stores. They are pills made of opium and morphine and simply scrumptuous. Burroughs says they are the only things that cure virus. I had just one last night and felt like I was in a warm pool.

Monday. I'm supposed to see the doctor now, so I'll end this. I'm feeling lousy again today. I think the kif has done something to my brain as well as my liver. I hope I will heal....When we came back from Arcila yesterday the water was running out of the car again. Right out of the motor this time and rapidly. Somehow it doesn't bother me. I've been using the car less and walking more lately. But I'll have to get it fixed. It must be cracked or something. Charles is always giving me lectures on my career. He says I am not enough of a politician. When I told him that it seemed from your letter that Susan had a TV show he said I should write to her. So I've taken his advice and written her a sort of friendly letter (with a slightly guilt-aimed subtext) not mentioning anything about TV or such and not asking for anything. It is awfully sour having to humble myself to her. I think I've always been too proud to use people, but I think in the end it is always done in one way or another. And I've got to learn how. Charles says success is just over the hill for me, all I have to do is work. I want so much to be famous now.

Later. At the doctor's I met the two dykes from upstairs and it turns out one of them has the same thing I do. It also turns out a vast number of people here now have the same thing. The idiotic doctor is too idiotic to realize it is probably a virus epidemic. It occurred to me to tell him how I'd been sick on and off since Fez and he then decided I had subictharyl hepatitis, a mild form without yellowing. And that I'd probably be better in a week or so. What a schmuck. I doubt there's a decent doctor in this country. Or probably in the world. He also said my piss probably turned color from the beets, but if it happened again I should come back immediately for tests. Oh, he's now decided there is a connection between the weather, the east wind and the liver.

I kiss you both. Love, Alfred

To Edward Field   Saturday,September 29, 1964
                                                     —Sidi Bujari 28, Tangier

Paidhi mou:

How do you like *Exquisite Corpses* as a title to my book? Or maybe *The Exquisite Corpse*? It isn't sexy but there's something nice. It's from that game where everyone draws another part of the body. Remy [Charlip] is here and we did it last night with Dris and Norman, very kifed, and they are gorgeous. I want to use one on my book jacket too. It's a robot's head with a childlike torso, a pile of sort of dead cocks at the groin (I drew that) and a kind of spiral whirlwind for feet. My other contributions were a torso with arms chopped off, two heads, Siamese twins, a skeleton for the pelvic area, a mandog being fucked, and a pair of feet torn from the legs with a hill and a crucifix on it and the inscription "Goodbye World." It makes me think I must be very sick. Am I?

I avoided Remy for the first couple of days but he hunted me out and then finally I was glad. He bought a painting from Dris for 1000 francs and is giving it to you and I told him he'd better say it was from both of us. Dris gave him another one free. D. is suddenly painting again, thanks to Chas. encouraging him and bringing him a fancy box of watercolors from Gib. The latest ones are simply gorgeous, sort of surreal and full of colors....Remy is traveling with Jayjay Mitchell, who spends all his time with the beach whores getting fucked. I think Remy is somewhat disapproving but I think it's nice. Norman and Remy have hit it off and Norman is being simply impossible showing off and being clever, so he makes me sick. Diana Athill says my liver condition is a result of 95% from my sense of failure and 5% as punishment for changing from Candida to Scott Meredith. She says SM will never do anything for me because he only cares about vast film and serial deals. I'd already written Norman Mailer again asking him please to ask Meredith what he is doing because he doesn't seem the slightest bit interested in me....I let Remy read one chapter (1-1/2 pages) the other night because he asked to. (He wanted to see how thick the book was so he could tell you. He adores you.) And he made no comment, but I'm sure he hated it. It's just the scene where Ismael wakes up in the hospital with his head like a toasted marshmellow and he screams for the mirror. The book is getting much more cohesive, at least in my mind. The secret of writing the novel is just to keep doing it; it becomes convincing just by the sheer weight of its presence, the quantity.

Remy says I look much better without the wig, but what else could he say?...Grove sent me proofs of Hubert Selby's book [*Last Exit to Brooklyn*] for a quote. They are planning a big push. I wrote that he is one of the most extraordinary writers alive and a lot of other superlatives. I believe it too. He is very good. But it is part of my campaign to become famous.

Your letter depressed me horribly. I mean about the conversation with Jean Ennis and then WBAI losing my tape. It just seemed like everything was working against me. And when you told me nice things about *Goliath* I don't believe you anyway; I think you are just throwing me a sop. Don't bother trying to convince me, lovie, it won't work.... Oh, I think I've been depressed partly because of being sick (which was sapping my vitality), partly because of Chas. Wright (who throws me into the idea of Big Time and I feel like a failure). And partly because of not smoking kif. I mean my book is really in a way a kif fantasy, even though it is all my old and own ideas. So without kif it seemed meaningless and I felt like a failure. But oddly enough the day of the evening that I went back on kif I broke through it and wrote two chapters and found that I believed in the book without kif too. When I rewrite it and put it into shape though, I think I will stay off the stuff altogether.

Sunday. I wish Remy would go. This is the third time this summer I've been stuck entertaining. He's having such a good time now that he cancelled his Fez trip and let JayJay go alone and will meet him one of these days in Marrakech. Meanwhile I am entertaining him because there isn't anything to do in Tangier, of course. Though Norman took him to the baths yesterday and they ordered boys. I was a little shocked. I'm supposed to drive him to Arcila at noon, but I think I'll have to conk out. I also get to bed late and I can't work in the morning because I've been so social....I've become a pill maniac suddenly. Every morning I take two liver pills, an amphetamine, a B complex, a one-a-day vitamin....Oh, I woke up this a.m. dreaming about you. I dreamt you were hot for a man who made fireworks. And I was jealous but pretended that I didn't understand why you liked the fireworks, not why you liked the man....I love more and more the title *The Exquisite Corpse*. Don't tell it to anyone.

Monday. Remy is going today. He'll give you some information on rugs, I got him a beautiful secondhand blanket rug for $11, enormous. Do you want thick matting or whatever it's called? The price of new rugs is incredibly high. He also bought three djellabas and a stunning blanket. I got the whole thing for $37. But I nearly collapsed, I mean I did collapse of exhaustion about eight in the evening and am still not recovered....The first gigantic rain fell last night so perhaps summer is over. Though today is sunny. D and I went to the beach but couldn't stay. I was thinking I am very unhappy with my book, that it is flat, boring, pointless, no good and yet somehow it's the first honest thing I've ever written. Maybe it is like that poem of yours that you sent to everyone years ago. If it has a moral it is that the extraordinary is just as dull as the ordinary. All the fairies, freaks, murderers, transvestites are bores and bored. The other moral is that nothing is inevitable; everything is gratuitous even the inevitable....I told Remy about my old Pinocchio idea and now I'm dying to write it. Is it true that Irene [Fornes] is a success? Am I the only failure left?

If you are all alone I kiss you twice as much as usual. xxx love xxx Alfred

Tuesday. Larbi has been begging me for a year to get him the address of the Whitney Foundation. Paul simply refuses to help him do anything. Could you please get it and the forms if possible....Last night, when I was kifed, I had a revelation about promoting ourselves. You must keep it absolutely secret. We're going to invent a movement called DURATIONS. I'm already figuring out the principles behind it and am inventing a couple of other writers, including a man who invented DURATIONS. You can mention them when you go on your reading tour. In fact you should refer to certain of your poems as DURATIONS. Never mind which, the principle comes later. Then we have to run a personal ad in the Voice for about six months with the one word DURATIONS. Then print up postcards with just that word and send them to editors, book buyers, reviewers, smart people, etc. Say 1000 postcards every month or couple of weeks for a few weeks. Then gradually start publishing things. What do you think? Your *Sex Stories* can be DURATIONS and my novel of course is. Please advise by return.

I had a letter from Scott Meredith and we are back at the beginning. I wrote Norman [Mailer] to get him cracking, but I'm beginning to despair of his ever really doing anything.

To Edward Field   October 4, 1964—Sidi Bujari 28, Tangier
Dear Edward:
I have only two more short scenes to write, and then I will have the first draft. Will you believe it? Of course most of it is a mess and

exists more in my mind than on paper. But like the lady says, the work is finishing itself. And you're right, I'm a great writer. I think the book isn't gratuitous at all, but I'm not paying attention to that side of it. As far as I'm concerned it's irrelevant nonsense. But somehow gorgeous and wonderful. I love it. The end is so stupendous and ridiculous. It's only about 130 pages or so (I've not paged because of the way it's written) but will probably end up closer to 200 than 150. Some scenes repeat themselves. Also, half a dozen scenes have yet to be written. I hope I can put it into shape real fast and then I'll come back to New York, at least for a few months, and you can tell me what to do about it. I am really exultant, but scared, like I violated the law of my own failure. I feel like I'll be struck dead. You're very smart to notice that I'm fooling around with going crazy again. I will do my best not to. Like the last time, I've lost all sexual desire and it is bothering Dris. Oh, he is painting like a demon. And you can't imagine how good he's getting. I'll send you one. He has now sold three, to Norman, Remy and now Charles. Charles says he will buy two more as presents when he goes to New York. Charles is completely mad, completely, and scares me. Last night I thought he was going to start a fight with me and Norman. And earlier in the week when I was alone with him I thought he was going to kill me. He started reenacting a scene with a hustler and he got carried away and quite violent.

No, Evergreen mustn't publish my piece as it stands. Please. [Barney] Rosset is in Morocco, according to Paul. I saw a couple of new Evergreens at Paul's and really I hated them, they were like trade magazines. I ran into Paul and he dragged me up the Mountain to his house. Larbi fed me majhoun and I got terribly depressed with the records, tape recorders, books, magazines, culture. You know: Iamafailure set in. And the whole horrible subtext conversation....I can't bear "Pilgrim Soul." I really can't bear anything I've written until now. I feel like changing my name. Just after I was crazy, but when I was still a little crazy, I started a diary and wrote just one entry. It said: I am new. It made me very sad and depressed and I wasn't sure it was true, but I suspected it was.

Monday. Well, I've done it. I've done the last two scenes, though very sketchily because I got up this morning so nervous and thinking I would have a gigantic block. So I just raced through the two chapters, putting them down. It needs a great deal of work, especially the first (piddling) half of it. But I think I will be true to myself for once and show the way it really did grow from a sort of nothing to a gorgeous nothing. Anyhow, I want to go away now for a couple of weeks, to the Sahara, but probably won't be able to leave just yet. It is conceivable that I could have the next draft ready by the end of the year.

I had a letter from Epstein: "I had hoped that Jean Ennis would be able to work up a lecture tour, and I'm sorry to hear that she has been unsuccessful; an outcome which I'm sure will lower your opinion of Random House still further." I've written back asking him to add a paragraph stipulating promotion in the contract to reassure me of his honorable intentions; I said that I had the feeling he wanted nothing more than for me to break the contract. I also asked what he'd done about paperback. Nothing, I'm sure....If you think I should wear a wig, you'll have to order it for me because it takes a month or so....I've given up the codeine and eubyspasme (opium) now because I feel good. Now I'm down to vitamin pills and amphetamine. Don't worry I'm not going to get hooked on anything. Are you still taking peyote?...I don't think [Jean] Garrigue is ridiculous at all. She is probably right in what she says about Lowell. He has always been her Achilles heel because he is her "junior" as she puts it. Of course, he has already had all the prizes except the Nobel anyway. What is Jean like now, poor old wretch?

I just this minute got a letter from Holt asking me for $1150. Candida once gave them $350 off some advance or other. And I'm going to write them and ask for it back since it was they who breached the contract.

Could you please send me a copy of *The Warren Report*? I understand there is a paperback for $1. Time's summary doesn't convince me, though there are lots more eyewitnesses than there used to be. And now the RR overpass is guarded on November 22. It wasn't last March.

They also don't explain why officer Tippett was miles off his beat, why Ruby was standing opposite the assassin's window and how he knew to arrive at exactly the right time to kill Oswald, one hour later than the expected time of Oswald's exit from prison. They also seem to have changed the story of the 90 seconds between the shots on the sixth floor and finding Oswald in the lunchroom on the second floor drinking a coke out of the machine. They now say he was outside the lunchroom. But I don't think it was the Rightists at all, and I think finding Hunt's book in Ruby's pocket is the same kind of crude criminality operating behind the whole thing. I bet you Johnson was behind it. It was a coup d'état. I hate, hate, hate, hate Bobby Kennedy. How could he say he accepts the Warren findings? Well, maybe he is just becoming a politician.

I bought a pair of stunning lorgnettes at the flea market in an embroidered pouch with velvet (purple) flowers. Round lenses and marvelous tortoise shell stem. I'm going to put my own lenses in and be even weirder than weird.

Lots of love and kisses to both my darlings, Alfred

To Edward Field   October 7, 1964—Sidi Bujari 28, Tangier
Me agin.

I'm feeling nervous and even a little hysterical about my novel. I don't dare look at it. Like I've been fooling myself the whole time and now I'm faced with making it into a book.

Please send me the list of colleges you wrote to, a copy of your curriculum vitae and your covering letter. I think I will write and ask for engagements March and April. Or is it too late?

Burroughs is going on a tour and getting $500 a time.

Wednesday. I had a letter from [Evergreen Review editor] Fred Jordan last night saying they want to use the piece ["Glory Hole, Nickel Views of the Infidel in Tangier"]. First I got all shattered. Then

I got high and thought, oh how nice. I started feeling famous and paidattentiontoagain. He says they want to run it with illustrations or photos and asks for names. I suggested Remy as I can't think of anyone else. Though I said if he wanted to run primitive mosques and medinas I'll send him Dris's latest. They'd look gorgeous. I also said I wanted to make some changes in the piece, but now I'm feeling maybe I shouldn't. I'll see. I will have to get out of Morocco before the piece appears, you know. I hope Paul has a stroke when he reads it.

The Tangier piece is too exalted. It embarrasses me.

I was thinking that maybe I should ask Evergreen to run a full page ad of *Goliath* along with the piece rather than pay me. Wouldn't that make Epstein shit? Can you find out how much a page ad is, so I could figure out if I'm winning or losing. And how much do they pay? It used to be $5 a page, but now the pages are bigger. I really feel alive again. I need a public, I really do. I'm a performer, I guess.

What should I do about [Scott] Meredith? He doesn't do a thing except write me notes saying he will write me notes. Yesterday: "At the moment I only want to reassure you that everyone of the aspects, both foreign and domestic, are being handled actively. Some of them, especially the foreign, require extensive checking and followups, but we expect to straighten this out soon." This sounds to me like big-time double talk. Checking and follow-ups, what bullshit!

I was thinking last night how you got me published the first time in Europe and how now you have done the same thing again for the new me. So since you run my career, you better figure out what I should do with my novel. Should I ask Grove to publish it? (It isn't very sexy, just very disgusting.) Would they promote it? Would Rosset do that to Epstein?

Thank you, *qelbi*, for restoring me a little to celebrity. A million kisses. Alfred

To Edward Field   October 25, 1964—Sidi Bujari 28, Tangier

Poopie:

Did I really write you a subtext? A mean one? I wish I had an unconscious to blame it on. I can't really believe it, though. Are you sure? I keep racking my brain. Maybe it was a heavy joke? Was it about "The Moving Man" where I said I thought you identified with the boy? That's not subtext Edward. I don't feel bad because I can't believe it. But I'm sorry it upset you. I know kif makes you do it, most people do it, but I know I've only done it—or only caught myself doing it when it's been done at me too much. And then I feel ridiculous being Machiavellian when I'm not. Anyway I love you, so I didn't mean it.

I am down to one half a dexamil a day now, so don't worry. Vitamins or something have given me energy. I feel better, though I have two teeth rotting out of my head, so I seldom take the others. Ira though says he'll get me some LSD to try, and I want to. Just once.

No, I don't live in the medina. I live out past the European quarter in a neighborhood Souq l Bkar, beet market, formerly. In a huge mansion converted to apartments. I enclose some photos....I've been very worried about Dris, his foot. It's been more or less bad for months and it's been getting worse. Swollen at the ankle and painful. We've been to a few doctors and taken xrays but nothing helped. Now have gone to the English hospital and seen a young bearded American who admitted he didn't know what it was, but is trying arthritic remedies. It seems to be helping.

Days later. I've had a terrible crisis because of a letter from Scott Meredith and also because of a pile of Book Weeks Kluger sent me. Enter the world and my life goes to pieces. I hated my book, etc. Though I'd been so happy rewriting it. Am all right again now and back at work. The Meredith letter upset me because I'd written him to check the thirteen paperback houses that Epstein listed, and he answers "We've taken a sampling of three of the houses; we've called them; and they've all confirmed that they did indeed reject your book. We have every reason to assume, therefore, that the others have seen it, too, and rejected it." That is ABSOLUTELY the only thing he has in three months told me about getting *Goliath* into paperback. I wrote him a strong letter and if I don't have anything concrete when I get back from the trip, I'll just fire him. I can't get into another frustrating relationship by mail.

We'll be going in a day or two probably. Paul stopped by yesterday with his new (ugh) boy, and gave me lots of tips about where to go in the desert (probably it's a trap). Norman and Hajmi are coming with us.

Love, Alfred

To Edward Field and Neil Derrick   Tuesday, November 17, 1964
                                    —Sidi Bujari 28, Tangier
Lovelies:

I've been back since the weekend but I'm still shattered. 3000 kilometers. I drove practically all of it myself. Dris helped a little but there were too many cops stopping us all the time and he doesn't have his license yet. No rugs for you so far. Not in the south or here. I was at the flea market again last night with Charles and again found nothing. At this point I hate the kind of thing Remy got because it's so common. I can't stand the thick weave kind because it reminds me of mama's toilet. Blue is probably out of the question. Until you say stop I'll just go on looking. (I anyway go to the market two or three times a week just for fun.) Don't send money. I've decided to enter a higher price range and see what happens. I'll pay half as a gift because I'm so rich. Don't think I'm being too fussy, because I'm not. Dris has wanted me to get a rug for us for ages and I've never found anything I could live with. So I mean I'm not being fussier for you than I would be for me.

I have so many things to say I don't know where to begin. Anyway, I've fired Meredith. And I sent a wire yesterday to Candida asking her to take me back. (Charles says she's dying to, but I'm not so sure.)

I'd written Meredith before the trip asking if he would find a magazine that might want me to write about the Sahara. [William] Shawn of the New Yorker is very interested and hopes I'll write a long thing in the $3000 range. Of course this made Meredith all eager, but at the same time it was still apparent that he hasn't been bothering with paperbacks or foreign rights.

Dear Edward, you shouldn't get a job, we should open a shop together and sell Saharan goods. I'm sure my brother would back us. My burnoose could easily sell for $75 or $100 in New York. Handwoven white camel's hair: It is the most beautiful thing I've seen here. Dris wore it (worsened it too at little) to Arcila yesterday and his mother said he mustn't wear it again because he'll get the evil eye from people, it's so spectacular. It cost $25. I bought calfskin slippers ($1) and enormous lanterns with colored glass, very big and beautiful, made by hand of pressed sardine cans ($1.50 each). These remember are retail prices. We bought fancy yenty colorful cushions in Tiznit. A marvelous iron charcoal brazier for 50 cents. *Sebsis* (kif pipes) for 10 cents. A gorgeous breen and brown straw *haiti*, for the wall around the bed. From *hait*, meaning wall. *hyot*, plural. A green date pouch woven from palm leaves by a boy who sat with us while we picnicked in the oasis in the valley of the Amelne outside Tafraoute. We gave him 25 francs.

While eating supper last night my right ear, cheek and jaw suddenly went numb and blew up gigantically. It went down after awhile but I phoned Mme. Roux anyhow and she said it sounded like an allergy to something I was eating and not to worry. (Maybe the olive oil from the Sahara in the salad.) But I made an appointment for today for Dris. The English doctor said it might be gonorrhea in the foot. Remember when I first came we had it for months? Infecting the tendon. So half the trip he took antibiotics but they didn't do anything, and the doctor said if it was gonorrhea the foot would react. I think myself it is affected by bad weather because during the summer it bothered him on the same days that Skoura had epileptic fits. And she always had fits just before the weather went bad. Yesterday she had two and yesterday his foot was very bad. But in any case it keeps getting steadily worse. He showed it to his family and they all said at once it was some Moroccan disease that had to be cured by a *fqe*. Holy man. So he went to the hammam twice yesterday to purify himself and is going to see a couple of *fqes* today. Jane says it is a good idea for Moroccans to use both their own doctors and western medicine men. She says Sherifa always wears lemons on her forehead and also takes penicillin and it works together. When she's sick. As for Dris's brother Hamid, I've given up on him because he won't cooperate. (I just went to the toilet and wiped my ass with Jenkins, Bobby Kennedy and JohnJohn Kennedy. Did I tell you España ran a frontpage headline saying the Goldwater people accused Bobby Kennedy of murdering Marilyn Monroe? Was this current in America?) I don't think a rat ate up Hamid's toe because he feels pain, terrible pain, in the foot. And there is this ugly blackness on it like mold. Leprosy is not the same here as elsewhere. Though it occurs to me now that his nose is smaller than the others in the family. I must go take another look. But he won't let me take him to the doctor. He breaks appointments, etc. He's 38, so I can't just haul him away.

I've heard that when Paul first came here in 1933 with that composer [Aaron Copeland], can't remember the name now, very famous, who wrote the Mexican suite and lots of Americanish stuff. I keep thinking Kazin. Because he was on the plaque in my cabin at MacDowell near Pearl Kazin. Anyhow, I heard Paul went to Fez and some caid or other fell madly in love with him and locked him up in his palace and fucked him like mad and that is his big sex experience. Paul himself has talked about it to me though he never mentioned the fucking. Moroccans like white meat. Very much. But—didn't you read my story?—the thing they like best is what is available. I hear there is prejudice but I hear this only from Africans. Moroccans say you can never get syphilis or gonorrhea from black meat. There are lots of high yaller and black marriages. No one takes note. There is an American Negro girl around now and lots of Moroccans are in love with her. Charles [Wright] claims there is prejudice (he is practically white), but I think he is annoyed that everyone doesn't fall in love with him the way they did in America. Including me. (He gets very competitive

222

for my attention when Dris appears, and starts talking a blue streak to divert me from D. I have to be quite rude to him sometimes.)

If a Moroccan has a choice, he will choose the youngest first, next the fairest. Anyway, it's very complicated because funlaughter enters all this, also meat, and also money (sex is a commodity). Also very important is the Moslem bit. The fairer you are means the more Arab (semite.) The blacker people are African. I've noticed in the horrible Rabat-Casa bourgeoisie that they like to have very black servants. But I think that's imitation Europe-America. (Like the way the Greeks have all the French prejudices because they think they're chic.) Like they also pretend to be horrified by homosexuality. Any foreigner who looks more than 22 or 23 is approached by a Moslem at least as much for money as for sex. (Though this isn't always true either, especially in Marrakech.) It's possible Moroccans may think American Negros are poorer. But I doubt it. Finally: it is natural for a Moroccan to go to bed with a friend. A friend is someone they can have fun with. And also not be ashamed of, like not have elegant, pretentious faggot manners. If color figures, I think it figures only when the object is also being rejected for a lot of other reasons.

You never know why a Moroccan doesn't want you anyhow. Hajmi admitted to me that he won't sleep with Norman because N once told him he'd once had little things like worms (polyps) cut off his ass. I threw Norman out of the car in Essouira because I got fed up with his queening it while Dris, Hajmi and I worked all the time: driving, cooking, cleaning windows, carrying luggage, etc. Whenever there was work to do (or a bill to be paid) he'd sort of wander into the desert to experience William Burroughs' "crystal blue silence" or Paul Bowles' stillness. He never bothered with Alfred Chester's labor. In Essouira I told him to wash the windows and he said, what do we have them (the Arabs) for? So I told him to work or get out and started screaming that just because he stole money he didn't have the right to consider himself a duchess and threw his bags at him and also a box of Quaker Oats (the scene was in public.) I was also annoyed that he was hiding money so as not to have to buy Hajmi the djellaba he promised him. Hajmi decided he'd better stick with the car, so I had to support him for the next three days. It was on the way back. I'm glad to be rid of him. And hope I don't have to be friends with him again since he's going to America soon, but I've already had two letters from him. He says Hajmi has turned into a juvenile delinquent because of his proximity to me and Dris.

I haven't looked at my novel in two weeks and am terrified. I'll get very kifed today and approach it.

No, I don't use the witch anymore.

I don't know why I haven't told you anything about my trip. Maybe next time I don't feel like it now. I kept some notes. The most exciting part was the big outdoor courtyard toilet near the Koutoubia in Marrakech. Like a Chirico in the moonlight with lots of cruising. The exciting part was I was high and stepped into a booth with turds all over the floor. One of the turds moved and then two big rats slithered into the shithole and disappeared.

Love and kisses, Alfred

To Edward Field and Neil Derrick   Friday, (date uncertain)
                                                —Sidi Bujari 28, Tangier

Boyeles:

The money changing scene here is getting nerve-wracking because the government has clamped down on dirhams going in or out of the country. The reason: 50% more tourism over the summer and 25% less foreign currency. Somebody squealed that John Mitchell of Fat Black Pussycat was going over with $7,000 so the customs stripped him naked last week but found nothing. He'd given the checks to an English boy crossing with him. All the money changers are in a panic and the expected devaluation doesn't seem likely now.

I'm exhausted because for some reason I've been seeing a lot of people since we came back from the trip and seeing people drains me.

Charles comes over night and day and I don't know how to get rid of him. I have my little package of LSD now and I keep waiting for the right moment to take it. I'm beginning to hate it. I never before just sat around with an experience waiting for the right moment. I keep imagining the dose is wrong or too much, etc.

Dris has gone to the *fqe* three times and I actually believe his foot is improved. The lump seems somewhat smaller and he walks a bit better.

Love, Alfred

P.S. I don't know where you can get a copy of Jane's book. It's being republished in England next year.

To Harriet Zwerling   Nov. 23, 1964

Dear Harriet: I've been wanting to write you for ages, but everytime I start, I start feeling cheated, meaning you won't answer me, or you'll answer me on the run, so then I stop.

We went to the Sahara for a couple of weeks and I loved it, though it exhausted me. Morocco is much better than Europe and you shouldn't waste your time going there (Europe).

I'm glad that you don't see Susan. In your letter in September you wrote, "I saw Irene the other day. You wouldn't believe who she has become." Who? But in this letter you say she's more to your taste. I wish you would tell me. I keep wanting to write to her but I keep imagining she probably still hates me, so what would be the point? She and I should go into the importing business. Where is she?

I fired Norman Mailer's agent last week because he really is *un con* and only interested in big deals. I too would like to be interested in big deals, but no one wants me to be. Some queer book club has taken on *Behold Goliath* so maybe I'll have a few more sales. Yes, I'm rewriting my novel now. If I tell you the title, don't tell anyone. (Edward knows it and so does Remy, the latter gave me the title.) It's called *Exquisite Corpses*. It's short and weird. And I want Morty Schleifer's P-Town photo of you on the cover. The jacket, I mean. If anyone publishes it. Oh, did you hear that Evergreen is publishing my piece on Tangier (that I wrote for Show but they wouldn't print it). "Glory Hole, Nickel Views of the Infidel in Tangier." It's nice but I'm terrified they may kick me out because of it. Evergreen may use some of Dris's watercolors to illustrate the piece. He paints in spurts, but he's not too interested in it really.

When your letter came the other day I was just going up on LSD which I'd never tried before. Your letter seemed like an ominous warning because of Bill's experience. But lo and behold, a blinding light entered my brain and it was divine. You should try it. At first everything was like a cartoon, Disneyland. After, like a box of jewels. Jack Smith must take a lot of it. I wonder why it was so horrible for Bill. Maybe because he took it at night. Whenever the sun went behind a cloud it got depressing. Everything sort of sagged. The life went out of everything. I'm dying to try it again.

In the evening on Saturday, when I was coming down, a girl named Rosalind was here and an American Negro writer named Chas Wright and we talked about the Art Students League. We were sitting in front of the fire and being nostalgic about NY. But the evening ended catastrophically because Dris, not knowing there was anything wrong with the word, hugged Charles affectionately and said, Nigger, nigger. (sometimes I call Dris "you big nigger" even though he's more or less white.) So that's probably the end of Charles, and I can't say I'm sorry. The scene here is really pretty grotesque.

I'm at the bottom of the page. Will you write me? Hello to Louie. A kiss to Milo and lots of love to you. Alfred P.S. You were in a photo in Time at some play. A lot of people sitting on stage including Allen Ginsberg. You were sort of in the back with your head cocked to the right. Remy saw it too. A sort of weird German play I think.

To Edward Field   Nov. 25, 1964—Sidi Bujari 28, Tangier
Qelbi:

I have a terrible cold and someone has given me American antihistamine pills but they don't help. I finally took the LSD on Saturday and I loved it. I'm still not completely out of it; reds attract me very much and luminous blues. But patterns don't interest me so much anymore. It made me very sick at first, like too much amphetamine, plus making me very nauseous. So I took a cab down to Ira's because I thought I was going to die and then suddenly the Socco Grande turned into a carnival and all the people into freaks, everything in technicolor, Disneyland. I roared with laughter. Ira's palace, with all its tiles and campy furnishings, turned into a box of jewels. I've been thinking about it a lot since, and I believe that what it does is not only quicken the senses but slows the mind. You see things before the brain can tell you how to feel about them. So you really see them. Like people getting shorter and longer. They really do, as they move toward or away from you or at different angles. Only you really see it happen, and your mind isn't straightening it all out, I didn't have any real hallucinations except the wall up on Ira's roof, very mildewed and rotten, and that sort of moved in and out of focus and turned into paisleys. I ran back and read your letters later on peyote. I noticed you mentioned paisley. Also the sun. The sun was very important in my high. Everytime it went behind a cloud, I came down. Everything sort of deflated and went dark. I can't wait to do it again. Rosalind says that the natural stuff (mescaline and peyote) is warmer, that this is very sharp and chemical. Quite true. It isn't a soft high, but a cold hard sharp one. Very odd: I kept wanting to get high when I was high, like to smoke kif or hashish. Ira says that's very usual.

I'm moving, I think. To the house Paul had during the summer on the Mountain. He really is such a louse. He told me it had been rented by an American for two years. But I found out he was lying. Fifty dollars a month. About five rooms in the most enormous forested property you can imagine. On the cliffs over the Atlantic. I nearly changed my mind last night because it's so scary up there and because this apartment is so cosy now. But it's really too small with the dogs and all. Dris can now raise chickens and goats like he wants to. But he's not too happy moving up there. Charles is going to take over this flat. I wish you would both come and live with us. There's plenty of room and there's even another little house which belongs to me a little down the cliffs. Why don't you come and be my guests?

I have my proofs from Evergreen and it's making me nervous as hell. Oh, I've written my ad. Full page. It has two quotes. The Burroughs and something from one of your letters.

Oh, Dris did a marvelous picture last night. He did one the other day of the walls of Tiznit (combined with Marrakech) and it is sort of boring, so I told him to do it again only better. So last night kif gave him a great idea. It is blue sky with thumb prints, the red brown wall of the desert with a tower and a couple of green trees behind it (one a palm, the other a sort of Rousseau) and in the wall, extreme left, is a white arched doorway, trimmed in green with a strange red flower floating in the middle. Lovely and quite shocking.

Will they throw me out of Morocco for the Evergreen?

Charles brought over something from the Times book review about how you don't know nowadays which Norman, which Alfred, or which Lionel people are talking about. If I'm so famous, why don't people buy my books?

I'm getting back into *Exquisite Corpses* but it's boring me, I really want to write another book but I must redo this one....What does Susan have to say about camp? I hate her.

Thursday. I didn't take the house. The heating problem is gigantic, and it's very cold and rainy up there. Besides, I guess I'm getting too old to sacrifice my cosiness here for even that spectacular place. So I've rearranged the apartment a little and made the laundry room into my office. I've put a board over the huge sinks and that's that. Only it's a little too sunny.

Charles came to dinner last night with some horrible American friend economist. Charles never eats here (it makes me very annoyed) and the friend was too busy being boring to notice the food, which was spectacular. A chicken tajine with potatoes and cauliflower, sort of gingery. I'm glad Dris doesn't take his cooking personally, but I do, so I was annoyed. But I'd given up those antihistamines and taken a bunch of codeine tablets and a lot of kif so I felt divine.

Mme. Roux is now treating D.'s foot. She said it is rheumatism and is giving him a lot of cortisone. If that doesn't work she will try something else. And if that doesn't work she says we should go to Moullay Yacoub near Fez for the baths. We were there in the summer did I tell you? It's in the middle of miles of crumpled yellow deserty hills like the moon.

I long so much to see you. Alfred

Enc. Ad for *Behold Goliath*

"One voice speaks through these pages like an electric scalpel; Mr. Alfred Chester writes like white lightning." William S. Burroughs.

"Nobody has testified like Alfred Chester, with such a chorus of voices and the ringing of bells. In his writing, the history of mankind speaks; even the ape has a voice, or whatever it is we came from; there is a sigh from the original jelly fish and the wail of the first Jew." Edward Field

To Edward Field   Nov. 30, 1964—Sidi Bujari 28, Tangier

Dearest Edward:

I envied you your dull Thanksgiving dinner. The day went by unnoticed here. I have a terrible cold and the weather has been colder than it's ever been before in Morocco, for the last two or three days. I think it's because the rain still hasn't come and something is fucked up in the atmosphere. All you usually need here is the sun to make things warm, and we have plenty of sun, but it is probably around 40 degrees. Maybe more really but it feels terrible. Everyone just complains about the weather the whole time.

I was just down at the beach sitting with Charles and his dull

dull friends. He has three American visitors, and I made the mistake of entertaining one who is sort of like a petrified demented thinner [theater director] Cyril Simon. I think Chas is annoyed that I haven't invited the latest ones to dinner. We were sitting in the Spanish bar and Hajmi turned up and they all got a letch for him, especially this big white monster named Jay with bloated white hands. So I asked Hajmi in Arabic if he'd consider and he screamed with laughter, but finally said 3000 francs. So I told the monster who I think would have except Chas was frowning on so exorbitant a price. Hajmi looks like what Julie Perlmutter would look like if he were brown and a movie star and had a beautiful body. Anyway the scene annoyed me. I came back home to work but found your letter and the letter from Scott Meredith asking me to reconsider. (He is hot for the New Yorker deal.) I won't.

I've finally begun working again and this new chapter where Ferguson meets Baby PoorPoor and they turn into John Doe and James Madison is entirely unexpected. Thank God it doesn't matter whether there's any logic in the book at all. I wish I were finished with it so I could write the Tangier murder mystery. (I'm getting somewhat kifed as I write which is good because I haven't written you kifed in ages, and you should know Him as well.) Paul came over the other day and it was fun being with him. I mean I can handle him much better now and he is really so fascinating. In his kif world where every motion and word matters and is like a little chess man being pushed into some important place. I want to write a story beginning: "When I gets kifed, I love to think about Paul. First, I heap the fire up with big dry logs, then I light the candle in a lantern from Marrakech and stick up sticks of incense all around the place. Then I take a big glass of mint tea, my metui full of kif, my sebsi, a pack of cigarettes and matches and put them on the floor near the fire. Then I turn off the electric light and lie down on the sheepskin with the fancy pillow from Tiznit under my elbow. I get as close to the flame as can without my eyeballs getting sunburned. It is the most beautiful place on earth here, with the colored glass playing out of the lantern and my nose full of jasmine-flavored smoke. (European writers used to think Morocco was evil because it was Paradise and since they knew they didn't belong in Paradise they thought it was a trick of the devil's.) Getting higher and higher and higher, I watch the fire and think about Paul. I think of every move he makes and every word he pushes into the arena, etc." Anyway he told me that Larbi (who has a two month visa to the States) suddenly got passage on the Independence (Burroughs is also on it, going to St. Louis for Playboy magazine) leaving from Algeciras, but that the Moroccan police turned him back from the port of Tangier when he was trying to board the ferry to Algeciras. Paul of course thought it had to do with the trouble in the Congo; he would. That was on Saturday and the boat doesn't sail until eight tonight. (The Independence doesn't, not the ferry. That sailed.) Yesterday, Sunday morning, Larbi appeared here and said he thought he might have an easier chance getting out into Ceuta. (A Spanish port colony about sixty-five miles from here on the Mediterranean.) The reason they don't like to let Moroccans out is they think they're going to work abroad, and they don't let them out unless they have prearranged contracts, so the government can take half the money as the man earns it.) Larbi is going for a lot of reasons, including selling jewelry that he makes, and also going to Belgium from America so he can work in a mine or a factory there and send money to his wife and kid, not the government. So would I drive him? So I drove him, Dris coming along, and this hideous American girl with juicy pimples all over her face. I don't really know what she was around for, presumably to help Larbi cross borders and maybe to get fucked by him.) Though both Dris and Larbi were horrified when I asked Larbi if they were going to share a room in Algeciras; Larbi and the girl, not Larbi and Dris of course.) This is becoming like a Jane Bowles letter, it is taking me forever to get to the point. Kif.) When I'm kifed I sometimes think that when I went crazy last spring, I actually had a stroke like Jane. I have heard that she had a stroke after eating some majhoun (hashish fudge). The majoun showed her, I'm sure, some unbelievable but true picture of herself, and all the alcohol that she'd been drinking for years to blur the true picture rose in one big loyal gesture of combat against the kif and just knocked out that part of her brain which contained the true picture. By the way, when I'm kifed I know that I'm still not altogether recovered from last spring. I mean I realize I am still a little crazy. The kif me, who is talking now as you've probably noticed, is absolutely sane at least he thinks he is and is very objective about all my acts. (Oh, important. That other night after Paul left, it occurred to me that I might have to kill my mother. Better burn this.)

To get back to Ceuta. So we got him through. It took some doing and about two hours. Dris and I couldn't get in, one, because he doesn't have a passport and, two, because I didn't have what is virtually an exit visa. (Sometimes I get scared that I'll never get out of here.) I mean we couldn't get out of Morocco to drive them into Spain, Ceuta, but we saw them off in a taxi. It was very moving. I mean emotional. (Not the taxi was very moving.) Larbi was ridiculous at the border. He has a valise full of trinkets for his jewelry. Ah-hah, what is all this, asked the customs police. Larbi said: To sell. The man almost exploded. The whole point is not to be making money and he admits the whole thing. Dris, however, came to the rescue, by telling the man that Larbi was lying, that he was ashamed to tell the truth which is: That he's making trinkets to give to girls in America, so he can fuck them, because if you give a girl little trinkets like that in America, they let you fuck them. The man was so taken by this that general virile conversation ensued and the valise was closed to loud chuckles of laughter.

Paidhaiki mou, the point of all this is: The Independence lands on the 8th of December. Could you please meet Larbi if you can spare an hour. Tell the customs man he is just bringing presents to his friends about the trinkets. He has a few hundred dollars so is all right for money. Do you know anyone who might like to be fucked by Larbi and so would put him up for a few days? Like Samartino maybe? (Though I don't think Larbi is much interested in sex; he is too sick religious somehow; he even went behind the customs shed to pray.) (I take all that back about religion; it was nice his going behind the shed.) He's only staying a few days before going on to San Francisco. He has to see [Grove Press editor, Richard] Seaver, etc. Or maybe just stick him into a cheap hotel. I feel guilty asking you, especially with the movie and all, but it is sort of horrible to think of Larbi dropping into New York. (Dris could handle it all, I'm sure; he even handled the cop the other day who came into the café and confiscated the kif; the cop gave the kif back.) Maybe Muriel could put him up. He's very sweet. Or do the Ross's need a babysitter? Or a dogsitter. He sat with my dogs when we went to Marrakech. I told him you can't, so he doesn't expect you to offer. I told him I'd write to ask you to meet him. Anyway, give him Irene [Fornes]'s address, because she speaks Spanish, and she can talk to him for a little while. And Harriet's. Who also speaks Spanish. (I didn't have time at the end to give him any addresses.) You don't have to feel too bad if you can't endure going because the American girl is there, and I think she could manage (though she's from S.F. and doesn't know N.Y.) She anyway. There is her big pocketbook with its fat mouth gaping open under the customer inspector's face, and she drags me away suddenly to say that her pocket book is full of kif. I told her to grab the bag away and she did and we rushed to the car and there was a swift exchange between her and Dris of oranges and kif. Everyone saw, I'm sure, but nothing was said. (The customs shed is open air, on the curb next to the car.) Larbi was meanwhile being frisked and maybe even stripped to see if he had any money with him.

I completely forgot. It turns out the old French woman downstairs has a bunch of Moroccan orphans weaving rugs she sells to France. You even make your own design, choose your own colors, thickness, etc. Please let me know at once, so I can get a definite estimate. Or, if you want, I can choose some Berber designs or something. But decide positively on colors and thickness. Size five-by-eight, did you say? And send pattern if you want to invent one.

Habibi: I wrote the enclosed when I was kifed last night but will send it anyway, though it seems rather boring this morning. It occurs to me now that Seaver or someone may be down to meet the Independence because of Burroughs, and that Burroughs himself is sometimes kind. I mean, if you would hate meeting Larbi, you don't have to.

No, I don't really look so well. My face is very dry and full of little ugly wrinkles, and sags. What should I do about it? Also I have the eczema that I had last year, or whatever it is, that I wrote about in the Tribune, on my right eyelid, in my right ear and on my cock. But I have a cream for it which helps a little. Dr. Roux has given Dris cortisone since she says his foot is rheumatism. He seems to be a little better actually. I was thinking last night that it's very odd how he doesn't bore me, Dris, because we can't really talk about too much together. Also it is sort of nice how we cannot sometimes, like eat a whole meal without a word, and I never feel any tension like I used to with Arthur or even Walter.

Dris says if Grove buys the pictures he will give his mother 5000 francs and his father 5000 francs and his brother Hamid 5000 francs and me 10,000, and he will buy presents worth 5000 each for you, me and himself. That adds up to 40,000, so evidently he expects eighty dollars....*Fqe* is pronounced fkay; I use the usual French spelling; expect the q represents the letter *qaf*, which is pronounced like k but comes out of the throat.

I'm going to end this letter now so I can work on my novel. I woke up this morning thinking I want to steal something from Irving's book, a bit about that poet Marshall who picked up a man who made him wear a dog collar.

Love to you, Alfred

To Edward Field   Thursday, Dec. 17, 1964
Dear Edward:

I had, what the doctor said was an acute attack of sciatica last Saturday. It's really been unbelievably painful. It subsided yesterday, but I got out of bed and it was raining and I drove (it kills me putting my foot on the clutch) to try to get my legal problems organized. So the pains came back very severely, and this morning I'm sitting here full of codeine (and pain) and it's hard to gather my mind.

I sent you the wire after making no headway with lawyers here. I had a letter from the Clerk of the Court on Monday. "We direct your attention to the fact that this action was instituted after a warrant of attachment was issued against you. A warrant of attachment would tie up any funds not exempt from execution of which the plaintiff is aware." I don't understand this at all but it makes me terribly nervous. Would you tell the lawyer about this and ask what it means? Anyway, here is a rundown of my view. Joe Fox (now at Random House) took me on at Holt. He was trying to get up a bunch of literary writers for them. When he left Holt in September 1960, he took some of the writers with him to Random House, but not me, claiming that my stories were too dirty for Bennett Cerf. That Holt unloaded all its serious writers after Joe Fox left is evidenced even in Esquire of June 1963 in their chart of the literary establishment, when they said that Holt did not have a single literary writer. Anyway, the point is, as Cohen says, that after Fox left, Holt told Candida to find me another publisher. So how can they sue me for breach of contract? I've asked Candida now for all the relevant correspondence, but she hasn't answered and I don't know if she will. The question is: Why, if Holt wanted to get rid of me, did I agree (or let Candida agree for me) to a payout schedule [returning the advance] and even let her take $350 out of my check from Lippincott and give it to them? The real reason lies in my psychology. That was the summer after Arthur left when I went to MacDowell. I mean, I was trying to make I, Etcetera into a book and feeling hopeless about it. I suppose I actually felt very guilty. I never knew anything about a payout schedule. All I knew from Candida was that Holt bugged her for money from time to time. The whole thing was very confused in my mind and I was under the impression that they would never really press hard to get their money back. I didn't know whether or not they were entitled to their money back. I suppose I assumed the law was on their side (the law is always on their side) and the best thing for me to do was be sneaky about it rather than take a position. Anyway, what I really have to know is: If Candida as my agent agreed to this payout schedule, or rather, if I through my agent agreed to a payout schedule, which I now think of as illegal, am I obliged to fulfill that payout schedule? As I wrote to Arthur Cohen: Whatever the details of the matter, there can be no doubt about the fact that it was Holt who was giving me the air and not vice versa. I do remember months later asking Candida if she couldn't get Holt to publish *Behold Goliath* and she said no. I abandoned *I, Etcetera* in November of 1960 and there is probably a case to be built around this, for me, I mean. That having been sent away by Holt, I felt too depressed to continue with.

Here are some things I have to know: Have I been legally served? I mean, is a summons delivered to me in Morocco legal? Also: Can I legally change my mind about a debt? I mean, is it possible for me legally to agree they (Holt) have a right to their money in 1960 and then later question this debt? Is it legal for a publisher to tell a writer to get another publisher and then sue him for breach of contract? Because they are suing for breach. Also: Would it be better tactics for me to make a countersuit?

For the $350. And also for the psychological damage done me as a result of their getting rid of me when Joe Fox left? After all, it destroyed my novel. I'm trying not to implicate Candida in this mess because, frankly, I think it would be bad politics. But there's no doubt she is really to blame for the whole thing. There is no doubt that if she had been truly working for me, when Holt told me to get out, she would have refused the idea of giving them money. Anyhow, the immediate problem is not the suit but the answer to the summons and to find out what the clerk means by a warrant for attachment. Am I already attached?

I can't be very gossipy now what with lawsuits and sciatica. I keep worrying a little that I am going crazy again. Especially when I have visitors. A lot of people have been visiting me these last few days when I've been in bed. I mean everyone here is so nutty, I feel as though I'm going to explode for lack of communication or any real friendship, even on the Harriet level. I get very paranoid and think it is all some horrible plot to keep me in this hole. Maybe I should come to New York even for a short visit. But then I think I mustn't interrupt my book just now. I did that with *I, Etcetera* and it was fatal.

I read about Susan in Time.

I saw your poems in Paul's Evergreen. Also Susan's article. I glanced at it and I thought: How did she know? I mean about the true depth of a work being in the surface. Which is what my book is.

Paul and Jane have come over a lot lately and I quite love them now. Especially him. I feel I finally understand him and the way he has had to organize his life and his mask. He is really my only friend here. He has a boy now, which is making him very happy and I hope he manages to keep this one.

Edward, I start getting hysterical every evening about my leg. I think there must be some connection between it and Dris's foot. Though Mme. Roux says no. The trouble is there isn't a single doctor here I trust. My pain was so awful on Saturday that I actually sobbed. It went from buttock to foot, left leg. When Dris paid the cab at Mme. Roux's, I was on my knees in the street, I couldn't stand up. And he had to carry me up the stairs. She took me off the suppositories and told me to take a series of vitamin B shots for the nerve. But that was before I did all that running around yesterday and got the severe pains back. I get so scared.

I can't go on with this now. I'm sorry to bother you about this legal business, but that's what you get for being the only person to whom I can turn. There is so little time left for answering the summons, what with Christmas in the middle, that I don't know what will be if I have to answer any questions. You can wire them if necessary and I'll wire back. Please let me know as soon as things are straightened out, so I can relax about it. They are really such dogs. Arthur Cohen. He's doing it because my letters to him were so cold and smart aleck. He wanted me to grovel and be humble and inferior. And all I wrote was that I wanted my $350 back.

Lots of love, *habibi,* and thank you. Alfred

To James Broughton   Dec. 19, 1964

Dearest James:

Your letter came over a week ago, and my impulse was to answer immediately. However, I was struck down by (what the doctor say is, and what I'm not at all sure is) sciatica. It's been unbelievably painful and this is the first morning I've faced without the help of drugs and dope. But if I sound a little dopey it is partly because I naturally am and also because I probably got a thick white veil of codeine on my brain. I really think it isn't sciatica but gonocchocal arthritis which, according to Merck's Manual, can cause serious tendon damage very quickly. I think my Arab darling has the same thing, though, as antibiotics haven't cured him very rapidly (which they are supposed to do); the doctor thinks he has rheumatism and our two cases are just coincidental. There isn't a decent doctor in this hole.

Anyway, to stop kvetching for a minute, I was, as you can imagine, delighted to hear from you. Even though you are writing to another Me. I have changed vastly since the last stories in *Goliath* were written. The most violent of the changes have occurred during the last year-and-a-half, or since I came to Morocco. The most severe crisis of my life having taken place last spring when I finally went crazy. (A little afterwards, I stopped wearing my wig, though this is still somewhat difficult for me.) I don't think I've really completely recovered, but I'm very changed. Anyway, I've written a novel since, and am now rewriting it. I have given up all that ridiculous criticism that I was writing. I don't know if this novel has "come smashing through out of the whole core of my life" as you put it, nor do I think I've found how to tell my own story. The book is completely unexpected, though it emerged from older material.

When I was still nuts I sort of said to God, well, I will accept whatever you give me. And then every day I sat down and recorded what was given to me. Rewriting it is hard because I have two distinct impulses. One is that its whole rightness depends on the raw state it's in; my purpose was to displease rather than to please. The other impulse is just to clean it up and give it a certain pattern. Obviously

I'm trying a middle ground between the two. Already, though, I feel the book is over and want to go on to the next. For the first time in my life I'm not interested in making what I'm working on into a *chef d'oeuvre* but am merely (wrong word) interested in seeing where I will go from here. In its way *Exquisite Corpses* (title is a secret please) is a parody of a novel, a ridiculing of what I once valued most. Also it abandons any effort to find my own voice, an admission of not having one.

I knew you were married since I had your announcement. And I knew you had a baby because Eve Triem told me so. (Her letter came when I was emerging from the center of my madness and I couldn't find any way to answer her; I still can't really.) I suppose I envy you too, and maybe the gods will one day smile on me as they have on you and give me that joy which is so accessible to most of mankind and yet so far out of my reach. But what I want most of all now is, I suppose, what I've always wanted: to be me. I used to want it in life. Now I want, rather, now I believe the only place to find it is in my writing; and maybe, as I suspect, the real discovery of me is in the fact that there is no me. How am I then to be me? Shit.

I'm glad you liked *Behold Goliath*. It sold virtually no copies, though now some queer little book club has taken it on and maybe it will sell a few for me. Everyone tells me how famous I am, but no one seems to buy my books....I saw a story of Evan Connell's called "The Corset" in Esquire, which a friend brought the other day to keep me company in bed. I could hardly believe it, it was so bad. I had a little news of Max Steele from Mary Lee [Settle] in those days three years ago when I saw her fairly often and let her trample over my soul. The last time I saw her (no, the next to last time) she did a whole little play about menstruation for me. Grotesque. About how she hadn't had a period in five years or something. Then, while I was there with some other people, she went and took a bath, and lo! she came out cleansed and pure and radiant with a choir of cherubs singing, and Mary with ecstatic eyes saying, it cometh, it cometh. Apparently, Act III, in the bathtub: She bled. The last time I saw her, it was a reading of a dialogue she'd written in St. Thomas's on 5th and 53rd. She kept holding my hand in a pew. I escaped and never returned.

I saw a few of the other Paris people while I was in NY. But not many and not often. Oddly enough, I had news of Zev recently, from a mutual friend in Rome, Norman Glass. Also of Eugene [Walters]. I suppose you read poor Marguerite [Caetani] is dead. That made me feel bad.

Life is boring in Morocco. I have few friends and most of them profoundly unbelievably hugely dull. Paul Bowles is the one exception. We've spent most of the last 18 months fighting, but slowly I've come to respect and admire him enormously. It takes a lot of knowing to see through the horrible exterior he has built for himself. He's created a persona that never justifies itself and which leaves it to you to discover if there is anything, or what there is, underneath.

I'm going to stop this now and try to work a little. I hope you'll answer me. My most serious blessings on your house. And as always my love to you. Alfred

P.S. I wish I could recommend an agent to you for your play. I fired two this year, one of whom I rehired and am probably about to fire again.

To Edward Field   December 21, 1964—Sidi Bujari 28, Tangier
Paidhaiki mou:
The lady just finished the pattern of your rug and it's enclosed. The colors are my choice, based on the color of my apartment, the main colors, which are like yours. I really love it myself. The patterns, the design, are authentic Berber, mountain stuff; oriental Arab stuff is more citified. Anyway, now this is what you have to do: Either like it enough to tell her to go ahead, hate the whole thing too much to go on with it, or suggest your own alterations in the design and also your own colors. I'm enclosing the wool samples for her pattern which I think scrumptious.

I'm feeling somewhat better though I seem to be getting my lumbago back on the right side now. I walk more or less like a cripple. So does Dris. He is embarrassed for us to be seen together in public, and so am I a little. It is so ridiculous. Rosalind says all we need is to go out with Skoura and Jane, and the scene would be perfect.

But my week in bed with drugs and pains has given me a surge of energy and belief in my book. So anyway I'm working. I should really trade this typewriter in for a portable because it's high keyboard always strains my back. The lady *praticante* who gives me my daily shot of vitamins, thiamine, I think, says she now has four cases of sciatica among Jews, and Pepita the concierge is sick with lumbago. So maybe it isn't gonococcal arthritis. But what should I do about Dris? It seems not to be getting worse, thank God, but it certainly isn't getting better

I just reread *Nightwood* for the first time in twelve years and I realized that *Nightwood* is the game I was playing with my ladies all these years. Susan was Robin. Irene was Jenny. Harriet was Nora. I, of course, was Dr. O'Connor.

We have a big wood burning cuisinière in the kitchen and Rosalind was thinking of cooking a goose on it for Christmas. So I'm trying it out today with a little duck scrumptuously stuffed and surrounded by oranges. It is taking a long time to get hot, but the fire seems okay.

I hope you've done something about the lawyer. If I don't answer the summons, I forfeit the case and they will attach my royalties if not my bank account, plus legal expenses and interest. Please make the lawyer go answer the summons. I'll send him a check.

Merry Xmas to you lovelies. Lots of love, Alfred

Tuesday. The cuisinière isn't very good. I left the duck in for six hours and it only barely got dry. Finally Dris threw it into the fireplace and roasted it Arab style. It was amazingly delicious. Except there was a nigger in the woodpile: Charles Wright. He came over. And he never eats here. I gave him a plate of food and he just tasted it and then made his hysterical talk, which is supposed to prevent me from getting into conversation with Dris but actually only prevents me from saying another word to Chas. I withdraw into monosyllables or outright silence. I loathe him more and more.

Don't send me a Xmas present. But it would be nice if you sent Dris one since he loves them. Any kind of clothing except a tie which he never wears. Or something like very Amerikanish and portable (souveniry I mean) that he could show off in the cafes. Yes he remembers you very well. You have the distinction of being my *amigo*; I mean when he just says to me, *tu amigo*, he means you. Or else he calls you Wedwood. Which is probably what I call you. Norman is Wawmin and Ira is Iwa.

I am feeling good this morning, leg and all. I had a marvelous high last night. Your rug may have had something to do with it. I mean, it was an interior-decorating high. I told Charles (who is going to flip out, by the way, any minute now; his time is coming, and I'm afraid because I believe he can be dangerous) I wanted a house full of beautiful things. Morocco has done this to me, also LSD. I started imagining this red room. And he tried to be helpful by giving me suggestions for it. But every specific suggestion seemed contrary to the room. Like even when I thought of red brocade walls, it somehow was wrong. Finally I said it had no windows and no doors; it was a state of mind. I'm still fascinated with it this morning. Is it a womb? Anyway I'm lickety split putting it into my novel. I lay in bed this morning for an hour after I woke up thinking about my novel. It is incredibly beautiful. It's form is, I mean. It is formless and yet its formlessness is exquisitely formed. It is such a pleasure to think about. All its piddling irrelevant parts add up to a gorgeous whole. I really am a great writer. Today.

I kiss you both. Alfred

To Norman Glass   Jan. 3, 1965
Dear Norman:
My New Year Resolution is to finish my book, or the second draft, by the end of January, so I'm off huge letters.
All the kif sellers were arrested yesterday, thanks to people entering

Spain and England and getting caught. But Ramadan ends tomorrow, so I'm hoping things will get cool. I went to the movies last night with Ira, Roslyn and an American guest of theirs named Martin who is in TV and who (of all things) had read *Goliath* in NY. This would make me be more optimistic about my forthcoming royalty statement, except that Holt has also summoned Random House and there is apparently a lien on my earnings. The case has become really too large. Edward paid a lawyer $250 to handle it. That's all I know about it so far. Also, my agent quit me (the one I fired, Charles's) because I believe she is responsible really for the whole mess and is nervous of her reputation.

I see Paul very often. He came over yesterday (with Janie, who didn't stop complaining about my seeing Rosalind and Ira) and I'm going over there tonight. My sciatica still hurts especially in this bad weather, but not so badly. But good news is that the mystery of Dris's foot has been uncovered by a Spanish doctor and a new Xray. He has a spur, which is also partially fragmented. The doctor says he has had some success curing spurs with some new medicines and we are trying them out. If that doesn't work, he'll have to have an operation. But it seems already that there is some improvement, at least Dris says so. The lump is softer truly and he walks much better. He is also so happy about it that he is being angelic over the place. *Insha'Dris*, as you say.

Charles has gone. Yesterday. I can't tell you how relieved I am. He was getting really flippy toward the end. On New Year's Day he had disappeared altogether and Jay, Mustapha, Hajmi and I (his creditors) ran around like the Mafia all over town looking for him. Hajmi (who unaccountably had been in C's apartment at four o'clock on New Year's morning, though of course they did nothing) said Charles had had the *mijma* on full blast and the place was full of fumes. He was worried Charles was dead and that the police would say he murdered him. Finally, we [went to his room and] woke him up. I think he was up all the time but just owed too much money. He also had been telling people he was getting $2000 for his new book, when in fact I saw the letter and it was virtually a rejection. He did a big drunk scene, also he did the mad scene from Lucia in blackface. I got disgusted and said

I was broke (which was true) could he give me back some money. Instead, he did another scene from another opera. So I left, and he chased after me down the stairs, so I went back, then he started getting violent so I left again. He chased me down the stairs again and gave me 5000 francs but even so I wouldn't go back. He pretends he will come back to Tangier soon.

Otherwise things are much as you left them. How was your visit to Diana Athill? What are you doing there [in London] aside from freeloading? You'd better not let your U.S. visa expire because your arrest will give you great trouble if you have to reapply. Better find out if, in order to extend it, you need more police things. You haven't had any mail except half a dozen letters from Rabat, hysterical about your departure. I am not forwarding them for fear you will suffer guilt over having abandoned Mohammed.

Love, Alfred

To Norman Glass   (undated)

Dear Norman:

Thank you for excusing me my bad wit. You can stop entertaining your little horror fantasy about the AlfredDris combine overpowering the great love between you and Hajmi. The romance is still perfect. Actually, I've only seen him when he came to have your letters read, or his written. I told him I was not going to invent anything as his secretary, but would put down only what he said. He is a very nice boy and very sincere, and you should not get all nasty simply because he is who he is. He is really very fond of you. You suggested in your letter that he might come visit you in England. He was suggesting the most practical way. Should I have told him you were only having a little fantasy? I didn't.

I'm very curious to know whether you lied to me about Paul's offer to send in your manuscript. He has several times, and in the presence of others, told me that he had never said he would send it, nor would he now. I assumed he was lying of course, but later I wondered. He has gone to Casablanca now for Holiday and then he goes to America for a couple of months. He is as crazy as ever.

I had a wire from Charles Wright telling me he is coming back tomorrow. Ugh.

There is much more optimism and friendliness in the air here than when you left. I have become quite good friends with Ira [Cohen]. They are painting their palace and have an income from a tenant. I see Jay [Haselwood, owner of the Parade Bar] rather often. A millionaire nymphomaniac has bought the property where Paul lived last summer.

I finished my book. Charles is supposed to bring me the carbon paper and I'll type it up and send it to NY. I don't know how good it is. It is probably very strange, but it seems now commonplace to me after all these months. I want to write my Pinocchio play for Remy's ballet theater next, and then a novel: *The Tangier Murder Mystery*.

The two Italians near Cape Spartel are dead, both of them. They died within fifteen days of each other last fall. I just found out. The younger one took sick and went to the hosipital, and then the old one died alone. It was three days before his body was discovered. Later the younger one died. There is now litigation over the property.

Dris is fine and doing a lot of paintings with fancy chalks and magic markers. His foot is being treated again, but it may require surgery. Edward and Neil are coming in May for a month.

Your lowermiddle-class values seem to be reasserting themselves. I mean, of course, your strange reference to Lower East Side sneers and scowls. Paul says you are hopelessly bourgeois. I hope not hopelessly, but you should watch your tastes as well as your suffering. What you like is who you are. Of course, I will be gracious to your chic American girl. As I hope my friends in England were gracious to you....I note you have a satisfactory address and a gallery. If you improve your accent a little, you'll be able to pass.

Write soon.

Love,

Alfred

To Edward Field   Jan. 6, 1965
Beloved Poet:

The Evergreen arrived while I was in the doldrums after having had a (I believe) wisdom tooth pulled. You restored me at once to my senses. *Paidhaiki,* "Lower East Side" is ingenious, aside from being funny, sad, and generally delicious. It is an ideal example of the Principles of Art I have discovered through writing *Exquisite Corpses*: No comment, no generalizations, no sociology (or hardly any), no psychology, no philosophy. I mean it. It is very far superior to the other movie poems which all have a concealed, not-so-concealed message. I only wished it were longer, which I suppose means it is just the right size....You know, I often think how I have never said a word to you about "Letter to Alfred." I really can't. I feel so shy about it and grateful.

I also read Susan's piece ["Notes on Camp"] through, or as much as was manageable. As Nietzsche (rightly) says: Susan was carefully listening to Alfred all those years, wasn't she? Except she is fake. Does anyone know that? When she talks about feeling, I feel embarrassed because she is lying. The excerpt in Time about her Camp article sounded not so good. And she got $6500 for her criticism. Do you think I lurk in her dreams? I liked the Beckett play. Actually, it was sort of a fun issue. Though most of it is unreadable.

Edward, I want to ask Dris to make the witch in Arcila work for you for the National Book Award. Should I? I think it would be hopeless to ask her to work for me, and if you are eligible it would be nice for you (and me) if you get it....I had a letter from Meredith again, only not Scott, Sidney Meredith. His son? He pretends I didn't fire them, and says that C.M. Heath wants to know the dates and places of my stories' first publications with a view to selling them to English magazines. I'm thinking of answering, also because I would like them to get in touch with Mailer about my case. The lawyer hasn't written me. Do you know if he answered the summons?

My book is called *The Exquisite Corpse*. That wasn't really the title I wanted, and I don't care if it sounds like a murder mystery. I remember when Remy said to Norman right here: Did you ever hear of The Exquisite Corpse? And before he explained even, I was wishing it were the title of my book. I am back on the Dear Dr. Franzblau chapter....Did I tell you Norman went back to England a few weeks ago and got caught in Dover with kif? He was arrested and fined €50 partly because it was Christmas, partly because he had so little, and partly because his step father is Lord Mayor of Manchester... Charles too is gone, *hamdullah*. To New York.

Friday. Your letter just came and filled me with joy. I'm so glad you like the rug pattern. It was becoming a serious problem to me. I'll tell Mme. Pinatel to go ahead ... How can [Robert] Lowell be such a pig? He seemed so sweet and quiet that night I met him. How can he want the National Book Award? He is preposterous. Do tell me to go ahead with the witch, if only to spite Lowell....Ramadan is on full blast. Which means almost constant quarrelling, everybody is in such a bad mood. Dris though isn't. He is angelic. His foot seems to have improved a little from these shots. I'm a little nervous about an operation. He already went around bragging to everyone that he's had one. He calls it "reparation," Spanish pronunciation....He told me his brother's foot is being eaten up rapidly. He will die soon I know it. I think maybe Skoura will too. She is getting stranger and stranger. Now she falls asleep sometimes and it takes a quarter of an hour to wake her. I think brain damage must be spreading.

My sciatica is much better but still there. I think you're right about the impulses going astray.

There is a banyan tree in the Mendoubia Gardens, where the mosquitoes came from in your hotel. I was never inside as it looked forbidden, but Rosalind told me to just go in. (She is Ira's girlfriend.) So I went today. It is spectacular and even more spectacular is this: I had mentioned to Paul the other night, the same night that Rosalind was there, and mentioned the banyan tree, about the strange white flower someone sold me last summer. Remember? It opened up in the night, big and white and sweet lemony (did I tell you that there are sweet lemons in southern Morocco? Delicious), and then fell apart in the morning. Paul said it must be night-bloooming Cereus. But today

I saw that the leaves were exactly like the banyan tree. So I asked the guard if the banyan tree ever gave flowers, and he said no, it gave rubber. So how can that be? The leaves were very strange, but exactly like the banyan. And yet Paul, Ira and Rosalind said it was the only banyan tree in Morocco. I still have the dried pod and leaves and wish I knew how to plant it.

I had a letter from Stein & Day asking to consider my novel. Richard Kluger spoke to them highly about me. Do you know anything about them? I thought they were Catholic. Anyway, there is no getting away from it that everyone is going to consider *The Exquisite Corpse* an experimental novel. I suddenly see it from the eyes outside. I mean, it is the last thing anyone expects a novel to be, even me. The trouble is I think that I'm really much cleverer than I am talented. If only God would give me a little more talent I would be genius. As it is, I'm just a pest, a smart aleck, and a nasty kid like my relatives always said. A fat spoiled Jewish brat. Still there are parts in the book that are quite good.

Everyone is so sexy now. Ramadan. They're really not supposed to fuck for a month. But they do at night. Then they have to rush to the hammam. Dris is always wanting sex but I got fucked up with my exchange and we haven't had hammam money. Anyway all the boys look and act like they haven't had sex in a year. Their baskets seem overloaded with cum. Now that the weather is better. It was nearly freezing over last weekend, the worst it's ever been here ever. I worried for the car because there's no such thing as antifreeze. I spent all of one day in bed with a hot water bottle….Paul came over yesterday with a new character, Gordon Sager or something. A writer. I never heard of him and couldn't bear him. He is one of Jane's eunuchs. She collects anglosaxon eunuchs.

Sunset. The cannon just went off. Now they can all eat. You can hear them running and hooting through the streets. Them. The Arabs. There is music most of the night from the mosques. At dawn the cannon goes off again and they wash their mouths and fast. The men sit up in cafes all night. Dris comes home at three in the morning, stoned out of his head. They smoke all night too. At three he eats eggs, bread and butter, tea, sometimes the leftover hereira, the soup that breaks the fast. I feel bad that I can't keep my eyes open and sit with him. But I usually go to sleep at ten. (I'm smoking kif now, so although there was a logic in that apparent non sequitur I can't remember it now.) Did I tell you how my memory is going going? I've forgotten millions of names out of my past, completely, though I remember the people. And often I can't even remember when a recent thing happened and who was there. Events get confused with each other and I feel like I have Walter's mind. That mud in his head, his brain. Incidentally, I think I've completely recovered now from my madness. And I am a much stronger person than I was. Paul is being sinister again but it doesn't even bother me. He has secret tape recordings and records everyone without their knowledge. He is trying to get on my nerves over Dris again, and it isn't working a bit.

Saturday morning. I have to go to the dentist again. Maybe pull another tooth. We both have terrible colds. I prayed to God this morning like you said, I don't know yet of course whether it has helped, but I trust. I remember when the book was beginning I prayed and said I would accept whatever God gave me and then it all came. But I really have no self-confidence. I was reading Jane's book last night (which is now being finally re-published England; actually first being published in England) and I got depressed thinking she has a voice. Everyone has a voice. All 1 do is over-write. "When he blew anyone in a public place, he secretly dislodged his teeth and stowed them in his pocket, then holding the cigar at arm's length between thumb and index finger, he bent from the waist as if bowing, but didn't remove his hat. Sitting down at the Comet he would spread his dark, luxurious genitals out across his lap with good natured generosity like someone offering to share a lunch....Baby Poorpoor, who like many others loved Franco and went to the Comet every night because of him, saw the dapper butcher speeding down the aisle and knew at once, by many signs, that tonight Franco was insane. Tonight Franco will not sit down beside him, will not take his hand, will not lead him blushing into the men's room, will not whisper in his ear of beloved Havana raped by the red tigers. As he moved through the theater with a blissful look on his face, Franco was putting all his rings on his right hand. One on the index finger, the third finger and the pinky; two on the ring finger. Rapidly and blindly, he jerked off anyone on whom his hand fell. Going from boy to man, from bum to queen, he discharged them all like a frenzied milkmaid. His right hand and five rings soon dripped and stank, glistened in technicolor radiance. In his trance Franco even sat down alongside his lovers or chased them through the house if they, out of heartbreak, refused him. Baby Poorpoor submitted to the ritual, tears rolling down his face. Why, why? he asked the cowboys on the battered screen. Indifferent as gods, they pursued their inexorable destinies....Inside the mad Franco lived a murderer named Tomtom Jim who longed for blood. He lurked in the forests of Franco's soul, hiding in the tropical darkness, black as the darkness, looking for victims. No passerby escaped his rage, his hunger for death. He never slept." All the characters are dreams of each other.

Thank you for letting me keep your picture. You are one of the myths of Tangier. The other night when we were for the millionth time planning some way of making a killing before Tangier becomes a tourist heaven, and we decided on a chic restaurant called The Majhoun Palace, and decided we needed a very special person to be host, Ira suggested you.

Must run. Kisses to you both.

Love, Alfred

(marginal note) Monday. I got a letter from Harriet and she says she hates my title() and artnouveau. Now I feel depressed about the whole book.

To Edward Field and Neil Derrick   Jan. 22, 1965

Boyeles:

Why can't Neil take more than three weeks off? Then we could take
a nice leisurely trip. Actually, since you both drive, the trip could be
leisurely anyhow. I keep imagining myself doing all the driving. Oh,
I can hardly wait to show you all the beautiful things I've found. June
is hot, though not too bad, hovering around ninety I guess. (If you
come in June you should come here first, then go second to Madrid
and London.) September is worse, because the heat and dust have
accumulated after four or five months without rain. May would really
be ideal; is that too early for Neil? Anyway Chauen and Fez are only a
very few hours from here. Marrakech is a day's drive; or better, a night's
drive. Tangier of course is never hot, hardly ever over 80 or 85. You
should check group flights before you buy your ticket. You might get
something, say, to Madrid round trip for $250. You should ask Harriet
who knows about these things....Yes, study Arabic. But make sure it
is Moghrebi.

We went to Larache yesterday with Mohammed Dumdum to give
blood to Hamid who is in the hospital again with peritonitis again. His
appendix, not his foot. He was supposed to be operated on but never
went back, so he nearly died again. I made the mistake of taking the
car although that disc on the side of the motor block that keeps the
water in had already come out once on the road to Arcila and I had
never repaired it only pushed it back in. So of course we got stuck and
a shepherd kept running up and down the cliff to a little water hole to
fill up his boots for us. I finally got some putty and pasted it on and it
lasted us home; Dris prayed the whole way to all the saints. Anyway,
in Larache it turned out that three of the brothers had already given
blood and the hospital can't store it. They said they would operate
on Monday and if more was needed we could come then. Only I was
disqualified for having the wrong group. They are all, the whole family,
in a bad way now, as Ali the bus driver had an accident and was put
on probation. So about twenty-five of them are living off Abdeslam's
pinchito stall. So now I'm contributing to their welfare. There is one

rich brother who evidently is a criminal and smuggler and lives with a Danish girl but doesn't give his family anything.

The Ford Foundation gave a bunch of awards to the exciting new critics to encourage criticism. So Susan got $6500.

Did I tell you one of the leading characters in my book is called Mary Poorpoor? She lives simultaneously two distinct lives in different places. One is with Tomtom Jim who is helping her search for fairyland because the fairies exchanged their baby for hers. (Baby Poorpoor is also an infant all through the book as well as a huge fat man who is also James Madison.) She and Tomtom Jim have three other children together, a girl named Bijou and twin boys. In the end Tomtom Jim and Bijou get eaten on a movie location by fake cannibals and Baby pushes the twins into the river Smahaa, (pardon us). The other life Mary leads is one in which she keeps meeting the same woman over and over again and living with her and they never recognize each other. "Stealing themselves, the pilgrims continued along the path, and soon they were at the mouth of the forest where the pitchblack tamaracks seemed topless. They stepped forward, but didn't have the impression of entering; rather, they felt as if they'd been swallowed by the wood, sucked into it. It was an unusual place in many ways other than the color and height of the trees. The earth, if one could call it that, was all translucent blue stone, and except for the tamaracks, whose roots could be detected under the forest floor, there was no vegetation at all. Not a bush nor a fallen leaf. Not even any little trees. The light in the wood was yellow and it didn't come in from above, nor from anywhere else apparently. It was simply there, gentle and asleep, like a cat. But the most curious thing of all was that there was no smell of any kind. Mary and Tomtom Jim both noticed this phenomenon at the same time. Together they sniffed. Then Mary leaned forward and sniffed at his armpit. 'Nothing,' she said. 'Not a thing.' Tomtom Jim then knelt down and stuck his head up Mary's skirt. 'Hardly anything,' he said, getting up. But Mary could tell he was just being polite, and that whether everything else smelled or not, her cunt still stank. Feeling terrible, she pretended to be very interested in the height of the trees."

I have about eighty or ninety pages done, but surely can't finish the book this month. Next, hopefully. It is really a marvel. Though my moment of exalted delusion, during which I imagined I would make a fortune, is over.

Gordon Sager, whom I can't bear, cast my I Ching. I had asked what the oracle thought of my book, but inside I was asking, Would I ever be rich and famous? The answer was Oppression, and the change was Breakthrough. I am going through one of my unbearable periods. Everyone seems to me unbearable. I haven't seen Paul lately because he got on my nerves finally over the kif. As Larbi went away, he didn't have any. Though Dris started buying and chopping for him. Then one day Paul told me the new lot was terrible. Did I tell you this? I tasted it and it truly was terrible. But I knew it wasn't Dris's fault as I'd tasted it while he was chopping. Paul had put something in to make it taste bad. But I just said, Speak to Dris about it. He didn't of course talk to Dris, but everytime I saw him after that he had something new to say about it. He found out it was inferior stuff, etc. The last time I saw him he had decided it was fish and he'd put cloves in and it tasted all right. I said nothing but haven't seen him since, for fear I would start screaming at him again. Which is what he wants because nobody else gets emotional with him.

No, I don't like to fight with Harriet. I just don't like or trust women anymore. I've started identifying with men. She said that about my title to be destructive. That is the only comment or question about my novel she has ever made. She said she loathed it....The hammam is the Turkish bath sort of. It costs fifty francs. And then another fifty francs or sometimes a hundred for a man to scrub you. But since he [Dris] would have to go in the middle of the night, when there are no buses, it would mean another three hundred in taxis because of his foot. And for a week there we were living on money he was borrowing from Arabs. Anyway, it is all right now. The money came. I've never gone to the baths, chiefly because he makes such a fuss about it. He doesn't want me to go to the big steamy room but to take a little private room. And of course he won't go in with me lest they think we've come to fuck, the way people do in the private room. Also in the large rooms.

Who is the man who thinks Rechy and I should make up? Is that a joke of some kind or what? Are we supposed to be mad at each other?

Edward, I keep thinking I should go to New York when I finish my book and take care of my family business. Should I? What do you think? Dris says I could go for a month. Who is Buffie Johnson? The name sounds so familiar I'm trailing off into inconsequentials too.

Love, Alfred

To Edward Field & Neil Derrick   Feb 5, 1965

Quelbi:

An envelope was just slid under my door by the postman and it made me so nervous; it looked just like from myself. Same envelope. Same type. Only from Joan Michaelson. She says you met her in Gramercy Park. Why didn't you tell me? She makes the meeting sound very romantic. I am annoyed that she stole my novel from the Brandeis Library.

Poopy, please go at once and get us a press agent. Or anyway check into it and find out prices, etc. You are absolutely right, we need one. So don't waste anymore time.

Dris and I had a terrible fight four days ago. I flipped out and started screaming in the apartment and out in the hall. It was begun trivially, over going to Arcila, but Mohammed Dumdum was here, and Dris had to act like he was boss on account of him. We stll haven't made up. We hardly talk to each other. And please don't tell me I love to fight. I don't. I hate it. I even have stopped fighting with my landlady. He keeps trying to have sex in the middle of the night and I keep refusing. I still hate him.

Jane's book is getting bad reviews in England. The Observer even implies she imitates Beckett, though of course she preceded him. I went there last night with Ira to comfort her. Gordon [Sager] was there and also Flopsie of Flopsie and Mopsie, these awful Princeton queens who have lived together for years but pretend to be straight. Flopsie is a writer called John Hopkins. Sometimes to be bitchy I refer to them as Fluffie and Muffie because Jane's pet name for Paul is Fluffie. Anyway her book is so good. She deserves great fame for it....Mary Lee [Settle]'s new book is also reviewed. They hate it but they all adore *Herzog*. At last the square world has its voice.

So now you know what my life has been like, talking with all those hideous other voices coming out of me. Don't tell me things like you want to commit suicide over it, that hurts me; it sounds like a message, a suggestion.

Moghrebi is hard to learn from a book because of pronunciation, and because everything changes from region to region and most books are Rabat-Casablanca. I have three or four that I don't think would be too useful to you alone, but there is a phrasebook Norman bought that I liked. I'll buy it and run through it putting notes and airmail it to you. The grammar is virtually nonexistent. It is just a matter of memorizing a few rules and a small vocabulary.

Ramadan is over, thank God. On the 26th day, the day of destiny, light, truth, commemorating the prophet's reception of the best or largest part of the Koran, the devils and angels all came out to earth. Here, everyone walks around all night, including girls who otherwise never come out of their houses. Sex is forbidden. Dris was in Arcila with his family. I got tipsy on dry martinis and kif, and coming home at two a.m. stopped on a dark deserted street to pee. A man in a djellaba approached me and offered me a cigarette and began kissing me. It was exciting. But he was obviously dying of guilt and was so nervous that I got into the car and drove home. The last time I was unfaithful was with a very beautiful boy (who seems since to be turning into a real hustler). I fucked him in a pine wood on Malabatta. In the early fall, at twilight. I acted out little obscene fantasies with him and he went along with them, but was obviously more excited about driving around in a car. Lolita.

It has been spring now for ages. You would not believe how thick and green the pastures are and full of flowers. The Mountain is one huge burst of mimosa and everywhere perfume. It rains every couple of days heavily but doesn't get cold, thank God. I had a letter from Charles Wright saying how NY is cold and snowy. You never tell me about the weather.

I have worked away badly for the last week, and my New Year resolution has come to nought. I hope I can send you the book this month. After your letter I realized the book is full of "this" phenomenons. You can cross them all out and correct it. Please tell me the truth. I mean, when you said how that "passage about Franco at the Comet was brilliant, marvelous etc., I just screamed with laughter. Of course, I mean by the truth: tell me it is lousy. It probably is, but I can't be bothered caring. For years I couldn't write a book because I didn't have a reason. Now I have a reason: money and fame. So in reading the book you should think of that. Not whether I will be loved or critically appreciated. The critics will hate it, which makes me happy to think about.

When you be a chronic teahead, kif is virtually useless unless chopped fresh every day. You buy a *rabetta,* a little branch. You throw away everything but the flowers, then chop, sift, blow, crush, add the tobacco. You have enough for an evening. Paul buys for days in advance. I don't know how he gets high on it, but he claims he does.

I have about 150 pages of text. I am adding a new brief chapter about Isobel, the Yellow Rose. She is a fantasy of Ismael's, but takes on independent life. She tries to smuggle three strands of pearls across the world in her asshole and they get absorbed by her body and ever after her skin has a lovely glow.

Love and kisses to both of you.

Alfred

To Edward Field   Feb. 16, 1965

Beloved: I love you. I adore you. I worship you. I kiss you all over. If you didn't exist inside me, what would I do? You come to my rescue continually, like a knight in shining armor. I'm still grateful to you for your aid and comfort given so generously last night. Some friends of Remy's have come [Charles Stanley and Deborah Lee], and they are young and sweet. They've brought a lot of painting supplies from Remy for Dris. I have been busy entertaining them and it's been nice. Except I can't be with people so much. I get the horrors when my quiet interior days get lost in the traffic. Anyway they made New York seem terribly exciting. Things happening. Everybody doing things. But yesterday it was people all day and then Ira and Rosalind were here and then Remy's friends came, bringing a bottle of champagne. And flowers. And they talked more about HOW EXCITING everything was. And they all talked about drugs for hours until I wanted to vomit. It grew dark and there was no kerosene to start the fire with and I wrapped myself in my burnoose and thought: why do I not consider the Frug a great advance in freedom and civilization? Why do I still think it is boring to spend hours talking about drugs? And I felt so alone. Then, hero, you came to me. And I knew that you too would have been sitting there wrapped in your burnoose, feeling nauseous. There are tears of gratitude in my eyes now. We'd bought a big chicken imagining the Americans would be here for supper, but then I didn't want anyone here for supper. I just wanted to be here with Dris and the fire. So I didn't invite anyone until it was pretty clear I wasn't going to, and then I drove them all into town and said I'd meet them later so they wouldn't come back. I felt bad, of course, guilty, and on the way back, again you comforted me with the phrase: You have right to be yourself.

Adding to my depression last night was a letter from Epstein. It is nearly a year now to the moment when I went crazy and I think it may have had something to do with the turning of the season, because I do feel batty for a little, here and there. Especially the overwhelming rage and hatred comes up in me. But don't worry, please. I know it isn't going to be like last year. I have my book now, which also I should say was a source of comfort to me last night. I mean I could turn to my own people in my mind. Anyhow Epstein. I wrote him asking him to submit *Goliath* for the National Book Award if it wasn't too late, and I also mentioned my ad in Evergreen, and (it was all very polite) asked if he would watch sales for the next month or so as I was very anxious to know if there would be any results. He doesn't say a word about the National Book Award, so I presume he hasn't or won't enter it. "I'll let you know if the ad sells any copies, but if I were you I wouldn't plan any expensive parties." Isn't he horrible?

Paidhaiki, I can't think about the lawsuit now. I've had another nice letter from the lawyer, but I can't answer it, and it doesn't seem necessary now. I'll write after I finish my book, so if he gets in touch with you you can tell him that.

Paul got his Evergreen ages ago, but I never got mine. I sent them a card. As I anticipated, Paul tried to make me paranoid about the piece ["Glory Hole"], but I told him to stop. He says the piece is hyperbole but very amusing.

Remy's friends do beautiful things but fill me with a creeping horror that their things are part of a new movement. They bring their cigarettes in little fancy art nouveau antique boxes, like from Egypt. (As the boxes are small they run out of cigarettes very quickly and smoke up all of mine in their ugly wrappers.) They both wear steelrimmed glasses like [Village Voice critic] Soren Agenoux, etc.

Jane is not nice; she is really awful, but I can't explain why. I'll tell you, or try to, when you're here. She only SEEMS nice, but she and Paul are one person...Pot used to make me sexy. Now it makes me ticklish. I don't have any potency problems now. Though of course I did in New York; we used to talk about it. Rosalind once said in passing about how Jewish cocks get so tiny when they aren't erect, and I thought of this last night. It suddenly occurred to me that all those centuries of fear aren't so easily discarded....That little Arabic pamphlet is terrible so I'm not sending it. I suppose I knew much less when I first saw it.

So what should I do? I'm thinking of just preparing a bunch of lessons for you myself and sending them to you. It would be faster, simpler and truer. I think Sicily gets hotter earlier than here. Spring goes on here until July. You would go out of your mind if you saw the fields. They are like kindergarten drawings of pastures, full of wild splotches of color everywhere....We are thinking of taking an enormous mansion on the Mountain with Dale and Liz. It has about fifteen rooms and divides itself naturally into apartments. Huge grounds. Four baths. Terraces. About $60 a month. Dris didn't want to live up there before, just the two of us in a big house, but he likes the idea of dividing it into three apartments. And he's excited about maintaining the farm and raising chickens and goats and sheep. It has the grandest view, and has a mimosa orchard and a cedar orchard. If we move up there you can stay with us and be independent at the same time. If not, I will fix you up nicely. Would you like a darling little house in the Casbah? It would be my present to you? There's a very cute one, not lost in the medina but up, very bright and light and toyey. Probably that is a silly idea as I hope we'll be travelling. Oh, it will be thrilling to show you this beautiful Morocco. Oh, it will be thrilling to lay these lovesore eyes upon you and boyele....Dris and I made up. And I love him. He is always with me in a room, but he isn't much help when the conversation is in English.

I said three notable oracular things out of my burnoose last night. I said: Now that pop art is in bloom, they have a bowl of pop art in their room. And: It will have to become a priest society like in the Middle Ages. And: The problem, it seems to me, is simply how to stop talking about THEM. Neither to put them down nor put them up, but to concentrate on what is immediately round one....I have only about thirty or forty pages left to do in the book....I love you, *paidhaiki mou*. Alfred

To Edward Field   March 2, 1965

Darling boychick: Please stop worrying about your cock. I think basically the trouble is that too much attention is paid to it, not not enough. Can't you walk down a street and know, even if he isn't wearing tight pants, who has a big cock? They act like it. Even here in Morocco. But at the same time, here there isn't that competitive thing like in America, because they don't have big fantasy lives. In America I always expected to be rejected so how could I really get a big hard on, except when I was very young and went after sex because I really wanted sex not emotional security. Here, if you are friends with anyone, they expect you to go to bed with them. But even if the boy is someone you get off the street and you know he expects money at the end of it, unless it is a hardened hustler, he enjoys himself and you know he isn't measuring you or competing with you or having a fantasy about someone else. And also an immense cock here doesn't negate all the smaller ones, although it is proud. You know how sex is really for us, the acting out of a fantasy. That's why we're queer and Moroccans aren't. Because they are just making it. And they've been circumcized too and have the whole shame and guilt thing like the Jews about the genitals. I started having hard on trouble when I mixed up sex with psychological needs. It is very difficult for me to think these things out, as ever since The Mistake I can't think this way, in terms of explanations and generalities. When I can't get a hard on and want one, I usually look close around me for an answer. Like: I'm too tired, and then I don't force myself, since I don't feel obliged to prove anything. Or like when I felt like picking up a boy: Dris will find out so I get too nervous, or something like that. I mean, naturally your cock gets big at the Y when you're busy, not idle in your mind and concentrating on sexualemotional things. YOU SHOULD NOT BE PAYING ANY ATTENTION TO YOUR RELATIONSHIP. Neil is there to be your comfort and your aid. Don't pay attention to his fantasy life. It is none of your business and it is just part of the municipal disease. You should be doing your own business, which is your career, earning money, getting famous, just writing poems. (marginal note: I think maybe somehow you have to forgive yourself, to really pardon and love yourself.) You are beautiful and you have a beautiful cock and you should let people love you and it. Sex is really something nice that we spoil. The next time you are tempted to worry about your cock, worry about your career. They are both just distractions, but sex belongs to God and shouldn't be used as a diversion from boredom. I can remember only very few times in my adult life when I really wanted sex so much that I thought I'd explode. It wasn't frustrating, it was delicious. Desire is delicious, but I hardly ever feel it. Anyway, stop blaming your poor old parents for something that happened forty years ago. (Doesn't that sound awful, put that way?) And to tell you the truth I don't care anymore—no, that's a lie. I was about to say I don't care if I become impotent, but I just thought I do.

Anyway, it occurs to me if you had a bald head to worry about, you wouldn't pay so much attention to how hard your cock was or under what circumstances it best arose. You should read your poem to the left hand.

Charles and Deborah came back from their travels and are leaving for New York tomorrow. I like him very much now. We got very stoned on Dale's Christmas pudding, full pot, yesterday. There has been a lot of majoun around lately and Rosalind has been baking the little cookies of Marrakech. Yesterday was fun and we stayed high for about eight hours. Dris and I are drying rabbit skins to make *mettuis*, kif pouches, with. Shall we send you one or wait until you come?

I'll give Charles Stanley a book for you to study. It is Jane's. And is good enough. Here are some things for the moment to remember: [He gave a page of advice on speaking Moghrebi and a basic guide to grammar, pronunciation, and vocabulary, emphasizing the real language rather than by the book.] ...That is the way I talk, with my 12th Avenue Arcila Accent....If you talk the way I do people will love you more because they will think you love them and not an abstraction who talks like no one.

Your shoes arrived and they are acres big on him, though spectacular. We finally decided to trade them in for others here. Thank you, lovie.

We've quarrelled about them endlessly, as I felt it would be a failure of love not to wear them. I've changed my mind....Here are some handy terms in Arabic: *zubi f'soowetsek*, my cock in your ass, or *fummek*, your mouth. *Troll fl fresh* (the r in *troll* as in French), get into bed, *andi zub kbir a mezyen*: I have a big beautiful cock. *Radi* (French r) *nheb howik*, I will love to fuck you. *Radi nmshee howik*, I am going to fuck you. I think that last is wrong. I must ask Dris, but he has just gone to the hammam as we are going to put a black magic spell on the woman upstairs today to make her move. She has complained to the bank (which is agent to the landlady) that we make "nocturnal scandal," etc., and they wrote us a letter to leave by the 15th of March. The truth is she hates having a common Arab in the house; she is a Swiss Jew, an old maid with a big consular fantasy; she always has all the grand and the mighty (most, or many, of whom I know) in for cocktails and she is embarrassed by us. Paul says she is also hot for Dris. She has always made her hatred felt, though I never cared or ever even spoke to her. Finally when the letter came I tried to, and she ran screaming up the stairs saying she hadn't slept a single night since we moved in. Poor woman. Anyway, she always comes home from her grand dinners at 1 a.m. and clatters around in heels and slams doors, moves furniture, etc. Neil would adore her. I asked the concierge several times to tell her to be quiet. But the odd thing is now that she has done this awful thing she is scared silly of us and there is never a peep now. Anyway, everyone hates her and wishes she would go, she is bossy and snotty. So Miss Henry's maid has gone to the *fqe* today to get us some *s'heur* to stick under her door. (Dris has to be pure for it.) And Pepita, the concierge, is giving us a thermometer. We have to put that in our armpits and then break it at her door (*la juive's* door) and push the quicksilver under. That is supposed to make everything darken in her eyes and she will move. (All this is secret, naturally). It must be creepy finding mercury under your door in this day of science fiction and William Burroughs. Anyway, I wrote the bank that if I hear anything more of this I will sue for defamation.

I've only got about four more chapters (about 12-15 pages) to rewrite. There are some chapters I really hate, and will have to change again....Yes, I wrote you that I felt this book was like your poem. It happened very late to me though. "Stand Up," I mean. I am now the kind of person who is happy and at home in a room full of men. I don't need a woman around anymore. In fact I don't like women around. I go down to the Cafe La Paz and sit with all the Jewish businessmen. Oh, Old Irving, (not Irving Rosenthal), Old Oiving from the Garment District is opening a little hotel here and I will fix you up a room there. He is very cute. He has decided to call the hotel, the Tangier Hilton. Actually the Atlas is really very nice only it is in that French quarter and rather expensive. Do you want a bath in your room? We didn't take the house on the Mountain nor the house in the Casbah. The Parade is where all those alcoholic faggots and nymphomaniacs go, like Tallulah Bankhead's sister. Smokers don't go there....If *La Juive* moves, I will take her apartment too, because I do need more room and put a stairway up from the terrace (or a ladder) and you can stay here. Unless you don't want to. *Paidhaiki*, you must say frankly if you want to stay with us or prefer to be alone. I would prefer to be alone. I mean, if I were coming here. But I would prefer to have you stay with us....Dris is sending you and boyele some new pictures with Charles Stanley. We are going out with them to Arcila to have couscous with my in-laws. Oh, what do you know, after all these years, Hamid's foot is cured. It was limited gangrene and would have gone years ago if he had bothered about it. I think it is all a lie about his having a million doctors. Anyway, he has to go back to have his appendix out and then he will be, *insha'allah,* as good as new....The summer ended and we have been having gigantic equinoctial rains again. Yesterday was like a hurricane. There have been two hailstorms and hurricanes.

Such terrible things have been happening. The season. Some women were raped by three Arabs in the *Forêt Diplomatique*, French women I think, and one was a virgin. So they captured three guys, who knows if they are the rapists, and tortured them and knocked their teeth out and hung them by their heels outside the gendarmerie and admitted the public at 50 francs apiece. Then the sultan ordered them to be hung by their wrists until dead, no water, just a crumb of bread per day. Last I heard one was dead. Probably the others now. All the Arabs approve of this, including Dris. Because she was a virgin. Also, a little boy was raped by the barman at Merkala (cf. Larbi's book) and I heard the boy too was dying. A boy was murdered in the Medina and his djellaba was sewn up like a sack. Another detail from Paul, about a murder that took place two months ago. The boy's asshole was sewn up and he was left at the door of his parents' house. It all sounds terrible, but you have to remember that any little thing immediately gets great notoriety here.

How can you say such silly things about yourself? You are the wisest, most wonderful person I have ever known and besides that, a great poet with your own voice. You are also dashingly handsome and with full cheeks doubtless irresistible. All you need is a little more meat on you. You should allow your cock to be worshipped and adored, the way it deserves to be.

This is the dedication of my book: "This book is dedicated to the memory of the two old Italians who lived for many years in a shack with a tin roof held down by rocks, opposite the ocean, on the solitary stretch of road between the Cape Spartel and the Grotto of Hercules, Province of Tangier. They died in the autumn of 1964, within fifteen days of one another. I do not know their names." I felt awful when I found out they both died. I cried. The younger one got sick and was taken to the hospital and the older who was about ninety and had an enormous white beard and wore a big Italian hat and a sort of winding wine-colored girdle around his waist stayed on alone. The boy who brought the bread finally told the police that the old man hadn't been visible for three days, so they went and found the body. The younger one died two weeks later. The old one used to come out to me on the beach with all their dogs and try to talk me into becoming their partner. They had a kind of ramshackle bar setup and they'd fixed up their piece of land to look just like Italy with bocce and all. The old one dreamed of turning it into a big tourist resort. The younger one was like an embittered wife. I am told there is now litigation over the land. When Dris and I went out there the other day there was only one dog left, practically starved. I brought her some food. Do you think it is terribly corny to dedicate my book to them? I cried and cried and cried over them and felt they should have some memorial. It was rumored that the old one made *s'heur*, but he denied it.

I have been hours at this letter.

Love and kisses to both of you, even you, oh avuncular one.

Alfred

P.S. Yesterday was a year since I sent you that telegram!

When are you coming? You can extend the 29-day tours with a doctors note. I can get you one.

Please look around for a good portable radio to bring me. Not a little awful one, but something that really gets shortwave. And tell me the prices.

To Edward Field.   Saturday. Undated.

Paidhaiki mou: Your carpet is ready. I just saw it. It is unbearably beautiful. You will have to change your whole living room around it. It's simple but very ritz. The problem is, what shall I do about it? Madame Pinatel is ready to pack it in sacking and let me take it to the post office. However, I'm afraid you will have a terrific duty on it. You can't take it on the plane with you. It weighs a ton. It looks good enough to eat.

I was up late last night because Charles Wright returned, so I'm feeling shitty today. He is really such a bastard. He didn't bring me the carbon paper that I wanted. I'm supposed to be typing up my novel but am only on page two because I keep changing things.

I had some opium last week, a little sliver in front of the lower teeth. It dissolved bitterly. It was mild but lovely, only it made me a little bit irritable. Now I know why they always lie around on shelves dreaming. They don't want to be disturbed.

I told Charles I was afraid he was going to become our James Baldwin. He acts just like a celebrity. He came back smelling successful, injecting a hollow tube that kept saying to me: failure, failure.

Chapter Two: "Noon in the garment district. The sunny streets swarming with hungry people hunting lunch. Joy swam in the air, as did lint, clots of fur and multicolored fuzz. Even Baby Poorpoor, lost for a moment in the appetite and freedom of the crowd, was happy. He mingled, smiling, and fell in love with everyone he saw—the slender secretaries, the strong boys pushing racks of dresses, the manufacturers with little puffs of hair sticking out of their ears and nostrils. No one looked at him nor loved him back, but this didn't bother him until a cloud passed across the sun, turning everything gray. Then his rapture darkened. He grew sad, but not bitter, and very tired suddenly. It was exhausting not to be loved back. Maybe if he gave his hair a blond rinse? Or lost some weight, say fifty pounds? Or stole enough money to buy rich blue contact lenses instead of these flaring pockmarked (from where the rhinestones had fallen out) tortoise shells that used to belong to his mother? Baby gave a long painful sigh, scaring himself because the sound came from such depths."

I have to hang up now and finish the chapter. Love and kisses, Alfred

To Edward Field   March 5, 1985

Dearest Heart: I finished the revision. It's 158 pages. My pages. So I guess it will be about 170 regular type, long enough. God be praised. Would you ever have believed it? There are three or four chapters that really stink and must be altered before I type up the copy to send. There is a great deal of lousy writing too, but that can come out presently, and I hope you will read it carefully and note all things you think should be changed. I haven't read it yet, so I assume it stinks, but it doesn't matter. The next one will be better. So don't be afraid to note as many bad things as you like. I am a little tired of the title now, but it seems right. The book is a mystery really.

I'm not feeling exhilarated about the novel. Strangely enough. What I would like to do is go to Chauen and Fez for a few days to get it out of my mind, so that I could read it all new when I come back. Maybe I will.

I've just spent the last few minutes touching the pages of my book. It is nice to touch.

I got tired of Charles Stanley and Deborah Lee. I felt she gave the show away. They do this number about living in the present. I think Susan's camp article must have been about people like them. He is good at it, but Debby is like a member of the CP or the Church or Zen. For instance, I told her she could read such and such a book on the airplane, and she said, Oh, no, I like to give my whole attention to the plane, it's such fun. They do elegant little things that are really very cheap, I think I told you. Like carry cigarettes in fancy art nouveau boxes that hold about two cigarettes; so they run out of smokes in a minute and use mine. Or just sit around being high forever and eternally eating in my house. Or saying how they meant to bring such and such, but didn't, like a gift to Dris's family for the couscous dinner. Although actually they did bring a bottle of champagne when they first came.

Are you going to take a lot of luggage to Morocco? If not, if you are under your fifty pounds each, will you bring me some things? They are easy. What I would really like is my phonograph—that little tiny one I gave Harriet. It weighs about five pounds and my two Mozart opera albums. I would also like a portable radio, but if I go to Gib to mail the book, I might buy one there. I'm terrified of leaving Morocco because I'll have to cross two frontiers twice, not looking like my photo on the passport. And also I have to go to the cops here first for my exit visa. And then they might say go away and don't come back. Or bring your financial statements, and prove you aren't changing money on the black market.

Dris is doing a lot of pictures. I want to go and ask the Tangier First

Gallery to put on a show for him. If you tell me when you are coming maybe they will do it then. On the invitations it will say "...In the presence of their lovelinesses Edward and Neil.

Love to you both, Alfred

To Edward Field   March 19, 1965

Lovey:I'll send your carpet next week as soon as Mme. Pinatel comes back from Casa. It will require a great deal of running and doing, which you would go mad doing here (five different government offices). And you can't take it on the airplane. I feel terrible about the customs, I mean the duty you'll have to pay,

Well, three weeks is better than no weeks. I can hardly wait. Where shall we go when you come? I think Dris and I may be going to Fez for a couple of weeks after I send you my book. To the thermal baths at Moullay Yacoub. If that doesn't help his spur, then he will have to have an operation, and that worries me because all the good doctors have left. There's supposed to be a good hospital in Madrid. Did I tell you his brother is practically cured?

I had a letter from Kluger offering me $1500 payable quarterly for six reviews (including short ones) during the year beginning next September. I've accepted. I think something must be going for me in NY.

Extro refused bail because he is happy in jail. The beatniks here love getting arrested. There are dozens of cute little beatniks here, I, or anyone could fuck. The idea appeals to me, but then when I think of having to pretend to be interested in them I get turned off. I've sent away to England for mescalin. I have a piece of opium and I suck a sliver now and then. It makes me very tired, but also it tells me to accept myself, whatever I am. It turns sex off completely....Monday was Dris's 23rd birthday and we had a party. I bought a huge cake with candles, only Columbine ate half before anyone got here. It was nice anyway. Charles Wright ruined the party however. He sat not eating or smoking or saying a single word. I had a chat with him a couple of days later and gave him to understand I didn't want him around.... Dale is opening a bar [The Lion and the Lizard] and may hire Dris as his bouncer. This doesn't make me too happy, but it makes Dris happy. And boys have to grow up after all. The whole town here is charming youths and aging queens. But don't worry, the youths always win.... Dris is inventing new things in his paintings. Please bring him lot of magic markers and those nylon-tipped pens, all the colors you can get hold of. Remy's chalks haven't worked out too well, nor the rice paper. He liked the colored wrapping paper better.

I'm on chapter 8 of the retyping of my novel. Of course I'm rewriting again, so it will probably be weeks before I send it. Chapter 8 has turned into the most obscene thing wherein John Doe makes James Madison (who lies around in a pink brassiere and yellow panties) shove four tampaxes up his ass.

Next day. Saturday. An extraordinary thing happened to me last night. Dris was in Arcila to show off his new clothes (pants from Chas. I paid for them and a shirt, new birthday shoes from me, and a fancy watch he is buying on the installment plan from Mustapha of the PussyCat), and I took a bath and decided to go out on the town. I'd been working hard and unsatisfactorily on Chap. 8 all day. Then your letter came. Then I wrote you the first page, smoking a little kif. And all of a sudden I realized, reading back both my letter and your letter, that the reason I lose my voice while writing is that I forget whom I'm talking to. I always have. So I sat down and rewrote the chapter to you. It took a half hour and slid out like a dream. Five pages. Now it is in carbon copy already and I feel inspired. The trouble with me is that I am really a coward. I remember over and over and over and over again the most important thing you ever said to me one night in your apartment. I don't know what we were talking about, but you said: "Well, Alfred, maybe you don't take enough risks." It was such a bombshell, and it has never stopped exploding. Until then I had always thought I was terribly daring. And I had never even dared try to be myself.

Paul came over just as I finished the chapter last night. He's been to Casa for Holiday Magazine. He brought me Baudelaire's *Paradis Artificiels* as a present. We got terribly stoned. I am handling him quite well. Whenever he makes subtext, I immediately say, oh, like me? Then he crawls out of it. I hope this makes him stop. Jane came to Dris's birthday party and I subtexted her into silence. She is a rat. I loathe her. Anyway, they are going to America for two months and I'll give them your address. I'd give them the rug if I thought they were human....We did the *s'heur* with *la juive*. Dris soaked a special paper in magic incense, then buried it at an abandoned grave. Then he burned a piece of special paper each day for four days. The story is that when this is done we will forget the *juive* as the grave has been forgotten. It seems to be so. She has suddenly discovered, Jane tells me, that I'm a celebrity and now speaks well of me.

I drove out to the lighthouse at Malabatta the other afternoon because it was beautiful and because I had my eye on a boy I'd seen there recently, a cute very young dark scowly dirty little shepherd. He appeared, but alas I had picked up two hitchhikers whom I knew vaguely from the Pussy Cat. One of them, it turns out, is a mercenary in the Congo and is returning. I had to control myself not to put them out of the car. He was just what you'd expect. He says they hardly ever get paid, but they blow up the banks as they capture a town and take all the money....No, it isn't odd to like dark rooms with pot. You want a soothing atmosphere, and one that is steady, so that you can learn. I am so grateful to kif you can't imagine. I sometimes feel like kissing Paul out of gratitude....I want to hire a bunch of Gnaoua musicians to come and meet my boyeles but I'm afraid you'd be put off by the show. *Paidhaiki*, everyone here is looking forward to meeting you, and you will be terribly bored with them, but please don't show it too much. You can imagine how bad the scene is if I thought Charles Stanley exciting.

I liked *The Messenger* [by Charles Wright] too, though it turns out Vercelle (his editor) rewrote it line by line. I wondered after I read his new ms last summer how he ever could have been so coherent. He wasn't. Vercelle was.

One of the most interesting things about you is that you are always a man instead of a beautiful object. You made your looks seem unimportant. How is that? I know what Neil means when he says you're fortunate, etc. Does that bother you? Ira told me the other night that he'd run into Charles in the Socco Chico (*souq ndakhil*) and they talked about me, and Ira said I was the best adjusted person he'd ever met. This doesn't bother me; it makes me think though I must be a terrific hypocrite. On the other hand, I enjoy myself immensely. I mean, I really do like people and things. I only hate to drink now. It makes me quite sick.

Kluger offered to send me *Herzog* but I don't want it. I only like to read things with strong plots now and lots of suspense. Story....I meant Chas. was like Jimmy [Baldwin] because he was acting like a celebrity when he got off the plane. But the fantasy dissappated very quickly.

Wasn't Fritz Peters Mary Aswell's husband? And didn't he write a queer novel? If you own that Gurdjieff book [*Boyhood With Gurdjieff*, by Fritz Peters], please bring it with you. You know I used to love him.

Oddly enough I don't feel the slightest sympathy for Extro. He doesn't mind. Remember when we got arrested in New Jersey? He was very happy about the whole thing. He is very bored and empty inside.

Love and kisses,

Alfred

To Norman Glass   March 30, 1965

Dear Norman: Thanks for your letters. I hope we're not going to have to discuss our RELATIONSHIP. You should go out and have some sex instead. Most of the Englishmen I knew were circumcized, though it's true they don't look it.

Hajmi was over with your letter which I read in a somewhat edited version, I confess. To tell the truth, it embarrassed me to have to say those things. I expect people don't make a very deep impression on you which is how you can abstract them into your fantasies when they're not with you. Or even when they are with you. I'll write a letter for him as soon as he comes over again. (He was supposed to have been here yesterday.) I have tried to explain about going to England, though you are crazy to think he couldn't divert himself. If you think you really want him then please do something about getting him there. Personally, I don't think you do. I think you just want to write your romantic letters like to the boy in Rabat. This isn't too fair to Hajmi. Nor really to me as the go-between.

Ira [Cohen] said he wanted to write an article on majoun for money and I encouraged him since I thought it was a natural. So he finally kvetched it out and it was quite astoundingly beautifully written. I sent it to my agent last month, and we heard yesterday it's been sold to Playboy for $1000. He is in seventh heaven, needless to say. And I'm glad too.

Paul and Jane have gone to America. I had a card today from the Madeiras where the ship stopped for a couple of hours. Have you heard anything about those riots in Casa and Fez? What do the English papers say? Here we get only very different stories.

I had a birthday party for Dris two weeks ago. Columbine ate half the birthday cake before anyone arrived. But it was nice anyhow. Except of course Charles sat not eating, not talking and ruined everyone's fun. The next day I had one of my famous SHOWDOWNS with him and haven't seen him since. He sits in Pinero's night and day, poor duck. But I can't suffer his character with him. I've also had another fight with Jay [Haselwood, owner of Parade Bar], thank God, and I hope he doesn't try to make up.

I'm about halfway through typing the carbon of my book. It's taking so long because of course I keep rewriting. I hear that publishers all over the place have their tongues hanging out for it. Of course they haven't seen it, and each writing makes it weirder. Holt, the publisher who is suing me, has offered to forget my debt and give me another $2000 if I give them the book. Also the Tribune has made me a, what I think is, spectacular offer.

I hear Brion Gysin is coming back next month, but Bill Burroughs isn't because he loves NY. Probably he has a lot of adulators there.

Write soon. Love, Alfred

To Edward Field   April 2, 1965

Paidhaiki: I'm mailing your carpet today. The delay isn't my fault but Mme. Pinatel's, who thought there was this horrendous procedure to go through. It is true you need more papers, but otherwise the shipping process is the same. So when my maid comes this morning (I'm up at six these days) I'll have her sew up the burlap sack and haul it off to the post office. I'm ordering one like it though I asked Mme. P. to try a design with some bright colors thrown in. Liz is going to order a tapestry with a lion and a lizard for the bar.

I've typed sixty pages so far and, because I'm rewriting as I go along, it's come out to 85 pages. The book will be over 200 pages at this rate, which I don't like. But I think it's much improved. There is a new scene in which Xavier and Death take a walk through the garden at night together. And also one in which John Anthony (Walter) gets fucked by Satan's tail on the quai in Paris. I've taken out that bad chapter about Franco at the Comet that I once sent you.

Epstein writes: "I want very much to see the new novel, and will do everything I can to make it a success if we decide to publish it. But I would not like to discuss the contract at this point. Let me read the book first, and if I see the possibilities that I fully expect to see, then we can discuss an additional advance as well as promotion and advertising plans….I promise you that if we are enthusiastic about it, we will do everything under the sun to make it a success." What do you think? Shall I send it to him? Or maybe you shouldn't think about it until I've sent you the book.

[Richard] Kluger writes that Cohen is dying to publish me and offers to drop the suit and give me an additional $1500-2000 advance if I give him the novel. You'd better tell that to the lawyer, the ass. Lawyers think people are so simple. Like themselves. So Kluger phoned Epstein to see if he'd let me go, but now everyone thinks that I'm going to be a hot property. Kluger says I should offer Holt the next book after this. But I'm tired of this publishing dance I've done and I want a publisher who'll pay up all my old publishers (Holt and Lipp, and Random, or any other combination thereof) and get me free of Vanguard's clutches.

Dris started working for Dale yesterday. 800 francs a day. They're interior decorating now, and I'm running the whole show. It's gold and black. I think they're overdoing the black, but it may work. Dris looks so glamorous at the bar. If I get rich soon, though, I'll buy him a fishing boat, so he can be who he is.

Did you hear about the riots in Casa? D's cousin who works for government TV in Rabat says 150 people were killed. The police shot into the crowd. There were riots also in Fez. And I hear also in Marrakech. The day before yesterday the cops went into a school here and arrested twenty students. It is calming down, though. But doubtless it's the beginning of the end because even the women are on the side of the students. My dentist expects a bloodless coup ultimately, like Egypt, by the military....Did you read about the terrible air crash off Cape Spartel? This is such a strange place. I guess because it's small. There is enormous community feeling. I mean, everyone cares, like about a plane crash. Even me a little.

I saw another gorgeous movie, "Topkapi," which according to Liz spells "I pack pot" when read backwards. I pegged it for LSD the minute it started going. Oh, I got my shipment of mescalin, five grams for $30 (ten doses), but won't do it until the book is done....I want to write my Pinocchio play before I write my next novel. I have to catch up with the old things. Like I am really writing *I, Etc.* now, just like you always said I had to. Then I will write the *Tangier Murder Mystery*. I have quite a few ideas for it. I have a general idea of my direction in writing now.

Paul and Jane have gone. I had a marvelous time the last time I saw them. I sat with a huge lump of opium dissolving under my lip. And everything was so clear. They were such a ridiculous and pathetic pair. Ira tells me Paul is afraid to show me his new book because he thinks I'm a famous critic and would do him harm if I hated it.

I've been working on dexamils and been having very little sleep, so today I'm really feeling pooped.

It's very strange, everyone loves me these days. Dris told me a friend of his heard that I am the father of the American community here. Even the kids and the beatniks love me, though I guess they always did. And I'm just as fresh and bossy as ever. And I might as well tell since you'll find out when you get here anyhow, I still have quarrels very often and I'm usually not on speaking terms with someone. Or several someone's.

I'm thinking of calling my book *The Exquisite Corpse, An Artificial Novel*. Does that sound pretentious? Please answer. It came to me when I was high on a white cookie....Be careful with Gurdjieff. Now is no longer the time to observe yourself. Now is the time to work.... It's funny you say you didn't keep after Grove because of shame and self-contempt. Fighting wouldn't have done any good anyhow. Look at me and Random House. I've discovered that you have to call things by their names right from the beginning. I mean, there is no point fighting after. You have to make yourself understood first.

Oh, I had a revelation for you the other day. You have to start writing rhymed poetry. It is going to come back within the next few years, so you might as well be the one to bring it back. Between now and the time you come here you must write fifteen rhymed poems. This will be the big thing in your new book, not the movie poems. The rhymes come in the first section, followed by the other poems. Keep this a big secret so no one else catches on first. And don't publish any of the poems in magazines until you're ready to send the book away. They should be short narrative poems. Like the movie poems. (Ira thinks your movie poems are lovely.)

This is your job. Trust me. I know. Love, Alfred

Going to mail rug now.

Queen magazine in London is publishing "Ismael."

Lovey: Tragedy has struck. After writing you the enclosed I went to the PO with the carpet and it turns out it is too long to go parcel post or whatever they do here. It has to be no more than one meter fifty. They said I should just fold it over, but I didn't like that too much, so I went and asked Mme. Pinatel about it. She says no. For a day or two yes, but a month would leave it with a permanent crease where the fold went. So I am back where I started now. Find out how I can send the rug and make sure they send an airmail letter to whoever is in charge here INSTRUCTING or ORDERING them to take the rug and ship it. It must be an ORDER. They don't understand please.

I woke up Saturday morning with one of those awful dizzy attacks I had often last fall. Maybe it really is liver, from too much coffee, pills, tobacco and kif. Greasy food. I'm not feeling dizzy anymore but I'm not feeling well. I'm working, but like with cotton in my head and tired eyes. I slept twelve hours last night, from 6 p.m. to 6 a.m. What do you think it is? It's like being on a rocking ship, seasick sort of. xxxxx Alfred

To Edward Field   April 14, 1965

Dear Edward:

I've been reading Ron Landau's book about Morocco which is pretty awful, but I keep thinking where you and Neil would like to go. Chauen is essential and besides is only a couple of hours away. Tiznit is also essential but is probably too far and will probably be too hot. I'd really like to go through the Draa Valley and see the casbahs, but of course it may be hot there too. I doubt if it would be terrible though. Have you thought where you want to go? Distances are not really too large. From here to Fez (via Chauen and Ouezzane) is only about 200 miles, half a day's drive. If you didn't feel like sightseeing we could go along the Mediterranean into Katama Province (the Rif mountains) where all the kif comes from. That too is close. Marrakech is a day's drive, via Rabat and Casa. Those are really the main things in the north. I've asked everybody about the Sksawa and no one has heard of them. Where is it exactly?

Ira hired the *djillala* musicians (trance, self-flagellation, etc.) to come to his house on Saturday night and invited a million people, Arabs and Nazarenes. It was marvelous. Dris turned into an Arab again, but I was afraid to let him dance on account of his foot. The house looked as it had when I took the LSD, like a jewel box. We're going to hire them again for you and boyele, though I doubt if you could take it until three in the morning. I stayed on after midnight only out of obligation to Ira. The trouble was the couscous was served just before midnight and then after that everything was anticlimax. But earlier, extraordinary things happened. Everyone was high on something or other anyhow, but about between ten and eleven, it really became magic. I felt the whole house take off like a magic carpet. I saw that reality was a gorgeous mosaic facade floating in a pale blue sky. Everything moved and ran and flowed and flew. Excuse me for being literary, I have a terrible cold. (I'm not joking.) I can't describe it is really the point and you will have to see it for yourself.

You will be high in Morocco from the minute you land until the minute you leave. Don't worry. I'm glad you smoke a lot. My book will be more interesting to you. I'll keep some mescalin until you come. And Ira has ordered one hundred mgs. (five hundred highs) of LSD which we are splitting. It should be here before you. I guess I have about sixty more pages to do on my book. There have been a lot of festivities here, and also Dris was working and I had to run down to the bar ten times a day to see him and boss them around at the bar. Everyone thinks I'm the owner. Yes, being high is really the only way. What a pity we didn't know that years ago. What were we doing? On the other hand I don't think I could have learned so much from it years ago....Dris's job is over temporarily, as now Dale has to wait for the liquor license. He spends his money as fast as he earns it, buying presents for his relatives. He bought me a gorgeous wooden vase for flowers. Japanese, I guess. Sort of like a tan mah jong tile. With dragons for ears. It is one of a pair, and Ira bought the other one. D. paid 800 francs for ours and then the bazaar owner made a fuss, claiming that it was worth 20,000. He wanted it back. His assistant had sold it when he was out. We didn't give them back. My house is beautiful these days, wait until you see all my schmattas and fancy lamps. Last night, I had a fantasy of you walking in and looking around, especially at the walls, and saying with a gasp: "Alfred, it's the Exquisite Corpse." Also it is full of flowers here. The world is full of flowers lately. I wish you could see the countryside. I never saw anything like it. I've got five bowls of flowers in this room right now. The prettiest is a bunch of wild flowers a boy sold me on the mountain, with blue daisies, orange daisies, bunches of little lavender things of all shades like pink and mauve and fuschia. The Japanese vase has dark purple irises and tall yellow things.

I got very depressed last week about my house. I decided none of it was me. (I think a lot depends on what chapter of my book I'm working on.) That I was bare and empty. And that all this beauty around me was a lie (facade floating in space). So one afternoon I got high and made a list of all the things in the house, deciding which was me and which wasn't me. And in the end I realized that even what wasn't me was me. I also told myself not to worry about imitating and being unoriginal. I think I am in a funny phase, really. I'm picking and choosing who I am going to be. I never was anybody, so now I'm making myself up. Revelation at *djillala*: The world is illusion, illusion's the only world, all the world is illusion, God is illusion.

Chapter Three. *Aid Kbir*. This is the festival celebrating Abraham's sacrifice of the ram instead of Isaac. Every Moslem house no matter how poor kills a ram, big or little, or if they are very poor a male goat. Dris invited me to Arcila and at first I didn't want to go. It was Tuesday. For weeks now those poor rams have been dragged through the streets or carried in carts or carried in baskets on burros. I was terribly depressed about it on Monday, so was Ira and Rosalind and everyone who wasn't an Arab. Dris went to Arcila Monday night and told me to come Tuesday at noon. As I knew the sacrifice would happen in the morning, I knew he was trying to protect me from it, and like I should just come for the meal. Although of course he doesn't really understand why it would bother me. He only knew it would. Anyway I woke up Tuesday feeling shitty and began to work. I also went out of my mind over all the baaaing and maaaing (it's sort of country here) of animals being dragged. Then all of a sudden, I thought, maybe it's about time I stopped being a lamb, a bull, an incinerated Jew, old dead Italians, etc. Part of this was the I Ching the night before at Ira's house. I got Earth Below and Earth Above, The Receiver, I think. Very female. I'd asked whether I should go to the sacrifice. Anyway, one of the things it said was: a tiedup sack, no praise, no blame. I thought, it's nobody's fault it happens and I just have to accept it, because that's how it is. So to my surprise, I jumped in the car and bought five dozen roses and drove to Arcila practically in ecstasy. Anyway, it was like driving through a flower market. And the country people were all out in their fancy nylon rags, you know those phosphorescent colors. So anyway I got there and I sat through it. It was the most horrible thing I ever saw. The father did it, while the brother-in-law Hassan and Dris held it down. It was a great lovely ram, tied up in the kitchen, sort of smelling the floor and people's feet, and really quite happy. (We are just putting one of it's legs into the oven downstairs now; Miss Henry is out and her maid is doing it for us.) I, of course, started working myself up to be sentimental, but then things happened too fast. The knives were sharpened. The ram thrown over and it's legs tied. Meanwhile all the million children and women are running around making bread on the charcoal fire and this and that. Two of the brothers were out killing sheep for other people. The father took off his djellaba. They gave me a chair to sit on. The mother poured a tablespoon of flour and a glass of water into the ram's mouth. Dris told me it was to make peace with him, so that when he goes to heaven he will have no complaints against the family. Anyhow, it ate, poor thing, lying on the floor with its eyes bulging. I think I must have gone into a state of shock then. Did you ever see anything killed, *paidhaki*? It now strikes me how really far I am from reality if, like, the killing of a lamb is a major experience for me. Anyway, the father cut its throat in one stroke, I guess right through the windpipe and the gullet and jugular. The blood shot across the room like from a hose and kept coming. The ram jumped around. The women were already washing the floor. No one but me was paying too much attention and I was in a state of shock. I don't know whether I actually rose in my chair; in any case no one even noticed me, which is good because they never would have understood my reaction. I really wanted to scream. And my mind was saying the whole time This is the Truth. This is the truth. It was really horrible. It probably only lasted a minute or so, but it seemed forever, that jumping and the blood shooting out and a horrible noise like snorting that I think came from the windpipe and the lungs. Finally, it made one violent shudder and looked floppy and dead. But it really only dies in pieces. It was twitching even after it was skinned. (I'm getting the skin, since I gave most of the money for the sheep.) Anyway, then the father went back and sat on the sheepskin and went on cutting his kif. Hassan, the brotherinlaw, did the rest. He cut a slit in one leg and then shoved a long hollow hard twig up the length of the leg. He blew into it and the sheep started swelling up like a balloon. It was upside down and finally got as big as a hippopotamus, I guess. Enormous. I think it's to make skinning easier. I was still probably in shock then because metaphysical things were still happening to me. Anyway. its balls swelled out like melons and it got an erection. That was especially awful, the white bled cock coming out of the foreskin. God. Then he let the air out and skinned it. Neatly. It was just meat by this time. He kept filling his mouth with water and driving it into the sheep's asshole. It was hanging by the legs now from a door jamb. Things and blood and things kept shooting out and I got covered with blood. This was the only thing that upset the family, that I got blood on my clothes. Then he eviscerated it. The guts came out in a neat bland bunch. The blood is the thing. The death and the blood is the real horror. Everything else is just meat. He dropped all the guts, everything, in a big basin of water and the women started fixing the liver. That's the first thing you eat. On skewers. With spices. Yummy. I didn't feel the least bit guilty. It was the best meat I ever ate. I'd really paid for it. So had the ram. After that, they quickly threw together a tajine of liver and heart which we ate with the most gorgeous spiced bread, full of anise and other things I don't know. Later, they ate the rest of the tripe after it spent the day drying in the sun. But we went back to Tangier. Yesterday was couscous of the head day. D. went to Arcila and brought some back and a great leg which we're roasting downstairs. Today is meat day. It goes on for ages.

Here are some thoughts. The bullfight is a farce because it is a contest, or a fake contest. The sacrifice is the truth because that is how life is. The ram was innocent. The father said after he killed it, "*El pobre, mira como sta delgado. No ha comido asi dos semanas porque nadie no queria andar con el hasta el campo.*" Anyway there isn't any moral to the story. Except that's probably the worst part of it. I felt very happy afterwards, clean. And good that I had faced it....Oh, then I saw another one killed. Because we had to go help Hassan kill his. But this time it was just a sheep being killed; not really, but almost. It didn't protest as much. Except as its throat was cut, it wagged its tail for a long time.

Next day. I'm very depressed, maybe because of my cold. I wonder if I hadn't eaten, say for a month, how I would have felt about the sacrifice.

Dris got his passport yesterday, finally, after years of trying. This is going to mean daily conversations about when are we going to use it. He can go to Spain without a visa, so maybe after you go—or maybe we should meet in Madrid actually and drive down? No, that isn't too good. *Paidhaiki*, please don't do anything but rest in London. I keep thinking that after a week of travelling by the time you get here you'll be tired. And you should save all your energy for here. I mean, your interest. Oh, you will be interested. You will really be interested.

One of my merchant friends at the flea market comes from Ifni and he is just like a merry Ifrit. A movie *djinn*. He lies in his goods in his white dress and turban and laughs at me for being so cheap. Today he said: *Safi, Safi,* (which means more or less *ça y est,* or, it's done; it's like the Hebrew *sof,* meaning the end, and it's used constantly), once you can talk Arabic, Tangier has got you forever. You'll never get out....I think that added to my depression. Also of course I think my book is so truly truly bad. And yet I don't. Remember once I wrote you it was the first honest thing I'd ever written? Well, I think I meant it was the first thing I'd written that showed what a fake I was, Maybe the next one will be better.

I told Dris you were studying Spanish to talk to him and he was thrilled. But then I said I was going to write you not to strain yourself as he only likes to talk about sex and money anyhow. He pounded the bed and pretended to sob. But he was really amused. I guess he likes being teased, though I never realized this before. He has changed a lot. He isn't too much of an Arab anymore, and sometimes when we quarrel he shouts at me: You still think I'm a Moroccan. Anyway, sex is good lately because I've discovered that I get turned off a lot simply because he always makes the advances. As he is so much younger I never used to get a chance to. Now, when he starts I make him stop and wait, and then I make the advances. Besides, it is summer.

Sunday. Easter Sunday. Dris's father died yesterday. Abdeslam came early in the morning to tell us and we drove out. I guess he was about seventyfive but you wouldn't have thought he was much more than fifty. He was lovely. I guess he had a heart attack. He apparently complained of indigestion and then just died. He was buried just in a shroud in a field near the house at noon. But by that time the funeral had sort of turned into a party, the way everything does here. I wish I had been born a Moslem. Ira and I often talk about converting. Marc Schleiffer converted, but into a black muslim. I'd want to be a brown one.

Dris will stay in Arcila for a few days so I'm here alone. I stopped at the river inlet on the way back and the water was warm enough for swimming, but the wind was up and chilly and I still have a cold, so I only went in up to the knees. The fields have turned blue since the other day. Also there are wild poppies and tiny little orange things.

Monday. I've been in a terrible mood for days. My kif has been bad lately. I think it's the season, and also I haven't had an evening smoking alone in ages. People keep visiting or I have to go out. If I don't smoke alone at night I lose my book. Though I read parts of it yesterday and to my surprise loved it. It was very funny. I think it could sell a lot of copies, if readers can give themselves to it. I'm past the most difficult parts and hope I'll have it done before April is over. That's only twelve days.

Cucumbers were in the market today. 200 francs a kilo and I grumbled. I just had some on bread with anchovies. I think Dris will be back tonight. I hate him. I feel rejected because he is in Arcila so long.....Oh, I had a letter from Dennis with three horrible cancer stamps on it, like he was my enemy....There is Dris at the door. He brought a pile of fish with him. I don't hate him at this moment. Yes, you can drink pot, though you have to boil it for ages and ages. You can brown it and chop it into powder and mix it with dates, figs, honey, nuts and what you like, and you have majoun. Or you can boil on a low flame for twelve hours with butter. Cool. Collect butter off surface and use for baking white cookies of Marrakech. Or you can boil it with tea or coffee, but it needs a very long boil. We tried to poison Marty Tucker this way, and must have used a quarter pound of kif finally. But no one got high. Not enough boiling.

Wouldn't it be nice if people weren't people? Rosalind said I should smear my manuscript with LSD and musk to turn the editors on....I'm thinking about my next book which is going to be far more interesting than my present one. It's going to be me. I have to get a tape recorder for it too, because I really like talking better than writing. And letters, and day-by-day recording. Should I give myself a time limit do you think? Like, say, start it on the first of June or whatever and then set an arbitrary final date? Like a month? Or two? On the other hand, I thought yesterday that if I set an arbitrary ending date, I might start dramatizing my life to make it interesting and then it would be fake. I should probably—oh, I know! I know! I don't know if I could stand it. Maybe you should decide. When you feel bored one day or whimsical, you can write or wire STOP. It's awful that I even have to have a starting day. I wish I could begin it without noticing. It will also be the *Tangier Murder Mystery*. Oh, did I tell you my book is *Coming Attractions?* Sometimes it's *coming attractions*. It is also all subplot. There is no main plot. I'm throwing out three or four chapters, since I have more than enough pages and don't really need them. I have to do something about the chapter where Ferguson (John Doe) first appears, since that really jarred me yesterday. I didn't like the fake exalted tone. I'm throwing out the chapter with Ismael at the hospital since it isn't really necessary and it's sort of nice the way he comes in again at the end. I'm on Chapter 36 now. About 50-52 altogether. This is the chapter in Gramercy Park where the ladies wheel empty baby carriages and tell abortion stories. Mary leaves Emilio home because she is so ashamed of having a real baby. And one day he climbs out on the landing while she is in the park with the ladies and falls down and just splatters. The ladies walk around him not noticing. But he is alive again a few chapters later.

Stuart Gordon, one of the local Americans, was taken away to the loonie bin at Beni Makada. He got me scared a little just before they got him. He carried on at the La Paz Cafe in a weird way and punched a waiter in the stomach. He's a big fat soft Jew. He invited everyone to a housewarming and no one went except Charles Wright (whom I'm still not friends with). Stuart was sitting under a tree across the street with his little boy (son). He lifted the kid up and slammed him down on the ground. He bled but didn't die. Anyway, the cops came and found all his kif and took his wife away instead of him. Just like in real life. Stuart went and hid on the boulevard, but they evidently finally got him.

Wednesday. This letter is getting longer and longer. Chapter 36 is splitting into two. It turned out to be a terrible problem. Sometimes I get all worked up about my logic and then when it is all carefully organized I throw in the most illogical thing. Anyway I'm thinking of throwing Chapter 37 out. Though I feel it is one of the key chapters. Of course, it is meaningless, but I mean it could throw a whole phony light on the book. *Paidhaiki*, I think my book is really a put on. It is a total fraud. Yet I take it very seriously at the same time. I guess you won't be able to understand until you see it, but then I guess you'll see.

Thursday. I love Dris. Though he isn't like himself these days. I mean, I guess he is very sad about his father.

I don't want to throw out chapter 37. I mean the one about Isobel. Early in the book, Ismael writes a long letter to Dr. Franzblau and he pretends to be a girl named Isobel. Chapter 12. Then, 25 chapters later, Isobel is on the run from a sailor. The sailor himself is a role played by John Doe in another chapter. In that chapter James Madison is a lady called Madame X. Oh well, you'll see. What I really meant about the book being a put on is that it is all full of clues and phony keys that smell like meaning but really aren't.

Friday. Your letter finally came. I also got a letter from the lawyer with copies of things to sign in front of the American Consul. I'll have to get it notarized somewhere else, as I surely won't go and ask Schutz [the Consul] to do it. I've been embarrassed ever since I went up to him with Paul's threatening letter. Strange I just thought of it last night. And stranger still, in the same mail now as your letter and the lawyer's, a postcard for Dris from Paul in Florida with a picture of a huge bridge spanning some huge sea. He is really in league with the devil.

No, *paidhaiki*, the last thing I'm trying to make of my book is a masterpiece. I'm just trying to make it into a book. I'm doing the carbons now of 36 and 37. They came out all right. Maybe I will put that Comet chapter back. There would then be two Chapter 4's, but why not? Or whatever it is, Chapter 8. I like the way I change my mind in the middle of it and decide not to use Franco. But then I thought if I wasn't going to use him why put him in? But I guess that's the kind of book it really is, also putting in what I'm not going to use.

The magic wood is still there. No, not *The Exquisite Corpses*. Just one. *The Exquisite Corpse*.

Will write you in a few days to give you a list of a few little things to bring. Oh, don't bring magic markers.

Love and kisses to you and Neil, Alfred

To Edward Field   April 27, 1965

Dearest: I've become a nervous wreck and so have started rushing things on the book. I hope to finish it tomorrow or Thursday. In any case I've set May 3rd, next Monday, as my mailing deadline, either from here or from Gibraltar. The postal rates are cheaper there and besides it would be nice to let Dris use his passport. I figured that it had to be sent by next Monday in order to give you and boyele even just the vaguest amount of time to read it. I know you hate telegrams, lovey. But could you please just wire me one word when it arrives?

I have a splitting headache and also lumbago slightly from sitting such long hours at the machine. So please, correct errors. If some words or phrases are left out, fill them in if you can figure it out. If you can't, make a note of page and send it to me. Also, maybe you can figure out how I can make the first half better. Or maybe it is all right the way it stands. I got high last night and thought about it, and laughed and laughed. I love thinking about it.

Helen DeMott sent me the Voice review of Irene's play. I'm glad for her and would like to send her a note. Maybe I will. Her play sounds a little like my book. Except I felt put down when the reviewer made a distinction between high and homosexual camp.

God, my back hurts. I hope I don't come down with sciatica again. I want to go to Moulay Yacoub next week for two weeks with Dris for his foot and my back. I'll put the dogs into storage I guess. Oh, I want to tell you *paidh*i, that it is about 5050 chance you may land a flea in Tangier. They are one of the plagues here, and if you do, please don't think it is the dogs. You get them in movies and cafes. Or just anywhere. People carry them. If you have a chance to do a little shopping for me, bring [a long list inserted here]....Also if you can think of anything that is cheap and plentiful for children, bring some for when we go have couscous at my in-laws. Your *mettuis* will be ready I expect by the time you get here.

Back to work now.

Love, Alfred

To Edward Field   May 4, 1965

Lovely: I'm going to the PO as soon as it opens (I've been up since 5:30 a.m.) to mail you the book. I finished it Thursday but kept it over the long May Day weekend. The first 40 or 50 pages are perhaps not too interesting, but persist, *paidhaiki mou* and you will enjoy it maybe. If you don't find it too funny, smoke some pot and read it again. I find it funny with pot.

When all is said and done, whether the book stinks or not, it is really quite ingenious, and oddly enough, even felt. Right now I think it is very good except that opening. Also, I had a nervous breakdown over the weekend when I realized the whole Mary Poorpoor thing is stolen from *Candy*, but I don't mind anymore. Originally, the whole book was supposed to have been stolen. Anyway, maybe I'm wrong and the book is horrible. If it is, maybe don't give it to Meredith. I'm writing him to say you will bring it. Give him a little pep talk. And tell him that I need at least a $5000 advance, etc.

We're going to Moullay Yacoub tomorrow, *insha'allah*, for D's foot. Fez is only ten kms. from Moullay Yacoub and we may stay at a hotel in Fez and drive in everyday for the baths. If luck is with us, you should have the ms. by next Monday, the 10th. I know that doesn't give you much time, but it's only 205 pages and reads like a children's book. It is in fact a children's book.

Rosalind has been bothering me to ask you to bring some underwear for her, as her pants fall in the street and she has no brassieres. So I told her to ask her mother to phone you and if you agree to take things for her she'll bring them over to you.

I think the last half of the book is stupendous. I think I can make a fortune off this book. Today. I'll probably be sick after I mail it, ashamed, etc. But it is MY book. Good, bad or indifferent, it is mine, which is the nicest part of all.

I took mescalin with Ira the other day and turned into the person I was before I came to Morocco. I rejected the new me. I was all fake love and guilt and trying to settle my problems in life rather than art. I rejected all the lovely things I saw and got all hung up in

RELATIONSHIPS, though with women (Rosalind). She turned into the feathered bird goddess. It was a very powerful experience. But writing a book is a better one. I loved Ira with Mescalin, and I was relieved because he claims to love me and I have always felt slightly guilty not loving him. But I'm right not to love him, because he really doesn't love me. He just wants me to love him. It made me terribly hot for Dris. And I still am. Sexy in general too. I also bought a turban and have decided to become elegant. It is hard with my bald head, but I must try. I think maybe I should have about a dozen wigs, all styles and colors, and other elegant headgear, because I really have to dress around my head.

Lots of love and kisses, boyeles, Alfred

To Norman Glass   May 5, 1965

Dear Norman: I was glad to have your letter, though of course you left out all the details of your ax-maniac. Please write me fully. Everything that happened that night. Never mind going to analysis. My mind is fogged. It's six a.m. and we're leaving for Moullay Yacoub today to take the baths. Mainly for Dris's foot. Partly for my sciatica, (still have it) and a holiday. If his foot doesn't get cured there, I'll take him to England now that he has his passport. Oh, Edward is going to London on the 18th of this month on his way here. I'll write him your address and tell him to look you up. I sent my novel away yesterday finally. It came out to 205 pages. I like it now. It is really very funny and could make a lot of money, I think. I hope.

Forgive me for being incoherent. I'll write you again from Fez. Rosalind and Ira may be going with us, and I wish it was you and Hajmi. I had a fight with Ira yesterday. It has been stewing in me for some time. It is really because—I can't go into it now because my mind is too fucked up just at the moment.

Dris has been working for Dale and Liz at their bar. Earning 1000 francs per day. I don't know if you met them before you left. They're opening the old Puerto del Sol. That was that big restaurant and bar opposite the little gardens where we used to sit sometimes. You know, where we figured out the letter to your uncle. I've helped as interior decorator. The inside is black and gold. It is quite chic and will be a great success, I'm sure. I took mescaline on Saturday and looked at Rosalind in the bar. She was all sprinkled with gold dust and turned into the bird goddess. I saw all those Aztec symbols and gods just like you're supposed to, but I didn't pay attention. I turned into the person I was when I first came. Love, and blab. You remember. And I thought my book was awful and that the person I had become was awful. I really thought it was nice to be that fake love, sentimental, guilty, creepy thing. Like Ira. Anyway I'm glad to be the new me. I've been madly in love with Dris lately, I don't know if since the mescalin or because I finished the book (last Thursday) and feel more relaxed.

Will be away 10 or 12 days....I've had a couple of subtexty postcards from Paul Balls in Florida. He says Bill Balls is having enormous success. His books are on sale in the supermarkets. Brion Balls is coming back next month. Jane Balls, by the way, have you read her book? *Two Serious Ladies*? It is one of the great novels of this century. I am not joking. Better get a copy. Did you see that "Ismael" was published in Queen Magazine? Fifty pounds. I haven't seen the money or the magazine. I'm sending a p.c. to Diana [Athill] today to ask for a copy. Aren't they publishing *Goliath*? Did she tell you anything?

Hajmi was around with your letter, but missed me, went back to Arcila, and was supposed to return yesterday, but didn't. He tells everyone you sent him 10 pounds....I guess I didn't tell you that Dris's father died. It was sad. It happened suddenly and fast, heart attack I suppose, and Abdeslam came early in the morning to wake us. Dris now has dreams about marriage all the time and for the first couple of weeks he used to walk around sighing: "*Hay algunos tienen padres y hay algunos que no tienen padres. Suerte.*"

Must close now. Have to pack and drive Rosalind's maid to the hospital. Will write from M.Y.

Love, Alfred

To Norman Glass   May 22, 1965

Dear Norma: We've been back from Moullay Yacoub since Saturday
(today is Friday) and I've begun a dozen letters to you. The problem has
been that I was writing the letters with a carbon stuck in the machine
as part of a plan for my next novel. The thing is that I became very
self-conscious and stilted on account of the carbon and couldn't go on.
This letter doesn't have a carbon, so I'll have to ask you to save it and
those that follow until I ask you for them. Is that all right?...Dris didn't
get cured at Moullay Yacoub, so our next plan is England. I guess we
will drive up later next month *insha'allah*. Can you check around for
bone-specialists or orthopedic specialists? You might ask Diana (why
the fuck doesn't she write to me?) He has a spur, remember?

I am very glad about you and Jamie. It would be perfect if he didn't
have any literary pretentions, but of course you wouldn't know that.
Even so, it is nice. Too bad about your job. Why doesn't Jamie take out
an insurance policy and both of you come to Morocco for the summer?

It promises to be a lively summer with lots of special New York
people appearing....I'm thrilled to pieces about *The Exquisite Corpse*.
I spent all last night and this morning being high and thinking about
it, and laughing. Edward wrote that it kept him and Neil in stitches all
the way: "And afterwards I felt high—it is a high triumph, a novel that
is completely original, all you, all the best of you." If we go to London,
I'll bring my copy. If not, I'll try to have a copy made to send you. I
think it is so sweet of God or the Devil or whoever to have given me
this book to write. I think it may make my fortune.

I read Irving [Rosenthal]'s book [*Sheeper*] at last, finished it
yesterday. All but the first eighty pages which are missing in this ms.
It is very good and beautiful, though a bit heavy, and it should be cut
into half. What it needs most of all is what he said he wanted it to
have: Space. It is too airless. But it is honest and charming and often
high poetry. I wonder why, in spite of all its virtues, I find it tedious
and, finally, trivial. It is too literary, I suppose, for my taste. It needs
a haircut, besides. Also the image of a little boy playing with his own
shit (which is what the book is) is good and true. It is a perfect image

of my generation (you included), but the reader has to be more of a shiteater than I am. Reading it, I felt like Ira was in the room and had grabbed me by the collar and NOTHING but NOTHING was going to make him stop talking. A monologue, a performance. Often brilliant. Flashes of genius, but too much.

Ira and Rosalind didn't go with us to Fez. At the last minute Rosalind decided to be nervous about their maid who is in the last days of pregnancy and skinny, sick, etc. So they stayed, meaning to join us in a day or two. The maid had twins, and a couple of phone calls went back and forth (via Dale's bar). But they never showed. Finally, last Saturday at 5:30 p.m., as Dris and I were just coming into Ksar Kbir on our way home, D. said, "Mira, Rosalind." As we'd been saying that to each other in all unlikely places for the last ten days, I hardly bothered looking. But there they were, hitchhiking, on their way to Fez, Rosalind in a black Chinesey cocktail dress, and a new boy with them, some kid up from the Living Theater in Rome on a mission to bring kif back. Anyway, Rosalind acted like we'd ruined her whole vacation and wanted us to turn around and go back. But I had no more money and, besides, was exhausted and, besides, was secretly delighted that I'd had my holiday without them. Ymmy. Yummy, I mean. I like Ira, except he talks too much. I mean, he even follows me into the toilet, on and on and on. And that mescalin trip I wrote you about gave me the idea that he might be rather less than I had imagined. Though who isn't? Except Paul Bowles. I miss Paul. My mind is getting cleaner and cleaner without him here poisoning it. But at least something interesting happens when I see him. I mean there is always a lot to think about afterwards; you know.

Jay has taken a furnished apartment not too far from here. Charles [Wright] is wrighting two books, one on kif, though what he knows about it I don't know. Maybe it will be a fantasy. We aren't friends, but I saw him the other day at Dale's and then the next day got a letter from him asking for money. I read a James Bond book in Moullay Yacoub and loved it....Oh, we took the baths. I really hated Fez. The people are just the way they are supposed to be: dour, proud, shrewd, etc. Very unsensual. The whole air is of a colony the French have abandoned. Though lots of French still there. And marvelous French market with fruit and veg, I'm sure flown in from motherland. Bread and strawberry tarts, *tartes aux fraises*, scrumptious. And the lovely gardens. Did you get to see the gardens the time you were there? With the rivers all over? It was full of roses now. And students, pacing back and forth with books in front of their faces. They were all doing "The Student Prince"; I hated them. Anyway, Moullay Yacoub—oh hot as hell, so was Fez—over a hundred, surely, every day. It all smells of sulphur fumes and the hills are soft. Glare, heat. It's holy, so we were very holy the first few days. But then we started suddenly fucking like jackrabbits. And I got weaker and weaker and had to stop the baths for a couple of days. My sciatica is better though. But not his foot. It does marvels for the skin. Also you lose your appetite, so I took off ten pounds. Got very dark. Went off every day to swim at the raselma. We stayed at the Grand Hotel Moderne. It was just like going to the Catskills with mama in 1933. All Jews, but 1930's Jews. Dris was the darling of all the Yiddishe Mamas and some of those evil-looking middle-aged French ladies around too. I took amphetamine and kif every night and would sit at the cafe over the baths watching the procession to and fro. The rich Moroccan ladies arrive in little fat groups. In the most outlandish costumes you can imagine, layer upon layer upon layer. And things on their heads. One girl looked like she was dressed in lime jello. And followed by their little slaves. The kids are nice in Fez and M.Y. and don't pester. I had a few little friends at M.Y. who came to sit with me every evening, Mbark and his cousin. My Arabic improved. Anyway, I was glad as hell to get away, though the first few days I imagined I could live that life forever. The baths themselves are nice. Very hot and salty and smell and taste like rotten eggs. You practically faint from the heat and the fumes at the beginning.

Anyway, so now I'm back and have finished my novel. I saw John Dav's quote [for *Behold Goliath*] in the Observer. As Diana would say: "Dav is an old dear for coming through." I know him, you know. There was a quite good review in the Sunday Times last Sunday, but reading it again yesterday I suddenly got the feeling that the reviewer really hated the book and was being blackmailed somehow into pretending he liked it. Like because he thought he might not be chic or hip or something if he admitted to hating it. That's the only review I've seen so far. They are fucks for not telling me the book was out. Will you please look through Queen magazines for April and May and send me the copy with "Ismael" in it. What is the matter with them there in England? And tell Diana to send me by air at once a copy of *Goliath*, their edition.

Part of Bat Palace collapsed the other day. Luckily they [Ira and Rosalind] were out. You remember that ballroom on the roof? Well, it broke and fell through the skylight. They could have easily been killed. Or blinded, blinded, as Rosalind keeps saying. You should see my apartment. It is so beautiful, you wouldn't recognize it. I've been collecting odd things from the flea market all winter. The other day I bought a strange tree for 300 francs. And I bought a *haiti* from R. & I. that we're going to run around behind the bed. And today I'm going out with Liz to get foam rubber and some cloth for cushions to throw on the bed. I want the place to look pretty for Edward and Neil. I wonder where they are....I went off with the cocksucker one afternoon before we went away. He was much better than that other time. He said I could fuck him, though only indoors, not in those bushes on Malabatta. But you have made the idea of his cock so repulsive, that I don't want to see him naked. He asked after you and I said you were in England working. He said, well, if you have any other friends who want to do things, tell them about me. I saw him yesterday by chance coming out of school in Emsallah. I'm glad you're writing your book. Love, Alfred

To Norman Glass   June 3, 1965
Dear Norman: Yesterday was Sade's birthday. 225 years old. I know because, never mind.

Did you get my long letter after Moullay Yacoub? Paul Bowles speaking: But I don't understand....How can you quit your job two weeks after you've been given a month's notice? Ah yes, the gesture.

Anyway, it sounds defiant. Paul will be back in a week. I miss him. Edward and Neil are here, or rather travelling. I expect them back today. We went to Chauen together and I invited Hajmi to come with us as a playmate for Dris. It was simply gorgeous there. Like a dream, like a dream. It gets more beautiful each time I go. Drenched with green and Bavaria and incense and Morocco. I am high on just two pipes. D and I are mad at each other, or rather I at him. Edward bought a bunch of little Japanese toys for Dris's relatives and I was dying to open one or two of them, but Edward forbade. Today I found D had taken half of them to play with at the cafe. So I'm mad because they are ruined and because I never got a chance at them. I've ruined the rest today.

I guess we are going to drive to London about the middle of the month. I wrote to Diana that they might phone her from the frontier to say she is sponsoring Dris. She hasn't written, nor have they sent the book or reviews or anything....Oh, *The Exquisite Corpse*. Everyone agrees it is a masterpiece. Ira sort of sweetly and exquisitely backhandedly even gave me to understand it was a better book than Irving's. So that is a nice compliment. Or actually, it isn't any compliment at all come to think of it. But Edward loved it. Anyway, everyone loves it, and of course Random House doesn't want to publish it because Jason Epstein is baffled as to whether it is a novel or a poem and what my intentions are. My intentions are: to divert, to instruct, to elevate the morals of the young of course....Dris is packing again. He has been for the last five or six lines. We had a fight about the toys again. Would you believe, Norman, that I'm going to be 37 on my next birthday, *insha'allah*. I am ignoring him.

A little later. We have made up. I'm a little high, so I just kept laughing while he packed. That's good as a principle. When they pack up, laugh. Except they have always packed up behind my back and sneaked away,...Ira wants to publish *The Exquisite Corpse* and unless I get a very large offer from an American publisher, which I doubt, I'm going to let him. I can see your hackles rising. (I have never written about hackles rising before. Is that correct?) The Lady Mayoress hackle is getting nervous about vanity press, etc. But, no, there is method in all of my madnesses as you should know by now. However, I want you to save this letter for my book, and I don't want the public to know, so it will have to wait until I see you....Poor Norman. If only you were here tight in my kif smoke. Remember the fun we used to have getting high? I don't think I've had a good gigggggle since you left. Oh, well. Angus Stewart has been with his nurselike wife staying in Paul's apartment while Paul has been away. He is going mad. Naturally. He really likes boys and once got into trouble over a 13-year-old in Tangier. Anyway marriage isn't suiting him and kif is, so he is flipping out. And afraid to face it. Run back to England and looking for friends. May be some money there. Looks it. New car. He is a writer, published....I had a cocktail party for Edward and Neil. A roaring success. I made an orange punch with black market rum from Dale's bar. Very potent. Ira had some Congo hash which everyone smoked. So they all got very drigh (drunk plus high) except me. I looked stunning though. I wore my new gold turban and my purple and gold embroidered waistcoat (up to the neck) and shades....I am going to be very outrageous in London. Prepare yourself. I want to get into all the papers. Dris and I are going to be the new beatniks. Tell Diana to get the press out....Oh, I've just smoked some hash and am even higher. There was another roundup in the medina. Strange how you are never here for one. It makes me suspicious of you. Twelve Americans pulled in. Trial today postponed until next week. The U.S. consul came to the trial and protested the mistreatment. Imagine.

Friday. As I was writing the above, Edward, Neil, Rosalind and Ira all appeared at the door and the rest of the evening was spent out. Edward disappoints me a little, I'm sorry to say. He is a little oldmaidish....Ira says the Tangier First Gallery has now opened a gallery in London. Go see them. Dris has suddenly started painting again and struck an extraordinary vein. Maybe he can have a show there and earn some money for us.

I have to run out and pay bills and go to the police for my re-entry permit, etc. And to the flea market to look for a few decent jackets, etc., so that we can look rich coming into England. I'm terrified of that English frontier partly because of Dris-Moroccan and partly me with my passport photo looking different from the new me. And partly because in the fifties I used to cross it often and they always made me feel lousy. I hope you know where pot is available in London. Also where we can stay cheap.

Love, Alfred

To Norman Glass   June 13, 1965

Dear Norman: I had the letter of invitation from Diana, so that's all right. We should be leaving later in the week, like Thursday or Friday, which *insha'allah* means we'll be in London between Sunday and Tuesday of next week. Diana offers to put us up until we get somewhere to stay, but I'm not too eager to take her up on the offer, so please please look around and see if you can't find a room with maybe cooking facilities which would accept us two Moors. Maybe we could take a tworoom apartment together, though that might be ghastly. Anyway please don't find something that costs a pound a day. That's too expensive.

Dris is taking along his new pictures which are truly incredible, Norman. Wait until you see them. You won't believe it. Every morning there's a new one on the wall and they're gorgeous. A whole strange fantasy style in brilliant colors. If he goes on like this, he'll make a fortune.

Nothing is happening with my book. My agent stupidly sent it to some kid at Harper's whom I know through Jean-Claude Van Itallie. But Harpers could never publish it. Meanwhile, other publishers are after the agent and me for a look at the book.

Next day I've been in a very irritated state since Saturday morning because of my lawsuit. Norman, I am really quite crazy. Literally.

Paul and Jane are back. They got back last Wednesday I learned from Ira who went by to see if they were home. Saturday evening I found this in my box: "We made a *petite visite formelle* at 5:30. Jane says to tell you we'll be back tomorrow at 5 p.m. Best, Paul." Sunday (yesterday) afternoon I left a note on my door saying I'd gone to the beach and hoped they could come to dinner on Tuesday at 8. When I got back Dris said he'd seen them and they left a note: "We did come, and missed you. Jane says that she would love to come Tuesday but at 8:30. Why don't you telephone her tomorrow? Best, Paul."

It is 6:30 a.m. and I'm not feeling too communicative.

Love, Alfred

To Edward Field and Neil Derrick   June 16, 1965

Dearests: It is one week, one day, and 10,000 years since you left. I'm finally listening to the Mozart. We're supposed to be leaving for England tomorrow but Dris is sick with the grippe, sore throat, and I think reaction to his vaccination, though I'm afraid to mention this to him. He has been doing the most gorgeous paintings. Drawings. He moved on from those *haitis* to other strange things.

Paul and Jane are back and I had them for dinner last night. It was a horror. I asked Ira and Dale and Liz over for champagne before dinner (new Moroccan champagne, very good but tasteless, with a special artifically added explosive to blow out the plastic cork: 50 cents a bottle). But of course it was hard getting rid of Ira and in the end he left without saying goodbye, in a rage. Do I have to have people to dinner if I invite them for a drink before dinner? Jane was impossible. I haven't had her to a meal in a year. Never again. Paul brought the pants for Dris, disgusting cotton things. Dris gave them back to him. I was glad. Paul is impossible but interesting. Random House turned his book down and he gave it to Seaver. He saw Susan in New York. She is in London, so perhaps I will see her.

Your letter just this minute arrived. And now I know I will spend hours on this letter when I have 10 million things to do and meant to write just a note. I'm wearing your red shirt. I haven't stopped wearing it since you left. I look so good in it. I need butchy lumberjack things, I think. I realized what is wrong with your friends. They are too old for you. Young people are ghastly but the energy flows the right way toward you. You eat them instead of being eaten. I have so many things to tell you; like that brilliant observation, but can't now and I'll probably forget the way I do everything. Anyway it doesn't matter....You had the necessary rug paper [for export]. There is only one necessary paper, the one on the back of the rug itself, which I warned you about. Anything else he [the Moroccan customs official] said is a lie and blackmail. NO NO, don't send him cloth, that wicked man. I just read that to Dris and he is all ready to go give the man a piece of his mind. I'm glad your letter came because I was actually playing with the idea of taking some hash with me, but now I remember about borders. Do you think the English will fuss over my book? I think I'd better mail it to myself from France....Diana sent the invitation and also a rather reluctant real invitation. She is also checking on doctors....I wrote a bunch of ferocious letters to Imboden [of the Scott Meredith Literary Agency]. George Plimpton, he said, is starting a Paris Review Press with Doubleday and is dying to see the book. I've had a letter from Sam Lawrence who ran Wake, then AtlanticLittle Brown; now runs his own house in association with Delacorte. Offers large advance, promotion and 100% reprint rights.

Next day. We're not going today because Dris is very sick. We went to the doctor last night for a note to show at the frontier because they are so lousy about letting Moroccans out of the country, and the doctor said D. should stay in bed a day or two. It is a combination of vaccination and grippe. He's still very feverish this morning.

It wasn't that you were too much for me, it was just, if you really want to know, that I felt in danger of judgment. Isn't that strange? And you have always been the one person in the world I felt never judged me. Among the reasons for it I think is that you've always been the older brother; you know how we talked about how you take charge of things on the assumption that (like on Sullivan Street) Neil or I couldn't do it. As I've been older here than most of my friends I've become used to accepting their helplessness. Anyway, all this doesn't matter....I love Neil more than I ever have before and wish he would write to me or at least trust me. I mean, he feels nervous of MY judgment. Aren't people crazy?

I ran around all day trying to get hold of some pesetas. Getting out of Morocco is so complicated for us natives. I can't take money out. Ceuta is the best border to pass for Dris, as they are more lax there. But once in Ceuta, we need money for the ferry to Algeciras, food and lodging overnight so that I can go to my bank in Gib and get dollars. So my Belgian lady has promised to try to get hold of 3000 pesetas for me tonight or tomorrow morning. Anyway, it exhausted me.

I've put my chinning bar up but it hurts my sciatica. If I don't do exercise though, I settle in toward my middle. Why didn't we talk about all these things when you were here?

Paul says Brion Gyson runs around New York marking up subway posters with: "Please drop the bomb on us now.".…My plants very happy.…I'm still enchanted over our trip to Chauen.

I've had a correspondence with Durant Imboden, really trying to fire him. But they are holding onto me with all their teeth. Is it because they think I will bring money or because of prestige? Imboden writes: "Well, to a certain extent, I agree with Epstein your book is more of a poem than a novel. But there's nothing wrong with poetry that I can think of, other than the fact that it seldom brings in as much money as does more conventional or popular writing....Corpse is brilliantly written. Some of the scenes, in particular, are beautifully done. The scene involving the impotent sailor and the woman who wants to be raped is especially good. It will probably offend many people morally, and it doesn't fit in with my particular sexual sensibilites, but it's brilliantly written. And literature is to be judged as literature, after all."

The real horror of living here is that Paul Bowles is my only equal (or superior) in intellect. It really matters.

Love love love, Alfred

The beatniks were all deported. Ira's LSD arrived, and he is busy making mixtures and is high all the time. Dale almost has his license. Paul and Jane get very upset that I have a friend who runs a bar. They deal with people in a complete hierarchy....David Herbert is the Hon. D.H. where I had dinner with Cecil Beaton, remember? He is the ruler of Tangier really. He is even responsible for the present ugly condition of the Socco Grande, I hear.

What an awful scene with Gnaoua [magazine edited by Ira Cohen, which U.S. Customs tried to confiscate]. I wish I owned a deathray machine, don't you?

My life is dreary and empty without a book to write. I want to write my Pinocchio play, but I can't calm down long enough in between comings and goings....Paul says Susan has apartments offered to her in London and Paris and that she may come here. You know, I think she is afraid of me.

It took me at least three days to recover from you. Then I felt a little crazy. As a matter of fact I started feeling I'd never stopped being crazy. The first day I was so depressed that you'd gone that we went to Jay's for lunch—I mean dropped in and he invited us for lunch—and got terribly drunk on absinthe. Finally in the evening I decided you had landed and had never really been here at all. And I still feel that way. I wish you would come to Morocco. I mean it really is a million years since you were here. It's so strange how the present is so insistent here, isn't it? Then suddenly you are here and you've always been here.

I realized if I don't get a substantial advance we can't come to America in the fall. I can't start scrounging again and being poor.

Hooray for Irene. Jane was making dinner talk last night about the evil state of the theater etc. etc. Broadway she meant. I said I didn't expect drama to come out of Broadway anyhow. Yes, she agreed, no money in it. It was idiotic NY talk. Pretending to take Broadway seriously. I was rather high on some majoun and the champagne and during the long pause following the dialogue on theater I said: "Oh, well, that wasn't too interesting," meaning our conversation.

There was a circus here over the weekend. Dris loved it, and I liked some of it. Except there was a little bald man who handled all the animal acts (bears, horses, an elephant) and I felt self-conscious everytime he appeared. So that ruined it. Also the planks were hard to sit on. And one aerialist looked just like Jackie Kennedy.

Diana has arranged for me to be on the Third Program. I wrote her I also want to be on TV and in all the newspapers. I wonder if I'll really have the nerve.

Later. Dris may be beautiful but he isn't wise. He is a pill. We just had a fight about Mohammed, who is staying with the dogs. I want to leave the money with Pepita because (just think, you now know all these people), as I told D, no Moroccan could hold on to 20,000 francs over a month. He would spend it immediately. So he was insulted, though it's true....Fat Jay and Chas Wright are just coming up the steps now....I must close. Will write from England.

Love, Alfred

To Edward Field   from London, July 2, 1965

Darling *paidhimou*: Diana Athill came over last night with your letter and I read it before going to sleep and had nightmares about you and Neil all night. I think maybe because you signed your letter Neil. I don't know whether it's a joke or an accident, but it shocked me and I got all confused retroactively. I'm in the western world again where those things matter. We're staying at Norman's, the three of us in one big room. We got here the day before yesterday after ten days travelling and a car accident outside Biarritz. I'll tell you about the trip in a minute. Anyway, Diana came for dinner and Dris whipped up a lamb tajine and it was a pleasant evening. I let her take away *The Exquisite Corpse* and we're seeing her Sunday. She says Harpers has turned it down, and that Sam Lawrence has written to her asking please to write him about the ms. the minute she sees it. I expect Plimpton has it now. Anyway I can't occupy myself with my career until I get something straight about Dris's foot. We have an appointment with a bone surgeon for noon today, but I'm canceling it and going to see Robert Romanis who is a GP writer for Deutsch to lay all my cards on the table about National Health etc., and try to find out the best way to go about things. Dris is sleeping still and Norman has gone out to see a doctor for tranquillizers.

The trip took ages and was a horror. In the first place we couldn't get started on account of D's fever. Then I got caught at the border with 2100 pesetas, which the Moroccans confiscated. This took so long that we missed the boat and had to spend a day in Ceuta, then another day waiting for the bank to open in Gib. Spain is monstrous and so hot that the car overheated all the time and we had to drive 40 kms an hour. In Madrid we couldn't get a room because they thought we were beatniks and crooks or something, so we went back to Aranjuez where Paul had said to stop in the first place. It is like Versailles there and lovely and we stayed an extra day. We'd also stopped at Granada and went up to the Alhambra but Dris didn't want to go in as the ticket cost 50 pesetas apiece and he was shocked. Anyway, all this took a week. And finally coming across the French frontier, just outside of Biarritz on Sunday morning, a German car with a Spanish family ran into us. They crossed over into our lane and left fenders smashed. Their car being new was very damaged, the way new cars can be. Ours is just the fender. But Dris banged his head on the rear view mirror which broke and he got a cut on his eyelid. They took him to a doctor who did nothing but call an ambulance, and he was taken away to Bayonne without passport or money, while I was left in a state of shock at the scene of the accident surrounded by kindly gendarmes. D. had whispered to me he was all right and just thought this was the way to our fortune, and maybe it was but neither of us could go through with it. The car was finally hauled into a garage and the cops said for one franc I could get a bus to Bayonne, but all I had was foreign money and no place to change it, being Sunday, and when I told them this they shrugged and left me. So I had to walk all the way into Biarritz and finally changed pesetas at a hotel, went to Bayonne and found that Dris had run away from the hospital. It took me all day to find him, because the last place I thought to look was at the police. But he was there, having gone to them and insisted they feed him and take care of him. So they did. (This typewriter is making me write like Norman.)

Anyway, we left the car in Biarritz for reparations and took the train here. There was a little trouble getting in on account of Dris, and they gave us a month only in the passport but that can be lengthened. All the frontiers were difficult. In Algeciras they searched every inch of the car for kif, including the doors and cushions. I haven't smoked now in nearly two weeks and I miss it though not terribly. My head felt more and more elegant the further north we came, and Diana says it looks very good and would look very good on TV. I don't wear a *tageeya* [skullcap] outside or in. I missed Tangier terribly at first but now I see again I could live more or less anywhere. Anyway, if Dris is with me, I mean. So I'll write those letters to America, but I don't feel too hopeful. I don't seem to have that kind of energy anymore, convincing people that I should be lecturing or anything....Diana says *Goliath* isn't doing too well.

I read all about Lowell [refusing invitation to] the White House. And then Dwight MacDonald wrote a letter to Time saying it is true he signed the petition supporting Lowell, but the next day got an invitation, so he changed his mind to serve God and country. I think that more or less is the level of seriousness and commitment of all those bullshitters. Bellow was quoted as sounding like a pillar of the establishment. The whole literary thing including Susan makes me want to vomit and I haven't even any kif to make me feel amused about it.

Norman has Hajmi's photos all over and it looks strange here.

I have absolutely no interest in sightseeing or even in seeing people. Here at Earl's Court, it's really like the Village. Though I do want to go to the movies. I have lost all belief in the importance of anything in the world except beauty and peace. All the nonsensical moneymaking activities etc. depress me. Europe is really dead. That's probably why I got so hung up on Gurdjieff in the 50s. I'm afraid to think of my book here, as it must be so out of context with this civilization which has nothing to do with pleasure.

I've changed my mind about turbans and things because my head seems the most elegant disguise I could wear....Dris is the handsomest man in London. Diana wants to buy one of his pictures for five pounds, but next week Norman and I will mount them and take them to galleries. This letter has exhausted me. I'll stop now. Write me c/o of Diana.

Lots of love to you both, Alfred

To Edward Field   from London—Saturday, July 18, 1965

Paidhi Norman is using the typewriter to make copies of my book so you'll have to endure my handwriting.

Talk about my letter making your day beautiful and exciting! *Your* letter has given me virtually the one breath of peace I've had since leaving Tangier.

First: about Dris's foot. At last, after more than two weeks of running around to guinea-a-minute specialists of horrifying ignorance, smugness and indifference, we got to (I hope) the right one yesterday. Thanks to a Jewish GP who persisted in connecting Dris's foot with gonnorhea, despite the fact that *les grands specialistes* and surgeons of bone and orthopedic said no—though they didn't have a clue to what it was, but smelled that there wasn't much money to be had. (Bill so far 35 guineas. Because it takes months to get to the specialists on National Health.) So he sent us yesterday to a venerealogist in N.11 who agreed to see Dris at once. He identified the condition at once as Bright's Disease, a result of a nonspecific VD condition) which I think I've had since 1954—remember the way Baby Poorpoor pisses? That's why I went to the naturopath in London years ago. Anyway, they don't know really anything about the disease except that when it is affecting the joints, that part usually clears up when the VD itself clears up. In D's case, they can't find anymore trace of the VD, and the venerealogist says he thinks it may be that the reason the foot hasn't cleared up by itself is that he hasn't rested it. So they want to put his foot into a plaster cast I don't know for how long. I think they'll do this on Wednesday and I'm hoping we can leave London the next day after that. Dris kvetches constantly because he's so anxious to get back to Morocco, but he has done a lot of painting (he hates going out into the street here—it's even a constant battle getting him to the doctors) and made extraordinary progress. He's sold 5 paintings at 5 pounds each, one to Howard [Griffin], two to Diana Athill, two to Deutsch's promotion lady. We'll probably go around to the galleries on Monday to see what they say. I've been mostly just Dris's mother, his interpreter, his business manager and his slave here in London. Every now and then I get disgusted and announce to the general public that I'm not doing any more interpreting but will now speak for myself. Dris pays no attention to this so we end up in glum silence, hating each other. But just a little. He has turned into a real prima donna. (I guess he's always been.) And has to be the center of attention (or his paintings) constantly. I don't mind—or wouldn't if I could just sit quietly and watch the fun like everyone else. Luckily I got a great lump of hash as a gift from someone here so things haven't been too bad. (Whoever said pot isn't habit forming was a liar. It is, but it is better that it should be.)

So the few moments I've represented Alfred Chester here, I've looked forward to, but they've been even more exhausting. My picture appeared in the Evening Standard in Arab gear with a few inches of silly type and sillier quotes. Yesterday I was taped at the BBC, being interviewed by hideous stupid Brian Glanville. I was stoned out of my mind, having had amphetamine and hash before going (to make me talk) and having been filled up with Scotch—in the Duty Room—just before the interview, to loosen me up a little. I dragged Norman along with me to the BBC's chagrin. (I didn't dare take Dris as I knew nothing could keep him quiet.) Oh, D was a riot when the BBC producer came to meet me at Diana's—this whole square scene trying to tell me how much they loved Burroughs (Can you imagine? They assumed I must love him) and Dris going on and on and on about some Swiss woman who was in love with him when he was 16.

Anyhow, the interview, I feel, was charmless. (Norman said I was endearing.) The only interesting thing I said was that Daisy Ashford was a much better writer than James Joyce. Also, I put Howard Griffin down though I didn't mention his name.

Howard. Is he an alcoholic now? He says he is 47 but he has turned into a doddering old queen. I've seen him now three times. The last time, at his place, he brought one of Terry's friends around, a painter and teacher, sweet boy (and wife) to give Dris some helpful hints on oil painting. The boy was quite overwhelmed by D's paintings and said he liked them better than anything on Howard's walls. (I agree.) But Howard was horrible to me all evening. Bitchy queen subtext, but not so interesting as Paul. Anyway, that evening made me loathe him and I don't want to see him anymore. Actually I think now he may have been hating me because of the boy's response to D's pictures. And a whole horrible subtext all evening long about Terry and his paintings. Poor Howard! He is so so so so so so dead!!!

I said on the BBC: "Yes, I used to worry about that identity question a lot. But now I know who I am—long pause—"I'm no one."

Dris is up and wants all my attention now. It's one p.m. He immediately wanted me to go out and get him mounting paper for his pictures. You know, I never really believed he loved me until the last couple of weeks in London. He really does. Isn't that amazing?

Dris refuses to eat out (except at other people's houses.) So it's just like Morocco here. I've been dying to go out and have Indian or Chinese. We haven't done anything except pinball machines and a striptease (where we had a terrible fight, but I'll tell you about this another time.) Not even a movie.

Susan [Sontag] has said nice things about me in London, nice but bitchy.

About my book. Diana was cool about it though claiming to like it. She said she was worried about what Andre [Deutsch] would say. The day I asked for it back (last Monday) for the typing, she suddenly came on about how one of the other editors was mad about it, so I think she is a little worried she isn't getting the ms back, and maybe pretended to be cooler than she was so I wouldn't mind a small advance. I'm not giving the book back to her, but will tell her straight that I need a big advance and if she is agreeable to that, to get in touch with Meredith.

I haven't written about the lectures because I am so decomposed here and in constant motion. But will when I get back. Pepita wrote the police want to see me about some accident in Casablanca. God knows what that means. I hope I'm getting paid back for the accident in Biarritz. There won't be much labor involved as there was no damage except to the fender. All the man needed to do was bolt on a new fender which I think may well cost over $100 on account of importing etc.

I did something awful on the radio too. I said I hated western civilization, then added "all civilizations." I meant I wasn't a Communist. I'm a little ashamed of myself but not very.

Edward, it's not that my head is separate, simply that I feel it's my dominant physical quality. Isn't it? Anyhow, I'm bored being elegant and I'm bored by Arab drag, so I'm just me again, though no hat. In fact I must get one as my head is almost always cold here:. The weather is terrible terrible. Rain and cold, worse than Tangier winter. The streets are frightening at night. Dris and I go into a panic if we come back late.

Assuming we leave Thursday, I guess best write to Tangier.

Dris (who is the handsomest man in London) "*Manda muchos recuerdos a el y a Neil.*"

Me too and xxxxxx , Alfred

To Norman Glass   Monday, August 2, 1965 Tangier

Dear Norman, Leslie, wives and children: This will have to be a municipal or communal letter, since I don't have much time at the moment, what with trying to straighten out insurance and being convoked to the police; and Dris in bed giving orders, dogs, debts, concierges, etc. Hajmi is also here. I can't stand doing the shopping, cooking, etc. And of course Dris doesn't trust the maid to handle our food, so we settled on Hajmi who seems glad about it, as the fishing has been bad. We are giving him meals and 250 francs a day. He will shop and cook and of course give his ass, which as you know he is very generous about. No, he will sleep at his sister's. He has a big ugly beard and his skin is bad. He's really a sweet boy. He's here now but is going out to shop and will add to this letter later.

The weather is lovely and hot and breezy. My bronze is back. My back is bronze. I am enormously fat and am going on a diet. Dale's bar is booming and fun to go to. The thing is that everything happens very slowly here, so that you can't start earning the minute you get off the boat. For a bar, you need a personal liquor license which takes anywhere from a week to three months (Dale's case), depending on how and who you bribe. Dale bribed the wrong man and refused to bribe any of the right ones. I think the Pussycat may still be up for sale, and I'll check. Would you consider a partnership, Leslie? Because there may be something already going that wants to expand and needs new capital. There is certainly a tourist if not boom then expansion going on. The beach places are doing record business as are the bars and hotels. Coming down the Costa del Sol last week, I knew it must be crowding over here. It is too horrible there. Anyway, I think this will be the last cheap year here, I mean on buying in. I'll find out what's going on. Dale himself I know is interested in investing more money (he has more), and in fact we'd talked about if I got a big advance going in together on a fishing boat, big one, which Dris could manage except now he is such a successful painter. Florence wants two oil paintings for her apartment, she was so overcome by the drawings that Dale and Liz have put on the Ladies and the Gents. (It is very interesting to see people trying to figure out from the paintings which is the Ladies and which the Gents. It seems somehow so appropriate in Tangier.)

Norman, I think you better hold off a little with Anthony Blond. I had a practically hysterical letter from Diana in which she very carefully doesn't offer 1000 pounds advance, but leads me to believe that is what they're going to offer. Then the next day came a letter from Andre himself, asking for the book back and enclosing a letter from the director of Penguin Books who is interested in making an offer for the complete works of Me, though he wants to see the new book first, which would probably screw up the works. Anyhow, I haven't answered either Diana or Andre yet but have written to my agent to get in touch with them. I'll probably write them to get in touch with my agent. Meanwhile he writes that everybody and his brother in New York is trying to get a look at the ms. And I think things must be good there, or promising, because lo and behold I've had a letter from Susan Sontag, saying how I am much on her mind and would I like to see her for a couple of weeks. That whore. Of course, I've written back saying I'd love seeing her. She wants her Roger Straus to see the book. I guess she will be here next week. God.

The trip down was uneventful, except at La Linea, thanks to the hash and those really marvelous tranquilizers that Tintner gave me. Please find out what their names are, so I can order them here. There is no news to give him of Dris's foot since today is his first day in bed, having gone to Arcila for three days. His brother Hamid looks like he is dying, but not of the foot. Pneumonia? Anyway he is supposed to have a drain in his lungs. He sat on the floor in the angle of the *mtarbas*, surrounded by cushions, sort of gasping, and all the women around him with their tits out and babies hanging from them and the smell of the female thick in the air. No wonder he is dying. But of course neither he nor they would let me take him to a hospital in Tangier, though they will call the bar if he a) worsens or b) dies. I'm reviewing a book about Amazon savages and they have much in common with Moroccans. Which reminds me I saw Paul Bowels [sic] on the Calle Libertad as I was driving down with Ira, Rosalind and their new son (a charming ex-junkie with a huge motorcycle). As usual, I honked and stopped. As usual, he didn't hear, didn't see, vaguely reacted, started, startled, turned, heard, didn't hear, and finally looked after the car blindly as I roared away in a cloud of smoke. Ira says the same thing would happen if we passed each other in the Sahara.

We saw a very bloody bullfight in Granada. Grizzly. We had a delicious lunch at Charpentier's in Paris, rue Mabillon. Nothing changed but the prices. In the evening before taking the train we ran into Walter [Kerell]'s (John Anthony's) old wife with a young Yugoslavian gigolo. It brought the whole past back for her, etc etc. I was glad to escape to the train. The car is here and the fender is still in the back seat, and I am blackmailing my insurance man, so he will blackmail the other insurance company. I should be at the police now and I should be looking for a garage, but I'm sitting here writing you. Dris is in bed doing seascapes he's already done. Success is making him repeat himself. He was surprised just now when I told him I never wrote the same thing twice. He did one oil painting, terrible, but it is impossible here. We really need a bigger place. The whole place stinks of turpentine and I've got paint all over....I've seen Charles and Jay a couple of times. They are unchanged. I don't feel settled yet, or really home yet.

I will close now and go about my tasks. I want to thank you one and all for your kindness and hospitality and generosity. Even Norman.

Love to one and all. Alfred

The Visit

To Edward Field   Aug. 5, 1965

(Marginal note: When I came home, almost my first thought was: Were Edward and Neil really here ever? I loved the nightshirt. Dris wears it constantly:)

Paidhi mou: We've been back for ten days and I've been trying to write to you nearly every day but can't seem to get a letter out. Of me. I'm just beginning to get relocated and identified. Today is Dris's fifth day of thirty in bed trying to heal his foot. Finally, they didn't put his foot in a cast, since the rheumatic specialist said it could do more harm than good, and the best, if not the only, thing to be done is get off the foot for a month. Also he is on a heavy dose of cortisone. So far there's no change, though he looks marvelous, fattened up a bit. Me too. Though I don't look so marvelous. Hajmi is here to help with the cooking and the shopping and the entertaining of the very demanding patient. It is funny to see Dris acting just like me and getting all upset because somehow Hajmi isn't putting the right kind of heart and love and enthusiasm into his task. Last night, while high, I discovered I had a real dread of Dris, I mean of his displeasure. He is so imperial and thrilling. I suppose that is what an Arab wife is supposed to feel. Mme. Susan Sontag is coming to Tangier soon. She wrote me saying I was much on her mind and she would like to see me. Would I like to see her? Etc., Etc. A very strange twisted letter that makes you wonder why she wants to come here. Really to see me? Is she doing an article? Is she afraid I will become famous and powerful and be her enemy? I will try to fathom her black sinister depths.

The car is ready today. It will probably cost about $50. They didn't fix it in Biarritz as the value of the car in France is less than the value of the fender alone. France. So we drove it away fenderless, but otherwise in perfect health. The trip down was calm and lovely.

I read *The Nightclerk*, the Formentor Prize book by Stephen Schneck. I like it quite a lot. It reminds me of *The Exquisite Corpse*, though it is snappier and cleverer. His book is. Only he is very self-conscious and has to keep explaining how his book is magic (magick) and is all an imaginary cut-up. Genet is like a big tree from which all

313

these little fruits have fallen. I've read also Peter Mathiessen's new book to review for Kluger (he is reading mine at the moment according to Imboden). All right, but deeply deadly dull. I am glad Meredith is my agent. I think already my value in the publishing world has gone up because of the change. Please write me.

Lots of love and kisses, Alfred

To Edward Field   Aug. 18, 1965

(Marginal note: I'm reading Stations by Burt Blechman. Did you say you liked it? It's so fancy and pretentious. But mostly it makes me wonder how Epstein didn't love my book.)

Dear Edward: Do you think great fame and power will always be just out of our reach? I don't think Susan's celebrity is so strange. Remember, there is a millionaire behind her, she is beautiful, she says things or thinks things that really couldn't upset the establishment, and that whole dead New York liberal literary crowd was dying for a new face. Or voice. Remember what they were offering me? I am glad now I rejected that world. Oh, a letter for Susan came from Straus, and holding up the envelope to the light I could read some of it. (I am too lazy to steam it open.) Her book *Against Interpretation*, which I assume is essays, is apparently coming out in the fall. She will be here next week. I have had two letters and so has Paul and we compared them and roared with laughter as they go together so interestingly. A woman, Paul kept saying, she's a woman. Naturally. I think she is trying to make us compete for her. I still wonder why she is coming. In her first letter to Paul she says she is coming with Carlos somebody. In her second letter to me, she says she is coming alone. And the whole hotel situation threading between me and Paul is a riot. In the end she will wind up not having a room as no one is getting her one.

Hajmi's pants came yesterday and Dris has been practically tearing his hair (beatle hair since London) out. He says you were supposed to send him a pair like that, etc. Is that true? Even if it isn't, please send them immediately. He says you took his measurements and everything. Also, you'd maybe better send him one of those sweatshirts too, or whatever it is you're sending Hajmi. There is terrible sibling rivalry going on. Uncles Edward and Neil are being roasted over the coals along with papa here. So please. I'll send the money. He's in the middle of his third week off his feet. He isn't off his feet entirely, but practically entirely. There was quite a radical improvement after the first four days (I'm practicing on you for my letter to the doctor). But I think that was probably symptomatic relief due to the heavy dose of cortisone. Then everything slowed down to nothing and I got very unhappy and suffered over it, because I kept thinking if this doesn't cure him, where can we turn next? But I do think that during the last three or four days there has been further improvement. I would say the swelling has gone down by about a third. Paul says he should just go on with the cure even after the month is up, and I broached the subject today and Dris took it quite calmly. He is getting fatter and fatter. Could it be the cortisone? He eats like ten horses, as the fatter he gets the more beautiful he finds himself, so he stuffs himself more. At first he was throwing up after meals from eating so much. Now he can keep it down. Hajmi is still with us and I long for solitude. Yes, it's lovely having Dris a prisoner here, but it means I'm a prisoner too. Hajmi runs off hustling all the time, comes back with money and promptly loses it to Dris at cards. So I finally tore up the deck and Dris is now painting. He's done some gorgeous elaborate women with robes in some of which are other women, houses, etc. They're beautiful. Oh, Hajmi says to send dark blue for the sweater. Send whatever color you think nice for Dris.

I've also been depressed about *The Exquisite Corpse*. Kluger hated it and said Straus won't publish it. The Paris Review hated it too and turned it down. They didn't understand it and said it was offensive. Straus has it now. Charles Wright read and said he liked it, but I don't believe him. Not paranoia; I could tell he was lying. Paul now has it and I suppose he will hate it too. The only nice thing is that Deutsch is swamping me with letters asking for it back. I'm going to try to talk them into giving me a large advance, like 2000 pounds, as a risk. To cause a little excitement in America. Of course I'm not even sure they'll want it. Paul says I have been promoted from one kind of schlemiel to another. He says publishers always consider you a schlemiel, but there are different levels or categories. Oh, I read his book. Simon and Schuster gave him a $70,000 advance. I found it sort of boring, but will go through it again as I missed a great deal. It's a mystery story, a sort of parody of *The Sheltering Sky*. The best part is the beginning, which is like Jane's book and describes him and Jane. (Oh, I finally saw her yesterday. He dragged her over and we had a row about my doorbell. I was high and was getting furious, then suddenly my eyes met Paul's and I began to laugh and couldn't stop. I adore him this week, which usually means that he will do something horrible. He lures me into dropping all my defenses, then does something monstrous. I'm dying to know what he's cooking up for me and Susan.)

Dris's brother Mohammed Larbi just arrived. The mother sent him to tell us to take Hamid to the hospital, as he is dying. I made all the arrangements last week to smuggle him into the hospital here, and when I went to get him he didn't want to go because the mother had to stay with the daughters who were suddenly dying of grippes. He couldn't go without his mother. Besides a witch had told them the day before that evil spirits entered him last month and she would cure him in three days. Did I tell you all this? He has gangrene not only of the foot now but the intestine and evidently the lung. He looks like death. I flew into a rage and screamed that he would die and it would be on their heads. But of course it was like talking to Columbine. I also screamed at Dris that he wasn't acting like a man. But there you are, the truth is the women here run the whole show. (Mohammed Larbi just told us some boy in Arcila murdered his young wife last week. I don't blame him.) Anyway, I said I washed my hands of them. Now he is here saying go and get him. And that means starting the whole process of faking his Tangier residence again. And it's hot. And I don't really care if he dies, except it will be so awful seeing those idiotic women screaming at the funeral.

Next day. Dris's foot seems to show definite progress. Today he's quite willing to spend another month off the foot, mostly because he wants to get fatter. We're bringing his brother tomorrow to Tangier probably. D. wants to move to Arcila so that we can run the pinchito stall, as it's falling to pieces since the father died and with Hamid so sick

I think I will stop now. I know this has been a dreary letter. But it's not as dreary as I am in person these days. I give you both kisses.

Love, Alfred

[*The letters break off here during Susan Sontag's visit to Tangier, which is traumatic for him, and are only resumed a month later.*]

To Edward Field   Sept. 16, 1965

Dear Edward: Could you please if possible write me another letter?

Love, Alfred

To Edward Field   Sept. 17, 1965

Dear Edward: Your letter came today. I'd sent you a note yesterday. Your other letter, the strange one, I burned about two weeks ago along with a lot of other papers and diaries, though not your other letters. I kept reading that letter and it kept filling me with horror and finally I burned it, wishing it would go away.

I've been through hell for the last month and consequently have ended up mistrusting everyone, including you and Dris. I don't even believe you are writing your letters. Susan's visit was catastrophic. I didn't entertain her at all because I was nuts, out of myself or induced, I don't know. Are you really Edward? And how can I know?

Why are you suddenly talking about the third eye? Please answer these questions. What do you mean: "I made stuffed cabbage the other day for the elephants [nickname for two overweight friends] it was magnificent. They are astrology buffs you know, and they say October.... etc." If *The Exquisite Corpse* is the book you told me to do for practice, why did you say it was so marvelous? Yesterday and today I've been looking over parts of it to send out to magazines (I think there is a conspiracy not to publish me anymore) and I think some of it is most beautiful. What did you mean try curing Dris's foot with hypnosis? It is very bad again as a result of the last month. I feel responsible for it, guilty over it, as if I gave him the urethritis. I feel as if I am a bearer of cancer, that my brain was destroyed by x-rays when I was seven....I didn't do the books Kluger sent me for review. The Matthiesen, no. And then *La Batarde* by Violette LeDuc, I couldn't read this since it seemed to be about me. Like a horrible joke publishers are playing on me, not that I can blame them. Am I really such a villain? I'm sorry also for those nasty reviews I used to write. I don't know what to do now. Kluger is sending me the new Capote book to review for January, and I don't know if the $1500 contract is still in operation. I'm terribly anxious to earn money, and can't think how. I want to stay here and don't want to stay here.

I can get you that blanket in Tangier too. If you'll tell me what it looks like again. Was it soft cotton or stiff?

I haven't smoked in a month. I think I was being fed LSD and various other drugs, and I feel as though Susan was taping my hysterical babblings.

I would start a new novel, but I keep thinking soon I'll be broke. Maybe I should go to America and ask my brother for a job in the fur business...What should Dris forgive you for? Anyway, I'm sure he has. The question is will anyone forgive me, and for what and why not? I have three live scorpions in a box on the table with some dry bread. I went scorpion hunting with Paul, and a country boy caught six for us with spit at the end of palmetto leaves stuck down their holes. They have had their stings and poison sacks cut off by Paul and the boy. They frightened Dris at first, but now he is used to them. I am terribly lonely. I wish you lived with me, if you are really Edward. I made an ass of myself in England and am terribly ashamed. I don't understand people. Or myself. I feel as though I've had a lobotomy by long distance, that my dreams are visible, that my thoughts can be read, that I've been fed yage.

Please write me by return of mail. Do you remember when you lived off 2nd Ave and we acted out a play in front of the fireplace? Do you remember what play it was?

I love you, if you are Edward. Alfred

To Norman Glass   Sept. 23, 1965

Dear Norman:

Everything seems to have come to pieces here, especially me.

It's raining today. The first rain. Dris says, Now comes the time of flowers.

I'm rewriting parts of *The Exquisite Corpse*, partly to send to Transatlantic (and other magazines), partly to make it cleaner and perhaps more publishable. No one seems to want it. I haven't heard from Deutsch.

How is Leslie and family? I wish he seriously wanted to go into business with me here, as I suppose it is crazy imagining I will ever earn a living off writing. The Pussycat I believe is sold. I wish you were here. I think I have been mad (crazy) and perhaps still am. I was certainly mad in England. Was it (is it) induced from without or within?

Susan was here. Her visit is impossible to describe.

I would be very interested in reading that psychiatric book you talked about (to whose author you wrote). Could you possibly send me a copy?

When I think about it, after all, I don't know who you are really.

Sometimes I think you're an actor hired to play Norman Glass who doesn't exist. Sometimes I think you are that psychiatrist you wrote to.

I'm trying to get back into the review business.

I don't see anyone except Paul lately.

The air on the terrace feels lovely after the rain.

Love from Alfred

To Edward Field   Sept. 27, 1965

Dear Edward: No, I don't really know it's you, but what can I do? And here you are giving me another address to write to. About recent events, what I want to say is that I don't think I have been crazy, or yes I have been crazy but that it was induced by a mixture of drugs and suggestion, or God knows what. I know you aren't going to believe me, or are going to pretend not to believe me, so though you can say I'm crazy I'm not going to accept it. I think now also I wasn't crazy last year either, but was driven to it. If I told you some of the things that happened, and that I know for a fact happened and were not imagined, you would be even more convinced that I was crazy. It is an unhappy situation because I have to go on accepting from people altered versions of what took place....Anyway, I'm here with a lot of problems. The bank wants me to get out of this apartment and refused my rent. I can fight of course, but I don't have the energy, and besides need a larger place, especially if Dris starts painting again. He stopped because I burnt two of them during the drugging. But I don't think I really want to go on living in Morocco. I'm too lonely, and it makes me feel too old somehow. I see no one nowadays but Paul. I'm very worried about the picture in my passport. I went with Susan and Dris to the consulate to change it, but no one waited on us though people were lurking around watching and listening, and Susan kept trying to make me talk about really delicate subjects. I think the intelligence section is watching me. Anyway after an hour I felt too miserable to wait anymore and besides I felt that they were exposing me to xrays and radioactive things....Also Dris's foot. And I must go and find out what my ug system has. But it scares me....I feel as though someone has spent a lot of money to have some fun with me.

Your new apartment sounds nice. I wish there were one for me next door. I am truly miserable here except when I work. I'm writing a story ["Safari"] about when Paul and I went scorpion hunting. I've written the rough draft and am now struggling to put it into shape.

I don't know what a demonic writer is, and it doesn't cheer me up being one. I'm feeling pretty hopeless about my writing anyway. I've been doing a little revising on *The Ex Corpse* to clean it up a little, if that will make it more publishable. But then I stopped and began this story.

The play we acted was Hamlet. You were Hamlet and I was Ophelia. We did the "gettheetoanunnery" scene...When you were here you upset me terribly by asking if I'd made my peace with my past yet, or something like that. What did you mean I wonder?

I don't understand how my one-line letter came a week or ten days after my long letter, when the long letter was written afterwards. You see how funny things are? I wish you would tell me about you and the third eye, since that is what I was being led to believe I had. Ira suggested it. Then Jane (when Susan was still here) said she wanted me to meet an old lady friend of hers who was involved in third eyes or something. Then your letter came.

The thing that started the whole recent episode in my life was Paul's book. It had extraordinary similarities to mine, and they can't be coincidental. He had for example two chapter thirties. Remember when I wrote you about two chapter twelves in my book? No one else knew but you and me....I don't see Ira anymore and don't want to give him anything for his magazine.

I gave a lot of thought recently to considering whether I was dead or not and in purgatory. I thought perhaps I died in Mexico coming back from Veracruz when, because of my grief and a very heavy fog, I nearly drove the car off the cliff. The boy I came back with grabbed the wheel only just in time. Lately, I've been wondering whether maybe he didn't grab the wheel in time.

Do you really have optical migraines? Everything makes me feel something very odd and horrible is going on. Your comments on Curt's book make me paranoid. Susan asked me about Hortense Calisher. I think she saw her in Yugoslavia at the PEN meeting.

It has been raining and hurricaning for a week, like December. I don't have a driving license anymore. My NY one is valid only in NY. (They got me. Maybe all the crazy letters I've written in the past have finally ended up in one dossier.) My international one isn't valid at all. And I failed the Moroccan one and can't try again for six months. Dris took his first test today and failed, and I'm furious since I paid 26,000 francs to an auto school. He'll take his next test Saturday. You fail if you miss one sign on the cardboard. I think they want them to fail so that we won't have the use of the car. I think I'm persona non grata in Tangier.

I'm reading *The Delicate Prey*. He writes so beautifully sometimes, almost like Lawrence. Maybe I'll write an essay about him. I wonder why he's so ignored lately. He's better than almost anybody. The monster. Here's what I say about him in my story: "Sometimes I think Gerald is God and sometimes I think he's the Devil. I have the strange feeling his mind can make things out of nothing like the road we were on, the plain we'd just crossed over, the mountain above us. I know this is insane. Probably I am insane. None the less I think a madman can be logical and right. If I see too much of Gerald he spreads insidiously through my life like ink on blotting paper. I go out at night and hear a strange bird cry in the trees and I think: that's Gerald. Or a dog baying. If I'm with someone I may say, 'Do you hear that bird? It's Gerald. He can turn himself into a bird.' Or possibly the crying birds and baying dogs are paid off by him to noise themselves at the most appropriate moments. Who, for example, is the laborer in blue jeans and blue denim jacket? Who is the middle-aged man who parks his old blue car opposite the Garden of the Frog every night and then walks distractedly up and down the path where the musk lilies bloom, hiding a twig of them behind his back? Is he just out for a stroll? Is anyone ever just out for a stroll? Is there any innocent pleasure left the stealing of a flower, walking through a park at night, the cry of a bird that is really a bird, the bay of a dog that is really a dog, a strange feeling in the body that isn't poison or malevolent magic?"

Don't tell me it's a masterpiece. I'm writing now because I have to earn my living.

It was sweet of May [Swenson] to say nice things about me. I wish I lived in New York and was friends with her.

Do you remember the bits of cactus we picked at the beach cafe when we had drinks with Dale and Liz? They are growing nicely. I never go to Dale's bar anymore because they make me feel like poison.

I love Edward and Neil and hope you are they. Alfred

Please be circumspect in your letters about any subject one should be circumspect about.

To Edward Field   Oct. 6, 1965

Dear sir: Thank you for your long interesting letter with tearsheet photo of Genet and kindly subtexts. Hell is not so bad a place to be so long as the post office operates.

I am not broke at all. I don't know why you keep imagining I am. How are you living I wonder?

I'm very suspicious of my suspiciousness. In fact, it all goes away when I don't see anyone or hear from anyone, when I just isolate myself. However, even I need human contact, and when I have it, I find that those I have it with are interested in aiding and abetting my paranoia....I meant by burning Dris's pictures during the drugging that I have not been crazy, I was being drugged. I believe that I already said that to you.

Yes, I am mistrusting you out of retribution for breaking off with Poor Harry [Goldgar]. This is the first I've heard of it, but it's retroactive. Only practically as long as I know you you've been breaking off with

Harry. Are you trying to suggest that the American intelligence is investigating me and therefore have I been driven crazy or drugged or whatever? You keep mentioning having changed and not being a hypocrite anymore, etc. I don't know how you've changed except that your letters are so bitchy. They sound like you learned weaving from the same spider that taught Paul Bowles. But I can't say that turning pitiful, valuable, talented people away from your door is new to you or reprehensible.

I had a letter from Diana Athill last week which truly brightened my life for several days, though it is very guarded and coded: "I waited to hold my peace until I had definite news for you, but it still isn't through yet. I think, though, that it's safe to say it's coming so hang on a bit. It won't be world shattering but it should be good." End. For three or four days I felt happy, but then I came to realize this is just part of the new torture program in my life. The point being to raise my hopes and then come down with a crushing blow....I am curious to know if, in fact, your new apartment is the size of mine how you could squeeze into the living room a couch, a table and that huge breakfront and complain about too much space. And how you could possibly eat in the kitchen.

Your cure for nonspecific VD is a wow, especially when the water is scalding and with a little chili pepper thrown in with the salt. You must have felt delicious throwing that little xray treatment bomb into the paragraph about my forcing coincidences. I would be glad to have details about that....I heard from the man who is making an anthology, and I wrote him saying I didn't want my piece to appear in his anthology. I sent a carbon to Meredith. Now I've heard from Meredith (our letters crossed) saying that he'd already given permission. Nonetheless, I don't want it reprinted....I don't know if Susan is really a rat. I think she is just very much at home in the world....Paul has brought some boy who buys manuscripts, letters etc. I asked for his credentials, which I found upon inspection wanting. He is obviously contemptuous of me and I think never heard of me before and believe that what he wanted was letters from Paul. Anyway, he offered me $400 for practically all the things I haven't burned over the years, except your (Edward's) letters, which I didn't want to sell. I also later withdrew Susan's letters since they are so personal. (Footnote: Besides, the withdrawal didn't bring the price down.) Though all the letters, everything in fact, he claims can be officially sealed here at the consulate. In any case $400 doesn't seem worth parting with my few papers for. Perhaps he will give me the money just for Paul's letters. They came over yesterday, also with his boyfriend, who took movies of everyone and is tiny and wore tight white jeans. He, the buyer, is sort of vaguely Truman Capote, though taller and better looking. They are coming today again and I will refuse their offer.

Ira claims to be going to the States soon. I have seen him twice this past week and in a moment of weakness agreed that if you (Edward) let him have a piece of my novel for his new magazine I would agree. I've changed my mind however and don't want to publish in his magazine. So please don't give him anything.

I look forward to the distress your next letter will cause me.

Love, Alfred

Friday. Today I sadly wish you were Edward because Deutsch is taking *The Exquisite Corpse*.

I must ask you to do something you'll truly hate. Phone Walter [Kerell] at the Catholic Worker. I want him to read the book. If he's very upset by what he reads I will have to change the book somewhat. I could disguise the Worker I suppose by locating it in Harlem, which would in any case be more topical. I would prefer to leave it the way it is, but it might hurt Walter terribly. I've written him several times during the last two years, but he doesn't ever reply, he is so angry. Could you please assure him that I could change John Anthony beyond recognition if this is what Walter wants.

I went to Arcila yesterday and walked out to the country. (My car is in storage on account of no license.) And I thought: Why is Edward writing to me in this way? Should I tell him to go to hell? Should I not answer him? <u>What is going on, Edward?</u>

I decided yesterday to move to Arcila where Dris feels happy and where people ask me how I am and actually notice how I am and don't merely act like Paul and Ira and Susan and your letters. I am really horrified at your letters, and if you write me any more subtexts I won't answer you. I would also like an explanation.

I found a nice house in the Arcila medina, fairly large and cheap and just remodelled, though no water, toilet, lights, etc. I can do that myself. It has a huge empluvium [stet] and three rooms downstairs (sort of like Ira's house) and a large roof with two rooms on it upstairs.

Miraculously, Hamid is cured again and out of the hospital. He looked like death when I took him to the hospital, and even when Susan saw him (convalescing) she thought he was dying. Now he is plump and jolly. Maybe, as I often think, this isn't the real world at all, but a kind of purgatory of mirrors. With no escape.

I love you if you're nice to me. Alfred

To Norman Glass   Oct. 8, Saturday, 1965

Dear Norman I was glad to have your letter, uninformative though it is. How did you manage to leave England? I mean, financially. The last I heard you seemed quite happy chez Leslie, and now you say you collapsed after my visit.

In the letter Leslie didn't forward to you, I said I thought you were either an actor or a psychiatrist, possibly the psychiatrist who wrote that Penguin you think so highly of. Or perhaps you're involved in some secret organization. Anyway, I'm enclosing a check for $20, though I think you are rich, just in case you aren't. I'm sure (I think) if you go see Gait Froge at the English bookstore, rue de Seine, she will cash it for you if you are too broke to wait for it to clear. Also give her my warmest regards. I peered into the bookshop when we passed through Paris but was shy of walking in.

Good news. I had a letter from Andre Deutsch Thursday offering 500 pounds for *The Exquisite Corpse*. After taxes and agents, I will get just half of that, and am hoping my agent can up the figure a bit.

Though of course I wouldn't dream of refusing, am in fact grateful since the Americans hate the book so. I think now, though, I should have an easier time getting a U.S. publisher.

I wish you would send me your criticism of *The Exquisite Corpse.* Yes, I think I was very crazy in England.

Who do you see and whom do you do? Is sex interesting in Paris? I saw Hajmi the other day. He has a mustache and his hair looks marcelled. In Arcila, I found a very nice house there and will probably move. There's no point staying here in Tangier among the poisoners. I see no one except Paul and I wonder if too much slimy water hasn't flowed under the bridge for us to really be friends. Besides, you never know when he'll strike next. Ira, I understand, has left for New York for a month where he intends to make a fortune and come back.

You are the only person I've met since coming here who I think I could call a friend, though probably you are involved in an elaborate conspiracy with all the others.

Yes, my arrangement with the Tribune is still operative, only, having been drugged for a month by persons unknown, I thought my brain had been damaged and that I couldn't do reviews. Anyway, my brain feels better and I will be reviewing Truman Capote's new book *In Cold Blood*, nonfiction, about a horrible murder in Kansas.

It's been raining nearly solidly for almost a month. And dreary and cold. I don't have a driving license anymore. Today, Dris has gone for his driving test. If he doesn't get his license I guess we'll sell the car.

I wish you were here. I feel very differently about you since England. Are you serious about going to Israel? I'm sure the embassy would help you if you said you wanted to migrate there. I've thought of it myself. Paul says, though, it's like the Bronx. And besides the new Israelis seem so humorless.

Dris has made the laundry room into his atelier and done his first oil painting, incredibly good. An orange fish. His watercolors would stagger you. I keep wondering who he really is. Who you really are. Where I really am. The question is no longer Who am I?

Love to you, dear friend, Alfred

To Edward Field   Oct. 20, 1965

Dear Edward Dris said last night "If I knew anything about what had happened, would I keep you with your heart so full?"

Please, Edward, why do you keep me with my heart so full? I keep thinking that anything that has to do with you must have good as its meaning. But my anguish isn't good anymore.

I wanted to write to Mrs. Schaefer [N.Y. psychotherapist], but couldn't find her address in the phonebook.

I guess I am going to leave Morocco soon. Dris wants to go work in a factory in Belgium. I want to go to New York but am terrified.

I keep asking myself—is it possible you really hate me?

Love, Alfred

To Nadia Gould   Oct. 28, 1965

Dear Nadia-ele: I was glad to have your letter, though sad to see that you too are in on the plot. Does it make you hate yourself? I love you anyhow.

I am suffering over Edward. I have to assume that anything he's involved in can mean me no harm. I reread his old letters and think yes of course they are sincere, because perhaps you can imagine, the doubt has entered my mind. I mean, is it possible he hates me, has hated me for ages? Anyway, I sent him a very sad letter last week and then immediately after mailing it tried to phone him. They told me that his number had been changed, was now unlisted and so I couldn't reach him. I wanted just to hear the sound of his voice. It was really one of the most horrible hours of my life, maybe the most horrible. Please ask him to write to me and to send me his new phone number and to let me phone him. If I sound abject I don't care. Also, I don't know how much you know about what I recently went through. It felt very dangerous to me. And I hope that Edward is as informed as he imagines.

I think I want to go home. What for, I don't know. Dris wants me to, for one thing. The idea of getting out of this hole doesn't exactly displease me either. But I don't think I have much to look forward to in America. I can write of course, which is the only thing that makes me glad anymore anyhow. And I do have friends there; I mean, I hope you're still my friends. Anyway, if worst comes to worst I can always come back, if I don't get murdered en route. Oh, speaking of murder, I think I will have to kill poor Skoura. She was the first thing to get wrecked here, and I guess there is no point dragging her back. Dris says to leave her with his family, but that isn't fair and would be awful for her and his family....They are a lovely family, the nicest family I ever had. His sister Fatima is like my cousin Marilyn, remember? And his mother and father are (were—his father died last spring) like what my parents would have been like if they'd been human. I really love these people. I suppose Edward told you about them. Fatima was the young one who had just given birth when E. and Neil came. I don't suppose they remember her too well. The room was crammed full of women. She has a little boy they claim looks just like me (because she looked at me a lot when she was pregnant), and they are worried his hair will fall out at age seven too. Oh, God, to have that on my conscience besides.

This is the eighth letter I've written today, and they've gotten progressively more depressing. I wanted to write Harriet as well but will save it for tomorrow, lest I burst into tears in the middle. Would you like me to bring something special for you, Phil or the kids? I plan to bring little gifts anyhow, but if there's anything you particularly desire, let me know. I think I wanted to get you a caftan once and also for Harriet as I remember. Well, I'll count my pennies and see. Please write soon, and please get Edward to write.

Love to you and Phil and the brood. Alfred

To Edward Field   Nov. 6, 1965

Dearest Edward: Please write to me. It is so dreary not having your letters to hug and kiss. Stand up, friend, with me, indeed.

In spite of everything I have been keeping myself busy and productive. I am feeling very well adjusted when not feeling completely insane. The nicest thing though that has happened lately is a letter from Kluger signed "Your friend." I am hungry enough for a friend to offer up my asshole in tribute. It seems not to be too unhealthy an offering either; I finally went to a urologist and had my blood and urine analyzed. And I don't have any diseases, and my prostate is all right. Dris's foot seems improved. God knows what that was all about.

I wrote a very amusing story called "Safari" about the scorpion hunt and sent it to Meredith to sell to the New Yorker. I also did my review of Capote, as you doubtless have heard. What I really want to do now is write another novel. Will I be able to do it in America, do you think? Anyway, I am going there you might say, being driven there. I guess next month. I would like you and my brother to meet me. (I wrote him, but I expect he is waiting for clearance before answering.) I have decided that you love me and I'm not going to change my mind about it again. I do wish you'd send me your phone number, though. That was probably the worst thing that has happened to me....Dris says he will go work in a factory in Belgium and we should meet back here in six months. I'm going to buy two little tape recorders to write to each other with. I wonder who he really is. I keep accusing him of being a spy, but even if he is, he has made me happier than any of the devoted nonspies I ever lived with. So can I really complain? And whatever has gone on, I have been happier here than I ever was before. But now that all the support has been ripped away, am I any stronger? And more practically, is any sex life possible for me in America? I have been reading (or trying to read) *Herzog* and New York sounds so ghastly. Perhaps though it will be different without the wig. Who knows? I am sitting here wearing the sweatshirt you sent Dris. He doesn't like it. I like it, though....I've bought the most beautiful suit. Had it made. $50. I think the shoulders are a little bulgy but otherwise most elegant. A sort of dark blue with faint stripes. When it was finished I realized it could have been something my father wore, but nonetheless, it is elegant. Though perhaps a little elderly. Of course I am a little elderly. Also, I bought a gray feathery fedora. I wore the outfit to the synagogue to make it Jewish and to ward off Black Magic, the notorious English chocolates. If the New Yorker takes the story I will have another suit made, a gray, like you said. Otherwise I will get a cheap corduroy at the market. Should I actually affect a cigarette holder? (As Susan said: "But Alfred, you're practically middle-aged.") Ain't she sweet? A-whorin down the street.

I want to bring a lot of presents. Not for anyone who's been here, though. Shall I bring Mrs. Schaefer that blanket? Does it have to be just like yours? Where will I stay in New York? I keep meaning to write Harriet, but I don't think I really want to live in the middle of The Scene.

I hope you will answer me, my dearest friend,

Love, Alfred

To Harriet Zwerling   Nov. 7, 1965

Dear Harriet: I woke up briefly very early this morning and the eucalyptus tree out the window had turned gold as if it were mimosa. Then I fell asleep. Dris says it means I will be very rich within six months. But maybe it just means it is autumn there *aux États Unis*.

I will probably go there next month. Somehow it seems exciting to arrive before Christmas. Is Milo still my godson? I hope so? Do you know of a place for me? To live, I mean, if New York is bearable. Not so far east as you evidently are. I don't want to be right in The Scene. Cheap of course. I'll take Columbine back with me but will have to kill poor Skoura.

By this time you've probably seen Susan. I don't know for sure if she was here. Paul says she was and others do too. There was a dark lady, much less lovely than our Sue, and dressed like you, and with your belly, who hung around a lot in early September. I don't believe this was Susan.

Do I look sad or pained in my photograph? Probably because being photographed is for me a sad and painful thing. Though less so lately. Then, when those pictures you saw were taken, I was very happy. Or I imagined I was.

I have heard that Irene is going to be on Broadway this year, starring in Twinkle Toes. Do you think there is a part for me? I could play a sort of W.C. Fieldsy part, and you can dye your hair and be Mae West. Or vice versa.

I just took an interlude for brunch, it being Sunday and suddenly filled with severe pangs. I had what my father used to make on Sundays, salad and eggs with lots of bread and butter, but no onion rolls or bagels, alas. I can't wait to have fried matzoh again with Edward. How lovely it seems to see my darling friends again. Even you, now that you have a baby.

Speaking of Susan, I've been going to the movies a lot lately. I saw "High Wind in Jamaica" (*les grandes personnes ne vous disent jamais rien; il faut tout deviner*) and yesterday I saw a lovely (Egyptian?) Arabian Nightsy film in color about a slut who turns saint. When she is old and dies in her hut in the desert, her beautiful young self emerges with a chorus line and they sing and dance their way up to heaven while millions of the faithful gaze up in awe. Most surprising was that most of the film was a sermon (with a lamp floating over her head on the night of illumination) and the audience ate it up. Me too.

Write and tell me if there is anything special you want me to bring you. I will bring something nice for my godson of course. And see if there is some apartment for me.

Love, Alfred

I want my phonograph back!

To Paul Bowles   Monday, December (?), 1965—Tangier

Dear Paul

Since I hope to be leaving today, I'm writing this note to say goodbye. Sorry I missed you the other day.

I wrote my bank in Gibraltar to sent to your account in the bank here $30.50 to cover the 15,000 francs I owe you.

I hope to be staying at my mother's; 1530 E. 8th St., Brooklyn, NY, if you care to write.

Thanks for everything. Best to you and Jane.

Alfred

Madness

Alfred returned to New York in December 1965 acting very strangely indeed, with instructions from the "voices" to marry Susan Sontag. He followed these "orders" by first going to bed with her—if the story he told me afterwards can be believed. The evening of this attempted coupling, which may have been on the Christmas Eve following his return, was almost comic. She agreed to sleep with him because, she told him, she went to bed with men when she wasn't in love with a woman and he was the most fascinating man in New York. Once in bed it was a disaster, alas, since, as he told me later, she diddled him a bit, as women do who are bored with "it," and when no erectile response occurred, turned over and went to sleep. Afterwards, he went around muttering darkly about "the black hole of Calcutta."

As practical and unscrupulous as ever, he adapted her remark that he was the most fascinating man in New York as a quote for the book jacket of *The Exquisite Corpse*, which was about to come out. But when she saw it, an indignant Sontag had her lawyer threaten to sue, resulting in the book jacket having to be pulped and reprinted. After these two fiascos they never saw each other again.

In Chester's letters from exile in New York, there were repeated appeals to Bowles to allow him back into Morocco. "Dear Great Man, Monster,

whoever you are

whatever you've done to me,

you gave me the greatest gift I've ever had, by which I mean, in short, of course, what else, Morocco. Or whatever other name you want to call it.

Please, Paul, give it back to me again."

His feelings for Bowles, in all their complexity, continued to obsess him as he repeatedly declared in letter after letter, how much he loved him, though, "I also hate, despise and loathe you, which in my idiotic language means I love you terribly." And again, "I love you as I loved my father whom I hated. But I do love you, because like him you gave me life."

If Bowles was Alfred's "magic father," Morocco remained the lost paradise he longed for for the rest of his short life. There were several attempts to reenter the country by air and sea, and in 1967, he succeeded in returning for a year, but I have little documentary evidence of this stay, since he no longer believed I was "the real Edward" and didn't keep in touch with me. In his one letter to me during this period in Morocco he reported having made 18 plane trips and run through the lump sum his family gave him and was living off the largesse of his brother. Nor was there ever a reunion with Dris, who first went to Belgium to work, and reportedly drove through Germany with a German woman, before eventually drifting to Holland, where he got married to a Dutch woman who owned a restaurant.

Aside from some psychotherapy sessions in New York and a brief stay at the R.D. Laing Foundation in London, arranged by his editor Diana Athill, who has written about Alfred in her memoir *Stet*, he had no psychiatric care and continued to drink heavily and take pills to silence the "voices." His personality disintegrating and his creative powers disrupted, the rest of Alfred Chester's life was spent in anguished wandering, with brief residences in Capri, London, Paris, Greece, the U.S, and finally Israel. On August 1, 1971, the Israeli police broke into his house in Jerusalem, and found his body. According to the autopsy, the cause of death was heart failure, brought on by a combination of alcohol and barbiturates.

Appendix
The Final Letters

To Paul Bowles   February 8, 1966—71 St. Marks Pl., NYC

Dear Paul

Your book arrived today from the publisher. And thanks. I've only looked through it quickly. It looks the same but different.

I love your photograph. And you. I also hate you.

I just heard from my agent that Simon & Schuster has made a definite offer for *The Exquisite Corpse.*

I'm revising *Chariot of Flesh* at the moment. And I think I've finished the rough draft of *The Foot.*

I almost never go out. I don't know what New York is like. (Or maybe I know too well!)

I hope I'll be back in Morocco next month. I want to have fun and lots of it. Is that possible?

Hello to Jane.

Love, Alfred

P.S. Good picture of Seth too.

To Paul Bowles   March 1, 1966 71 St. Marks Pl., NYC

Dear Paul

Thanks for your letter.

I don't have anything to tell you about, except my longing to go back to Morocco. Tears. Moaning. And wailing.

I am more alone here than I ever was there in spite of what Jane said. I hope that she's well and you too.

I'm having family trouble. Of course. And am trying to gather money to go back to Morocco. A deal with Simon & Schuster for *The Exquisite Corpse* is in the air, as well as Grove. (Please keep these publishing things quiet.) But it is all in the air. (Yes, Penguin wants to publish *The Exquisite Corpse*.)

I saw a review of your book, and he seemed not to understand what you were doing. Not that I did. But what little I understood, he didn't.

Dris wrote me from Belgium saying he hadn't found work and needed money to go home. Would you, perhaps, on a nice day go out to Arcila and see if he is there and how he is?

I've sold some things to Andreas Brown who is in New York, and I am, I hope, seeing him tomorrow to sell some manuscripts.

I don't want to live here. I want to go back to Morocco.

I haven't seen Susan since Christmas Eve.

I'm working on a novel called *The Foot*.

Oh, I did see Ira, Rosalind and Irving a few times. And Peter. They all seem well and not unhappy to be here.

I haven't spoken to Yacoubi, but perhaps will this week. I can't believe you're serious about teaching in Washington. Unless for a very short period.

I wrote a rough draft of a play on Pinocchio and thought of doing music for it. But the dialogue is awful. It should probably be mime.

When will I see Morocco again?

Love, Alfred

To Paul Bowles   March 5, 1966 71 St. Marks Pl., NYC

Dear Great Man, Monster,

whoever you are

whatever you've done to me,

you gave me the greatest gift I've ever had, by which I mean, in short, of course, what else, Morocco. Or whatever other name you want to call it.

Please, Paul, give it back to me again.

I love you as I loved my father whom I hated. But I do love you, because like him you gave me life.

I wish it were three years ago again, so that I could know what it was you were offering. Though of course I still don't know.

Could you please like my magic father promise me Morocco again?

I love you and Jane very much.

Alfred

To Norman Glass   July 28, 196(?)
                              —20 Chesham Pl., London SW1

Dear Norman: They (They always get first mention) delivered your letter this morning and are allowing, giving, me to answer it. By machine. The typewriter goes back to Diana tomorrow. I've been thinking (ha!) that I would ask her if there is a job for me in London. I would like a job. Even a blow job. (They will make me a welder next.)

Would you like to go see "Ubu Roi" at the Royal Court? I'm afraid to go myself, knowing it will be about me and thinking of the intermissions when I will have to overhear people talking about me. I'll pay for you if you continue to pretend you can't afford to pay for yourself.

My bridge will be ready next Friday, the 5th of Aug. And where do I go next? Grease again? And I'm thinking They're tricky and may leave me financially in the lurch. Even if all the rest of it wasn't real, I don't want to be poor anymore.

My radio works. Such a blessing. I heard an arts program last night, probably like the one I talked on. They were complaining about sexy books again. Offhand, y'know, I can't think of any sexy books to complain about. I'm a little embarrassed about *The Foot,* not because it is so dirty, but because it is so personally dirty. I will probably deliver it to my agent before I see you, so if you haven't already read or written the rest of it, you will have to wait.

Your letter was interesting. You're awfully hung up on colonial and colored folks, aren't you dear?

Great Expectations is very good and whoever wrote it a genius.

Today a month ago was my first full day at the Mamounia [hotel, Marrakech]. I swam in the swimming pool and air-conditioned myself and in the evening they walked me in a rigid trance around the jmaa el fna [square] and part of the medina. The moon was over the gardens and opposite my balcony. Is the moon real, Norman, or just a lamp in a balloon? I mean this question seriously as you perfectly well know.

To Edward Field   Feb. 12, 1967—
                              18, rue Sidi Mansour, Asilah, Morocco

Dear Edward Has the time come yet to speak the truth, or to speak at all, or to write letters to each other? Can I tell you anything you don't already know? Can you tell me what I don't know? I ask you please, if you can't reply to this letter honestly, not to answer it at all. If you have a choice.

I'm here in the house where Paul lived when we first came to Morocco, living more or less entirely in the room where we slept that first night. It's changed but the windows are still on the ocean, so that's nice. I'm more or less alone. More than less. I don't know where Dris is. I saw him for a week in September, then I went back to my English prison where he was supposed to join me but never did. So I came back here in November and have been here since, except for a week in Paris (I got back yesterday). I'd thought to go from Paris to New York, only because I hoped that there (New York) maybe the time had come for the truth to out. But once in Paris it was made evident that I had to come back here. So here I am, in a manner of speaking.

I have to move soon, to a house outside the medina. Facing on the beach, but with a road in front where the cars and motorcycles can get me. On the back and side, the old cemetery turned wild park, where the kids can get me. And with me, my head, and my nerves, where They can get me best, or worst, of all.

But things seem to have improved, though this isn't the first time I've been led to imagine it.

My vast fortune of last spring is all gone and I'm living off my brother, if he is my brother and if the money I get is his. All spent on 18 airplanes, on a car I owned for about two weeks (taken away by the Spanish police). You must know all this.

There is a very young boy here who goes by the name of Mhand. He says he is 18. As I don't dare go out hardly ever, except every few weeks to take an airplane to nowhere, Mhand shops for me and cooks a supper that we eat together. For the rest I'm practically always alone, panting for breath, though I'm hardly ever off the bed, exhausted though I do nothing but live the horror of my life unveiled. And the (almost) incredible thing in my brain. No writing. Virtually no reading for fear of the torture books hold for me.

Why do I tell you all this when I'm so sure you know and that if you write me you will deny knowing and so hurt me even more?

I wrote you an unmailed letter in November and ended it by saying "If I sign this letter love do I mean it and do you hear it?" And then on the wall of that house with the courtyard and the fountain where the dogs used to stay when we first came here I saw written "*L'amour n'egziste* [stet] *pas.*"

So how do I end this letter to you, so long and little known (you by me)? Maybe you know better what my heart is like than I do—in which case you know how this letter should be signed.

To Paul Bowles   Sept. 8, 1967 ⁃
                         11 rue Yaacoub el Manzor, Asilah, Morocco
Dear Paul
Maybe we could see each other some time? You could come here for a day or stay overnight. If that wouldn't be too horrible. Or I there?

Can you please advise me what is the best tape recorder available in Tangier? Prefer the rechargeable kind. Also, if I buy one would you be kind enough to record some of your tapes on others? At my expense.

I'm enclosing a check for Jane for 5000 francs. Thank her for loan. Best wishes to both.

Alfred

To Paul Bowles   Feb. 5, 1968
                              Villa Palme, Vieille Montagne, Tangier

Dear Paul

As it's difficult to reach you by phone, will you call me?

I'm having of all things a teeny tiny cocktail party (tea for you, or maybe I'll even buy a bottle of Dubonnet). It's for next Sunday the 11th of February between 5 and 7. I can't imagine you appearing but would be glad if you did.

Anyhow, phone me.

Love (not without hatred), Alfred

To Paul Bowles   May 17, 1968 Tangier
Dear Paul

The boat is supposed to leave early tomorrow morning, so I won't have time to see you. Please give Mhand fifteen thousand francs (15,000) making a total of twenty thousand I owe you.

You can write me c/o my brother, Herman Chester, 3077th Ave.

Goodbye and love and thanks.

Alfred

P.S. Also if the maid Habiba comes, give her some money please.

To Paul Bowles   June 5, 1968 Chelsea Hotel, NYC

Dear Paul

I'm sending a check for $40—is that right? to you c/o William
Morris Agency.

I'm here at the Chelsea with dogs since last Thursday. Yes, New
York is horrible.

I can't write. Please write to me, with nothing awful in it.

Alfred

To Mhand   June 12, 1968 Hotel Chelsea, NYC

Querido Mhand:

*Yo he mandado a ti cinquenta dollares que falta venir al societe de
Banque, al lado del correo a Tanger.*

*Yo estoy a un hotel con los perros. No me gusta New York. Quiero
vuelver a Tanger.*

Muchos recuerdos.

Alfred

To Paul Bowles   July 19, 1968 Hotel Chelsea, NYC

Dear Paul:

I'm leaving today on the Yugolinea (Jugolinija) "GROAN KOVACIC"
scheduled to land at Tangier on July 27. If they let me land. Could you
please meet me with the car so I can put the dogs into the kennel at
Malabata? (They're not allowed in taxis.) You can check exact arrival
time with Duborgh Jugolinija on the rue Dante.

Mhand may be in touch with you as I'm writing him.

See you soon?

Alfred

To Paul Bowles   Nov. 3, 1968 via Tuoro 22/c, Anacapri (Naples)
Dear Paul

Are you there? It would have been nice to see you at the port when they didn't let me off the boat at Tangier.

So now Capri.

I've now written to the Sureté Nationale at Rabat and the U.S. Embassy to ask please let me go back to Morocco.

Will ever see you again?

Love, Alfred

To Paul Bales, San Fernando Valley State College, Northridge, CA.
                    Nov. 25, 1968—Anacapri (Naples)
Dear Rat:

I knew you weren't there. What would Tangier be without your ratcheese?

The embassy and the Sureté Nationale haven't answered me, and yes I am more or less back in Arcila. Even without you there I would go to Tangier if there is or could be a Tangier without you.

My driver's license arrived so I'll buy a car. If they don't let me go back to Morocco, I will go to Asia as soon as I can get rid of the eight puppies that I now have.

Where should I go? Cambodia? Will you ever be in Tangier again? Will I? Should I go to Tunisia?

If you will be in California forever, should I come there?

Please answer *par retour de courrier*.

As ever, I hate you, I love you.

Alfred

But America is horrible. The worst.

To Paul Bowles   June 26, 1969
                    10 rue Ernest et Henri Rousselle, Paris 13

My darling Paul

Please forgive me for trying to write you on a French typewriter.
Your letter just arrived. I can't tell you how happy I am to have it.
Almost as happy as hearing your voice. I am about to go and see my
house. It's paid for and above is the address. I think, hope, I move in
tomorrow. Very chic of course.

Later: I've just cane back from visiting my new house: "*Les chiens
vont faire toujours pipi dans le jardin?*" "*Mais non, madame,*" etcetera,
etc. It's even harder writing in French on this damn French machine
than in English. Anyway, while I was away, Towszer, my female dog,
tore your letter to pieces so I can't cherish it as I intended to. Our
phone call, fifteen minutes, only cost $10, so Jane can call me anytime.
Of course $10 is something I would never expect you to spend on a
phone call. The number is 331 53 13.

Tell Jane if they let me back to Tangier I will lie on the floor with
her as long as she wants, provided I can keep drinking and taking pills.
I do love her, maybe not as much as I love you, because I also hate,
despise and loathe you, which in my idiotic language means I love you
terribly. But the practically nicest thing about Jane was that she really
was glad that people loved you. I might say that she is almost not a
woman and that both of you are almost not human. I better cut this
out as the lights are blinking terribly.

Why should Baudouin [the landlord?] hate me? Because he made
so much money off me? If he is responsible for getting me out of
Morocco, then you should tell him to get me back real quick, as there's
still lots more money.

I sent you a telegram from Capri saying I was coming to California
to be with you. That was in April or March or something. The wire was
returned and they said you'd left California and gone back to Tangier.
Nonetheless I went, since I hated Italy. (Why do French typewriters
have q's where a's belong and periods in impossible places?) America
wasn't so terrible but it was naturally uninhabitable. Besides my

brother gave me the idea that he could get me back into Morocco. Mhand also gave me this idea last December. So off I went with the dogs first class in an airplane. As you know the bastards didn't let me in. How's this for a non sequitur: I haven't had sex in a year which probably doesn't interest you, but does me....If King Hassan doesn't love me he is a fool. Meanwhile the Moroccan Embassy here is trying in appearance to be helpful and the U.S. Embassy is trying to appear nasty. I'm trying to get a teteatete with the U.S. Ambassador. Anyway, your prayers would be more useful, and surely Jane's. I am reading *Howard's End* for the third time. It is still gorgeous. Only *A Life Full of Holes* stood up thrice for me. So much for Hassan. My affectionate greetings to Louise de Meuran. For you and Jane I sign idly with love.

Yours and yours and yours, Alfred

To Paul Bowles   Aug. 20, 1969
                                   10 rue E. et H. Rousselle, Paris 13

I am going to Israel tomorrow. I'll never forgive Morocco now and probably it isn't important whether I do or not. It is hurting me terribly, but I'm just spending huge amounts of money in this hole, and I know I will never see you or Tangier again. Maybe Jerusalem is something like Tangier. Maybe I will suffer less and find a place that wants me a little. Paul, I will never find again. And this seems somehow more necessary than Dris under the circumstances.

If you think any correspondance is necessary you can write me at 21 Square des Peupliers, Paris 13. I'll write the bitch where to forward letters. My brother has vanished, with few regrets.

It's terrible never to see Tangier again, or Paul or Jane. There is no point going on.

If I never see Tangier again or Paul or Jane, it would be nice they imagine to know how I kissed them and hugged them and have loved them.

To Paul Bowles   May 20, 1970
                                          188 State St., Brooklyn

Paul

I hated Israel. (Israel = *Bit el Qots*? what does *Qots* mean?). So I
came back here last month. Yes, the dogs went with me and are here
with me now. I wanted to go to black Africa, but everything was so
complicated with visas, and I'm back here. It isn't so awful, but I loathe
it. Yes, imagine even if they did let me slip through at Casablanca,
would I be supposed to stay in hiding in Tangier, and then after three
months would I apply for residence, or go to Gibraltar and then
not be let in, etc.? Maybe I will write to the Moroccan Embassy in
Washington. In Paris the Moroccan Embassy said why did I always
try to get in through Tangier? Why didn't I try Rabat? And the U.S.
embassy said: "Our people in Morocco tell us you better stay away;
if you go back you might be arrested, etc." And now half of *The Foot*
has been published in the New American Review. They will hate me
more for having loved them so much. I had a letter from Larbi (now
spelled Larbe) while in Israel and told him to tell you to write to me
through him. If I ever come back to Morocco maybe Jane would get
well. I thought of going to Spain to see her {in the sanitarium], but
didn't know where to go or how to start, and I'm still afraid of Spain.
Extro (Eckstreau—a town in the south of France) reappeared for a few
days. I was utterly unprepared for an activity I thought gone forever,
and he only helped me out the first night. After that I was on my own
and I don't know what I thought of it. I wanted a houseboy, and he
said he would be it and go to the supermarket for me, etc., because it
is so horrible. But after three days or so there was this and that and I
threw him out.

Imagine, the autobiography of Paul Bowles. If he has a lot of years
ahead, I wonder if it is a good idea. But maybe he will never exist
again.

But you did say on the phone you thought I would come back. Why
don't you make it happen (or get me out of here)? And now after two
years, it frightens me to think of going back, even legally.

Grass here is terribly expensive and not much fun. They sell pornographic pictures in shops openly.

I have a dreary basement apartment, $300 a month, but there is a bit of back yard for the dogs to shit in.

What may happen, did you ask?

Love, Alfred

To Paul Bowles   June 5, 1970
                                                      188 State St., Brooklyn, N.Y.

Dear Paul:

Is this crazy? I've had, and since reading your letter—your unreal letter—just now, I have very strongly the feeling that I can go back to Morocco next fall, October or November maybe. I don't even know if I want to. Sometimes days go by without my wanting to. And also, I'm terrified that if I do go back, if they let me go back, tape in the going back, it might be a trick like *Bit el Qots,* and the running around business will start all over again. But this requires, going back to Tangier requires, I believe, a letter to the Moroccan Embassy in Washington. Now that I have a typewriter maybe I will do it. I bought this very chic remodelled Royal portable for $45 yesterday around the corner on State St. I mean Court St. for God's sake. Among many other things on Court St. are a pornographic movie house (to which I have never gone) and a pornographic bookstore with lavishly illustrated magazines costing $4 each. I sent Extro to buy one and he brought back "Young Teens," which turned me on to him excessively. Though he is thirtytwo tomorrow. And Edward is I think 46 or 47 tomorrow; but I never see him. I don't see Extro either anymore. We parted, rejoined, and then parted so sweetly I felt it was The End. And it seems to be. So I rushed out and bought another magazine, "Big Boys" which is rather more interesting. All of which leads me back to what I wanted to say: that it is appropriate that I use this typewriter for the first time for you. But you know, I imagined that while I went house hunting in

Tangier you would let me stay WITH THE DOGS in Jane's apartment. Jane would. If it should happen that I come back, go back.

Later. It's only after six but I'm *tvupif* (is that the word? From your childhood diary?), because Dennis came with a little giftie for me because, says he, there is a grass panic on. And there is. At least *chez moi*. I'm starving for lunch, as I suppose are the dogs, but I can't start that scene yet. What I was saying was, I probably won't hear from you for weeks, but maybe you would know somewhere I could stay with the dogs. A hotel, I mean. While I look, if I look. The Dutch kennel at Malabata is awful because of ticks and other reasons. Though maybe in the fall there aren't any ticks. Just scorpions. Stop. One of my problems in writing the Moroccan ambassador is I don't know if you write on the envelope: The Honorable or His Excellency or what. And if the letter should begin Dear Sir, Your Excellency, Dear Paul or what. Dennis says to phone the library, but my phone is on the blink since last Saturday. Nearly a week and they keep promising and promising. Now they've said immediately, in the phone booth. This letter may be unreal, but it's long. Which reminds me of my belly loneliness.

I haven't read Mrabat's second or third novels and haven't seen them anywhere. I haven't been anywhere. Don't mail them to me though I'd love to read them, because I never know from one day to the next where I'll be. Or if I'll be. I've been writing too. I've written more or less two longish short stories and am preparing myself for the reassault on the very long thing I wrote in Israel and have been revising here. Bed again. It would be nice to get a play and that forthcoming novel out of my system.

Now I'm feeling nauseous. While we got *tvupif,* I drank a long bourbon flavored with vodka. And it doesn't seem like a good idea at present. Imagine Boujemaa being He of the Assembly. Now I want to read it all over again.

Why do they call it *Bit el Qots*? Why don't they call it *Motta* or something like that? Is it a *bit*? It didn't look like one. And I was only there six weeks. Then I went to Tel Aviv and found a house somewhere north of it. I would have to get a new passport for Morocco.

Does Mhand, Mohamed of Asilah, still exist? And if so would he be available to horrify me next fall when I may appear? So he could dogsit while I look for a house. If. I sent Habiba $50, thanks.

This letter sounds like what I've been writing lately. Who dun it? I got a 72 cents royalty lately, so I'm not too badly fixed. But the jets continue relentlessly continuing. And of course I spend a lot more than I earn. This luxurious garden apartment is heated even on hot days, and even on a cold day like today I have the air conditioner on. The garden is weeds but they are blooming prettily and some rambling roses from my neighbors stage right rambled over the fence and into my garden. I noticed this morning though that they'd been dragged back. My two mostly finished stories are called "Three Corsages" for Dennis who never promises anyone a rose garden (or *Nous ne savions pas comment vous les offrir*" and "The Death of Sammy Levine Perhaps." The first was written by Irene, Susan and Harriet. The second was written by Doris Lessing and John O'Hara (who writes much better since he died).

I see I am down now. Normally, *ness pa*? I am terribly horny. Please take me home, daddy. Well, lunch time again. Good night, sweet prince.

Love, Alfred

Made in the USA
Columbia, SC
20 April 2024